NABOKOV'S SECRET TREES

NABOKOV'S SECRET

TREES

Stephen H. Blackwell

UNIVERSITY OF TORONTO PRESS
Toronto Buffalo London

© University of Toronto Press 2024
Toronto Buffalo London
utorontopress.com

ISBN 978-1-4875-5442-2 (cloth)   ISBN 978-1-4875-5443-9 (EPUB)
                                   ISBN 978-1-4875-5444-6 (PDF)

Library and Archives Canada Cataloguing in Publication

Title: Nabokov's secret trees / Stephen H. Blackwell.
Other titles: Secret trees
Names: Blackwell, Stephen H. (Stephen Hardwick), 1965– author.
Description: Includes bibliographical references and index.
Identifiers: Canadiana (print) 20240338413 | Canadiana (ebook) 2024033843X |
   ISBN 9781487554422 (cloth) | ISBN 9781487554446 (PDF) |
   ISBN 9781487554439 (EPUB)
Subjects: LCSH: Nabokov, Vladimir Vladimirovich, 1899–1977 – Criticism and
   interpretation. | LCSH: Trees in literature.
Classification: LCC PG3476.N3 Z586 2024 | DDC 813/.54–dc23

Cover design: Tom Eykemans

We wish to acknowledge the land on which the University of Toronto Press operates. This land is the traditional territory of the Wendat, the Anishnaabeg, the Haudenosaunee, the Métis, and the Mississaugas of the Credit First Nation.

University of Toronto Press acknowledges the financial support of the Government of Canada, the Canada Council for the Arts, and the Ontario Arts Council, an agency of the Government of Ontario, for its publishing activities.

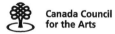

For Gabriel, and Timothy, and all the trees

Contents

Acknowledgments   ix

Abbreviations   xiii

Introduction   3

1 Nabokov's Origins in the Poetry of Trees   22

2 Trees on the Mind: Consciousness and Memory   44

3 Twigs, Shadows, and the Ramifications of Art   65

4 "Knowledge-Amplified Love": Trees and Epistemology in Nabokov's Worlds   82

5 Trees in the Frame: Art about Art about Trees   120

6 *Ada*'s Exuberant Trees   151

Epilogue: In and Out of the Pines   175

Appendices   189
   Nabokov's Invented and Real Trees, in Images   191
   Lists of Trees in Nabokov's Works   208
   All Trees (and Effects) in Nabokov's Poems, by Year   210
   List of Trees and Shrubs Mentioned in the Works of Shakespeare   216

Notes   217

Works Cited and Consulted   263

Index   273

Acknowledgments

Generous financial support for this book has been provided by the University of Tennessee Exhibition, Performance, and Publication Expense und; even more generous support was contributed by the Department of World Languages and Cultures. I benefited greatly from my fellowship year at the University of Tennessee Humanities Center in 2019–20. Research trips were also supported by the university's Lindsay Young funds. I am very grateful, as well, to the Vladimir Nabokov Literary Foundation for its encouragement and support of this project throughout my work.

This project germinated for many years, and during that time I benefited from input and assistance from many, many friends and colleagues (and I feel sure I am forgetting a few). It grew almost by accident, from the paper I presented at Brian Boyd's "Nabokov Upside Down" conference in 2012, which led me to my first "interesting tree," the reflected elm in *Pnin*'s chapter 4, and then to many others; Brian also sent me invaluable tidbits of tree-related material as he would come across them while working on other projects, especially from the *Letters to Véra* materials. I was similarly helped by Robert Dirig (who sent pressed leaves from Ithaca), Bobbie Ann Mason, Julie Loison-Charles, Olga Voronina, Gerard de Vries, Paul Grant, Heather Hirschfeld, Marijeta Bozovic, and by the sorely missed Gene Barabtarlo. Tatiana Ponomareva led trips to Rozhdestveno and its Vyra, where I could first see the descendants of the lindens and oaks so important to Nabokov's early years. She also, with Olga Skonechnaia, gave me immense assistance with a side project that was partially incorporated into chapter 1. Randy Raskin led me to my first two wild chestnuts. Andrei Babikov first led me to the *Pyrospodia* tree and we shared many spirited exchanges. Lisa Pearson of the Arnold Arboretum helped me track down Professor John George Jack. As always, my cherished friend Dana Dragunoiu read most of these chapters and provided essential criticism and feedback along the way; my gratitude to her, and to Andrew Wallace, knows no bounds. Generous responses to individual chapters or conference presentations were provided by x Acknowledgments

Tatyana Gershkovich, Eric Naiman, Stanislav Shvabrin, Neil Batt, Bruce Stone, Lisa Vermillion, Matthew Roth, David Bethea, Jenefer Coates, Marie Bouchet, and Agnès Edel-Roy. Lyndsi Barnes and Emma Davidson at the Berg Collection (New York Public Library) were a pleasure to work with, always extremely helpful and efficient; I am also grateful to Andrew Wylie for expediting requests I made for special access to restricted materials.

Michelle Tipton, as my undergraduate research assistant, created the first instalment of a spreadsheet organizing all mentions of trees in Nabokov's works, which has been the basis for many expansions in the past eight years. Without her excellent work, this project would have gone nowhere. Many meandering conversations, and meanderings, with Allen Dunn have sustained me through many seasons.

My earliest mentors and enduring friends, Robley Evans and Vadim Liapunov, have been a constant source of stimulation and inspiration throughout this project and everything that proceeded it. It all begins with them.

I also feel a profound debt to the natural world, and especially the trees, for everything they have given me and continue to give, in every facet of my life.

The seven artists who created original work for this volume, Susan Elizabeth Sweeney, Valerie Hird, Alexandra Kent, Tatjana Bergelt, Beauvais Lyons, Randy Arnold, and Eric Pervukhin, inspire me and fill me with admiration; it is a high honour to have their work here next to mine. I feel sure that Nabokov would be pleased to see his imaginary trees branching out into new creative minds, with magical and unpredictable results. Stephen Shapiro and Christine Robertson of the University of Toronto Press were kind and efficient in their handling of all stages of the project; I offer warm thanks to Anne Laughlin for her meticulous, generous, and thoughtful copy-editing. UTP's anonymous readers were attentive and extremely helpful with their suggestions, which I hope I have put to good use in the final result.

I am deeply grateful for the friendship and mentoring of colleagues who departed the earthly plane as I worked on this project, all of whom left many imprints on its pages and my life: Deborah Martinsen, Natalia Pervukhin, Gennady Barabtarlo, Dieter Zimmer, and D. Barton Johnson.

My family and loved ones have bravely (and indulgently) withstood my constant chatter about all the arboreal beings around us these past several years; I could not have written this book without their love.

All remaining errors are mine alone, reflecting the imperfection of my nature, but perhaps sharing a common spirit with an irregular, quirky wood grain.

The researching and writing of this book have been supported by the University of Tennessee, Knoxville. The land on which the University is built is part of the traditional territory of the Tsalagi peoples (now Eastern Band of Cherokee Indians, Cherokee Nation of Oklahoma, and United Keetoowah Band of Cherokee Indians) and Tsoyaha peoples (Yuchi, Muscogee Creek).

Permissions

The ornaments of this book are set in Trees, a typeface by Katie Holten. The Trees font is available to download for free from: https://www.katieholten.com/books#/abouttrees/.

"Topolia" (The Poplars) by Vladimir Nabokov. Excerpt of the previously unpublished poem "Poplars" (Topolia), copyright © by the Vladimir Nabokov Literary Foundation, Inc., used by permission of the Wylie Agency LLC.

The poem "The Rain Has Flown," copyright © 1970 by Vladimir Nabokov, is used by permission of the Wylie Agency LLC.

"Acreana bush," © 2024 by Beauvais Lyons

"Porphyroferous and black-leafed limia trees," © 2024 by Randy L. Arnold

"*Vallieria mirifica*," © 2024 by Susan Elizabeth Sweeney

"*Pyrospodia*," © 2024 by Valerie B. Hird

"*Quercus ruslan* Chat.," © 2024 by Eric Pervukhin

"Shattal apple," © 2024 by Tatjana Bergelt

"High-mountain willow," © 2024 by Alexandra Kent

Abbreviations

A	*Ada or Ardor: A Family Chronicle*
BS	*Bend Sinister*
CS	*Collected Stories*
CE	*Conclusive Evidence*
Df	*The Defense*
Desp	*Despair*
DB	*Drugie berega/Other Shores*
EO	*Eugene Onegin.* Trans. with commentary by Vladimir Nabokov
G	*The Gift*
Gl	*Glory*
IB	*Invitation to a Beheading*
KQK	*King, Queen, Knave*
LD	*Laughter in the Dark*
LL	*Lectures on Literature*
LTV	*Letters to Véra*
L	*Lolita*
LATH	*Look at the Harlequins!*
M	*Mary*
PF	*Pale Fire*
Pn	*Pnin*
PP	*Poems and Problems*
RLSK	*The Real Life of Sebastian Knight*
SP	*Selected Poems*
SSRP	*Sobranie sochinenii russkogo perioda v piati tomakh*
SM	*Speak, Memory: An Autobiography Revisited*
SO	*Strong Opinions*
TWS	*Think, Write, Speak*
TT	*Transparent Things*
SL	*Vladimir Nabokov: Selected Letters, 1940–1977*

NABOKOV'S SECRET TREES

Introduction

"Do you know the name of that tree?" Professor Nabokov asked one of my friends, an aspiring undergraduate author who had come to Nabokov's office for some professional tips. "No," he replied, after politely glancing out of the window in the general direction of Nabokov's gesture. "Then you'll never be a writer," said Nabokov.

Alfred Appel, "Remembering Nabokov"[1]

A writer knows the trees. This, it seems, is the simple and inescapable message contained in Alfred Appel's anecdote presented above. Nabokov apparently believed it to be true that knowledge of trees is both foundational and definitive of being a writer, and this fact makes us approach his art in a new way. When we do look at his work from this angle, we start – very quickly – to see how deeply and deliberately trees are woven into the heart of nearly everything he did with words. The phenomenon is so extensive, and so thematically rich, that it forces us to look for new ways to envision the interface between a human being's artworks and the products of the natural world.

The reasons for considering butterflies' role in Nabokov's world are clear enough – after all, he was the opposite of shy about their central role in his formation as a conscious, acting human being. But trees? Nabokov had no professional interest in trees to match his lepidopteral pursuits: he did not look for new species of trees or new taxonomic systems for their classification. An attentive reader can't help but notice that trees are mentioned with some frequency in various works – might they not be simply there for atmosphere, decoration, or even botanical accuracy? They might indeed, but the goal of this book is to demonstrate that they are in fact much more than chance verbal and visual texture. A closer and deeper look reveals that trees form a central and essential part of Nabokov's worldview, his intellectual/epistemological habits, and even, perhaps, his metaphysics. Let me explain.

Trees, in daily life, are everywhere and nowhere – everywhere, because except in the most barren cityscape, in a desert, tundra, or steppe, or at sea, they

4 Nabokov's Secret Trees

stand by in practically every imaginable outdoor environment, whether wild or cultivated; nowhere, because that ubiquity renders them partially invisible. In Nabokov's works they have a similar quality: trees are often mentioned in passing, occasionally serve as key sites of plot action, and only rarely do they become a central focus of narrative attention. Nabokov repeatedly pointed out how unobservant most people are towards nature, and it appears he knew the same phenomenon would play out in his artworks' reception as well. While barely noting them, one can view the trees in Nabokov's works as simple examples of life's detail and variety, its richness and complexity, so evident to a close observer of the world. This mimetic, representational role of trees should not be dismissed or underestimated. And yet, on close examination, trees are doing more in Nabokov's works than standing by and imparting natural "realism" to various scenes. Something about these trees – as a totality and, in many cases, individually – calls out to the reader for specific engagement and reflection.

How should we – or, rather, how are we invited to – see and experience trees in Nabokov's works? How do we even detect the invitation to engage in such experiencing?

Nabokov's artistic world is a capacious domain, and it has many entrances. Nabokov challenges his readers to approach his worlds (and those of other writers) as empirical fields for the intentional play and work of consciousness. His pedagogical desire that a linear narrative should become like a non-linear painting illustrates the way that texts, for him, are gateway phenomena, leading to transformations and expansions. A narrative is presented to a reader: What is it? At a fundamental level, it is something to be experienced and, gradually and with never-ending refinement, something to be known. In this basic and approximate way, a text is like the world – consciousness can work to know it, progressively, at greater depth and detail. The task of knowing the world is really the only purpose of consciousness in the rawest sense (leaving aside subcategories like knowing others, and ethically separate areas like loving, or Darwinian ones like producing offspring).

A tree can be experienced visually, tactually, olfactorily, emotionally, mnemonically, intellectually-poetically (artistically), and scientifically. Like most things, trees have metaphorical potential in how they relate to an experience of life's many aspects; more than many objects in our lives, trees have captured humanity's imaginative efforts to figure and explore its own essence – beginning with the Tree of Knowledge, with Yggdrasil, and other mythical or legendary trees that form parts of origin stories of various cultures. Trees have this role, most likely, because they are the oldest *nearby* living things in most people's experience – the only accessible parts of nature we can point to and instinctively know that they were alive when our ancestors were born – ten, twenty, a hundred generations ago.[2] Trees are, tend to be, *old* in a way few other living things we encounter are (various animals – some whales and sharks, various bivalves – can live as long as many common trees, but we don't see them much).[3] Whether we start from Nabokov's avowed fascination with time, or his demonstrated love of nature, or his passion for scientific knowledge – all of these phases lead us to pass through trees in his works. Nabokov's awareness of and love for trees comes out in his earliest artistic creations, to such an extent that we can say that just as trees are central to human origin stories across many cultures, they are also a core – perhaps *the* core – of Nabokov's personal creative mythology. This centrality ramifies in several directions – aptly branching into various creative forms over the course of his career.

Further to the anecdote told by Appel, Nabokov produced two more lessons about the need to know the trees around us. The first (chronologically) is from his lecture on Kafka, in which trees serve as the epistemological centre of three types of individuals in a rural environment:

> Let us take three types of men walking through the same landscape. Number One is a city man on a well-deserved vacation. Number Two is a professional botanist. Number Three is a local farmer. Number One, the city man, is what is called a re-alistic, commonsensical, matter-of-fact type: he sees trees as *trees* and knows from his map that the road he is following is a nice new road leading to Newton, where there is a nice eating place recommended to him by a friend in his office. The bot-anist looks around and sees his environment in the very exact terms of plant life, precise biological and classified units such as specific trees and grasses, flowers and ferns, and for him *this* is reality; to him the world of the stolid tourist (who cannot distinguish an oak from an elm) seems a fantastic, vague, dreamy, never-never world. Finally, the world of the local farmer differs from the two others in that his world is intensely emotional and personal since he has been born and bred there, and knows every trail and individual tree, and every shadow from every tree across every trail, all in warm connection with his everyday work, and his childhood, and a thousand small things and patterns which the other two – the humdrum tour-ist and the botanical taxonomist – simply cannot know in the given place at the given time. Our farmer will not know the relation of the surrounding vegetation to a botanical conception of the world, and the botanist will know nothing of any importance to him about that barn or that old field or that old house under its cottonwoods, which are afloat, as it were, in a medium of personal memories for one who was born there. (LL 252–3)[4]

Nabokov would have identified with the farmer as concerns trees, and with the scientist (and farmer too, partially) in relation to butterflies. But what is most inescapable here is the fact that all of these stories of subjective knowledge be-gin with and emerge from trees, from the city man who can't tell an oak from an elm, to the scientist who knows all the taxonomic and ecological relationships, to the farmer who knows all the rich local interconnections and their relation

6 Nabokov's Secret Trees

to time and personal stories. This *starting with trees* is a quirk of Nabokov's own engagement with the world, but it appears to be a quirk with deep roots, one that gives us special insight into how he experiences his life as an artistically perceiving consciousness, and hence, just how his artistic worlds attempt to express something about the world lived in and experienced by the artist. Attending carefully to Nabokov's trees will help us perceive his cognitive-artistic domain more fully.

The third anecdote is, on its surface, an echo of a part of the second:

> Among fifty college students whom I once happened to ask (in planned illustration of the incredible ignorance concerning natural objects that characterizes young Americans of today) the name of a tree, an American elm, that they could see through the classroom window, none was able to identify it: some hesitantly suggested it might be an oak, others were silent; one, a girl, said she guessed it was just a shade tree. The translator, when tackling botanical names in his author, should try to be more precise. (EO 3:9)

This story revisits the iconic (for Nabokov) oak-elm confusion, but it also leads to a fascinating extended note on natural and literary history, which includes Nabokov's coining of the word "racemosa" for "cheremukha"/ "old-world bird-cherry," along with his laborious and adventure-filled discovery that the word *akatsiia* in the same line of *Onegin*, normally (and quite logically) translated as "acacia," is in fact not an acacia at all, but, rather, a Siberian pea tree viewed through the prism of Konstantin Batiushkov's poem "Bower of Muses" (1817), where it is also called *akatsiia*. Nabokov's note traces the species's scientific name, the colour of its flowers (in comparison to flowers in other candidate trees, such as acacias), and, of course, the deliberate parodic relationship between Pushkin's line and Batiushkov's poem. All of this is driven by Nabokov's methodological statement: "should the translator take the name of a plant at its face value (sticking to his dictionary, which says that *akatsiya* is "acacia") or should he find out what the word really means, in its contextual habitat, within the terms of a certain imagined place and in the light of a certain literary device? I advocate following the second course" (EO 3:12). (This same question will become very important for us when we think about the chestnuts in *Lolita*, below in chapter 4.) Even when an artist's use of a tree is a parodic quotation, as Pushkin's was, Nabokov still feels that we need to get at the real tree held in mind by the target of parody.[5] Pushkin, it can be supposed, cared mainly about Batiushkov's words, though he might well have had the same tree image as did Batiushkov in relation to the word *akatsiia* (it's hard to be sure). Nabokov wants to get the trees right – not just the ones Pushkin was looking at more or less directly, but the ones he "imports" from his literary sources. The depth of artistic experience, he implies across four pages of literary-natural history, depends directly on the precision of environmental awareness – the awareness of trees most of all.

Nabokov, I want to suggest, was a Kilmerite. Unfortunately, this word does not exist outside of Nabokov's coinage.

Early in his first meandering road tour with Dolly Haze, Humbert Humbert reports that he is "no Kilmerite," but he agrees with the author of his guidebook that the roads around "Poplar Cove" in western North Carolina are "narrow and poorly maintained" (L 155). Surely, the word "Kilmerite" puzzles many readers. We indirectly learn that Humbert has just followed these roads to a plaque honouring Joyce Kilmer, soldier-poet and author of the very famous "Trees": "I think that I shall never see / A poem as lovely as a tree" – lines once known by nearly every literate American, even if their author's name is forgotten by most. If we think about this passage for more than the few seconds required to read it, it becomes very funny. Let's zoom out and examine it at slightly lower magnification: "A boulder, with a plaque, in memory of the author of "Trees" (by now we are in Poplar Cove, N.C., reached by what my kind, tolerant, usually so restrained tour book angrily calls 'a very narrow road, poorly maintained,' to which, though no Kilmerite, I subscribe)."[6] It seems as though the purpose of all those extra epithets in the parenthetical aside is to put maximum distance between the word "trees" and the name "Kilmerite." But what does it mean to be "no Kilmerite"? The phrase "though no Kilmerite" does not really fit logically with the larger meaning here: why should being or not being a Kilmerite have any relation to what one thinks of roads, or guide book evaluations of them? Let's look closely: if we decode this part of the sentence with logic and care, it appears to say: ".... 'a very narrow road, poorly maintained,' to which, [*although I do not believe that I shall never see a poem as lovely as a tree*], I subscribe." Apparently, Humbert does not think trees are inherently lovelier than poems – or, perhaps more likely, he simply uses understatement and diversion to inform us that he does not care much about trees. In chapter 4, we will return to this scene to consider more evidence for Humbert's indifference.[7] In contrast, Nabokov probably was, sometimes if not always, a Kilmerite.

We see Nabokov's connection to trees throughout his own art, but also in the art by others that he valued highly. Take, for instance, poets and poems he happened to praise. In his interviews, three examples of these stand out. About Robert Frost, he said, "Not everything he wrote was good. There is lots of trash. But I believe that rather obvious little poem on the woods is one of the greatest ever written" (referring to "Stopping by Woods on a Snowy Evening").[8] This evaluation echoes (practically verbatim) the one made by Charles Kinbote in *Pale Fire*: "Frost is the author of one of the greatest short poems in the English language, a poem that every American boy knows by heart, about the wintry woods, and the dreary dusk" (PF 203); perhaps surprisingly, Kinbote ends his comment by stating that "with all his excellent gifts, John Shade could never

8 Nabokov's Secret Trees

make *his* snowflakes settle that way" (PF 204). This remark is especially interesting because just a year or so later, in an interview with Robert Hughes of New York City's Public Television station, Nabokov gestured to a nearby ginkgo tree, and said:

> This is a ginkgo – the sacred tree of China, now rare in the wild state. The curiously veined leaf resembles a butterfly – which reminds me of a little poem ... ["The Sacred Tree," about a ginkgo tree] by John Shade – by far the greatest of *invented* poets. (SO 58–9)

Leaving aside the bald immodesty (and, most likely, a barely concealed dig at Yuri Zhivago, a poet in that other famous novel), the fact that Nabokov wrote this poem, gave it to his character whom he considers the greatest invented poet, and cited the poem in full for the interview (it is presented and discussed more fully in chapter 4), highlights both this tree's importance for Nabokov, and also his urge to *make trees important to invented (great) poets*. As we will see in detail in chapters 4 and 5, the ginkgo tree plays a quiet yet outsized role in the novel's arboreal undercurrent.

My third curious example of a "praised poem" comes from another interview, with Costanzo Costantini of *Il Messaggero* in 1969. Asked – twice – to name preferred favourite writers, and particularly, Italian ones, Nabokov finally offered only to speak about the poet Gabriele D'Annunzio, of whom he said, "I read him as a young man, I liked 'The Rain in the Pine Forest'" (TWS 382). This was the only writer, or literary work, besides Shakespeare that Costantini could get him to name among "contemporaries" (as Nabokov said: "Always Shakespeare").

Of course, Nabokov was interested in many poems that were not about trees, and there are relatively few trees in the poems he translated into English. However, it may be that his attention to trees expands in the interviews of the 1960s precisely because this time coincided with the final crest of his second "peak" of arboreal focus, in his work on *Ada* and, to a lesser extent, *Speak, Memory*. The earliest years of his career had also been heavily laden with tree imagery, especially in the poetry, where we find trees in nearly half of his output; the percentage in the last decade of poetry writing is even higher (though the number of poems much smaller). In chapter 1 I will explore just how trees work their way into this early poetic craft, and into his own telling of his emergence as an artist, but for now I want to turn attention instead to a few poems by Nabokov's avowed poetic idol, Pushkin.

We can take it as axiomatic, I think, that Nabokov knew Pushkin's poetry nearly by heart from an early age. Certainly he would have completed much of this task before finishing university at Cambridge. One poem that Pushkin wrote in early adulthood stands out in particular: "The Muse" (1821). The poem's speaker reports that "she" (his muse) gave him a set of pan pipes (*tsevnitsa*) in his infancy, and his playing developed as he "From morn to evening in the mute shade of the oaks / diligently ... heeded the mysterious maiden's lessons," until, one day, she took the pan pipes from his hands and they were "enlivened with divine breath, and filled [his] heart with holy enchantment." Not only the long tutelage under the oaks is interesting here, but the musical instrument too: in Ovid's telling, the pan pipes were created when Pan pursued the nymph Syrinx, who prayed to be transformed into reeds to escape. (And the word for reeds later became synonymous with lilac – which has reed-like hollow branches and twigs – also known as "syringa," *siren'* in Russian.) She was transformed, but Pan collected her anyway, and played on the pipes made from her reed tubes to be near her music forevermore.

That 1821 poem seems not to be directly mentioned by Nabokov anywhere, though as we will see, its oaks practically fuse with his own life story. A somewhat later poem, "The Poet" (1827), however, has a fascinating and meaningful connection to Nabokov's own biography. This poem tells of how a poet, once touched by the divine voice (*bozhestvennyi glagol*), will flee from human society to the wave-battered shore and the "wide-noised oak groves" (*shirokoshumnye dubrovy*), suggesting that forests and violent shorelines are the places where art comes forth. We have no way to know for sure, but it seems most likely that through passages like these, Nabokov felt an immediate kinship with Pushkin, and we feel the presence of the trees not just in a large number of early poems, but – as we shall see in greater detail in chapter 1 – specifically in poems and stories about the source of a writer's inspiration ("The Quill," "The Wood-Sprite," "First Poem," "Recruiting"). We find this poem's importance for Nabokov, and his clear memory of it, on display in an epigram he wrote about his increasingly dear friend Yuli Aikhenvald, saying of him "there's a line of Pushkin in his name / 'the wide-noised oak-grove.'" Aikhenvald's name comes from the German for oak ("Eiche," transliterated phonetically) and forest ("Wald").[9] The fact that Aikhenvald – one of the emigration's most highly regarded literary critics – was also Nabokov's leading early champion closes the circle joining trees, poet, writer, and reader.

Nabokov knew his Puhskin, and he found him in Aikhenvald. Although I have not found research on this topic, it appears from the few examples collected here that Pushkin felt that oak trees and artistic expression were linked. In *Ruslan and Lyudmila*, they are joined by a golden chain:

By a sea arc stands a green oak,
 a chaine of golde hangs upon it
And day and night a learned cat
goes ever round it on the chaine[10]
going to the right – it sings a song,
and to the left – it tells a fairy-tale.

10   Nabokov's Secret Trees

Oaks are far from the most common trees in Nabokov, but they play very significant roles in several works – most famously, perhaps, in the novel *Quercus* in *Invitation to a Beheading* and, as we will see, in *Speak, Memory.* In the poetry, oaks are not especially common, but occasionally make striking or stealthy appearances full of meaning; I have in mind the late poem "The Ballad of Longwood Glen" (1957) for the striking variety, and the very early "Resound, my faithful verse, soar, oh reminiscence!" (1918) for the subtle. There is a period in 1918 where oaks and lilacs (*siren'*) flourish together, perhaps in echo of the trees and pan pipes in Pushkin's "The Muse." There are no oaks, it seems, in the collection of juvenilia published in the 1916 "Poems," written mostly during the love affair with Valentina Shulgin (but there are many other trees). Nabokov's explicit connection of oaks with Pushkin appears first in the letter to Véra with its epigram about Aikhenvald, and runs as late as *Ada*, where an invented tree known as "*Quercus ruslan* Chat." (*chat* being French for "cat") produces a direct bond between Pushkin's creativity and Nabokov's own. Another prominent reference to this part of Pushkin's mock epic appears in the *Onegin* commentary, as a digression (appropriately enough) from what Nabokov calls the "pedal digression" (EO 2.115). He writes, "In the extraordinary lines, among his greatest, that Pushkin added in 1824, four years after its publication, to the beginning of Ruslan and Lyudmila, –

Tam lés i dol vidéniy pólnï
Tam o zaré prihlïnut vólnï
Na breg peschánïy i pustóy

There wood and dale are full of visions;
there at sunrise the waves come plashing
upon the empty sandy shore

– these waves give birth to thirty handsome knights who emerge one after the other from the limpid waters." (EO 2.139). Nabokov appears to refer to the entirety of the "Introduction" that was written in 1824, beginning with the green oak, and the chain-treading cat who becomes the source for Russian songs and tales – including the tale of Ruslan and Lyudmila (as its narrator tells us). As in the works of Frost, Costantini, Shade, and Kilmer, Pushkin, "among his greatest" lines, intertwines trees with the wellsprings of art – a fact which Nabokov pays tribute to not once, but twice.

Inheriting and adapting, perhaps, Pushkin's folkloric and magical myth about his muse, Nabokov' playful 1921 narrative lyric "The Quill" ("*Pero*") mentions firs, not oaks, but the result of the poem's action is that the speaker receives a feather from a firebird (to be discussed at length in chapter 1). It's doubtful that Nabokov ever wrote with a quill pen, but he did for a time use a special penholder that would have had particular, changeable nibs.

A hand-turned oak penholder. Courtesy of author.

In the final version of his memoir, *Speak, Memory*, a series of photographs was added, some with extensive captions with their own rambling, even nested, digressions. The penholder stars in one of these mini-dramas, one of which shows Nabokov, in 1929, penning *The Defense*. We discover the following, among many other details: "The end of my robust, dark-brown penholder (a beloved tool of young oak that I used during all my twenty years of literary labors in Europe and may rediscover yet in one of the trunks stored at Dean's, Ithaca, N.Y.) is already well chewed" (facing SM 256). This is quite a pile of words to describe a pen – we almost expect to discover the tobacco-chewing-and-spitting manager of Dean's around the next corner – and, as always, the overabundance likely is in part a diversionary tactic. It diverts our attention, I think, from the audacious claim that the penholder is of "young oak": How could Nabokov possibly know this? Oak, certainly, but young? The twenty years of devoted use, and the "beloved" status of the tool – nearly forgotten by the sentence's end, perhaps – point to an item of great significance to the writer. Was it a gift, maybe something custom-made and bestowed by a woodworking friend, or acquired with a story from one of his parents? The clairvoyant tale of the magnified pencil from Treumann's in St. Petersburg, bought by his mother while he ailed at home, with a high fever, also comes to mind (SM 38–9). This young-oak penholder also evokes the "oakling avenue" at Vyra, where Nabokov first discovered time and his own self-consciousness (to be discussed in chapter 1). Although the penholder's real story appears to be lost – it is a pity that no one asked him, or Dmitri or Véra, about it while they were alive: he clearly treasured the object, associating his first decades as an artist with this implement and its oaky origins. Some secrets will likely never be revealed.

Nabokov's poetry is rich with trees of various sorts, and amounted to a first florescence that became more subdued – temporarily – when Nabokov turned to writing novels beginning in the mid-1920s. Trees are mentioned in about 192 of Nabokov's 482 or so published poems (not including the juvenilia in 1916's *Poems/Stikhotvoreniia*). This includes about thirty-three with trees in the title and/or first line; there are an additional five still-unpublished poems with trees in that prominent spot.[11] Oak was closely linked with poplar in Nabokov's personal origin story as a poet (see chapter 1): he did some of his first composing from an

12 Nabokov's Secret Trees

oak-panelled water closet in Vyra, looking out over imported poplars; this scene would become crucial in *Mary* and undergo significant reanalysis across the iterations of *Speak, Memory*. Iconic of this biographical detail is the fact that he wrote a poem in Russian called "Poplars" ("Topolia") in 1921, and another called "The Poplar" in English in 1952. In the first poem, the speaker declares, "My soul is an alley of poplars," and in the later one, the middle-aged lyric persona daydreams back to a poplar of his youth. In the 1946 long poem "An Evening of Russian Poetry," a student asks the narrator, "*Trees? Animals? Your favorite precious stone?*"; to which the lecturer's voice replies, "The birch tree, Cynthia, the fir tree, Joan" (SP 136). We will see (especially in chapter 2) these birches in poetry evoking the lost homeland, and the lost father, as well as in prose memorializing his first love. The fir, as already noted, is extremely common but especially significant in the fairy tale of the poet's magic pen, "The Quill"; they appear together in the important 1917 poem, "Sonnet" ("The cloudless vault and silence …").

Turning to Nabokov's short fiction, we find that the majority of his stories feature one or more kind of trees: forty-eight of the sixty-four stories draw attention to trees to a greater or lesser extent. True, the stories – the prose fiction generally – emerge straight from the Russian forest, in the figure of the "woodsprite" animating that very first narrative, to be discussed in chapter 1. Aside from extreme and special cases like "The Wood-Sprite," the trees in the stories, as in the novels, are usually demure, and in the majority of the tales, they may indeed be primarily simple properties of the natural environment. But we also see, in these shorter narratives, Nabokov exploring and experimenting with the significative and expressive potential of trees, with different ways to weave them into an artwork's fabric.

For example, "Gods," the sixth story Nabokov wrote (after completing the fourth, in late 1922, he seems to have fully committed himself to writing prose), introduces the idea of trees on the move: "All trees are pilgrims" (CS 45), the narrator proclaims, all heading somewhere in search of their Saviour. We see this motif recur periodically during Nabokov's career, with a culmination in 1957's "The Ballad of Longwood Glen," featuring a tall oak also described as a "grave green pilgrim," who is "passing by" (SP 150). There are rich, subterranean tree narratives to be found in stories such as "The Potato Elf," "The Return of Chorb," "A Bad Day," "Recruiting," "Spring in Fialta," "The Assistant Producer" – to name only the ones with the most striking arboreal presence; that presence abides also, but more subtly, in pieces like "A Nursery Tale," "The Leonardo," "The Circle," and many more. Although, as I will argue, Nabokov worked to soften and de-emphasize trees' presence in his art after the initial poetic explosion around the early 1920s, this was something of a losing battle for him, and even periods of restraint are punctuated with tree frenzies here and there. And in the 1950s he more or less lost all restraint, and didn't stop until *Ada* was complete.

Introduction   13

If in texts like "The Wood-Sprite" and "The Quill" trees play a primarily allegorical and mythological role, it is also worth paying attention to the metaphorical potential they hold, something that was ever-present in Nabokov's writings. There are simple metaphors, including some of Nabokov's favourites like those for time and memory. The *Quercus* oak (in *Invitation to a Beheading*) stands for time – the embedded fictitious novel's whole point is to explore how tree, time (six hundred years), and place intersect – and it stands for memory, too, in the way that it both facilitates memory of a place's history, and also holds traces of humans who pass through (in their carvings on its trunk, which receive an entire chapter within the work – one we do not see). The tree in the poem "The Poplar" is largely a figment of – or gateway to – memory, a time portal between present and past. Visually, we find trees hinting at other sorts of entities entirely: a bare poplar in *The Gift* looks like "the nervous system of a giant" (G 53); in *Pale Fire* we read of a "weeping-willow dog," but in *Ada* "Sealyham Cedar" plays a significant role (referring to a Sealyham terrier: this dog has a face often groomed with weeping willow–like features; one of Nabokov's favourite trees at the Montreux Palace Hotel was the weeping cedar).[12] The same conjunction appears in *The Real Life of Sebastian Knight*.[13] In the *Pale Fire* lyric reproduced above, a ginkgo leaf is perceived by the poet as both a muscat grape and a butterfly, "ill-spread."

We see such transformations early on, too, especially in a series of vignettes from letters Nabokov wrote to his wife Véra in 1926:

11 June 1926
It rained yesterday, today's sunny although chilly, and the wind is fluffing out the bright crooked acacia by the wall of the yard ... There is something birdy or parroty in my acacia. (LTV 71)

13 June 1926
Rain, rain, since morning … Such a pretty June, I must say … It drips onto the window sill, it crackles as if endlessly opening thousands of tiny cabinets, chests, caskets – senselessly and purposefully, in the dark, in the yard, where my crooked acacia receives the rain in its own way, with an obedient steady rustling. (Ellipses in original, LTV 73).

29 June 1926
In the mornings, the acacia by the wall in the courtyard bathes in its own lacy shadow, which rocks back and forth behind it on the wall and through its leaves, and interferes with the movement of the leaves: acacia in a shady peignoir. (LTV 106)

10 July 1926
Meanwhile, the weather cleared up, the acacia put on its shadowy peignoir. (LTV 135)

14 Nabokov's Secret Trees

> 11 July 1926
> The leaves on my acacia are already turning yellow and falling down, covering the ground with their golden tongues. But after the rain, a huge puddle gathered them up; some huddled together by the gutter grating, forming a brownish-yellow spot that looked like the slightly browned edge of an omelet. (LTV 137)

Here, notice that the metaphor emerges predominantly from the acacia tree's shadow against the wall, the entire scene transformed into a micro-drama of intimate wardrobe. And this is a key point to recognize about Nabokov's trees: their shadows, and the interplay of shadows, leaves, twigs, and surrounding objects that catch the shadows, are together an elaborate, pulsating, and changing matrix, shifting from level to level of perception and "reality"; the shadow on the wall "interferes with the movement of the leaves," in seeming violation of the laws of physics. Even if a tree seems to be just a tree, it is always ready, in Nabokov's world, to become something more. A tree together with its shadow forms a larger, more ambiguous and unpredictable whole.

This aspect of Nabokov's art presents an apt moment to consider what we find in the treatment of trees, as contrasted with rhizomes, in Deleuze and Guattari's *A Thousand Plateaus*. In that work, trees and their roots are taken as iconic of linear, predictable bifurcation, discrete structure, and the epitome of a reductive and oversimplified tendency of human thought when grappling with the world's epistemological challenges.[14] Without any suggestion that the authors are wrong to use trees as the vehicle in this metaphor and in the service of such an analogy, I want to make clear that in Nabokov's way of thinking about and presenting them, trees would never have been able to play this role, precisely because he so cherished (at least, as his art and letters suggest) just those aspects of trees' existence that burst past all restrictions that their rule-bound, physically discrete, and coherent elements might seem to imply. In all likelihood, trees in Nabokov's conception of them *already were doing* all of the kinds of things that Deleuze and Guattari saw in rhizomes, in large part because those philosophers were thinking strictly in terms of the embodied (mass-bearing) parts of the world for their metaphors, whereas in Nabokov's thought trees are always thoroughly embedded in the bodyless contexts of light and shadow, as well as in memory and creativity. It is those weightless shadows, and the light that helps produce them, that allow Nabokov to turn trees into unpredictable spaces of infinite interconnections, interweavings, and transformations, rather than ones of predictable linearity and bifurcation.

Deleuze and Guattari's analogy can suggest helpful ways to focus one of this study's guiding questions: What are trees *doing* in Nabokov's works, and how does their activity offer us meaning(s)? Considering that I am placing trees more or less at the creative epicentre of Nabokov's intellectual project, it becomes a useful question to consider here, despite the possibly extreme distance between these philosophers and Nabokov as thinkers and conceptualizers of the world. I should start out by suggesting that, if I am right about trees' importance for Nabokov, a more thorough study of the tensions and overlap between Deleuze/Guattari and Nabokov is warranted, but this book is not the place for such a venture; here, my goal is to do the first work of exploring how Nabokov uses trees artistically, and I leave it to future researchers to flesh out the theoretical implications that arise from these patterns and devices. However, a brief overview of some important points of contact or divergence is in order.

The most obvious and crucial difference between the Deleuze/Guattari use of trees and that of Nabokov is that the philosophers are interested in trees strictly as an abstract concept, and as a structuring metaphor that has guided, as they see it, most Western epistemological or analytical endeavours since ancient times. Trees' serially dividing branches, from trunk to final twigs, and downward into roots, mark a sequence of divisions of one line into two, in a bifurcating yet linear fashion. The philosophers are critical of the arboreal paradigm:

> The law of the book is the law of reflection, the One that becomes two ... One becomes two: whenever we encounter this formula ... what we have before us is the most classical and well reflected, oldest, and weariest kind of thought. Nature doesn't work that way: in nature, roots are taproots with a more multiple, lateral, and circular system of ramification, rather than a dichotomous one. Thought lags behind nature ... Tree or Root as an image ... endlessly develops the law of the One that becomes two, then of the two that become four ... Binary logic is the spiritual reality of the root-tree. (*Thousand Plateaus*, 5)

This movement from unitary centre to multiple peripheries creates an inevitably hierarchical system and worldview, the philosophers assert, with further implications or tendencies of tyrannical structures. Against trees and roots, they pose rhizomes, which have no hierarchy and connect more or less infinitely in any direction.

Before turning to a consideration of how Nabokov's trees compare with this vision, let's first revisit the question of whether, taken as a whole, Nabokov's works appear to conform to the constraints suggested by the Deleuze/Guattari "arborescent" model. Late in their discussion, they concede that American and English literature already had begun breaking away into more rhizomatic modes ("nomadic" is their preferred term, but they do not give a start date for this trend). We might say that Nabokov's works would fall under the arborescent and hierarchical model if they tend to offer and encourage a reception as a "Total Work or Magnum Opus" – or, put another way, if they tend towards a "unity," or what Nabokov scholars might call a "unitary solution."[15] Certainly, Nabokov crafted a persona that appeared to endorse authorial control and singularity of meaning, full of "puzzles with elegant solutions" where "dual solutions are prohibited." Scholars have often written about Nabokov's desire to control his readers and their interpretations of his works – to control his works' ultimate meaning. This is the "tyrannical" image of Nabokov, a relatively common feature of the scholarship for several decades.[16] However, there is a contrary line of thought proposing that, despite his feigned desire for absolute control, Nabokov actually structured his works on a model of interpretive openness.[17] This would place him closer to his friend and admired mentor of the 1920s, Yuli Aikhenvald, who unambiguously advocated for the reader's role in shaping a work's meaning. There is more work to be done, I suspect, in the exploration of this topic, but for now it can be said that the scholarly view of Nabokov's authorial control is decidedly mixed. If Nabokov's works are not designed to have unitary interpretations, they may qualify as among those more "rhizomatic" works that Deleuze and Guattari perceive within Anglo-American literature.

An important component of any approach to this question may be the fact that, unlike the *Thousand Plateaus* authors, Nabokov brings trees into his work first of all as ideas of real physical objects, parts of nature in the world around him. And once they are there, in his works, they very quickly begin to misbehave – that is, do things that trees don't usually do. They travel, and they metamorphose, and their shadows, sounds, and visual features lead Nabokov to use them in a great variety of artistic figures that allow them to connect a diversity of thought, imagination, and human experience. One of the goals of this book will be to show that Nabokov explored many obvious and non-obvious features of trees' existence and their place in human lives and cultures, including their ability both to ground human lives and to lead them towards new forms and possibilities. Along with being "just trees," Nabokov's trees are always more, and more complex, than an abstracted notion of a simplified tree could imply. In a way, he already defined his position relative to any exclusively abstract consideration of trees in chapter 4 of *The Gift*, where the early socialists' vision of trees is shown to be exceptionally distant from nature's reality. (More on that in this book's chapter 4.) We see that move echoed in the quotation above. Nabokov's trees may not represent rhizomes, exactly, but they do stand as complex, multivalent points in his texts that make connections in any number of directions, across temporal, ontological, and conceptual boundaries (perhaps more like the dendrites of nerve cells, or like what we now know takes place in the mycorrhizal jungle beneath the forest floor).[18] One of the ways these trees leap out of their linear bifurcations is through interaction with light, and

Nabokov's considerations of shadows and reflections form a prodigious network of tree-related phenomena.

We will visit many trees' shadows throughout this study, but a few of these shadows deserve special attention before we move on in this introduction. Nabokov's trees very often cast shadows (including a magical one in *Pnin*, discovered by Jonathan Rowan in 2016), painting, pawing, and enmeshing the objects, people, and animals beneath their limbs. What's especially intriguing is that even his *figurative* trees cast shadows, and not just in his fiction. Two striking examples from the 1940s: the first is "cast" by a taxonomic, phylogenetic tree in one of his major scientific papers – a moment that demonstrates both the rigour of Nabokov's thought, and his inability to resist an opportunity to exploit a metaphor in order to jump across ontological boundaries, even in his science writing.[19] Akin to this device, but vastly more complex, is the tree-as-artwork analogy, in chapter 7 of *Bend Sinister*, where *Hamlet* is compared to an oak tree, and its translation to an elaborate wooden kinetic sculpture designed not to *look* like the original tree, but to cast *exactly the same shadow* as the original, including all wind-and-light-driven variations on its state of being, or its being perceived. We will return to these examples at greater length in chapter 4.

An enormous, absurdly mechanical pseudo-tree, whose shadow is a perfect reproduction of an actual living, swaying, *real* oak's shadow, requires quite a leap of imagination. This seems to be the heart of the matter for Nabokov: trees are the perfect space and material for just such imaginative leaps. He invented at least eight imaginary trees – far fewer than the fantastical butterflies that adorn his book inscriptions for Véra and others, but not a bad day's work for a mortal. Imaginary trees were introduced in the early story "Terra Incognita," with the "acreana" bush and its fruits, and the "black-leafed limia."[20] In the foreword to *Lolita: A Screenplay*, Nabokov names the "*Pyrospodia*" tree under which he conjured some of the dramatized scenes (italics original: it seems to be a genus, and "*Pyrospodia*" could be translated as "fire-ash," evoking perhaps the firebird of fairy tales and the early poem).[21] *Ada*, in so many ways a culmination, produces four new species: a "semi-extinct mountain willow" (A 55), a "shattal apple" (A 94 etc.), burnberry (A 62 etc.; see Boyd's AdaOnline), and one we saw above, "*Quercus ruslan* Chat.," which of course leads us right back to that magical source of Russian tale and song: Pushkin. In an interview with Bernard Pivot for the French *Apostrophes* in 1975, Nabokov modestly took credit for only one invented tree in *Ada* (while regretting that he never invented any mammals; he never thought of it, he says [TWS 467]).

This expansion of "trees" to include shadows, inventions, and metaphors is one of the ways Nabokov used them to generate new semantic and figurative layers in his works. Another aspect of his approach was to carry the memory of trees into the wooden materials and objects that are made from them. Now and then, it appears, Nabokov decided to add nuance to his artistic use of trees (and to reduce their visibility) by shifting to a significant pattern of wooden objects. This strategy is especially visible in early novels such as *Mary* and *The Defense*, but also detectable in mid-career in *Invitation to a Beheading*, in "The Ballad of Longwood Glen," in *Speak, Memory*, and in *Transparent Things*. Although trees are far from absent in these works, we can sense acutely that Nabokov is pushing their signifying reach outward, metonymically, through wooden objects, which become tokens of the tree world and its interweavings with daily life. We see this phenomenon most vividly when Luzhin buries his first (stolen) wooden chess set "in a coppice"; when Cincinnatus places his head and chest onto an oak execution block; when we are told that Nabokov's "first poem" was sparked in a pavilion that was "in tune with the trees, dark fir and bright birch, whose sap once ran through its timber" (SM 215); in the "robust, dark-brown penholder ... of young oak," which we saw above, that Nabokov wrote with in his first European period (caption, opposite SM 256); in the "varnished" stump of the downed tree in "Longwood Glen"; in the "cheap pine" pencil of *Transparent Things* (6). Each of these objects openly proclaims the connection Nabokov saw between wooden objects and their tree origins – connections which, given Nabokov's urge to peer into the temporal depth of any object he contemplated, he will have felt in other, less explicitly marked, wooden objects as well.

In fact, it seems no tree-related reference was too abstract for Nabokov to include in his purview. When he read through Bobbie Ann Mason's dissertation, writing her a series of notes she used while revising it for publication as a book, he objected to her claim that "no trees appear" in *Ada*'s Part Five, exclaiming, "'No trees appear in the last part'? What about the 'Babes in the brown-leaf Woods,' top of p. 588?"[22] Those "Woods" have no clear referent in the characters' world, and have a partial literary background; Nabokov did not want the allusion to be missed, however fleeting, abstract, or slight.

Trees, in other words, do not only bifurcate, cast shadows, and generate metaphors; in combination with human imagination and craftsmanship (or, sometimes, brutality), they are transformed into new objects – some of which also become part of the creation of art (penholders and violins, for example).

As films have a soundtrack, one might say that each of Nabokov's works has a distinctive, deliberately crafted "tree-track."

Nabokov's works might be thought of, by analogy to musical compositions, as being in a particular tree key. Specific types stand out in each novel (and

Introduction   19

some stories), such that one, two, or three dominate and appear to offer a kind of structuring background. These sets of dominant and subdominant trees in the works are not necessarily reducible to particular thematic commitments, though in some cases there do appear to be certain recurring associations. Most likely the primary and secondary trees in a work do have particular significance: in some cases, this might be a connection to specific literary or mythological antecedents; in others, there may be more or less identifiable biographical resonances that we discover through overlaps and echoes with the memoir and various semi-autobiographical texts. There certainly must be some instances of tree-clusters whose deeper meaning was a personal matter to Nabokov, and was not necessarily accessible to readers. These details will be discussed through the chapters of this study, but there is a more general point that stands separate from the question of trees' possible meanings: that is, that the trees, collectively and in their broad texture as diverse groups running through a work, create a grounding natural layer underlying the works' worlds. This background is almost unnoticeable – because trees are almost unnoticeable to most people – yet it forms the essential substrate, the hidden fabric that generates the natural reality indicating the portrayed worlds' physical (as in *natural*, from Greek φύσις) and metaphysical (that is, what might stand outside of, or behind, nature) being. In nearly every work, the background offers a hidden but vital story of nature, that thing that surrounds us always but is never fully known, and often not even noticed.

This way of thinking about works of literature is perhaps unexpected, but it may have had power for Nabokov precisely because it was so easy to slip it under the reader's radar. Most works in literary history aren't associated with a dominant yet hidden collection of natural items: the few exceptional cases, such as *Moby-Dick* with the whale and the sea, or Woolf's *Orlando* with its oak, or perhaps the Mississippi River in *Huckleberry Finn*, represent something different, where the given feature of nature really stands at the centre of artistic gravity, around which all other components orbit and dance. Shakespeare's works are rich with diverse flora especially; it might be that they could be treated in a way similar to what I will propose here for Nabokov's works.

As the lists in the appendices may illustrate, there is a tangible flowing essence to the presence of trees within the works. There are various ways we can visualize the networked presence of trees in the poems, stories, and novels, and each approach reveals something different about what role they might be playing. The simplest, a numerical and essentially chronological presentation, offers an immediate sense of which trees come first and last, and most frequently, in a work. Thus, to begin with the earliest novel, *Mary*, we find brief references to palm and fir, but an immediate emphasis on lindens and birches. These are soon joined by emphatic but passing episodes with pines and with poplars, before returning to firs and adding in several more pines, a few alders, more birches and lindens, and some laurels.²³ The last trees mentioned by name are lindens, preceded by pines. The birches fade out by the novel's midpoint. The novel includes sixteen species (including some wooden objects), a fairly large number for such a slight work. I suggest that the novel's main key is *linden*, with secondary keys of *pine*, *birch*, and *poplar*. Given the autobiographical overtones of the novel, combined with its themes, these key trees (or tree-keys) make sense, and we will note later how Nabokov creates his own personal thematic code that creates a part of each tree's identity for him. On the level of its trees, and looking back through the lens of a long career and that of *Speak, Memory*, the tree-story behind *Mary* looks relatively straightforward. But even without delving into those biographical details, it is worth simply sitting with the fact that this is a novel dominated by lindens, pines, birches, poplars, and perhaps firs. It should not be forgotten either that all these trees had a tangible and specific natural reality to Nabokov; that through them, he felt part of his own personal connection to nature, that is, the deepest reality of the world as he saw and experienced it.

The question of whether to tackle this book as a work of "ecocriticism" came up in early and late discussions with colleagues as the project evolved. As I entered the most intensive phase of my research, I considered such a framing carefully, looking at other works that contribute to ecocritical discourse. Ian Helfant, in *That Savage Gaze: Wolves in the Nineteenth Century Imagination*, pursues an ecocriticism that "explores ... how humanity views itself in relation to nature and how these views vary between societies and over time, particularly as expressed in literature and the arts."²⁴ Thomas Hodge, in *Hunting Nature: Ivan Turgenev and the Organic World*, cites Cheryll Glotfelty's definition: "an earth-centered approach to literary studies ... [which] takes as its subject the interconnections between nature and culture," while also following Turgenev in being an environmentalist without adopting advocacy, exploring the author's "self-conception as a moral participant in the natural world."²⁵ And Jane T. Costlow's *Heart-Pine Russia: Walking and Writing the Nineteenth-Century Forest*, a work visibly closer to my own topic, "takes as its central focus the cultural resonance of the forest in nineteenth-centry Russia."²⁶ In some respects, Hodge's work is the most similar to mine, in that he writes about a single artist, suggesting that "we stand to learn a great deal about [Turgenev's] thought and literary technique when we read him in both cultural and environmental context" (14), and proposing to use Turgenev's nature writings (primarily hunting-related) as material for discovering how he represents a singular manifestation of a cultural phenomenon.

In the end, I decided that the ecocritical approach would not be congenial to this study, and might even be redundant, given the artist under review. Already because of his extensive commitment to butterfly research, both as an amateur and as a professional, Nabokov is probably the most nature-invested writer or artist in the Russian tradition, and second perhaps only to Goethe as a global figure who spans the gap between art and natural science.[27] It would be worthwhile, I think, for someone to collect passages in Nabokov's works that foreground his interest in the natural environment – especially in *Glory*, in *The Gift*, and in *Speak, Memory*, as well as in some poems and a few stories – and in this way situate Nabokov within a cultural context, either of Russian aristocrats or of émigrés, or of artists or some other grouping. However, my task is entirely different, and both broader and narrower: I aim to show how a key driving force of Nabokov's creativity is connected to one beloved, and to him powerful, phenomenon: trees. Although Nabokov demonstrably loved nature, and worked tirelessly to know and experience it, and cared about protecting it, often "nature" is present in his artworks only tangentially, metonymically, through butterflies and trees and other plants. The real question for me is, What is the arboreal ecology of Nabokov's art? How does his ever-expanding engagement with trees enable him to deepen his exploration of specific human lives within the natural and cultural domains? Because they are so extensive, and so varied, I want to discover not so much how Nabokov experienced trees in nature – though this at times is relevant – but how he crafted them into components of his art.

Why should we think of Nabokov as a "tree" writer, perhaps even more than as a "butterfly" writer? In a way, this question forces us back to more fundamental ones, about what it means to read (or receive, perceive, participate in) a work of literature or art. How and why does one create art, and how and why does one attend to or respond to that art with consciousness? Nabokov, carefully considered, is a "tree" writer because trees, in various guises, are clearly a driving force of his art from the very beginning, right up to the end. When we see this fact and explore it with the depth and care it deserves, we come to feel that by following Nabokov's trees we not only understand him better, but also, just maybe, we understand all of life a bit more fully, too. The reason for both of these results is that for Nabokov, and in the history of life and culture, trees ramify and intertwine in almost every imaginable way. This ramification, in complementarity with weaving and shadow-casting, emerges as an essential element in Nabokov's artistic universe.

Chapter One

Nabokov's Origins in the Poetry of Trees

... the trees beyond the gate grow agitated
as they endeavor out of turn to get
into my verse.

Vladimir Nabokov, "The Madman"[1]

The Arboreal Beginnings of Consciousness

The presence of trees in Nabokov's works has attracted relatively little attention to date. It's rather surprising to see that scholars have not thought much about Nabokov as a writer who was interested in nature per se.[2] His specialized knowledge in the narrow sphere of lepidopterology, widely studied by Dieter E. Zimmer, Kurt Johnson, Brian Boyd, and others, has not so far transformed into a scholarly consideration of Nabokov as a naturalist more broadly, and specifically as a lover of nature.[3] To some extent, this neglect may be due to the wealth of other topics and conflicts (psychological, intertextual) his works constantly present to readers and researchers.

Let us begin with a brief digression, and a disclaimer. "Tree" is not a taxonomic category, and I will be discussing various plants that are not, or not quite, trees. I might have more accurately and awkwardly called this book "Nabokov's Secret Woody Plants and Other Tree-Like Things." Although in my lists I have included species as diverse as cactus, honeysuckle, and giant sequoia, the great majority of examples I discuss at length are real trees (if, sometimes, small ones); honeysuckle is one important exception.

"Tree" is a somewhat vague term, poorly defined at the smaller end, and Nabokov clearly appreciated many small trees or shrubs as much as the large, stately variety. Colin Tudge offers a charming and lively discussion of the complexities in defining "tree," boiling it down to a modified "child's definition": "A tree is a big plant with a stick up the middle – or it could be ... or is very closely related to ... or it resembles a big plant with a stick up the middle. It is clumsy, but it will have to do."[4] Despite the fact that it seems less precise than we would imagine Nabokov preferring, I will follow Tudge's definition, especially the "resembles" and "could be" parts. As will become clear in the course of my study, Nabokov thought of trees in a different way than he thought of butterflies. He responded to them intensely throughout his life, and worked actively to expand his basic knowledge of them – his list of acquaintants, if you will – but he did not study them scientifically, instead working in vague categories that can create some confusion. For example, of the hundred or so species of oak that exist, Nabokov presents only a few vague subtypes, including one he invented. Nevertheless, he took his trees seriously, and he expected others to do so too.

It is well known that trees occupy a central position in European folklore and mythology, and Slavic culture is no exception. In a recent study, Zsuzsa Hetenyi has shown that the trees in *Lolita* are in conversation with mythological precursors, especially from ancient Greece. Nabokov himself (and in his footsteps, Bobbie Ann Mason and Brian Boyd) presents the image of the Tree of Knowledge as a central part of the Ardis environment in *Ada*, from Nabokov's late period. But this belated revelation, appearing as it does in *Ada* almost in the guise of a joke, offers only the merest hint of the full depth of the arboreal theme in Nabokov's works. To begin this chapter, I want to discuss a more local mythology: the mythology of personal consciousness, and thus of the theme of creative production (or perception plus creativity) that he weaves into the various incarnations of his memoir, from the magazine versions beginning in 1948, to 1951's *Conclusive Evidence*, the 1954 Russianized version, *Drugie berega/Other Shores*, and at last the final revision, 1966's *Speak, Memory*.[5]

One of the most intriguing of the discarded possible names for the memoir – names Nabokov listed in the foreword to the final edition – was "The Anthemion," from the Greek ανθέμιον. This word could refer, on the one hand, to a "palmetto" ornament; alternatively, as Nabokov writes, it is "the name of a honeysuckle ornament, consisting of elaborate interlacements and expanding clusters" – features with obviously attractive metaphorical potential – "but nobody liked it" as a title (SM 11). One can't be sure where Nabokov got his definition, but a strong possibility is his favourite English dictionary, *Webster's New International Dictionary, Second Edition* (hereafter *Webster's Second*), where under this word we read the following: "An ornament consisting of floral or foliated forms arranged in a radiating cluster, but always flat as in relief sculpture or in painting; the honeysuckle ornament." Judging from the closely paralleled expressions and the one named plant, he recalled this definition as he was thinking of names for his memoir. Honeysuckle (generally a bush, but see the disclaimer at the beginning of the previous paragraph) was one of the shrubs prominently located around his family's country manor house at Vyra.

24   Nabokov's Secret Trees

And not only at the estate. Not by chance, perhaps, did Nabokov reach for this "ornamental" name for his autobiography: as we will see below, the honeysuckle also plays a key role in his earliest creative – specifically poetic – imaginings. Moreover, an "anthemion" represents a stylized, aesthetic image of this woody plant, frequently serving as a decoration on architectural monuments of ancient Greece, including the Parthenon. This is not the place to explore the full history of the anthemion as a cultural and symbolic form, but for now it is essential to underscore its role embodying the penetration of a plant into some of the most important semiotic systems of the ancient world. The anthemion image introduces yet another thematic element, one central to Nabokov's concerns and highly visible in his definition of the term, though partly absent from *Webster's Second*: I mean the "elaborate interlacements and expanding clusters." In the beginning of *Speak, Memory*, such interlacements and patterns introduce the first "gleam of complete consciousness" experienced by Nabokov as a child:

> Judging by the strong sunlight that, when I think of that revelation, immediately invades my memory with lobed sun flecks through overlapping patterns of greenery, the occasion may have been my mother's birthday, in late summer, in the country ... Thus, when the newly disclosed, fresh and trim formula of my own age, four, was confronted with the parental formulas, thirty-three and twenty-seven, something happened to me. I was given a tremendously invigorating shock ... Between them, as they evenly progressed, I strutted, and trotted, and strutted again, from sun fleck to sun fleck, along the middle of a path, which I easily identify today with an alley of ornamental oaklings ... My father, let it be noted, had served his term of military training long before I was born, so I suppose he had that day put on the trappings of his old regiment as a festive joke. To a joke, then, I owe my first gleam of complete consciousness. (SM 22–3)

It is striking how the motif of "sun through the branches" penetrates this scene depicting the awakening of mental life. The numbers of the family members' ages blend with the shadows cast by the oaklings, as the young Nabokov proceeds, "strutting" from one sunfleck to another, among the shadows of those same oaks, in the luminous spaces of this complex pattern. Consciousness appears as a "reflection" or "flash" of sunlight, and the shadows – in other words, the trees – create the outline for this consciousness. Nabokov draws attention away from the trees, saying that he owes this gleam to a "joke"; the joke, of course, is important as well, but at the same time we have here the narrator's craftiness as he distracts the reader's attention from what is most important: the play of light and shadow in the steps, eyes, and thoughts of a small human being and his dawning consciousness. The notion of pattern already stands out in the first and second versions of this episode, in the *New Yorker* and then in the book *Conclusive Evidence*, where the awakening self-consciousness is juxtaposed with the image of bursts of light: "I see the awakening of consciousness as a series of spaced flashes, with the intervals between them gradually diminishing until bright blocks of perception are formed, affording memory a slippery hold" (CE 3). In the expanded Russian *Drugie berega/Other Shores*, produced just a few years later, this passage continues, "the flashes merge into colored radiances, into geographical forms" (SSRP 5:146, my translation). The flashes and flecks merge and mutate linguistically as well as visually, finally leading Nabokov to connect the movements of the branches, leaves, and sunlight with the awakening of consciousness and the establishment of memory, allowing him to determine the exact date which, "judging by the strong sunlight that, when I think of that revelation, immediately invades my memory with lobed sun flecks through overlapping patterns of greenery, ... may have been my mother's birthday" (SM 21).

The key addition in the third and fourth versions of this passage is the emphasis on the young boy's *feet* – that is, the unification of the mental and bodily aspects of self: the "I" who notices, understands, and connects these flashes and flecks, and the "I" who "strutted, and trotted, and strutted again" among them. Thus, Nabokov's consciousness takes its first steps in both the literal and figurative senses in that avenue of oaklings, in the pattern created by their interweaving branches and leaves, not unlike an anthemion. A few chapters later, Nabokov will talk about other trees with a similarly important influence on his childhood development, although those trees will be not real ones, but images crafted in paint.

As it turns out, not only the first flash of self-consciousness but nearly all the key turning points in the awakening of Nabokov's creative spirit are intimately bound to trees. Those steps in their connection with trees (or tree-related artefacts), and their shadowy patterns and elaborations, continue in the fourth chapter, which was first published in the *New Yorker* with the title "My English Education." Nabokov tells about the end of an ordinary day at the family's country estate, Vyra. The scene begins by showing how little Nabokov, as a toddler or small boy, mounts the stairs to the second floor with his mother, all the while accompanied by her repeated, metronome-like words, "step, step, step" (SM 85), as they make their way to his evening bath. The passage is interrupted by an unexpected and conspicuous digression about bathrooms:

There were five bathrooms in our country house, and a medley of venerable washstands ... The toilets were separate from the bathrooms, and the oldest among them was a rather sumptuous but gloomy affair with some fine panelwork and a tasseled rope of red velvet, which, when pulled, produced a beautifully modulated, discreetly muffled gurgle and gulp. From that corner of the house, one coud see Hesperus and hear the nightingales [the Russian version here mentions a poplar tree], and it was there that, later, I used to compose my youthful verse, dedicated to unembraced beauties, and morosely survey, in a dimly illuminated mirror, the immediate erection of a strange castle in an unknown Spain.[6]

That is, we have shifted from the climb to the bath to an extended digression on bathrooms and toilet rooms or water closets, and we wind up in one particular WC – not the one annexed to the bath where we are heading, but one from the future, where (in the Russian version) he would sit behind "oak paneling," composing poetry while looking out the window at the stars and the poplars. In the *New Yorker* (original) version of the chapter, and only there, he adds, "And it was there that I composed my first poem" ("English Education," 26). As we know, the story of Nabokov's "first poem" is complicated; soon, he would transfer its compositional location to other spots – parks, gardens. These places receive their full embodiment in chapter 11 of the two English memoir versions ("First Poem" in magazine form), which was not included in version three, *Drugie berega/Other Shores*. But the idea of the WC as a creative retreat persisted through all the versions, and in *Drugie berega/Other Shores*, we find a vivid image: "there, in years of lilac and fog, I would compose verse." Moreover, it is worth recalling that in the Russian version, and only there, Nabokov at this spot mentions that this recurring episode, the scene of his youthful verse-writing, had been transferred into his "first tale" (SSRP 5:193), that is, into what we know as *Mary*.[7] The short novel gives us a fictionalized version of this creative nook:

> In one wing of the manor house, between the larder and the housekeeper's room, there was a spacious old-fashioned water closet; its window gave onto a neglected part of the garden where in the shade of an iron roof a pair of black wheels surmounted a well, and a wooden water trough ran over the ground between the bare, winding roots of three huge bushy poplars. The window was decorated by a stained-glass knight with a square beard and mighty calves, and he glowed strangely in the dim light of a paraffin lamp with a tin reflector which hung beside the heavy velvet cord. You pulled the cord and from the mysterious depths of the oaken throne there would come a watery rumbling and hollow gurgles. Ganin flung open the casement and installed himself, feet and all, on the window ledge; the velvet cord swung gently and the starry sky between the black poplars made you want to heave a deep sigh. And that moment, when he sat on the window ledge of that lugubrious lavatory, and thought how he would probably never, never get to know the girl with the black bow on the nape of her delicate neck, and waited in vain for a nightingale to start trilling in the poplars as in a poem by Fet – that moment Ganin now rightly regarded as the highest and most important point in his whole life. (M 46–7)[8]

We have here a double-bottomed digression of Gogolian proportions: from the WC to the poplars, from the poplars to nightingales and, with them, Fet.[9] In this artistically transformed autobiographical world, we see the "overgrown," "black" poplars more clearly, and through them, among their branches, the sky and stars. Ganin (the protagonist), as far as the reader knows, is not a poet, but it is noteworthy that, with apparent narratorial approbation, he "now rightly regarded" his time looking at trees through that window, and thinking about Mary, "as the highest and most important point in his whole life." That "now" refers to the narrative present in Berlin, the novel's "now," living in emigration, and awaiting a reunion with the *real* Mary, who is coming to join her husband. We can only guess why this remembered moment is the "highest and most important"; perhaps this was the first, even only, time he had achieved something like an artistic epiphany, hinting at an ability to reach into the future and provide Ganin his first steps towards establishing his life's coherence. The moment also echoes important role the real-world double of this space played in Nabokov's own life, a fact reinforced by the twice-mentioned oak wood of the room and its paneling – recalling to Nabokov, at least, the oaklings attending his first glimmers of consciousness, and perhaps the penholder of "young oak" in his writing hand (the one discussed above, in the introduction). The absence of a poetic impulse distances Ganin from Nabokov, but the poetic loftiness of such moments by the velvet cord draws them together.

In its Russian presentation in the memoir, this special room announces its wooden features more openly than in any of the English versions, before or after. Only in Russian are oak and poplar and lilac mentioned by name, whereas in English we find merely "fine panelwork," and the nightingales sing without reference to their perches. One therefore wonders, why did Nabokov add such details specifically to the Russian autobiography, but not carry them through to the subsequent, final English version? It appears that in *Drugie berega/Other Shores*, Nabokov enhanced the tangibility of the tree-derived elements of the scene's first part as compensation for a reduction in wood-related specificity in the scene's second part. The mutations deserve a closer look.

After the excursion into the future – the tour of the oaken WC in the servants' quarters, with poetry crafting – Nabokov leads us back to his early childhood and that specific evocative moment, climbing the stairs to the rhythmic sound of his mother's "step, step, step":

> As a small child, however, I was assigned a more modest arrangement, rather casually situated in a narrow recess between a wicker hamper and the door leading to the nursery bathroom. This door I liked to keep ajar; through it I drowsily looked at the shimmer of steam above the mahogany bath, at the fantastic flotilla of swans and skiffs, at myself with a harp in one of the boats, at a furry moth pinging against the reflector of the kerosene lamp, at the stained-glass window beyond, at its two halberdiers consisting of colored rectangles. Bending from my warm seat, I liked to press the middle of my brow, its ophryon to be precise, against the smooth

28 Nabokov's Secret Trees

comfortable edge of the door and then roll my head a little, so that the door would move to and fro while its edge remained all the time in soothing contact with my forehead. A dreamy rhythm would permeate my being. The recent "Step, step, step," would be taken up by a dripping faucet. And, fruitfully combining rhythmic pattern with rhythmic sound, I would unravel the labyrinthian frets on the linoleum, and find faces where a crack or a shadow afforded a *point de repère* for the eye. I appeal to parents: never, never say, "Hurry up," to a child. (SM 85)

Yes, we are still in a bathroom with a little boy – in a WC a bit smaller, "a more modest arrangement," compared to the one that would later become home to his verse-making. From this little space, he looks through the half-ajar door into the adjoining bathing room. In all three English versions, the bath, with its "shimmer of steam," receives a more detailed description than in *Drugie berega/Other Shores*: the bath is "mahogany," we are told; but in the Russian, there is no mahogany mentioned, nor any wood at all in the vicinity of the bath. Clearly, this is some kind of mahogany panelling that surrounds or covers the tub itself, but in Russian it disappears. My hunch is that the Russian term for this wood, *krasnoe derevo* (red wood), did not meet the sonic needs of the moment, the way the English word does; in this second domestic language, the central topic of the whole chapter, whose title in the *New Yorker* was, remember, "My English Education," the word "mahogany" feels expressive and warm, while also underscoring the sense of luxury. Apparently the Russian term lacked, for Nabokov, this necessary sensuous quality.[10] Thus, its removal from *Drugie berega/Other Shores* is compensated for in the first WC's description, where we twice read of the room's oak panelling. The principle and presence of wood, and trees' names, are preserved.

And indeed, the scene is palpably sensuous. As noted, it begins with the sounds on the stairs – not only his mother's words, but the imagined footfalls at each upward step. These stairway words and sounds and the "step, step, step" resound again when the little boy, watching from his "throne," mentally overlaps the words and the dripping water from the tap (in the Russian, this pattern is continued by an alliterative, drumming butterfly – *barabanila babochka*), "combining rhythmic pattern with rhythmic sound" (SM 85). This perceptual transformation takes place while, "bending from my warm seat, I liked to press the middle of my brow ... against the smooth comfortable edge of the door and then roll my head a little, so that the door would move to and fro while its edge remained in soothing contact with my forehead." There he sits, looking at the bath and the linoleum floor, pressing his forehead against the edge of the wooden door, rocking in time with the dripping tap, the butterfly, and (echoing in memory) the beat of footsteps on stairs and his mother's voice. These patterns intertwine, creating a sort of "anthemion," preparing all the constituent artistic elements of the future wordsmith. It's no surprise that he cautions never to tell a child, "Hurry up!" He says this partly as a joke, for he is talking not just about imagination, but also about a small boy sitting on his potty, after all. Back on the stairs, he had already given an anticipatory warning that his readers should avoid thinking in Freudian terms.

After the bath described above, the scene moves to the bedtime routine; here we find the same defining, yet half-hidden, images of Nabokov's life essence. This "final stage" of the journey takes place in the bedroom, preparing to get under the covers. Near the end of the chapter's third section, just before falling asleep, the little boy sees trees not in an ordinary or natural setting, but in a context saturated with magic and imagination:

> above the icon, high up on the wall, where the shadow of something ... undulated in the warm candlelight, a framed aquarelle showed a dusky path winding through one of those eerily dense European beechwoods, where the only undergrowth is bindweed and the only sound one's thumping heart. In an English fairy tale my mother had once read to me, a small boy stepped out of his bed into a picture and rode his hobbyhorse along a painted path between silent trees. While I knelt on my pillow in a mist of drowsiness and talc-powdered well-being, half sitting on my calves and rapidly going through my prayer, I imagined the motion of climbing into the picture above my bed and plunging into that enchanted beechwood – which I did visit in due time. (SM 86)[11]

It is quite appropriate that Nabokov calls this moment the "final stage" of his "vague navigation": we have already witnessed various stages of the boy's experience of his world, his translation of sensory impressions into the mental dimension of feelings and imagination. We also saw how tightly trees are interwoven into the earlier stages of this "navigation" that leads Nabokov to full self-consciousness. And now, above him, this watercolour painting with its path leading into the woods. This is the first instance in the memoir of artistically portrayed trees, of trees within an artistic creation. The "navigation" is not only Nabokov's boyhood journey, but also the journey of the trees themselves, having awakened his consciousness and his imagination, from the "real" world around him into the world of art and invention. The trees in the painting blend together with the woods from the English fairy tale read to him by his mother, and this provokes his vision of climbing into the painting himself, into its world of imagined trees and paths, its "enchanted beechwood" (SM 86). It is only in the chapter's third version, in *Drugie berega/Other Shores*, that Nabokov adds that he did "visit in due time" the enchanted wood, but for some reason he does not reveal when and how it happened. That secret he brings forth only in the fourth version, *Speak, Memory*, where he introduces a new scene into the chapter – one that finally closes the enchanted circle.

The path through the woods and the painting that figures the scene fade for a while into the background, but in the chapter's fifth section (sixth in *Drugie*

30 Nabokov's Secret Trees

berega/Other Shores), the theme of drawing and painting returns to prominence. In the first two English versions, in harmony with its *New Yorker* title, the section was restricted to a discussion of Nabokov's "drawing master," an Englishman named Mr. Cummings. It is quite possible that Mr. Cummings was the artist responsible for the watercolour over the bed: we learn here that a generation earlier he had been Nabokov's mother's teacher, as well, and that his creations could be found on various walls around the house: "His little watercolors, purchased at different times for five or ten roubles apiece by members of our household, led a somewhat precarious existence, shifting, as they did, to more and more obscure nooks and finally getting completely eclipsed by some sleepy porcelain beast or a newly framed photograph" (SM 91).

One reason to think that Mr. Cummings made the bedroom forest is his well-described penchant for painting "wet little paradises" in watercolour; another is found in the fact (added in the Russian, and modified in the final *Speak, Memory*) that he "held a pencil with unusual elegance, and with its magical strokes would stretch the distance into one infinite, far-away point" (SSRP 5:199).[12] "Magical strokes," one might think, would be just the kind to use to paint an enchanted forest. Although Nabokov de-emphasized the magical quality of the pencil and perspective lessons in the final revision, he restored them in a new passage about Mr. Cummings' watercolours, which concludes with a painting of "a pasture ending in the black fringe of a distant forest, and a luminous river, repeating the sky and winding away and away" (SM 91) – very much in the mood of the receding forest trail. Although these suggestions remain speculative, the crucial information is to be found in the way that in Mr. Cummings, painting merges with magic, and how in those first lessons in perspective he teaches young Nabokov the most basic type of visual deception. The significance of this relationship is probably hinted at in Nabokov's comment, made to Alfred Appel, that he was "born a landscape painter."[13]

In the final version of his memoir, Nabokov decided to broaden the chapter's focus beyond the Anglophilia that shaped his childhood, particularly expanding the section on his art teachers' role in his development. It was this extension that allowed him to reveal what he hinted first in version three – that he had managed to visit the enchanted beechwood in the painting. The next visual arts teacher, S.P. Yaremich (who was well known), caused a newly adolescent Nabokov to "rebel"; but the final artist, the "celebrated" Mstislav Dobuzhinsky, associated with the World of Art and the Ballets Russes, made vital contributions to the teenaged Nabokov's navigation of the interplay of conscious perception and creative expression. Among many other described exercises, Nabokov relates that

> he tried to teach me to find the geometrical coordinations between the slender twigs of a leafless boulevard tree, a system of visual give-and-takes, requiring a precision of linear expression, which I failed to achieve in my youth, but applied

gratefully, in my adult instar, not only to the drawing of butterfly genitalia during my seven years at the Harvard Museum of Comparative Zoology ... but also, perhaps, to certain camera-lucida needs of literary composition. Emotionally, however, I am still more indebted to the earlier color treats given me by my mother and her former teacher. (SM 92)

In these "geometrical coordinations between the slender twigs of a leafless boulevard tree" we sense the same elements that are found in the regretfully rejected title, "The Anthemion." These coordinations (in Russian a "dignified, precious pattern" – *vazhnyi, dragotsennyi uzor*) he relates to his work at the microscope drawing the organs of butterflies, and also to the "needs of literary composition." Driving home his theme, Nabokov here again takes the opportunity to draw our attention to the connection between the forms of trees and the creative work of artistic imagination.

After the orderly, chronological tale of his childhood lessons in painting and drawing, Nabokov returns, through a fleeting overview, to the emotional experience of those years; and then, still another repetition, to a moving recollection about all his teachers and finally, to the eventual trajectories of the two British artists. In the chapter's final episode, added only in *Speak, Memory*, he again finds himself in the company of Dobuzhinsky, who became a friend throughout many years of shared emigration, and even a collaborator in his first years in the United States.[14] It may be that it was from Dobuzhinsky that Nabokov learned the fates of the other artists, as was certainly the case with regard to the first Russian teacher: "'And what about Yaremich?' I asked M.V. Dobuzhinski, one summer afternoon in the nineteen forties, as we strolled through a beech forest in Vermont. 'Is he remembered?'" (SM 94). There it is, that beechwood at last, which Nabokov finally visited in the company of one of his most important artistic guides: in this beechwood, they strolled along a forest path, recalling other teachers, other artists, and bringing a toddler's fantasy to life.[15]

Poems in the Trees

The textual record of Nabokov's relationship with trees begins in the earliest phase – in his youthful poetry, certainly including some that were crafted in the luxurious WC overlooking the poplars. So we have to start in those early creations to try to map out what kind(s) of role(s), and what kind(s) of importance, and what meanings, trees have in Nabokov's works during his "mature" period as a "major writer." Setting aside for a moment his juvenile collection *Stikhi* (Poems), in which fourteen of the first twenty poems include tree imagery, and turning to the next published collection, *Dva puti* (Two Paths), a collaborative venture with Sergey Balashov in 1918, we find that eight of Nabokov's twelve contributions mention trees, including three of the first four. The fourth

32   Nabokov's Secret Trees

Nabokov poem in the collection is particularly valuable, as it associates directly with the mythology of his earliest days as a writer of verse: this is the poem "The Rain Has Flown" (untitled in Russian; "Dozhd' proletel i sgorel na letu …"). This also happens to be the first poem in *Poems and Problems,* as well as in the 1979 collection *Stikhi,* which was selected and arranged for publication by Nabokov prior to his death in 1977.[16] Intended as a collection of his best poetry, its presentation of "The Rain Has Flown" at the front door of Nabokov's poetic world provides much to reflect upon.

Often associated with "The Rain Has Flown," the "first poem" episode from *Speak, Memory* is well-known and oft-cited.[17] There are many signature Nabokov elements in the scene: coloured-glass lozenges, the pavilion, butterflies, the bucolic setting of Vyra. But within this collection of personal memorabilia, trees play not just a crucial role, but the primary structural, thematic, and metaphorical ones – although this prominence is concealed behind a tapestry of words and other images. "A certain pavilion," he tells us, is where he was possessed by "the numb-fury of verse-making" (SM 215). The scene is presented in part through dreams (as a man approaching fifty, he reports that he dreams of the pavilion "at least twice a year"), which allows the memoirist perhaps more than the usual latitude regarding "facts." The pavilion is a "sturdy old wooden structure" with stained glass windows. The dreamscape takes a surprising shift, the pavilion revealed as "a trifle baroque, and yet in tune with the handsome trees, dark fir and bright birch, whose sap once ran through its timber." Note here how the dream-travel back to the youthful time of the first poetic inspiration has now launched yet another, less authorized, subsidiary sort of time-travel: a dream within a dream, as we (and the narrator) imagine the live trees, with their running sap, that pre-existed the pavilion, and gave themselves to it (we must suppose an honourable sacrifice, in the name of art, or of human-arboreal relations?). The pavilion is alive – alive with memory, alive with the spirit of its tree-bones, their sap-blood, its deep, transparent-thingy past shining through the surface as it nurtures the young consciousness and imagination sheltering within it.[18] Again, it doesn't matter whether this story is literally true: it is truth-like – *pravdopodobnoe, vraisemblable* – and Nabokov here *imagines* that it was true, ascribing to it the truth of art.

Consciousness is the main point here, and it figures in Nabokov's essential definition of poetry, offered during this scene, in the middle of the extended passages about the poem's composition: to write poetry is "to try to express one's position in regard to the universe embraced by consciousness" (SM 218). As the extended creative moment unfolds, trees accompany the young Nabokov (along with, of course, other iconic objects): he emerges from a poetic trance looking at "undulating plump shadows of alder foliage on the water" (SM 222); then, later, he finds himself on "a low bench in the park, and the live shadows, among which my hand dipped, now moved on the ground, violet tints instead of aqueous black and green" (SM 223). Even Sequoia National Forest would have seemed a natural waking spot in those youthful days, he claims, asserting further that "when the old trance occurs nowadays, I am quite prepared to find myself, when I awaken from it, high up in a certain tree, above the dappled bench of my boyhood, my belly pressed against a thick, comfortable branch and one arm hanging down among the leaves upon which the shadows of other leaves move" (SM 223).[19] Notice here especially the way leaves and the shadows of other leaves overlap and merge, both physically and in the young poet's artistic consciousness. Almost everything to do with this poetic, imaginative, creative state seems connected – bodily and mentally – to trees. And as the story of the first poem's emergence nears its conclusion, Nabokov presents his reader with the scene of composition against a background of artistically figured trees blending into the real trees around him:

> The family phonograph ... emitted from its brass mouthpiece the so-called *Tsiganskie romansï* beloved of my generation ... Their natural environment was characterized by nightingales in tears, lilacs in bloom and the alleys of whispering trees that graced the parks of the landed gentry. Those nightingales trilled, and in a pine grove the setting sun banded the trunks at different levels with fiery red. A tambourine, still throbbing, seemed to lie on the darkening moss. For a spell, the last notes of a husky contralto pursued me through the dusk. When silence returned, my first poem was ready. (SM 224)

As this image flows and unfolds, it is hard to tell which of these are scenes in the songs, and which are the settings within which young Nabokov listened to the songs: most likely, the two overlap, and the confusion or blending of worlds is surely deliberate. Perhaps reclining in that "pine grove," the boy poet stirs together the trees in his mind's eye and the trees of the song and the trees in the nearby sunset blaze; the trees of the pavilion and the tree whose leaves – linden, we know, because he tells us they are cordate – provided the first dripping stimuli to the poetic impulse: "drip, leaf, tip, relief" (SM 217).[20]

Nabokov's art will regularly return to the relationship between trees and consciousness, but for now I want to remain situated, if not in the world of a fifteen-year-old nascent poet, then at least in the early years of that poet's creativity. Nabokov began his writing career as a poet (and it can be argued that his prose, too, veers strongly into the poetic register), and if we are allowed to imagine that his lyrical writings of those years were at least partially "sincere," they too help us develop a sense of trees' place in the imaginative life of the writer.[21] This intimacy, so vividly charted in *Speak, Memory*'s chapter 11, sees a clear reflection in the proportion of early poems that included or even centred on trees. The first collection, self-published, of love poems written during the youthful romance with Valentina Shulgin, features twenty-seven poems (out of eighty-six in total) that include trees, of which eight have trees in the first line.

34   Nabokov's Secret Trees

These were written around two years after the initial inspirations described in the "First Poem" story).[22]

Nabokov's gateway poem is brief enough to present in full:

> The rain has flown and burnt up in flight.
>   I tread the red sand of a path.
> Golden orioles whistle, the rowan is in bloom,
>   the catkins on sallows are white.
> The air is refreshing, humid and sweet.
>   How good the caprifole smells!
> Downward a leaf inclines its tip
>   and drops from its tip a pearl.[23]

"The Rain Has Flown," to be clear, is *not* the "first poem" composed in 1914, but it captures (perhaps commemorates) that moment, or combines it with other memories in a way reprised in the *Speak, Memory* "First Poem" chapter. Despite some confusion about the matter, Nabokov does not imply in his memoir that "Rain" was the poem that emerged from that scene, and Boyd makes this clear, too, in his biography.[24] The poem's placement, opening *Stikhi* as well as the 1970 collection *Poems and Problems,* Nabokov's major self-introduction as a poet to non-Russian readers, marks one of at least five occasions in which he placed trees prominently within an origin story for his art. The poem could be said to include four trees, or three and a shrub. One of the trees is almost invisible, because it is nameless, and in effect we must project back onto this poem from *Speak, Memory* to recover it. On the poem's surface, we have, first, the rowan, and things immediately become a bit more obscure in the English version than they had been in the Russian. "Sallow" is a little-known word for "willow," whereas the Russian, "iva," is perfectly ordinary to a Russian ear. In the second stanza, the "caprifole" may not bring an immediate image with it to the anglophone, but it turns out to be honeysuckle, whose Russian "zhimolost'" is not nearly so esoteric a term as its chosen English mask.[25] One plausible goal of these odd-ish translations, far from "literal" in a standard sense – Nabokov had emphasized his literalist credo in the *Poems and Problems* introduction, while noting that it did not really apply to self-translation – is to smuggle in a theme of hiddenness, as these fancy, rare words obscure the simple Russian words and the "real" items they denote.[26] Additionally, these words may be meant simply to provide a feeling of distance, and alienation, to the non-Russian: Vyra's greenery was not, we can imagine, exactly the same as the versions that "honeysuckle" and "willow" would evoke to a North American (especially) or maybe even a Briton, so those standard terms may not be adequate to Nabokov's particular desire for specificity. Be that as it may, the real hidden treasure, the gem behind the pearl, is in the poem's final line, and it is hidden in both versions – if we grant credence to the image presented in the much later "First Poem" episode as standing behind both the 1917 poem and the memoir's chapter. In the memoir, we are told that the leaves dripping and tipping with raindrops are heart-shaped (cordate), and thus, with some knowledge of the landscape around Vyra, we can deduce that they are linden leaves; the name is withheld in the *Speak, Memory* scene (SM 217).[27] The shape and species of the leaf that "inclines its tip" in the poem is not given in either the Russian or the English of "The Rain Has Flown," but there is no reason dictated by the poem's logic to think that it must be rowan, sallow, or caprifole; "linden" remains an equally good candidate, and, based on the named trees in the parallel texts, and the way their leaves collect water – the most plausible of all. We can call it a "secret tree"; there will be more.[28]

A third arboreal origin story bifurcated into both verse and prose during late 1920 and well into 1921. A brief aside here is warranted, to note that Nabokov's deep love for Pushkin of course included the long poem "Ruslan and Lyudmila," one of Pushkin's early successes. As discussed in the introduction, the poem begins with an image presenting a font of folkloric stories: a cat circling a green oak on a gold chain, voicing tales and songs about wood-sprites, witches, firebirds, and other mythical creatures. Nabokov draws in part on this tradition in his first prose work (which, like other work in emigration, he signed "Vladimir Sirin" – the sirin being another mythical creature, a bird with a human head and breasts; the creature was popular among the Symbolists, whom Nabokov admired passionately as a youth). The idea of a special visit from a wood-sprite, or "leshii," connects a short story written in December of 1920 ("Nezhit'," published in Rul' the following month, translated as "The Wood-Sprite" by Dmitri Nabokov for the 1995 collected stories)[29] with a poem composed in June of the next year, "Pero" ("The Quill"): the narrator, in both instances, receives a magical visit from the forest. I want to focus first on the poetic version, although chronologically it came second, because it is more explicit. Nabokov did include this poem in his list for *Stikhi* (1979), where Véra published it, something of a very late affirmation or, alternatively, a fond recollection of the sentiment it expresses. The poem, never translated, is presented in a poetic voice whose first lines explicitly echo the rhythms of Russian folklore:

> To the little green, nimble grandkids
> The wood-sprite proclaimed in a pine-grove:
> "Among the black branches, among the toothy-ones,
> the firebird will flit in the evening;
> catch it, my little wood-spritelings,
> and this cage made of moon rays
> take from housekeeper-night,
> and do it so that Kashchei doesn't see."[30]

36 Nabokov's Secret Trees

We are deep in fairy tale territory here: traditional characters of country magic (wood-sprite; firebird; Kashchei [also spelled "Koshchei"][31] – a magical folk antagonist; personified night; with some whimsical additions by Nabokov: do wood-sprites have children and grandchildren?), and the formulaic, incantatory repetition, "Among the black branches, among the toothy-ones" ("Po chernym vetviam, po zubchatym"), with the second epithet given its own copy of the preposition, common in Russian folk genres.[32] The scene is domesticated, too, by the generational expansion of the wood-sprite family and the diminutive form "leshenyochki," a neologism whose cuddliness is roughly, and barely, captured by my translation, "wood-spritelings." Adventures and misadventures inevitably ensue, in accord with the folk-tale form, but the prize is in the final stanzas, where the speaker reveals the magical conclusion:

> But in the morning, like a live flame
> on my dusty threshold
> there lay a fiery quill
> with a colourful, elongated eyespot.
> Well so, and for this gift
> I thank you, my woodland friends.
> I'm poor, and my daytimes are pale,
> and how I'm gladdened [by this].[33]

There is a great deal one could examine in this poem, but the key point for my purposes is that the lyric persona has received the tool of his craft, an archetypal quill pen, directly from magical creatures of the wood, the "green folk" (*zelenyi narod*), who represent (or are) the "pine-groves," "lingonberry groves," and "fir trees" (it is unclear whether "folk," *narod*, might refer to the trees themselves, a possibility supported by other works, as will be seen).[34] Of course, the speaker takes pains to soften the audacious quality of such a myth: he is chosen by nature – by the trees, as it were – to be an artistic voice in the world; but the magical agents doing the choosing are deflated, rendered folksy and almost comical (their work seems to end in predictably folkloric misadventure, when the firebird escapes, instead of being delivered as planned in the moonbeam cage, to the "meek exile" at a "little brick house" in an "overseas land"). The quill's miraculous appearance at the door of the "poor" poet transcends all mishaps, and the poem leaves us with a few key images: a gift, the forest and wood-sprites, the gloominess of exilic reality, and gladness – crucially, a gladness that derives both from the woodland gift and the "thanks" that answer it, or, in other words, from the interrelationship of poet and trees. Is this Nabokov's self-parodying, deflationary revision of Pushkin's "The Prophet," in its common Solovyovian reading, or maybe a reply to his "The Muse"?[35] Notably, the poem makes no claims about the power, provenance, or mission of the gift's recipient. The quill comes without any charge – a "pointlessness" quite at home in Nabokov's creative world.[36]

The prose version of this sylvan visit, "Nezhit'/The Wood-Sprite," was signed a half-year earlier, and thus we can accept that its creative inception, as well, was the earlier of the two. Significantly, this is Nabokov's first published story, and apparently his very first completed work of prose fiction, introducing his pen name "Sirin" in print for the first time.[37] Unlike its sibling poem, the story does not draw attention to the act or art of writing: that the first-person narrator has also "written" the tale we read can be inferred, but this role is, at most, understated (he is tracing his inkstand and the outline of its shadow as the story opens). The visiting sprite, "leshii," or "wood-elf" as Dmitri Nabokov has it in his translation, is in every way a personification of the woods and groves of the narrator's Russian, pre-revolutionary youth – a "mossy-gray tuft on his temple," a "luscious-green" voice, eyes "like wet leaves." And, of course, he disappears, leaving behind a "wonderfully subtle scent ... of birch, of humid moss" (CS 3–5). There is little to this story except the act of greeting, perceiving, drinking in the aura of this emissary from former lands, this itinerant embodiment of most cherished memory. Those "wet leaves" for eyes call to mind also the leaves reflected in "The Rain Has Flown" penned a few years earlier – and we perceive the echo, extremely muted, of that rainy inspiration transferred from the trees themselves to their anthropomorphic representative visiting the writer in Berlin (where Nabokov was when he wrote it in December 1920).

Taking into account all of these texts with their refractions of the artist's "birth," we have four variations on the theme of a sylvan visitation at the onset of a writer's work. We find among the four pieces a certain symmetry: one prose piece explicitly links contact with trees with the onset of art (*Speak, Memory*'s "First Poem"), while the other – the first prose fiction ("Wood-Sprite") – simply describes the reunion of a man holding a quill with a part, or spirit, of his beloved (but lost) forest; one poem ("The Quill") creates a magical allegory of art's bestowal from the forest, and the other ("Rain") simply presents the responsive individual, invisibly, in the context of the sylvan scene, the poem itself only implying the result of that intense sensuous experience – the creation of the poem: just as "The Wood-Sprite" only implies that its first-person narrator has written it. We will discover trees entangled with the onset or growth of creativity in various ways throughout Nabokov's career, and there is little doubt that he considered trees and woodlands to be a major source and wellspring of his inspiration.

There is, in other words, a persistent, mysterious quality of trees in Nabokov's writing, beginning almost with his earliest works about them, and it deserves attention. The first time this tendency appears is in a very early poem from *Two Paths*, written sometime in 1917, called "Sonnet" ("The cloudless heights and silence ..." / "Bezoblachnaia vvys' i tishina ..."). This is the ninth of Nabokov's twelve poems in the collection, and the seventh of its eight that mention trees.

The cloudless heights and silence …
Sky-blue-ish snow; frozen stillness;
The mute branches' patterned weave
My land is a magical land.
> When in the gleaming snow it [she]
> Stands like a silvery vision –
> [My] soul is in love with the mysterious,
> In [my] soul [heart] there is peace and meek humility.

"Little birch, shapely beneath the snowy haze,
Are you bewitched forever, pray tell?
Most likely you were a tender lass [girl, maiden] …"
"Little fir, are you tired? Is the snow pressing [crushing] you?
Hold on, I'll gently brush the snowy load from your drooping branches."[38]

We can feel the Ovidian tradition here, in the suggestion that the trees were once people, transformed by the gods as punishment, protection, or reward; their personification and the speaker's attentive, meek concern with their well-being creates a blurry boundary between the human and the arboreal. But of course these trees are not transformed humans or gods, and what is striking here is the speaker's effort to find words and images to express not mythology in the Ovidian vein, but his own sense of deep, soul-driven, mystical connection to the trees. We see this in the poem's progression from an anthropomorphic, *Metamorphoses*-style fantasy to a direct expression of empathy for the non-humanized fir, and, more than empathy, a literal reaching out to lighten its load. Human touches tree, shares its cares, unburdens it in the magical land where different species can communicate without words.[39]

About five years later, Nabokov wrote another sonnet ("Sonnet": "A spring wood shimmers before me … wait" ["Vesennii les mne chuditsia … Postoi"], 1922). He calls the wood's green "sacred"; the wood is "both bright and shady" ("i iarkii i tenistyi"); and "every little leaf has a heart." This is the place, the speaker confesses, where he learned "the alphabet of the fragrant breeze from the lilies and deer." The speaker has an addressee in this poem, a "you" who enters the wood ("my wood") and experiences and understands all of its magic. The "sacred space" of the wood unites speaker and addressee, and binds them both to the inviolable world of nature, where "there are no complaints, no desires" – lines especially remarkable in light of their date, 25 June 1922, a scant three months after their author's father was murdered by monarchist assassins.

It makes sense that Nabokov calls the trees "my land," even "my country," in the earlier sonnet, though in a way those words were prophetic: they were written some months before the Bolshevik revolution, at a time when Nabokov could have had no inkling that soon, indeed, trees and forests would turn out to be his only constant "home," and trees around him his most tangible connection to a lost homeland. The intimate link was clearly forged early, in childhood even, but it served a vital purpose in helping Nabokov to traverse both into adulthood and into an entirely new world when the old one, and his home country, were shattered.

These years of earliest adulthood and exile were especially fertile in nurturing trees' generative role within Nabokov's creative vision, experience, inspiration, practice. By 1923, and not counting his 1916 book of amorous verse, Nabokov had written at least thirty-one poems with trees either serving in the title (thirteen) or mentioned prominently in the first line (eighteen); he had composed dozens more with trees as significant elements or even characters. One of the earliest poems, from *Two Paths*, hints at a theme that will recur several times throughout Nabokov's career, with intriguing metamorphoses. In this first formulation, from the lyric "The fields, swamps drift past" ("Plyvut polia, bolota mimo"), a train's motion is projected onto to the objects nearby, including trees, whose trunks "run out and then step away"; pines "jump aside into the ravine" to avoid the onrushing locomotive. This animation and mobilization of rooted trees is tentative here, not fully realized, especially as the phrase "jump aside" presents what feels like a dire fate for the pines, rather than any kind of liberation or expansion of secret essence. However, it marks possibly the earliest instance in Nabokov of trees shown to possess mobility – that is, trees that somehow transcend their rootedness. In this poem, the figure is clearly a pure anthropomorphism, capturing the sudden appearance of the ravine and the pine-covered slope's abrupt descent into it: the image blends the real motion of the train with the imagined motion of the surroundings, including the trees along with the idea of precipitous fall, even a leap to escape danger (that is, pines escaping from the train).

This notion grabs hold of Nabokov's imagination: ambulatory trees (and other plants) appear in various works throughout his career. He bestowed this vision of trees' merely illusory rootedness upon narrators as diverse as Fyodor in *The Gift* and Humbert Humbert in *Lolita*. The narrator of "Gods" calls the trees "pilgrims," travelling to reach their messiah; in the the poem "Poplars" (discussed later in this chapter) they are "marching" but "never reaching" their goal; in "The Ballad of Longwood Glen," a tall oak "passing by" is a "grave green pilgrim." There does not need to be a unified meaning for all of these ambulating trees, but what seems certain is that, having entered Nabokov's artistic consciousness while he was a very young, still-rooted poet, something about trees made him want to imagine them as transcending the state we see them in. This imagined quality evolved, grew, and diversified with the expansion of his artistic universe.

Perhaps the least surprising role trees play for Nabokov in the poetry is that of a direct contact point for nostalgia (like Proust, but maybe even before Nabokov had read him?), especially obvious in poems like the late "The Poplar" (1952,

40 Nabokov's Secret Trees

published 1959) – and, of course, the nostalgia was forced to blossom early. Two reminiscing, past-laden poems, one earlier and one later than the wood-sprite pair, offer a sense of physical contact, even intimacy, with trees that nourish the poet's soul or inspiration. In a 1919 poem, "A Dream on the Acropolis," written in Athens during a pause in the Nabokov family's escape by sea from Crimea to London, Nabokov was already exploring his visceral relationship to the trees he had left behind.[40] The fugitive "I" falls into a vivid, lifelike reverie:

> And there in the distance, between the field and the village,
> I see a wood, – like happy youth,
> a birchwood, pale green,
> and the glimmers of wayward paths …
> How one wants to surrender to their twists,
> wander, dream, tear the bark from the birches
> and embrace the amber, moist trunk –
> to press, press against it with breast and lips
> and drink in its honeylike blood![41]

Here, so freshly parted from the homeland (or at least, from Crimea – a slightly longer eighteen months from the St. Petersburg region countryside with its birches), it seems not enough to remember the trees, or to receive benign inspiration from them; the waking dreamer, having involuntarily fallen into the reverie, violently yearns to cling to the tree's trunk, to strip the bark away, chest and lips pressed tightly against the denuded wood; here, a traditional childhood pastime – drinking the spring sap flow directly from the trunk – has become a primordial element of the poet-dreamer's past and experience, now intensified in recollection, imbibing the tree's sap, its honeylike blood, as if trying to merge with the mysterious natural beings so passionately perceived. Some tension exists in Nabokov's choice of the sleep-related term (*son*, "sleep/dream") for the poem's title, whereas the closing line uses the word "mechta" (daydream, fantasy): "Thus – I paid in silver for a dream [*mechtu*] ..." (ellipsis in original). The dream, more like a vision or visitation, also includes Nabokov's beloved racemosa (bird-cherry), and alder catkins falling on the crosses of a cemetery; these crosses add an embedded marker, and a very concrete one, of the past, of what is left behind – dust, buried remains – and traditions of memorialization. But the physical mingling, the attempt to merge with the birch tree, stands out, the press of flesh on flesh and the transfer of blood implying or insisting on a kinship, a deep and permanent relatedness, that lies at the heart of what has propelled the exile into this dream. It's as if the trees themselves and the winding paths among them ("izvivy"), more than "home" or "motherland," are the things whose loss is most deeply mourned; the winding paths will be echoed in later works such as "The Wood-Sprite," whose hero used to "[tie] the

Nabokov's Origins in the Poetry of Trees   41

paths up in knots" (CS 4), and in *Glory*'s and *Speak, Memory*'s path through the forest, among other places. That the dream occurs on the Acropolis adds an ironic touch: the dreamer cares little for this ancient monument, itself a marker of memory, a former temple, but one of stone, redolent not of life but of death, even the nearby red poppies recalling the blood of battle.[42]

A related poetic image takes a sombre turn a few years later, however, in "At a Village Cemetery," written in November 1922, about eight months after V.D. Nabokov's murder at the Kadet party event in Berlin:

> At the cemetery there is sun, lilacs and little birch trees
> and drops of rain on the sparkling crosses.
> Here and there translucent strips have peeled away
> and rolled into tubes on the bright trunks.
> I love to kiss their amber wounds,
> love to caress their bashful leaflets …
> Now a honeyed breeze wafts from the neighbouring field,
> Now the scent of algae from a nearby river.
> The green shadows are transparent and humid.
> The crickets chirp – the bushes whisper –
> and the pale little crosses of the hushed lilac
> asperse moist crosses onto the graves.
> (19 November, 1922)[43]

Many of the images from "Dream" are revisited here. Again, we see repeated the image of birchbark peeled back from the trunk, this time naturally, and the sacral kissing of the trees' "amber wounds": echoes, perhaps, of the gunshot wounds that took the father's life (there is a hint of springtime in the poem, in its affection towards the leaves, and their size – "[I] love to caress their bashful leaflets" – perhaps reflecting early visits to the grave in May or June). Taking place in a cemetery, heavy with implication and the tension between nature's fecundity and the departed loved ones marked by crosses, this much subtler poem already appears to be exploring trees' further potential within the creative act. The crosses formed by the lilacs' branches, and by their shadows, mingle with the crosses on the graves, merging to suggest a communion of the living and the dead and persisting nature, a synthesis that here gives rise to the creation of poetry, and this very poem, which, without presenting him, implicitly commemorates Nabokov's father. This poem is one instance where the consonance between the lilac tree, "siren," and the pen name "Sirin" bears special weight.[44] If we accept that this lyric persona is an avatar of its author, then the combination of trees, selfhood, and love for a parent, along with the sublimation of grief into art and joy, offers an exceptionally compressed and efficient microcosm of this personal side of Nabokov's artistic sensibility.

42 Nabokov's Secret Trees

Nabokov soon left behind the kind of explicit folklorizing of his creative origins seen in the "wood-sprite" texts – he never returned to it so openly, in fact, and did not translate either of those works (or the other two poems just discussed) into English – but the afterimages and reverberations continued throughout his decades as an artist, sometimes expanding again into powerful subcurrents within major works. In fact, the "wood-sprite" itself receives a subtle yet significant echo in Nabokov's obliquely autobiographical last Russian novel, *The Gift,* in the name of the Godunov-Cherdyntsev country estate, "Leshino" – which might as well be "WoodSprightville"; another (though not tree-related) folkloric example rests in Martin Edelweiss's paternal grandmother's lineage (in *Glory*), with its surname "Indrikov" deriving from a mythical creature, the indrik-beast (his own last name is also botanical, a flower).[45] Meanwhile, Martin's mother hailed from a place named for trees, Olkhovo, or "Alderton." Quieter echoes can be found in such names as John Shade (trees' shadows and shade are crucial elements of Nabokov's palette from the earliest days, and he often mentions "shade-trees"), Hazel Shade (hazel trees; one of Nabokov's early poems is called "The Hazel and the Birch"), and Art Longwood. I've even heard it suggested by native speakers that Pnin's name looks like a mock-possessive form of "pen'" (tree stump).

I want to close this discussion of Nabokov's early poetic engagement with trees by looking at an unpublished poem from November 1921, written in Cambridge, called "Topolia" ("[The] Poplars").[46] Interesting for its place in the "ambulatory trees" arc of Nabokov's imagination, the poem has a feature more important for my present purposes – the speaker's sense of identification with these poplars:

> My soul is an alley of poplars,
> tall, dusky, soft ones, unrelentingly
> they march, march, and their joy
> gets no closer ... but if a far-off
> music wafts from the fairty-tale land,
> and the wind through the mournful dreams
> of those sensitive poplars fragrantly flows,
> then, having fulfilled their bliss and slightly,
> slightly having begun trembling, their dark foliage
> will suddenly shine, in undulating silver ...[47]

The speaker's soul and the trees are one: presumably, the poet, too, is trudging towards a joyous goal that never draws nearer, and he (like the trees and their leaves) responds to musical, entrancing breezes from afar; the trees, like the poet, "dream," the dreams and the breezes mingle, and make the trees shine in silvery light – just as, we could say, an artist shines forth through creative expression when responding to an inspiration from the fairy-tale depths of consciousness or of the surrounding world. This kinship in creativity between artists and trees appears to drive both Nabokov's (or his artistic persona's) relationship to them and his depictions of them at every stage of his career, in every kind of text.

From these early writings, we confirm that Nabokov was indeed a Kilmerite, a word that he invented with the help of his character Humbert Humbert. As I suggested in the introduction, a Kilmerite is someone who, following Joyce Kilmer and unlike Humbert, feels that there is no "poem as lovely as a tree." Aside from these images here reviewed, Nabokov's lyrical persona directly declares his love for trees in the poem "What my heart requires" ("Chto nuzhno serdtsu moemu," 1923, *Gornii put'*): "I love the beasts, the trees, and God."[48] In the fragments and poems we have looked at, we see that for the artistic persona Nabokov was crafting, performing, or simply "being" as a young man, trees play a number of vital roles. They are companions and beloved others, eliciting empathy and love; they are sources of personal feeling, blending with and nurturing the formation of identity; they are tethers to the past, personal and historical; they are exemplars and wellsprings of impassioned creativity and inspiration, often mysterious; they enable the functional fabric of everyday life, allowing creation of pavilions, homes, and food for other creatures and plants, and providing shade, drinkable saps, fruits, and visual and aural beauty almost by accident, as an afterthought, or no thought at all. If the writer's soul "is a tree," that will tell upon trees' place in the writer's art. Getting to know Nabokov's trees well must be a crucial step in coming to experience the depths of his works.

Chapter Two

Trees on the Mind: Consciousness and Memory

This book attempts to treat Nabokov's artistic career as an organic aesthetic development. "Organic" is already a loaded term, but it may capture better than the word "coherent" the kind of relationships I'm proposing: *organic* suggests a centrally originating, outward-moving, growth-oriented process of development and rising complexity. Organic growth, logically, can be centrifugal (as well as rhizomatic). *Coherent* development, on the other hand, is more likely to imply a centripetal process, by which everything continues to hang together within a proper form. Organic growth can produce things that spin off into infinity; coherent growth maintains the integrity of a whole.

In a book focused on trees, it is tempting to lean on the natural shape and development of trees as a structuring device. I have tried to resist this temptation, in part because to succumb to it would create too artificial an overlay pressing upon the way Nabokov's artistic creations relate to the trees he engaged with. As much as Nabokov loved trees, there is little to be gained by promoting the "artwork as tree" analogy; artworks, after all, emerge at least in part from consciousness, whereas trees emerge from entirely different natural processes that may have little (or little enough) in common with consciousness, despite the claims of philosophical idealism. However, as we shall see in good time, certain analogies between trees, art, and consciousness do occasionally hold (and are even occasionally promoted by Nabokov), and they can offer heuristic advantages. Nabokov, in his memoir and in his creative life, explores consciousness as the foundation of human experience, and while trees appear to reverberate with that interest, it would be more than reductive to claim that they are its source. They are, however, one of its primary outlets and focal points within Nabokov's work.

For Nabokov, trees have a particular relationship to human consciousness; or, perhaps more precisely, he regards an acute awareness of trees in the environment to be one of the markers of high-level consciousness in general – at the very least, of artistic consciousness. People's typical obliviousness to the trees around them clearly bothered Nabokov, as we saw in the introduction; the diversity of trees – both in terms of species variety, but implicitly, too, simply within their individual traits – was for him a wealth and an abundance that could feed and enrich even a materially constrained life (as his was in his twenties and thirties). Thus, trees in some respects *define* consciousness for Nabokov; they emblematize the richness and intricacy of the world, and they also embody those traits, bring them to us in real, physical form, as if nature is presenting us with an offering, and it is our assigned task to accept and explore it. To put it in rather crude, quantitative terms: for a person in moist, temperate climes, trees quite simply constitute the vast majority of the biomass that one encounters during most days,[1] unless one lives in a particularly treeless zone; even cities are (and were) well supplied with trees, and one can engage this dominant life form consciously and actively, or unconsciously, passively, even obliviously. When Nabokov claims that a writer must know the names of trees, he is arguing that a writer's primary aim is to live out heightened consciousness, and this means, at least, noticing and knowing something about the most common and visually striking natural phenomena. Otherwise, he suggested, we are like ghosts, hardly interacting with the physical world, which is barely even real for us.[2]

As with the origin of his poetic sensibility, Nabokov chose in *Speak, Memory* to associate what he called "the birth of sentient life" (SM 22), when he suddenly became aware of his own temporal relation to his parents, with a particular kind of tree-filled scene:

> Thus, when the newly disclosed, fresh and trim formula of my own age, four, was confronted with the parental formulas, thirty-three and twenty-seven, something happened to me. I was given a tremendously invigorating shock ... At that instant, I became acutely aware that the twenty-seven-year-old being, in soft white and pink, holding my left hand, was my mother, and that the thirty-three-year-old being, in hard white and gold, holding my right hand, was my father. Between them, as they evenly progressed, I strutted, and trotted, and strutted again, from sun fleck to sun fleck, along the middle of a path, which I easily identify today with an alley of ornamental oaklings in the park of our country estate. (SM 21–2)

These small oaklings, his mother's "coevals," may not be the only source of the sunflecks among which he "strutted and trotted" – flecks of light showing from between the leaves of still taller trees, more experienced travellers in time. In his narrative, Nabokov is silent about this layering, but the fact of his memory of those small trees, those shady areas and their flecks of light, foregrounds the fact that not only the parental figures, but the trees and their complex shadows, too, were key elements in the awakening of sentience (even though the little boy had no awareness of what the trees were called, nor even, perhaps, that the sunflecks were caused by trees). In sum, we could say that the first elements

46   Nabokov's Secret Trees

that appeared distinctly in the focus of Nabokov's consciousness, as presented in this scene, were mother, father, self, sunflecks (and shadow), trees, and time.

As Brian Boyd has observed, the first and final chapters of *Speak, Memory* are linked by the theme of consciousness's birth.[3] The correlation becomes even more striking when we examine the significant role of trees in both parts of the memoir. *Speak, Memory* is one of Nabokov's most tree-laden texts, and the closing chapter serves in some ways as a recapitulation of what has transpired in the preceding ones. The few pages leading to the final, suspended anticipation attending the "find-what-the-sailor-has-hidden" ship's funnel contain almost a whole guidebook's worth of trees and shrubs: yews, privet hedge, arbutus, pine, olive, oleander, orange, a maze of topiary, oak, evergreens, beeches, plane trees, general trees, forests and shrubs, box, hornbeam, honeysuckle, Lombardy poplar. That makes *fifteen* named types, and several other unspecified references, in the space of a scant six pages. These pages, devoted to the earliest years of Dmitri's conscious awareness, and their observation and attendance by his parents, are surely themselves among the most densely thicketed in all of Nabokov's works. The metaphors of consciousness arising from the forest suggest why this is so – more on that in a moment. The shift in the memoir's last pages from treescape to harbourscape, with the hidden steamer, marks also a deliberate shift from the parental consciousness to the projected or imagined consciousness of the child: little Dmitri's main passions at that time were such things as boats in the bathtub (and would one day be trains and race cars); it is as if Nabokov re-experiences the birth of his own consciousness in the accounting of so many trees, and then, recognizing the independence and distinctness of the little human he is describing, shifts to imagine a mental world where *different* sorts of things are what remain in memory when the shock of consciousness first awakens (and in a way, this shift in his *parental* perspective is a deliberate inversion of the one that took place in chapter 1, when *he* was the child with his parents). The span between the first and last chapters expresses the growth of Nabokov's consciousness, metonymically through the proliferation of trees (the oak is still there, now accompanied by many other species); but it also jumps sideways into the analogous world of another, independent, newly born consciousness.

During this concluding section, Nabokov writes, "I would like to have the ability Professor Jack, of Harvard and the Arnold Arboretum, told his students he had of identifying twigs with his eyes shut, merely from the sound of their swish through the air ('Hornbeam, honeysuckle, Lombardy poplar. Ah – a folded *Transcript*')" (SM 304). We will return to Professor Jack, but it is worth remembering that this statement comes in the midst of his recollecting his and Véra's first years of parenthood, their son's infancy and toddlerhood, and Nabokov's expressed wish to remember an inventory of "every small park we visited." This is the theme of chapter 15 – parenthood, the awakening of two new consciousnesses: the child's and the parents' (together as one, "we parents").

There is an abiding tension in the chapter between Dmitri's preferred trains, cars, and boats, and the trees that helped spark and inspire Nabokov's own mental world. The infant's eye, upon deep (and early) inspection, led into the jungle: "that swimming, sloping elusive something about the dark-bluish tint of the iris which seemed still to retain the shadows it had absorbed of ancient forests where there were more birds than tigers and more fruit than thorns, and where, in some dappled depth, man's mind had been born."[4] The paragraph (the fifth in the chapter) continues by turning around and looking *out* from the child's eye, echoing here Nabokov's own early burst of consciousness by suggesting that "the closest reproduction of the mind's birth obtainable is the stab of wonder that accompanies the precise moment when, gazing at a tangle of twigs and leaves, one suddenly realizes that what had seemed a natural component of that tangle is a marvelously disguised insect or bird" (SM 297, 298). Notice the "dappled depth" above and its echo of the sunflecks among which young Vladimir had hopped on *his* first self-conscious day; and here too, through the twig-disguised insect, in what seems his own more definitive version, we find the precursor of Dmitri's (imagined) chapter-concluding "find what the sailor has hidden." Trees being older than ports and steamers, it's no wonder Nabokov takes the former as archetypal.

But take another look at those swishing twigs of Professor Jack. That brief aside, another Gogolian mock-Homeric digression, really, creates a new character in the memoir and gives him a scene of action – sightless, yes, but astutely judging the subtle differences in the acoustics of air currents around clusters of branching twigs. We think of trees as things that enchant the sight; that humble us with their sublimity, or their age; that release pollens and aromas; that change colour and drop their leaves; or that murmur, rustle, or groan vaguely in the wind. Here, Nabokov proposes an entirely auditory knowledge of specific trees, a connection to their individual forms that gives them reality and presence independent of their visual and olfactory effects on us. It is also true that this story of Professor Jack is just that – very much a *story*, a triple-nested story, in fact, as Nabokov retells what Jack's students retold that Jack had related about himself ("Professor Jack" retired in 1938, so Nabokov likely never met him).[5] Nabokov wants, he says, that thrice-wrapped magical ability from the mythical past to be his; in a way, through the story-generating power of trees, he has had this ability all along.

Memory

Nabokov began as an artist of memory – almost before he was old enough to have any important memories, and certainly before he had experienced the great losses that would force him to rely on memory alone to access such concepts as home, homeland, father. Before all of that, Nabokov was already taking note of the fugitive nature of being, of the intense experiences that build up a living

48   Nabokov's Secret Trees

consciousness. Let's return for a moment to what I've been calling the "gateway" poem, the one the later Nabokov sets as the earliest boundary of his art's beginning, "The Rain Has Flown." What was not clear when he first published these lines in *Dva puti* is clear to us in light of the "First Poem" chapter from *Speak, Memory*: that 1917 poem is itself not (or not only) a reflection upon an immediate or just-past experience of May that year; it is also (perhaps primarily) a recollection of an earlier such experience, from 1914, when he was inspired by the rain in the trees and the drops pulsing off the linden leaf to compose his "first poem." The episode becomes another example of nested memories: the writer of the poem in 1917 remembers both the physical experiences that sparked the earlier poem and, presumably, the process of creating that poem (though in "The Rain Has Flown," that earlier time, and earlier poetic composition or activity, are completely concealed from view: only the poet knows they are there; they are a poetic secret). The fact that critics have been repeatedly tricked into thinking that "The Rain Has Flown" is the poem described in the *Speak, Memory* chapter appears linked to the poems' unified central vision. In 1949's "First Poem" (the chapter's original form, in *Partisan Review*), Nabokov must have been remembering *both* the 1914 experiences (watching drops of water, feeling inspired, composing) *and* the 1917 echo of that day or time ("The Rain Has Flown" as a poem about a similar, later experience, or perhaps it too was about the same, original experience of inspiration and composition from 1914 – or both: a new experience, and a recollection of an old one). This situation makes for a curious pseudo-symmetry: in "The Rain Has Flown," the original 1914 experience is hidden; in 1949's "First Poem," the 1917 poetic re-experiencing is concealed. Considering that in 1949, 1951, and even 1966 "Rain" existed only in an extremely rare volume (maybe five hundred copies, most of them lost),[6] and had never been widely published, Nabokov could assume that his nesting of memories was secret – especially from Anglo-American readers.[7] In both of these texts (the poem of 1917, and the prose of 1949), the act of commemorating is also an act of hiding, camouflage, or concealment (like the work of the imaginary Sailor in chapter 15).

At the conclusion of the "First Poem" chapter, Nabokov's memory of the poem's debut before an audience – his mother – is also richly accompanied by trees, though here, appropriately enough, the trees from the performance scene are now also trees *in artistic representation*:

> With a little cough, I sat down on a footstool and started my recitation. While thus engaged, I kept staring at the farther wall upon which I see so clearly in retrospect some small daguerreotypes and silhouettes in oval frames, a Somov aquarelle (young birch trees, the half of a rainbow – everything very melting and moist), a splendid Versailles autumn by Alexandre Benois, and a crayon drawing my mother's mother had made in her girlhood – that park pavilion again with its pretty windows partly screened by linked branches. (SM 226)

The layering here is striking: the man recalls the boy, who recollects his poem (inspired by and in part, perhaps, about trees and rain), and recites and remembers it while looking at paintings of trees and a grandmother's much earlier crayon drawing of the very setting of his just-experienced inspiration, "screened by linked branches." The grown man's memory takes in the eye of the boy's vision, which sees his grandmother's childish memory and reflection of the same trees and tree-built structure that occasioned the poem – another childhood artwork based on (and inspired by) trees. Notice how here Nabokov repeatedly refigures trees as his means to journey further and further into the past.

Trees of Memory

In chapter 1 we saw how in that first "canonical" poem, "The Rain Has Flown," memory was in effect hidden within the poem's apparent immediacy – a hiding that only becomes evident with the help of Nabokov's memoir from thirty-odd years later. In several of the arboreal poems, memory guides the poetic structure and the trees' role within the work's development. As Nabokov embarked on a prose-centred phase of creativity, especially with *Mary* in 1925–6, we find a body of work very much fixated upon memory as the centre of consciousness, and on the role of trees within the personal relationship to the past. Since memory remains such a dominant theme throughout Nabokov's career, and the role of Vyra's trees in his late boyhood is so firmly established, one wants to be careful not to spend too much time exploring well-trodden ground.[8] Nevertheless, attention needs to be given to the first two novels largely concerned with memory, *Mary* and *The Defense*, whose trees indeed are central and definitive of how those images are formed. At the same time, there seems to be something particular about the place of trees within the memories, or within the experiences behind the memories, that renders them more than simple tokens of commemoration and reminiscence.

The forced, intensified relationship with memory began in a stop in Athens as the Nabokovs escaped into exile. We saw above that while there, in May of 1919, just days after fleeing the Bolshevik invasion in the Crimea, Nabokov wrote "Dream on the Acropolis" ("Son na Akropole"), a poem that immediately begins the task of holding onto the past as it drifts further away. The semi-erotic quality of "Dream"'s evocation of birches (discussed in chapter 1) might be explained, in part, by the nature of Nabokov's first meeting with "Tamara," or rather Valentina Shulgin: "I discovered her standing quite still (only her eyes were moving) in a birch grove, she seemed to have been spontaneously generated there, among those watchful trees, with the silent completeness of a mythological manifestation" (SM 230). These are not just any trees, any birches, metonymically associated with the beloved in consequence of the particularized moment. The trees are "watchful," in interaction with Tamara's moving

50   Nabokov's Secret Trees

eyes; their implied agency and the magical nature of her sudden apparition convey a weightiness, a solemnity to their presence that somehow embraces the moment and connects the writer to the essence of his, or of all, being.[9] (That "mythological manifestation" almost makes one wonder if, while writing the memoir episode, Nabokov might have also been recollecting the dream from Athens, epicentre of so much mythology.) Appropriate to myth, too, is the fact that he first spoke to Valentina when she happened to enter, alone, the very same pavilion in which he had experienced the birth of poetic inspiration. In echo of that fact, he relates in *Speak, Memory* that he took her "to all those secret spots in the woods, where I had daydreamed so ardently of meeting her, of creating her. In one particular pine grove everything fell into place, I parted the fabric of fancy, I tasted reality" (SM 232).[10] The trees, the beloved, the creative urge, and the magic all come together in this scene of Nabokov's first love – which might be regarded as little more than a typical childhood romance if we did not know how intensely Nabokov valued *love* as a worldly (ethical) and perhaps metaphysical phenomenon.[11]

This love between the young Nabokov and Shulgin, which at least in its beginning existed almost exclusively among the trees, was transplanted creatively into the past of Lev Glebovich Ganin, the protagonist of *Mary*.[12] Although the entirety of the love affair is presented as a treasure and achievement of memory (achievement, because Ganin painstakingly recreates the complete sequence of events over a four-day stretch of daydreaming in Berlin, nine years later), the content of the memory, and the value of that content, are significant as well. An interesting act of distancing takes place, as Nabokov fictionalizes the episodes: little details are different, but the important contours are essentially the same, when one compares "Tamara" with *Mary*. In the novel, the protagonist, "strange to say" (M 44), did not remember with certainty when he first saw his beloved (unlike Nabokov, who asserts that he first saw Valentina in a birch grove [SM 230], which itself is anticipated in Ganin's emphasis on a "birch grove" as he gingerly approaches the topic of his love with the old poet Podtyagin [M 57]).[13] Ganin's first conscious awareness of Mary occurs at a rustic concert in a barn, a scene which also brims with arboreal and related material: he is surrounded first by birches, then enters the (wooden) barn, whose walls are decorated with pine needles while village boys sit on large piles of logs. Looking back, Ganin recollects his longing for a yet unmet Mary, from within an "oaken washroom" with a stained glass window (which recalls the glass in Nabokov's pavilion, and the washroom he mentions in *Speak, Memory*, chapter 4 [SM 85]), looking out on "three huge bushy poplars" and their "winding roots" (M 46), and at the starry sky through the poplars' branches that "made you want to heave a sigh" (*poglubzhe vzdokhnut'* [SSRP 2:79]), producing "the highest and most important point in his whole life" (M 46–7).

Entranced by Mary at the barn concert, Ganin cycles around the neighbouring estates, never knowing "where he might meet her or overtake her, at which turn in the road, in this copse [*perelesok*] or the next" (M 48). When he finally works up the nerve to speak with her, his approach is prepared by birches, alder catkins and pine needles, and leads to a recreation of the same "pavilion" (the one Nabokov would later describe in "Tamara" and "First Poem"), which he sees her enter "through the foliage" (M 48) whereupon he leans his bicycle against a tree and enters the magical structure, initiating their relationship. Their romance is accompanied by more birches, a mahogany boat (M 57), alders, pines, racemosa (Nabokov's word for "old-world bird-cherry"), pinewoods, laurels, acacias, and lindens, as well as various other undefined leaves, tree trunks, and twigs. Later, after their love had faded at the end of a year, but seems revived in a burst of letter-writing while Ganin is in the Crimea heading into exile, and Mary in Poltava, her letter makes it to him, and he replies to her, writing about the catkins and needles on the bridge to the pavilion, and recollects their first autumn together – from this remote Crimea, where "the velvety hush of the narrow cypress avenues, the gleam of the moonlight on the broad leaves of magnolias – all this only oppressed him" (M 90), perhaps because the trees are not the right ones. Note also that not only is his act of recollected and perhaps resurrected love accompanied by trees (albeit different, unsatisfying ones), but it continues the nesting pattern we saw earlier in "The Rain Has Flown," of the memory within a memory: for here, we see Ganin of 1926 Berlin recollecting the Ganin of 1918 Yalta, recollecting the Ganin and Mary of 1916 – and note further that trees are present meaningfully at each layer of the nesting process; one might envision the layers of memory as the rings of a tree; this structure is similar the one observed above in "First Poem."

Just as the novel's end brings a radical change to Ganin's plans, it also presents a transformation in the role trees play in the scenery. This transformation might be signalled near the beginning of the final chapter, where "From the black branches of some trees, just beginning to sprout green, a flock of sparrows fluttered away with an airy rustle and settled on the narrow ledge of a high brick wall" (M 112). This sudden flight occurs just as Ganin is about to meet the unsuspecting Mary and whisk her away from her equally unsuspecting husband, Alfyorov; he is feeling the best he has felt in a long time, and returns to the very bench near the train station where he had done much of the reimagining of his romance with Mary. This sentence fuses the locus of the present (the bench), the memories of the past and its love, and, for a fleeting moment, anticipation of the future: "In an hour's time she was coming ... and he, Ganin, was about to meet her" (M 113). Recall, too, that the bench is now also a locus with its own place in *recent* memory, where further *memories of past memories* were evoked or constructed. But the very next paragraph, consisting of one brief sentence, seems to change everything: he "for some reason" remembers how he had gone to break up with his recent lover, Lyudmila. And then, the focus shifts to a construction site beyond the little park: "Behind the public garden a house was being built;

52   Nabokov's Secret Trees

he could see the yellow wooden framework of beams – the skeleton of the roof, which in parts was already tiled" (M 113). After a quick description of the workers and their progress, Ganin sees how "the wooden frame shone like gold in the sun," and this repetition of the word "wooden" alongside the "frame" (*pereplet*) attracts attention: no trees are mentioned now (though they must be present in the cityscape, or in the garden), but the wooden material of the frame is mentioned twice, and shines like gold. In Russian, the words are more striking, in that the Russian for "wooden" is *derev'iannyi,* or "made of tree/wood" (wood and tree are the same word in Russian: *derevo*). The city bench, too, is most certainly wooden, and shortly after this scene, Ganin finds another wooden resting place, and this becomes the novel's final image: "As his train moved off he fell into a doze, his face buried in the folds of his mackintosh, hanging from a hook above the wooden seat." Instead of trees (*derev'ia*) we now have wooden items (*derev'iannye*) – specifically, objects of human craft and handiwork. Meanwhile the "old dying poet" Podtyagin, singer of the "birch groves," has been left in the abandoned apartment with the remembered image of Mary.

It appears that Nabokov has structured this work with his passion for poetry and for trees held in close association, and at the novel's conclusion, the old trees are traded, or transformed, into new products of human craftsmanship, while Podtyagin, the poet, and his birch groves are left behind in a moribund state. There is plenty of too-easy, and perhaps too heavy-handed, symbolism here, with spring, and the new leaves noticed by Ganin and abandoned by the sparrows, and the fresh new wooden frame creating the new house and suggesting Ganin's new path for his life.[14] Another way to read the image, of course, is to notice that he *thinks* he is leaving the past behind, building a new life like the new house behind the garden, but the trees, hiding in the wooden seat on the train, are riding along with him, clandestinely, perhaps into the world of prose that the novel embodies and performs, and which Nabokov had embraced as his primary artistic mode with this work's creation. Those trees are no longer, or at least no longer only, markers and facilitators of young love, memory, and the birth of art; most likely, Nabokov had noticed his heavy reliance on them in a narrow range of meaning, and began working to expand (and conceal) their suggestive and structural roles in his work. This is one of many shifts and transformations trees' roles will undergo during Nabokov's long career.

With its "huge bushy poplars" attending at the "highest and most important point" in Ganin's life, *Mary* invites us to think forward to another work concentrated on reminiscence: "The Poplar," the poem Nabokov wrote in 1952 and published in his 1959 collection *Poems*. The poem's speaker responds to a tree growing in front of his house, reading in bed at night, and envisioning a boy and a girl in the darkened window reflection: "He props upon his slender knee / A dwarfed and potted poplar tree." We are told that the scene embodies what the speaker last saw in July, 1917 – the pillared porch of the Rozhdestveno manor, we can assume – and the poem then twists towards gentle irony: "This is the silver lining of / Pathetic fallacies: the sough / of *Populus* that taps at last / Not water, but the author's past" (PP 169–70). Part of the "past" is the memory of the poplars seen through the window by Nabokov (and Ganin) as a boy, while dreaming up poetry. Is this new boy's poplar "dwarfed and potted" by the foreshortening of so many years? The "author," however, does "not care to make a scene"; "nothing is ever said"; he reads in bed, and resists the urge to rearrange the clothes hanging over the chairs that enable the illusion. Nothing much happens here, except the power of memory (and a tree) to connect the present and the past, combined with the reminiscer's ability to withstand the archaic intrusion.

The story "The Return of Chorb," written immediately after *Mary*'s first draft was completed,[15] helps us to sharpen our focus on what was happening at this moment in Nabokov's creative laboratory. Like *Mary*, it is centred on memory of a lost love – in this case, not a former romance that might be revived, but a beloved wife who died soon after the wedding. The story, like the novel, struggles with the relationship of the reminiscer to the memories of the past, the things that are gone forever, but the rupture here is more like the one Nabokov himself experienced on learning of his father's murder at the 1922 Kadet Party event. Chorb's wife, taken from him instantaneously by a live wire, embodies the fragile boundary between presence and absence, present and irretrievable past. Chorb, of course, makes elaborate *physical* efforts to preserve her image and his memories of her, but when we finally witness the content of his memories – perhaps his happiest moments with her, the night before they marry – the scene is triggered by the trees of the present season, spring, which call up the remembered scene from the autumn. It's a long passage but worth quoting in full, because it represents an extended reverie on the connections of memory, trees, and love:

> Chestnut trees now were in flower. *Then*, it had been autumn. He had gone for a long stroll with her on the eve of the wedding. How good was the earthy, damp, somewhat violety smell of the dead leaves strewing the sidewalk! On those enchanting overcast days the sky would be of a dull white, and the small twig-reflecting puddle in the middle of the black pavement resembled an insufficiently developed photograph. The graystone villas were separated by the mellow and motionless foliage of yellowing trees, and in front of the Kellers' house the leaves of a withering poplar had acquired the tone of transparent grapes. One glimpsed, too, a few birches behind the bars of the gate; ivy solidly muffed some of their boles,

54   Nabokov's Secret Trees

and Chorb made a point of telling her that ivy never grew on birches in Russia, and she remarked that the foxy tints of their minute leaves reminded her of spots of tender rust upon ironed linen. Oaks and chestnuts lined the sidewalk; their black bark was velveted with green rot; every now and then a leaf broke away to fly athwart the street like a scrap of wrapping paper. She attempted to catch it on the wing by means of a child's spade found near a heap of pink bricks at a spot where the street was under repair. A little way off the funnel of a workers' van emitted gray-blue smoke which drifted aslant and dissolved between the branches – and a resting workman, one hand on his hip, contemplated the young lady, as light as a dead leaf, dancing about with that little spade in her raised hand. She skipped, she laughed. Chorb, hunching his back a bit, walked behind her – and it seemed to him that happiness itself had that smell, the smell of dead leaves.

At present he hardly recognized the street, encumbered as it was with the nocturnal opulence of chestnut trees. A streetlamp glinted in front; over the glass a branch drooped, and several leaves at its end, saturated with light, were quite translucent. (CS 150–1)

Notice that his entire memory of that prenuptial night is replete with the trees around them, their textures, smells, interactions and ecosystems (ivy, rot), changes (falling leaves, fading colours, foxy tinges, decay), geographic variations, reflections in puddles, flight. (The oaks and chestnuts notably anticipate the same trees that launch the first attack-driven fit of reminiscence as Pnin walks through a park to the bus stop in his novel's first chapter.)[16] What was then happiest must now, in the present of the blossoming springtime chestnuts, be the most painful in its absence. This moment is surely the climax of the story, along with the peak of memory's beauty and joy, the poignancy of the loss it marks. Chorb's physical efforts to clutch his wife's memory continue (just as she had tried to clutch the leaves) – without, it seems, any kind of success or satisfactory results. If the story leaves us, and him, with anything, it is with the intense, detailed image from that night, and a few other fleeting moments from the honeymoon, but mostly the balletic and pungent scene with the trees. His attempt to recreate the wedding night with his ersatz "bride" in the hotel leaves him screaming, and his reunion with her parents dissolves in horrific silence. In its dark conclusion, the story leaves unclear whether Chorb will manage to preserve anything, even a coherent self. But the tree-filled street scene remains as something solid behind the ambiguity and the implied author's ambivalence. Brian Boyd notes that the story expresses Nabokov's anxiety at the possible loss of Véra (as he had lost so many other things by that time), and we find this suggestion reinforced by the trees, as well.[17] The dominant ones here are chestnuts, recalling Nabokov's first poem to Véra, "The Encounter" (*Vstrecha*), commemorating their first meeting at a masked ball: "And under the chestnuts, along the canal / you passed, luring me askance" (LTV xxiv, SSRP 1:611); a decade and

Trees on the Mind: Consciousness and Memory   55

a half later he signed off a letter saying he loved her "endlessly, inexpressibly, chestnuttily."[18] Clearly, when it came to the things that were most important, it was hard for Nabokov to separate them from trees in his mind, heart, and art.

Trees as the Foundation of Self, Memory, and Consciousness in *The Defense*

Memory of times past, per se, began to move out of the centre of Nabokov's microscope after *Mary* and "The Return of Chorb," but it is rarely absent entirely, and in his works that explore variations on human consciousness, memory is almost always a significant theme (*King, Queen, Knave* is one of the few exceptions, although it can be seen as less about consciousness than about appetite and the striking *atrophy* of consciousness). *The Defense* stands as something of a hybrid in regard to memory, since the narrative itself is presented as a collage of temporal perspectives – some anticipatory, some reminiscing, some anticipating reminiscence (a favourite Pushkinian theme of Nabokov's: consider the "My Africa" theme from *Onegin*, and the "creation of a memory" motif from his story "A Guide to Berlin"),[19] and even anticipatory non-reminiscence as well as retrospective non-reminiscence and non-anticipation. But consciousness is not exclusively defined by memory for Nabokov, and Luzhin's mental world emerges as an abstract, obscure realm where "chess forces," scraps of memory, and a hard-to-define engagement with the present physical world combine in the awkward protagonist. Luzhin's life as we see it is a constant struggle: he is, obviously, radically unlike those around him, and no one, including his parents and his eventual wife, manages to have any insight into his inner world. His fiancée-then-wife pities him but cannot empathize with him or understand him; his only real friends are those chess forces – and, perhaps, trees.

As it turns out, trees feature in several crucial turning points of Luzhin's journey. The novel's third paragraph already includes a first embedded anticipatory memory, in which we learn that "a ten-year-old boy knows his knees well, in detail – the itchy swelling that had been scrabbled till it bled, the white traces of fingernails on the suntanned skin, and all those scratches which are the appended signatures of sand grains, pebbles and sharp twigs" (Def 16). The twigs are present only through their mark in the skin, in their absence and as if an afterthought, but they might be compared to the "trace of melody" that "very softly manifested itself on Luzhin's side" of the board in his final match with Turati (Def 137). Anticipating later scenes in the novel, this "trace" becomes a trail through the woods by the chapter's end, as Luzhin flees the train ride back to St. Petersburg, a new name, new school, and the unknown:

> As if on a stroll he walked to the end of the station platform and then began to move very fast; he ran down some stairs and there was a beaten footpath, the

56   Nabokov's Secret Trees

> stationmaster's garden, a fence, a wicket gate, fir trees – then a small ravine and immediately after that a dense wood.
>
> At first he ran straight through the wood, brushing against swishing ferns and slipping on reddish lily-of-the-valley leaves ... lisping childish curses when a twig caught him across the forehead ... (Def 20–1)

After crying briefly and finding a trail he knows, he walks through the woods for ten minutes to reach the manor house; he breaks in and notices the portrait of his grandfather holding a violin, who "stared down at him, but then completely vanished, dissolving in the glass as soon as he regarded the portrait form one side – a melancholy amusement that he never omitted when he entered the drawing room" (Def 23). We will touch several times on this violin – the first example of crafted, artistically deployed wood in the novel – and we will return to the path as well. But for now, it is enough to take note of the fact that Luzhin's escape is by means of a forest path, a path which is "familiar" to him (and which reappears, freshly but most vividly, in the novel *Glory* – among other places throughout Nabokov's works). The house appears "through the bare lilac bushes" as he approaches. We learn, in the process, that his flight is motivated by fears and expectations of unpleasant new routines in his life, especially school – and, conversely, by his memory of city life as it had been, and his knowledge that this remembered world is now gone. His instinct is to retreat to the depths of the country house, nestled among the trees, which guide him there. The bridge and sawmill, with its sawdust, similarly evoke the role of trees in human affairs, but also the ominous destruction of trees.

The novel's early scenes are replete with encounters with trees and their significant by-products. Having begun school, Luzhin undertakes to spend two hundred and fifty recess periods sitting on a pile of logs, among "stacked firewood" (Def 29), every day he attends the school. The musical theme, initiated during his brief flight by the portrait in the drawing room, continues when Luzhin retreats to his father's study during a concert devoted to his grandfather's music (an event also marked by lilac, as the escape to the house had been – but this time, just the colour [Def 41]). As he listens to the music he dozes and contemplates a "gleaming dot ... on the desk – he did not know what: perhaps one facet of a paperweight in the guise of a heavy crystal egg or a reflection in the glass of a desk photograph" (Def 41). The musician comes to take a phone call, and begins "fidgeting" with something that turns out to be "a polished box that had been presented to [Luzhin's] father a few days before" (Def 42).[20] The object acts on Luzhin with magnetic attraction, and he accidentally makes his presence known to the musician by trying to peer inside the box when the man finally opens it, the contents revealed to be "a number of carved figures" – chess figures, of course, carved of wood. The violinist goes on to extol the musical qualities of chess: "Combinations like melodies. You know, I can simply *hear* the moves" (Def 43). With that, a kind of mystical unity is established between the "world of chess forces," as it will come to be called, and the sphere of pure music, free from written notation or musical instruments. Both, however, often find a partial route to embodiment in the physical world by means of wood. "Excellent chessmen," the musician states twice, but their real value is in what they lead him to experience mentally, the "melodies" of chess moves. That binary quality of pieces and game reaches a full dramatic pitch (along with musical accompaniment in the narrator's description) much later, during the final match with Turati, as they play for the right to challenge the world champion (Def 136–9). This telephoning violinist in turn evokes the earlier one (from the portrait, Luzhin's grandfather) whose music he has come to play, and the wooden instruments they both use in their art, also in anticipation of the wooden chess pieces.

Not only this association with music, but also the association with wood, that is, with trees, urges us to feel that chess resides on a plane along with other experiences of heightened consciousness and creativity, such as motivated Nabokov's poetic and autobiographical invocations of trees – though here, of course, the theme has been partially camouflaged and distributed to various fields of experience, and various transformations of the material at hand (which makes sense, since this is what art does, too). To hold briefly with the musical analogy, "trees" and their attendant "wood" form just a few of the many "notes" associated with Luzhin throughout the novel, but their "notes" may form the dominant key. When he plays his first game of chess with his aunt – incomplete, due to his father's interruption – he sets up the board (and the same musician-discovered pieces) on a "Turkish inlaid table." Soon after, when the geography teacher misses a lesson, Luzhin "distinctly heard a special sound, wooden and rattly,[21] that caused him to grow hot and his heart to skip a beat" (Def 48), leading to another interrupted game played by Krebs and "the quiet boy."[22] Right after his last game with his aunt's elderly admirer, an occasion to which the latter had brought "a whole bush of lilac" (Def 56),[23] Luzhin's family returns to the country estate, where Luzhin spent his time in his musician grandfather's "former study," with "windows that looked straight out on grim dark fir trees, whose foliage was so thick and intricate that it was impossible to say where one tree ended and another began" (Def 54). This room also contained a bookshelf filled with old issues of a magazine with a chess column. (Is it significant that now, in this room with its fir-filled windows and its magazines, music is reduced to a "bronze boy with a violin"? Or that the trees are removed beyond the window, as will be the trees when Luzhin awakes in the hospital?). Having finished all the chess columns, Luzhin wanders outside, and Nabokov inserts a scene that parallels his own recollection of newly acquired consciousness, but with greater restrictions: "The avenue was paved with sunflecks, and these spots, if you slitted your eyes, took on the aspect of regular light and dark squares" (Def 59).

58   Nabokov's Secret Trees

One wonders whether his discovery of the chess squares in the trees' shadows affirms the natural essence of chess, and its connection to consciousness? When Luzhin senior learns of his son's gift and brings chess into the open, the very next morning, "in the darkest and mossiest corner of the dense coppice behind the garden little Luzhin buried his father's precious box of chessmen, assuming this to be the simplest way of avoiding any kind of complications" (Def 66). This act creates a manner of ritual closure for the wooden pieces – buried among trees, they will decay and feed future growth, continuing the cycle of life and, perhaps, art. The moment also propels Luzhin into a more serious phase of his gift's development, as his father procures for him a master teacher and sparks his relentless momentum towards the competitive world of tournament chess.

Each key transition in Luzhin's early playing is marked with some tree-related feature (the carved-wood pieces in the polished box, the lilac bush, the coppice-burial); his move from the private to the public sphere of chess is ushered in by a photograph "in a St. Petersburg magazine," published after his "first, unforgettable performance in a chess club" (Def 68). "The photograph was taken the previous year, in the country: a tree in the garden and he next to it, a pattern of foliage on his forehead" (Def 69). These scenes echo the way a "twig caught him across the forehead" as he fled the train station in chapter 1 (Def 21). The scene in this photograph is especially intriguing; Nabokov, it seems, wanted to underscore the tree's presence – or, perhaps, its former presence: the photograph represents a moment from the past, the previous year, *before* Luzhin's chess gift had been discovered, sometime shortly before the novel's opening scene and its jumbled return from country to city. As for the tree, since it creates a shadowed foliage pattern on Luzhin's forehead, we can imagine it to be a tree with small leaves and a sparse crown: perhaps a birch; the cranial overlay speaks for itself, recollecting other "dappled" images in Nabokov's works and their associations with consciousness. In the same passage, we learn that "it was as if nothing had been" (Def 68) between the country chess games and the day of the photograph's publication, suggesting already a troubling distance from physical reality that may be presaged in the photograph's indication of the past's, and the tree's, absence.

Luzhin's late childhood and early adulthood are rendered a blur, presented as a non-chronological patchwork stitched together from his father's real memories and efforts to write a fictionalized novel about his son, some interpolations by the narrator, and Luzhin's own recollection of the past in his mysteriously presented first encounter with the future Mrs. Luzhin. Notably, just before that chance meeting we learn that his father has recently died from a chill acquired while visiting "a suburban wood" to look for mushrooms, and Luzhin's first conversation with his bride-to-be takes place – we must conclude – among trees, although the narrative structure does some work to keep this fact relatively obscure: time is being jumbled as in a kaleidoscope throughout this section, and it is more than hard to follow the chronology. Suddenly the reader is jolted sixteen years ahead, without proper markers, and sees both the new "future-present" and the new/old "present-past" through the later perspective: "The same paperweights bearing emerald-blue views touched up with mother-of-pearl beneath convex glass were on sale in the shops near the spring and ... the same maples were casting their lively shade over small tables where people drank coffee and ate wedge-shaped slices of apple tart with whipped cream" (Def 71–2). Among those "people," perhaps with different refreshments, are Luzhin and his new acquaintance, overseen by benevolent maples. (Luzhin now has a cane, undoubtedly also made of wood – a prop very much inviting interpretation: are trees still attempting to support him despite his life's eviscer-ation by Valentinov?)[24] The absence of details, and especially of trees, during his entire time with Valentinov contrasts ominously with all the previous ep-isodes, and with the key central ones around his courtship, engagement, and subsequent chess play at the championship.

The fictitious biography undertaken by Luzhin's father also lacks, as far as we can tell, any reference to trees – one of many reasons to doubt this father's depth of character and other qualities. The future fiancée, however, is linked to Luzhin precisely by her connection with trees. She first meets him when, by chance walking behind him, he keeps dropping things through a hole in a pocket: "Luzhin was walking along a path in front of her ... She gathered up only the handkerchief and the coin and walked on, slowly catching up with him and curiously awaiting some new loss. With the cane he carried in his right hand, Luzhin touched in passing every tree trunk and every bench" (Def 86). Her own relationship to trees is highlighted by the narrator, who reports that "Finland ... had remained in her heart as something more Russian than Russia, perhaps because the wooden villa and the fir trees and the white boat on the lake, black with the reflected conifers, were especially Russian" (Def 89). Also among her special memories are the "mysterious orange tree blossoms" in her family's old St. Petersburg house (Def 105), "mysterious" because they are as alien as they can be in that clime. Not long after their maple-blessed coffee, she decides to spy on him, to discover whether rumours that he sits alone in his room staring at a chessboard were true: "She made her way along the footpath between the oleander bushes to his window. But feeling a sudden awkwardness she went straight by without looking and came out into the avenue [*v alleiu,* alley of trees]" (Def 91); she makes her way back to the window and watches him remove his jacket and yawn, before rushing away in embarrassment at her own behaviour. These oleanders and obscure trees might seem insignificant, incidental even, until we consider them against the backdrop of contexts in the novel that are utterly devoid of trees.

Trees and Luzhin's chess daydreams continue to intertwine occasionally; once he is in Berlin, at his fiancée's apartment, we learn indirectly that when he had first approached her mother to request the daughter's hand in marriage, they had been in a "beech coppice" (Def 126), as she remembers it (trees, once again, anchoring the mnemonic link of present to past). The approaching match with Turati dominates all else in the section, pushing Luzhin's fiancée and wedding preparations into a hazy background, as the tournament progresses and Luzhin's connection to the physical world becomes more and more tenuous, giving way to the constant presence of imagined "chess forces"; during these scenes, trees are absent, just as most other physical objects struggle to be perceived by Luzhin as "real." What happens on the day of the match, however, is striking. When play is suspended at day's end, and Luzhin wanders lost into the world, having been told to go "home," the meaning to him is suddenly clear, provided both by memory and by some mysterious pull: "It was difficult, difficult to find one's way home in this yielding fog. Luzhin felt he should keep left, and then there would be a big wood, and once in the wood he would easily find the path. Another shadow slipped by. 'Where's the wood, the wood?' Luzhin asked insistently, and since this word evoked no reply he cast around for a synonym: 'Forest? Wald?' he muttered. 'Park?' he added indulgently ... And indeed – he was suddenly surrounded by trees, ferns crepitated underfoot" (Def 141–2). All is confusion, however, as Luzhin feels tormented by the chess gods, and of course he is not, as he thinks, on the path leading "home" to his family's country estate. Collapsed on the sidewalk, he is suddenly without home, without chess, without trees, and without family.

Luzhin's reawakening (indeed, his return to consciousness) also begins from the trees: "Tiny yellow leaves gleamed in this blueness, throwing a speckled shadow on a white tree trunk, that was concealed lower down by the dark green paw of a fir tree; and immediately this vision filled with life, the leaves began to quiver, spots crept over the trunk and the green paw oscillated, and Luzhin, unable to support it, closed his eyes, but the bright oscillation remained beneath his lids." And then: "I once buried something under those trees, he thought blissfully" (Def 159). Note especially the "speckled shadow," again associated with rising consciousness. He is on the point of remembering just what he had buried when he is interrupted by voices – much as he had been interrupted in the chess match, and in the two first chess experiences. That "something mysterious and happy" in "the bearded man's conversation" works to move Luzhin's thought away from the trees, to something that "trembled somewhere behind the tree – an enigmatic, evasive happiness" (Def 161). His fiancée appears on the scene a moment later, and the narrator reassuringly reports: "The fact that his life was illuminated first of all from this side eased his return. For a short while longer those harsh eminences, the gods of his being, remained in shadow. A tender optical illusion took place: he returned to life from a direction other than the one he had left it in" (Def 161). Somewhat ambiguously, the narrator here appears to be voicing a perspective that aligns with "the world" and the doctor's diagnosis and treatment, mixed in with some of the narrator's deeper insights (such as those about the "harsh eminences, the gods of his being"). What is certain is that in the weeks and pages that remain in the story, not a single tree appears in nature out of doors; a lone palm tree is seen indoors, and a Christmas tree (presumably rootless, dead) at a party. Aside from that, some birches within Luzhin's memories, a palm tree in a magazine, and some trees within a film – these are all that is left of the world of trees as Luzhin moves towards his fate.

In fact, the recovery itself, in the hospital, begins with trees at a remove – trees seen framed through a window, but not experienced immediately through all the senses. Thus, it may be that the hospital scene is actually a final departure of trees, as if through a train's window, rather than a recovery accompanied or facilitated by trees. These trees, because they are framed, seem to echo the ones in the photograph from Luzhin's last pre-chess summer, even as trees and chess remained quite linked through the first chess-filled period and during the games with Luzhin Sr.'s friend, the doctor. After the aborted match with Turati, the psychiatrist with "agate eyes" and Luzhin's new family all blame his chess obsession for his troubles, but the subtle role of trees in his life, and the connection between the trees and the chess, offer another perspective: the world of tournaments, mercenary chess matches, and championship possibilities appears to be one that draws Luzhin away from something purer (or at least more beneficent and nurturing) in chess, while entrapping him in an excessively power-, competition-, and dominance-driven relationship to the game. Compare the chess-playing doctor's attitude: "since he was really a first-rate player he derived enormous pleasure from these *incessant defeats*" (Def 67; emphasis added). This same doctor advised Luzhin "not to get too carried away by it, not to tire himself, and to read in the open air" (Def 67). Luzhin's father was unable, and Valentinov utterly disinclined, to help Luzhin follow the doctor's advice. But when he finally breaks down at the interrupted championship in Berlin, it is "home" and "the forest" he seeks, as if innately aware that something inside his consciousness or his world has come unstuck from its foundation.

Trees and the Boundaries of Mundane Life

Needless to say, Nabokov was not writing his novels *about* trees. But trees were helping him to explore and express some aspects of what he *was* writing about. In *The Defense* and in his next novel, *The Eye*, Nabokov appears to have been most interested in exploring and representing consciousness itself, especially in extreme forms. "Chess consciousness" is compared to "musical consciousness," traceable at least through Symbolist ideals to some of the purest notions of what artistic consciousness itself might be.[25] In *The Defense*, the artistic consciousness, the proximity of "chess ideas" and "forces," becomes fully separable from the larger human and (especially) natural domain – a domain which is acutely represented by trees, and of course human interactions with them. Separated from that natural world, Luzhin withers, collapses, goes mad, and "drops out of the game." In *The Eye*, a much simpler consciousness is offered to the reader (although Smurov is suggested to have pretentions of poetic ability), but it is also one which becomes, or imagines itself becoming, thoroughly isolated from the physical, natural substrate: early in the novel, the narrator begins to self-present as something of a surplus, inertia-driven consciousness, persisting on earth willy-nilly after his physical death. His protests at the story's end notwithstanding, Smurov's tale is not a very happy one; notably, and exceptionally, it lacks reference to a single tree. Bracketed by the preceding novel's fifty-five arboreal images, and its successor's (*Glory*) eighty or more, this absence articulates a rather "eloquent silence."

Leaping across the treeless *Eye*, there is a surprising link between *The Defense* and *Glory*. Early in both novels, the protagonist climbs through a frame, walks on a forest path, and looks at a painting (not in the same order, however, and not on the same plane of reality). Luzhin flees the train station, runs along a path through the woods to his family's home, enters through a window, and looks at a painting. Martin performs a similar act, in imagination and in reverse: he sees a painting of a forest path, and has reveries of climbing through the frame, entering the painting, and going down the path. Luzhin's *physical* action is outside to inside; Martin's *imaginative* one is inside to outside. Forest paths are key motifs in both sequences. What is at the heart of this kinship?

In his foreword to the translation of *Glory*, Nabokov writes, "among the many gifts I showered on Martin, I was careful not to include talent" (Gl xiii).[26] In other words, he is not an artist – he does not seem to have any expressive gifts or inspirations. And yet, he does possess acute sensitivity to the world around him, affectionately noticing and cherishing many details (most memorably, the jewel-like lights among the dark folds of hills, seen from a passing train: this gift comes directly from Nabokov's own life [SM 24]). As a perceiving consciousness, able to attend to and value things around him, Martin has nearly perfect pitch (*nearly*, because of his obviously tone-deaf responses to Sonya and other young women). Martin lives and sees and *feels* like an artist, the narrative wants us to believe; he is attuned to the nuances that an artist, too, would notice – something validated when the writer Bubnov, late in the novel, plagiarizes Martin's co-invented Zoorland, dreamed up with Sonya. In *Glory*, and in Martin (and to some extent in Martin's friend Darwin, as well), Nabokov presents readers with a purified notion of *perceiving mind*, one stripped of what he calls (again in the foreword) the "material," "practical," and "utilitarian." Through his protagonist, Nabokov asks his reader to explore "the most ordinary pleasures" and "the seemingly meaningless adventures of a lonely life" (Gl x). Martin's acute perception is part of the reason this novel offers the first high peak in arboreal species-count: about thirty-three, double each of the first two novels, and nearly quadruple the number in Luzhin's world.

Luzhin, in contrast, is confined to one gift, one talent – the gift of direct contact with chess-forces, the music and ideal energies they suggest. In a way, he is Martin's perfect negative image: Luzhin barely perceives the physical world at all, and its features fade away, so much so that even the omniscient narrator sometimes follows his murky lead: having only eight or so different tree species, *The Defense* is near the bottom of that list in Nabokov's oeuvre; and the narrator manages to avoid telling us the names of crucial characters, such as Luzhin's wife and her family, and even Luzhin's own first name and patronymic until the novel's final lines. Luzhin's distance from the "ordinary" reaches its peak during the game against Turati, dramatized when he "removed and placed on the table beside him what was no longer an incorporeal force but a heavy, yellow Pawn ... And having got rid of these two chess quantities that had so suddenly turned into wood the players seemed to calm down and forget the momentary flare-up" (Def 137). The energetic magic and music of the game, which apparently both players feel, hardly needs rehearsing here; crucial for the novel is the fact that, whereas Turati can navigate the passage between the world of physical objects and that of chess ideas, Luzhin apparently cannot. Strikingly, it is the wooden pieces that (like the violin) mark the existential boundary between the two worlds. (Recall, too, how the grandfather and violin in the portrait would disappear when viewed from a certain angle, in that oft-repeated game of Luzhin's.)

This pure, most real part of Luzhin's mind, his chess consciousness, is banished when he awakes in the sanatorium and, as noted, trees are banished as well, except for a last view through the window just as he wakes up (Def 159, 161). The fact that the trees are beyond the window, and that he does not reach them (despite looking for the "wood," "park," and "home" as he fell into his catatonic state), suggests that now his consciousness is even more removed from whatever might be its goal, its "home." It is thus hardly surprising that after several chapters looking (and feeling) lost, Luzhin again winds up seeking a *window* to crawl through – and he does so, to "drop out of the game" (Def 252). By this point in his life, Luzhin has been deprived both of his chess world and, it seems, a natural one in which he might exist – but there is reason to suspect, as I have suggested, that his mind is crafted by Nabokov specifically to explore the idea of a consciousness not at home with worldly, physical items. In some respects, trees (and their derived items: violins, chess pieces, canes) are the closest things to *familiar* and comfortable objects to Luzhin. Stripped of his chess consciousness, which really was the only consciousness he had, it is no wonder he lost his mind and "dropped out."

Martin's situation appears to be the opposite. Again, Nabokov's comments in the foreword are helpful: "The perilous path that Martin finally follows into forbidden Zoorland ... only continues to its illogical end the fairy-tale trail winding through the painted woods of a nursery-wall picture. 'Fulfillment' would have been, perhaps, an even better title for the novel," he writes – but Nabokov opted for "the oblique 'glory,' which is a less literal [than 'exploit'] but much richer rendering of the original title [*Podvig*] with all its natural associations branching in the bronze sun" (Gl xii–xiii). Right away we notice Nabokov's use of the metaphor "branching" here, and the overarching arboreal feeling in this image, which tells us something about the artistic energy he associated with Martin and his life. Martin chooses to "enter the picture" at his story's end – unwittingly, perhaps – because his effort to attract Sonia, his chosen mate, has failed. Martin, while mimicking his childhood imaginary act, steps *out* of the narrative into a *real,* rather than painted, forest (one we do not get to see, as readers). This earthy world of pure experience seems to be his real home, and he simply fades into it, merges with it while others, especially Sonia and Darwin, try to discover his trace. In the "logic" of ordinary narrative, Martin has been captured and shot by the Soviets. In the *illogic* of this story (see Nabokov's phrase, quoted above), drawn from a fairy tale and a picture, he merges with the wooded scenery and becomes art.[27] This is the situation we encounter and recognize only very slowly, as Darwin departs Martin's mother's home and leaves behind yet another wooded trail: "He said something under his breath, rubbed his cheek pensively, and walked on. The air was dingy, here and there tree roots traversed the trail, black fir needles now and then brushed against his shoulder, the dark path passed between the tree trunks in picturesque and mysterious windings" (Gl 205).

Because Martin's consciousness is attuned to the ordinary beauty of life, but not to either Darwinian survival or to expressive creation, his act is a logical end to an illogical idea. This idea is similar to the one expressed in *Invitation to a Beheading,* and in "The Ballad of Longwood Glen"; in the first, the protagonist (Cincinnatus) possesses a degree of consciousness and *being* that is so far beyond that of most of his fellow humans that they view him as an existential threat. Like Martin, Cincinnatus appears to have no extraordinary gifts, but plenty of goodness, keen awareness, and sensitivity. The ballad's Art Longwood, too, shares little in common with his family members, and is deeply connected to the natural world, being liable to "stare at a blade of grass all day." He climbs the oak and, like Martin and like Cincinnatus, simply leaves this world for another that is congenial to his essence. (Luzhin seems to have done likewise, but Nabokov did not create, or at least did not highlight, the positive potentials of his last journey.)

In the coming chapters, we will explore further how the oak in *Invitation to a Beheading* helps us think about ideas of consciousness, and how it leads to related branchings in the works that followed it. We will also see, in *Invitation* and *The Gift,* how trees accompany a shift into a more detailed and specific exploration of artistic consciousness in its own right.

Chapter Three

Twigs, Shadows, and the Ramifications of Art

In Nabokov's last two Russian novels, we find two oak trees viewed as if through either end of a telescope. In *Invitation to a Beheading* we see a huge old oak as if we are looking through the glass the right way, or at least we come close to this, and the inset novel *Quercus*, the central imaginary text examining an oak tree's history, gives this kind of magnified, close-up view. In *The Gift*, the telescope is flipped around; an oak opens the novel (its first word in Russian, "Dub"), but is so abstracted, at such a conceptual and focal remove, that we can barely even perceive it. We've seen already how the oak features in the story of Nabokov's awakening consciousness (in the oakling avenue in *Speak, Memory*, for example), and it makes sense to wonder whether these later oaks, as well, have a similar or related significance. In the previous chapter, we saw Nabokov exploring variations on consciousness in the development of his early art, with the talented but narrowly focused Luzhin, and the broadly sensitive but talentless Martin. Here we will follow a bend in the trail, as Nabokov shifts towards explorations centred more on individual essence (in the case of Cincinnatus) and, finally, the combination of all of these peaks – heightened consciousness, idiosyncratic essence, *and* artistic talent – in one character, *The Gift*'s Fyodor Godunov-Cherdyntsev. Both of these presentations are carefully populated with trees, serving as landmarks and guideposts, accentuating and reverberating with the key themes as they develop.

The pivotal role of the oak-story in *Invitation* may well be a marker of Cincinnatus's own awakening to a higher plane of consciousness at the story's end; by contrast, Fyodor is already fully conscious in the artistic sense when *The Gift* begins, and his narrative quickly moves from the epigraph's miniature oak to a tapestry of many trees that shape and reflect his creative motion. Fyodor's story appears to be one of moving into his artistic prime, and this transition integrates many complex tree-filled structures, while also branching into other major components of conscious human life. In this chapter, we will see how the trees give texture and substance to the relationship between love, individual perception, and art.

Oaks Trees, Boundaries, and Selves (*Invitation to a Beheading*)

As we have already seen, Russian literature includes some oak trees of mythical stature – literally and figuratively speaking. On the literal level stands the oak of Pushkin's "Ruslan and Lyudmila," which serves as the maypole of verbal art, which pours forth from the cat's mouth as it circles now rightwards, now leftwards around the trunk. And, as we also saw, Pushkin's poem "The Muse" similarly places artistic inspiration within an oak's dripline. Among figuratively mythic trees stand two oaks in Tolstoy: the one Prince Andrey sees in *War and Peace* on his way to and from his first encounter with Natasha, and which is iconic both of Andrey's emotional development and of the pathetic fallacy in literature; and the one at the end of *Anna Karenina* that is struck by lightning and nearly – in Levin's mind – kills Kitty and their infant child. In *Invitation to a Beheading*, Nabokov made the unsubtle choice of insetting a massive (three-thousand-page), though briefly described, novel about an oak tree. There is something deeply puzzling about this inner-novel's presentation in chapter 11, and its place in Cincinnatus's mind, his world, and his physical experience. This is one of the most memorable of the trees in Nabokov's works – perhaps the most memorable, and one of the few that receives focused scholarly attention as a significant moment within a novel's interpretation.[1] The scene establishes several important contrasts, especially regarding time and space: *Quercus*'s implied story spans "at least six hundred years," vs. *Invitation*'s twenty days, and its physical heft is many times larger than the slim volume that contains it. As Cincinnatus reads the novel, he (or the narrator?) offers the possibility that the work has artistic value – "unquestionably the best that his age had produced" (IB 122) (we cannot tell for sure whose voice expresses this view); and yet, its effect on the condemned man is to produce "melancholy" and "dull distress," along with an acute consciousness of the author's inevitable death. This, the author's eventual death, seems "funny" to Cincinnatus, because it is the "only real, genuinely unquestionable thing" offered by the book (IB 124).

One thing that Cincinnatus and *Quercus* have in common is their Roman/ Latin name origin: the novel's oak may live six hundred fictional years, but the word "quercus" is far older, as is the name "Cincinnatus." Still, the tree's lifespan is significant; its ability to outlast many human lifetimes, and many centuries, marks its privileged stature relative to *Homo sapiens*. And on a literary level, as noted by Marina Grishakova, Priscilla Meyer, and Rachel Trousdale, the novel about an oak recalls both Virginia Woolf's *Orlando* (1928) and a flurry of books about oaks in culture published in the late nineteenth and early twentieth centuries.[2] But what is *this* doubly fictitious oak doing, in *this* novel?

The scholars who have written in some depth about this oak-tree novel so far have, generally, treated it as an isolated phenomenon, and not in the context of Nabokov's intense engagement with trees since his first days as a writer. The inset work may indeed, as Grishakova proposes, "expose the conventionality of a narrative with a motionless and changeless spectator," but the described oak brings forth a host of relationships and considerations.[3] Surely the tree's ability to endure through centuries, compared with mere decades for humans, is particularly significant (though, of course, trees do grow and change over time); the novel's implied stretch of culture across more than half a millennium deepens this theme, and the tree's situation at "the edge of a canyon whose waters never ceased to din" draws in another, even longer, measure of time's passage – the slow carving of geological fissures into the prehistoric strata of rock.[4] Against such a backdrop, the brief lifespan of the book's author might indeed seem "funny" or ironic; juxtaposing the tree's life with Cincinnatus's shortened fate, an even more striking contrast is forced upon the reader. The novel's alleged "greatness" is intriguing, while questionable, and possibly not particularly relevant to its thematic role. In its size it recalls Proust's *In Search of Lost Time*, and in its detailed digressions on the tree's natural and physical history it evokes Melville's *Moby-Dick*.[5]

Another way of looking at the situation is to notice that this oak in *Quercus* is the first highly prominent tree in Nabokov's prose fiction; it is the first in a series of emphatically present trees (or, as here, their ekphrastic representations) that take on a significant role in a novel's network of meanings. Considering that Nabokov had written twenty-nine poems with trees in the title or first line (and over a hundred more with trees featured elsewhere) before 1930, the comparatively unobtrusive place trees occupy in the prose, between "The Wood-Sprite" and *Invitation*, marks if nothing else a noticeable artistic reticence in their use, perhaps in consequence of their abundant presence in those early years of poetic enthusiasm. As a result, the elaborate brackets surrounding this oak enhance its artificiality, heighten readers' awareness of the gimmicky quality of *Orlando*'s device, and form a barrier against any kind of unmediated sentimentality towards this tree (a striking contrast, say, to the renowned giant oaks mentioned above, from the life of Prince Andrey in *War and Peace* and of Levin and Kitty in *Anna Karenina*). An ironic tone towards such an imposing tree creates distance; this first *iconic* tree in Nabokov's prose is deflated, removed, wrapped in layers of culture and "knowingness." Surely, we can't take such a tree seriously, as a carrier of nature-inspired meaning in Nabokov's larger artistic structure?

And yet, what if it is exactly such distancing that allows the tree, in its authentic "tree-ness," to escape the hollowing effects of cliché or sentimentality? Somewhere beneath all the cultural detritus, behind the novel within a novel, a tree still resides, sharing something in common with the many trees Nabokov had considered, with apparent sincerity, in his poems, letters, and life. If this author-persona "loves trees," if his "soul is an alley of poplars," we must wonder how *this* tree fits into the overall artistic complex.

68   Nabokov's Secret Trees

In some sense, the oak in *Quercus* reflects a reader's position, with the key difference that the oak is almost perfectly passive towards the events surrounding it, as Grishakova observed. The tree is both a vantage point for observation, and an object of observation or study; but it is not an actor. It embraces space and time through its physicality and its life cycle. Of course, this is an imaginary tree, even from Cincinnatus's perspective, and doubly so from ours; what does its quasi-existence within a framed artwork mean? Despite its artificial qualities, this tree appears to reach out towards the "oak-covered hills" of the Tamara Gardens (IB 165), the tree-filled places that represent and even embody for Cincinnatus the yearning for and memory of something better, something more than the sham world he inhabits. As D. Barton Johnson has convincingly demonstrated, the gardens, primarily through their name, represent the "tam" (there) of the beyond, and this association and its various echoes are carefully preserved in the translation, especially where literal translation would weaken it.[6] In one case, the emphasis is preserved with the help of a tree: the "tamoshnie sady" (yonder gardens) become the "tamarack gardens," whose only common feature with the original is the syllable "tam" (which, in Russian, sounds roughly like our name "Tom," in American pronunciation). Tamarack, as Nabokov would have known, is a type of larch endemic to North America: he most likely found its name by looking to see what word comes after "tamara" in *Webster's Second*: it is "tamarack." These gardens are also the locus for Cincinnatus's growing early love relationship with Marthe (see IB, esp. 27–8, 64). Despite her flaws, the novel does not suggest that she is unworthy of the human love that he extends to her; whether she can truly return or share that love is another, more doubtful, proposition. Cincinnatus stretches himself upwards trying to see the gardens from his cell's small window, and looks towards them from the roof (IB 29, 43), and they represent one of the very few signs of hope and goodness in a world of rot, alienation, shallowness, and cruelty. (More tentative signs appear in Cecilia C., in the librarian, and in the books brought by the latter – including *Quercus*.)

The *Quercus*-oak, even in its artificial and distanced form, creates a link with the promise offered by the gardens, through their embodiment of something more, beyond what the ordinary (or degraded) world contains (that world, too, contains "oak groves," intermediate to the Tamara Gardens [IB 28]). How else to interpret what takes place after Cincinnatus, while reading *Quercus*, calls out, "Will no one save me?" And then, after his cry, "The draft became a leafy breeze. From the dense shadows above there fell and bounced on the blanket a large dummy acorn, twice as large as life, splendidly painted a glossy buff, and fitting its cork cup as snugly as an egg" (IB 126). This brief paragraph conforms to the absurdist mode of *Invitation*, and in particular it reinforces the motif of a staged "reality" that offers only rough simulacra of "real life." But since the novel is built upon a two-world model, and the enclosed, stage-set world is somehow surrounded by a superior, actually real, world, one feels compelled to interpret this scene as an early hint of what will take place in the book's final pages, when the set collapses entirely. The "leafy breeze," the "dense shadows" that replace the lit room's ceiling, and, of course, the acorn, all violate fictional causality – they should not be there in the cell at all. The acorn is not a "real" acorn, and the leafy breeze is indeterminate, certainly also staged in some way. But by whom? This violation of the cell's integrity surely hints to Cincinnatus at the illusoriness of his confinement, in a way that other strange episodes and pseudo-escapes earlier in the novel do not. The "dummy" (stage prop, *butaforskii*, in the original Russian) nature of the acorn further protects this "otherworldly" intrusion from a direct, sentimental, or otherwise reductive interpretation; note, however, that the object is "splendidly painted," reinserting a touch of authentic artistry into a moment that feels laden with mockery.[7]

All paths out of the deadening reality of Cincinnatus's situation are illusory, fleeting; and all are associated with trees, a fact which the *Quercus* episode both reveals and conceals. His last two acts (aside from counting) are to lay his head and torso onto, and then arise from, a "slab of polished oak" (IB 219), and it is precisely these acts that seem to set him free from his worldly bondage. Whether through death or some other supernatural transformation, the oak has delivered Cincinnatus to the world of those "akin to him"; it almost functions as a portal. (We will see a recapitulation of this process, along with other details, in "The Ballad of Longwood Glen.") At the moment when one might expect the hero's life to end, his head removed, the narrative itself is – if not beheaded, at least subjected to an amputation: the logical (physical) conclusion to the chopping action is itself lopped off; the protagonist, full of imagination, life, memory, continues on, while the would-be executing world falls apart. From the hints given throughout the novel, trees appear to be a significant part of the world where Cincinnatus is truly home, and to constitute a beckoning that draws him, or a link that maintains his contact with that world in his "life," which he also calls "semi-sleep, an evil drowsiness into which penetrate in grotesque disguise the sounds and sights of the real world." (IB 92). The puppet-booth environment appears complicit in the process of his transition to his proper place.[8]

The narrator – one of Nabokov's most inscrutable[9] – indirectly endorses the connection between Cincinnatus's metaphysical state and the natural life of trees. In a lengthy discussion of "the precious quality of Cincinnatus, his fleshy incompleteness, the fact that the greater part of him was in a quite different place, while only an insignificant portion of it was wandering, perplexed, here" (IB 120), the narrator runs through a series of descriptions of his hero's delicate, semi-transparent features, often using metaphors of incomplete or partially sketched drawings ("the light outline of his lips, not quite fully drawn but touched by a master of masters; of the fluttering movements of his empty, not-yet-shaded-in hands; of the dispersing and again gathering rays in his animated eyes"), but finally admits defeat and resorts to an entirely different analogy: "but even all of this, analyzed

70   Nabokov's Secret Trees

and studied, still could not fully explain Cincinnatus: it was as if one side of his being slid into another dimension, as all the complexity of a tree's foliage passes from shade into radiance, so that you cannot distinguish just where begins the submergence into the shimmer of a different element" (IB 121). Vaguely anticipating the "nervous system of a giant" in *The Gift*, this tree exists only as a figure of speech, another "imaginary tree" set outside the story's physical flow; its role as an indistinguishable transitional medium spanning two "elements" also recalls the significance of trees within Nabokov's early poetry. Notice, as well, the analogy between the tree's complexity, its relation to shadow and light, and the individual identity (or essence) of a person, anticipating as well the refractive identity of trees and selves found in *Bend Sinister* and the mysterious journey of "The Ballad of Longwood Glen," and, moreover, echoing the alignment between sunflecks (within tree shadows) and consciousness in *Speak, Memory* (to give just one example out of many highlighting that phenomenon). The narrator's analogy can also be applied to, or compared with, the tree in *Quercus*, a tree that is somehow both art and object, something of the past and the present, and which somehow appears to reach beyond its pages to send Cincinnatus a painted acorn. Exactly where these transitions take place is as indistinguishable as the boundary where foliage passes "from shade to radiance."[10]

Quercus provides another intriguing entry into a series of artistically (ekphrastically) represented trees, which began effectively with the watercolour of a path in the woods in *Glory*. Whereas in that earlier novel the artistically rendered trees and the path they bound call to Martin to enter into that artwork, crossing the life-art boundary in one direction, Cincinnatus feels no temptation to enter *Quercus*'s world (nor, it seems, does he feel any yearning to pass into the painting, encountered within a "glazed recess" during a sanctioned walk around the fortress corridor, portraying the Tamara Gardens [IB 76]). However, the sound of rustling leaves overhead in the cell and the falling "dummy" acorn indicate that boundary's permeability, if only ambiguously in the form of a stage prop rather than a "real" or "natural" acorn. The acorn still belongs to the world of art, being "splendidly painted," but it has leapt off the page (of *Quercus*), as it were, into the world of physical, tangible, three-dimensional objects made of material, not words. Trees embody many examples of transitions and boundary crossings (such as the play of light in foliage, mentioned above, but also in the transitions from under ground, to above ground, to sky), and this literalized boundary violation is merely a continuation of an inherent, ongoing Nabokovian theme.[11]

Let's return for a moment to the question of the inset novel's quality, which maybe isn't quite so irrelevant after all. Although the narrator's (and possibly Cincinnatus's) evaluation – "the greatest ... the era had produced" – does not commit to actual greatness, it's worth pondering for a moment whether this novel is acknowledged, diegetically, as being in any way connected to the concept of *art*. Because Cincinnatus wades through a thousand pages (a third) of it, apparently without disgust, possibly with some interest or admiration, I suggest that the novel *is* intended as an example of artistic creation; we can imagine some of its features, such as the detailed scientific discussion of the oak and its ecological companions (birds, beetles), or the interpretive catalogue of carvings on its bark (evoking Chichikov's lists of newly acquired dead peasants in *Dead Souls*), as rising to the level of detail that Nabokov celebrated elsewhere. Attention to "the throb of the leafy shadows," and the fact that "no little attention was devoted to the music of waters, the palette of sunsets, and the behavior of the weather" (IB 123), adds to the work's apparent authenticity, its aesthetic validity. If I am right that the narrator and Cincinnatus accept this novel *as art*, we might take its existence as a suggestion that, even in a world as dead as the one portrayed in *Invitation*, art still persists. And given Nabokov's creative history, it is no surprise that such a token of artistry in that world would be embodied in the portrayal of a tree. To offer another temporal juxtaposition: in contrast to the "funny" brief physical life of the artist, and even the implied six-hundred-year life of the oak, the artwork itself has the potential to last "forever" – at least, according to what Nabokov told his students.[12]

One striking result of the *Quercus* oak's role in the novel is a kind of bifurcation of significance – or a questioning and possibility of duality or split essence. Following Khodasevich's insight, noted above, that Nabokov's works were frequently, at their core, about the figure of the artist, we can view the artistically presented oak as a transition point between workaday existence and extra-mundane, creative, artistic existence. Alternatively, the tree's metonymic presence in the execution block, combined with the beckoning trees of the *Tam*-ara Gardens, suggests the possibility of a metaphysical or otherworldly interpretation of its significance. In fact, these two positions – attending or intimating the boundary between workaday life (*byt*) and art, or between this world and "the beyond" (the *tam* of the Tamara Gardens) – are among the most emblematic roles given to trees in Nabokov's fictional works. (Next on the list, perhaps, come situations surrounding the portrayal of love.) Should we make anything of this parallelism? Does art lead us to the "beyond," to *potustoronnost'*?[13] Are art and *potustoronnost'* two sides of one coin? These themes will achieve their most pronounced fusion in "The Ballad of Longwood Glen," also by means of an oak, as discussed in chapter 5. Nabokov's trees move around; they shift valence; they straddle boundaries between figurative and denotative meanings; they become ghosts. Trees are *different* from us in so many ways that they invite us, at a deep level, to imagine new worlds and new ways of being.

There is an intriguing connection between *Invitation to a Beheading* and *The Gift*. These are the only two novels whose composition extensively overlapped;

72   Nabokov's Secret Trees

in this case, as is well known, Nabokov took a break from *The Gift* to act on a sudden burst of inspiration that produced the shorter novel's first draft in a "fortnight of ... sustained inspiration" in mid-1934 (SO 68). Considering that the smaller (embraced) novel has an oak at its approximate centre, and the larger (embracing) novel has as its first word "[An] Oak," one feels driven to wonder in what way this attachment to the genus *Quercus* links the two works. We do not know when Nabokov selected the epigraph for *The Gift*; he had drafted only the fourth chapter (and the related story "The Circle") when he composed *Invitation*, but that does not preclude (or confirm) an earlier awareness of this epigraph text, and a plan to use it. Nothing in the novels gives a clear picture of why an oak is the chosen tree in each case, or of whether a specific set of associations (historical, mythological, literary) with oak trees is intended (although, as we have seen, there *is* a possible biographical explanation for Nabokov's interest in the tree in his penholder, alongside the avenue at Vyra, and the various literary precedents). The link between the two works is especially insistent in light of the fact that *Quercus* is a novel within Cincinnatus's world, but also a novel that appears to spark a violation of that world's physical boundaries (the dummy acorn and rustling leaves within the cell), whereas Smirnovski's grammar (the source of "An oak is a tree ... " in *The Gift*) is itself something adjacent to the outer edge of *The Gift*'s narrative boundary, a "real world text" (the reader's and Nabokov's "real world") set at the gateway to a fictitious one. The epigraph's status in relation to Fyodor-as-narrator/fictive author remains unknowable: Did he include this epigraph in *his* novel? If so, is *his* epigraph a "real-in-his-world" text, or does he invent it? A comparison to *Invitation* is useful here: that novel includes an epigraph from an *invented* source, Pierre Delalande, who seems to exist "as real" in Fyodor's world, but not in ours. The pseudo-epigraph to "The Life of Chernyshevski," in contrast, can be taken nearly unambiguously as Fyodor's invention, judging from his book's reviews and the fact that it has no attribution line, and is called an "apocryphal sonnet" as Fyodor crafts his book (G 204).

The Gift's epigraph is demure about its tree; one would hardly suspect that it augurs a novel in which trees play a meaningful role. Those first words, "An oak is a tree," lead us into its multiple examples of elided "to be" structures in Russian, ending with "Death is inevitable." In Russian, it reads, "Oak – tree. [...] Death inevitable"; the verb "to be" is usually dropped out in the Russian present tense, often replaced with an em dash, as shown here in the first parallel, but not the second.[14] Be that as it may, this prominent-yet-cloaked position for the tree, outside the main narrative, preceding and initiating it, off to the side in slightly smaller typeface, may be taken as a diversionary tactic, one which nevertheless, ever so subtly, hints at the significance of trees within the artistic unfolding still to come. And of course, as mentioned above, the quiet oak also holds important reminders of Pushkin and Aikhenvald.

Although not as densely packed with trees as *Glory* (or several later novels), *The Gift* does fit among the more arboreally laden of Nabokov's works, with at least one hundred thirty-four references to named trees and shrubs (supplemented by many unspecified trees and their shadows). Trees' open appearance within the tissue of *The Gift*'s narrative is delayed until the third paragraph, where they quickly take on a multi-dimensional role in the environment. We learn that the street is "Lined with lindens of medium size, with hanging droplets of rain distributed among their intricate black twigs according to the future arrangement of leaves (tomorrow each drop would contain a green pupil)" (G 4).[15] These lindens enter into a special relationship with the nearby moving van – first, when it emits a mirrored dresser "across which, as across a cinema screen, passed a flawlessly clear reflection of boughs sliding and swaying not arboreally, but with a human vacillation, produced by the nature of those who were carrying this sky, these boughs, this gliding facade" (G 6). Soon after, as Fyodor looks down from his new window, the trees encroach upon the van's roof, where "the slender shadows of linden branches hastened headlong toward substantiation, but dissolved without having materialized" (G 7). This van, with its laterally shaded, faux-three-dimensional letters spelling "Max Lux" and an additional decorative dot, already captures so much of Fyodor's attention that the scene stands out as an instance of creative seeing and reading, with the branches, twigs, reflections, and shadows playing a starring role. The trees adorn the street, watch over it (a green pupil soon to appear in each drop of water), and shade it (with twig patterns; later, with dappled darkness), enlacing the van which serves as an inspiring focal point for Fyodor's first moments anchored at this new location.[16]

We see a similar role for lindens in a slightly unusual setting in the story "Recruiting," in which the narrator describes a character he has been watching and wants to "use," or import into the world of fiction as a character. As the story progresses and we learn more about Vasily Ivanovich's thoughts and experiences at his sister's graveside and afterwards (all invented, we learn later, by the narrator), he comes to sit, "reposed on the edge of a bench," where he "found himself filled with an almost indecent kind of joy of unknown origin." And then attention shifts to the scenery: "Bees were ministering to the blooming linden tree overhead; from its dense festive foliage floated a clouded, melleous aroma, while underneath, in its shadow, along the sidewalk, lay the bright yellow debris of lime flowers" (CS 403). A moment later, the narrator reveals the trick, and the real subject of what he is writing, his creative apprehension of his neighbour, the spinning out of a fictional world for him; he even enters his created world briefly, sitting on the bench next to Vasily Ivanovich. As he sits, wishing that V.I. "might share the terrible power of my bliss, redeeming its unlawfulness with his complicity," he sees how the latter removes his hat and "the shadows of the linden leaves passed across the veins of his large hand

74 Nabokov's Secret Trees

and fell anew on his grayish hair." And although the narrator splits, it seems, with his "representative" in the final paragraph, that representative slides over into the spot vacated by Vasily Ivanovich, closing the text with this scene: "the same cool linden pattern that had anointed his predecessor now rippled across his forehead" (405). In view of the visual coincidences, it comes as no surprise that Nabokov wrote this story while he was also working on *The Gift*, in 1935. (There had been similar linden shadows in "A Nursery Tale," from 1934, there associated with Frau Monde's supernatural power over Edwin's world.)

There is one more hidden almost-tree in *The Gift*'s opening scene, as well: the street's name is "Tannenberg St.," referring specifically to a pair of well-known battles in which Russian armies participated, but tacitly also to fir trees by means of the German word *Tannen*. Firs and fir groves are among the common and affectionately evoked trees in Nabokov's early poetry (and Fyodor is, after all, quintessentially a poet at this stage of the novel). The fir's latent half-presence also recalls the trees mentioned by the wood-sprite who visited Nabokov's first prose narrator in Berlin in the 1920 story.[17] Later, in the novel's chapter 2, we learn that Fyodor's last contact with his father was through a screen of fir trees (G 132).

Trees, Shadows, and the Bonds of Love

"The Wood-Sprite"'s magical visitor finds another echo in the name of the Godunov-Cherdyntsev ancestral estate, "Leshino," derived from that same "leshii," the fabulous wood-sprite: as noted previously, the estate's name sounds like "Wood-Spriteville" in Russian. As an ancestral home, "Leshino" suggests that Fyodor's origins are in a magical forest, a land of sprites: he shares this special link with the narrators of those two early works. Such a heritage helps explain the mysterious, even magical, qualities Fyodor identifies in his father in his biographical sketches in chapter 2 (the chapter begins, we should recall, with Konstantin Kirillovich stepping into the base of a rainbow – something physical observers can't really do, but magicals creatures such as wood-sprites surely can). This mythical, magical lineage echoes the forebears of *Glory*'s Martin Edelweiss, with their roots in beasts and trees."[18] Martin (like Nabokov himself [SM 86], as discussed in chapter 1) was enamoured of a painting by his bed depicting a trail in the woods, but the name "Leshino" connects *The Gift* estate's magic more specifically to its sylvan essence. As a result, anything that trees do in the novel, such as create elaborate pulsating designs on moving vans, quietly evokes this charmed heritage. In a way, Fyodor himself *is* the wood-sprite exiled to Berlin.[19]

The novel's initiation (its inception, conception, and inspiration, even its implied future composition by Fyodor), and its creative force, are thus aligned with the presence and growth of the trees inhabiting its setting. It has this much in common with *Quercus* from *Invitation*. The trees and the novel are both budding, "leafing out" (the book's pages and the trees' leaves become analogous and mutually reflective here, a pun that works in both languages). This association of trees with artistic activity, with creation, we have seen already in poems and early stories, and in *Mary*.[20] That novel (like *Speak, Memory*) also explored a very strong link between trees and the development of romantic love, the spiritual-emotional bond between two people (something also implied in the poetry, especially the juvenilia written during the romance with Valentina Shulgin). We see that same pattern in this novel, too, with some additional twists. That loving connection, with a dash of the magical element, is also woven into Fyodor's relationship with and memories of his father Konstantin Kirillovich, and these developments add new richness to the way that Nabokov incorporates and implicates trees in such connections. (A metaphysical tinge in this connection drifts in from *Invitation*, inasmuch as Konstantin has died before the novel's action begins, and his post-mortem "presence" has strong arboreal associations.) These new angles will also lead to new perspectives on trees' essence, and new interpretations of their significance, by leading *The Gift*'s narrator and the novel's reader into questions of epistemology that were less prevalent (if present at all) in the earlier works.

If artistic creation holds first or second place among dominant themes in every chapter of *The Gift*, chapter 3 is the one chapter whose clear emphasis is on interpersonal love, both the history of Fyodor's loves and the inception and sudden flowering of his bond with Zina. This theme – so central to Nabokov's art – is immediately entwined with the theme of poetic craft, and of course this is not a surprise: Nabokov's earliest period of prolific composition accompanied his romance with Valentina Shulgin, and hence "true love" and verse-writing are biographically linked in the author's known life. And just as the stories surrounding Valentina and her reflection in Mary are suffused with trees, so also Fyodor's story as a young lover and, most importantly, as the loving partner of Zina, is marked very deliberately by trees that take root in this chapter, penetrating backward to the novel's beginning and forward to its concluding scene. These trees constitute the tissue linking art (in poetry) and love.

One of the crucial features of Zina's role is her gradual, subtle emergence from the background and scenery into the foreground of the narrative: "she always unexpectedly appeared out of the darkness, like a shadow leaving its kindred element" (G 177), Fyodor writes, and the novel introduces her this way as well.[21] Her presence is hinted as far back as the first pages of *The Gift*; her name pops up here and there in chapters 1 and 2, and in chapter 3 the meandering action builds towards her appearance and then shifts to the writing and publishing of "The Life of Chernyshevski," scenes in which she collaborates "as a regulator, if not as a guide" (205). In the course of twenty-odd pages culminating with the chapter's midpoint and Zina's formal introduction, Fyodor-as-narrator weaves metrical verse into the prose, producing a concealed lyric that turns out to be a

76   Nabokov's Secret Trees

love poem to Zina; the poem's final (third) instalment concludes immediately before she arrives on the scene. We learn that "they usually met in the vicinity of the Grunewald" (G 176) – the forest park in western Berlin, whose name translates as "greenwood" – and thus their meetings are given a sylvan tone from our first knowledge of them. The poem contains a few noteworthy repetitions, and of these the most interesting is the presence, in each instalment, of a linden, lit by a streetlamp, over a bench.

1. "Near that streetlight veined lime leaves masquerade in chrysoprase with a translucent gleam ...";
2. "A bench stands under the translucent tree [*lipa*] ..."
3. "Within the linden's bloom the streetlight winks ..." (G 156, 157, 176)[22]

This triple invocation of a particular linden and its environment establishes it as almost metonymic of Fyodor's and Zina's love (and the Grunewald also takes on, by virtue of contiguity, some of the emotional-ethical baggage here); the linden's heart-shaped leaves (reverberating with Nabokov's early poems [especially "Autumn Leaves," 1921], with this novel's first pages, and with *Speak, Memory*), combine into a renewed convergence of poetry, love, and tree at this crucial moment in Fyodor's story. As chapter 2 had begun with a rhapsodic and hallucinatory memory of Leshino, of Fyodor's walks through its forest paths and park avenues (to which we will return in a moment), his introduction to verse-making in chapter 3 began with rhyme-patterns such as kiss/bliss, wind-in-linden-leaves/grieves (G 147), leading to fulfilment in discovering his beloved, soulmate, ideal audience, and muse in Zina, a fulfilment celebrated by the triple linden. At the novel's very conclusion, as the lovers stroll towards the apartment whose key they unwittingly lack (each thinking the other has it), Fyodor muses, "one day we shall recall all this – the lindens, and the shadow on the wall" (G 366), clarifying the trees' vital place in the collection of sacred objects constituting the poetry of their union, also including "flagstones of the night," "the star," "the square," and "the church."

   Equipped with this information, when we return to the novel's beginning, the opening scene's trees – lindens – decorating the streetscape, casting shadows, reflecting in mirrors, and sending out buds, take on a new significance, especially as we know that the entirety of *The Gift*, or its looking-glass twin, is composed by Fyodor under the muse-like inspiring, receptive, and "regulative" eye and ear of Zina. The trees at the novel's beginning thus embody not only Fyodor's artistic engagement with his world, but also his loving complicity with Zina, even his dependence on her for his creative vision and drive (or, one could say, dependence on the "fate" that brought them together, hence enabling their love and his artistry; in his first announcement of the plan to Zina, Fyodor calls the book "something similar to destiny's work in regard to us" [G 363]).

The love between Fyodor and Zina is romantic and fundamentally creative, as presented in the novel, and that creativity shows in the trees that adorn it.[23] But there are other kinds of love, other – perhaps better to say – facets of the love force within human existence. Filial love, for example, plays a significant role in the novel, in Fyodor's devotion to his father, his admiring fascination with him, his yearning for his presence and approval. Although Konstantin Kirillovich is primarily associated with butterflies and Asian exploration, and his role certainly cannot be reduced to any single token or emblem, it is true that two of the most significant episodes related to him are freighted with trees: the day of his last departure from Leshino in 1916, and the dream sequence in chapter 5 in which he "returns" and greets Fyodor, telling his son that he approves of the "book" about him presented fragmentarily in chapter 2. The first of these episodes portrays Konstantin and his wife in a red "touring car," ready to take them to the train station where she will see him off; Fyodor and the others remain at Leshino. During this scene, the old watchman is "at a distance by the lightning-split poplar,"[24] and as the car drives away, it disappears and makes its penultimate sounds (change of gears), audible "from behind the fir trees," before reaching the high road with a "triumphant roar of the engine ... which gradually faded away – forever" (G 132). Fyodor heads "into the trees," reaches a "wood meadow," and takes in its butterflies. It is at this moment that he sees a swallowtail butterfly lift off from a chamomile plant, which then straightens and sways, a scene emphatically reprised in the chapter 5 Grunewald scene, to be discussed below.[25] He then observes a cabbage butterfly on an alder leaf and much more besides; the narrator concludes the scene with this powerful insight:

> All this fascinating life, by whose present blend one could infallibly tell both the age of the summer (with an accuracy of almost to within one day), the geographical location of the area, and the vegetal composition of the clearing – all this that was living, genuine and eternally dear to him, Fyodor perceived in a flash, with one penetrating and experienced glance. Suddenly he placed a fist against the trunk of a birch tree and leaning on it, burst into tears. (G 133)

The tears at this birch tree become significant, because it will be – two pages later – Misha Berezovski who will lead Fyodor, in Berlin, to "call immediately on [Misha's] uncle, the geographer Berezovski" (G 135), who informs young Godunov-Cherdyntsev of his father's reported death. As we saw earlier, "Berezovski" encodes "birch," "berëza," an echo which suddenly adds almost clairvoyant sense to Fyodor's tears at the tree in the scene above. These tears, and the associations they evoke, also recall the lyric hero's response to the birches in the final Petrograd poem, in 1917, as well as the 1922 poem "At a Village Cemetery," with its hints of another father's death – Nabokov's own.[26]

78 Nabokov's Secret Trees

This collection of material, trees and all, is revisited in chapter 5, when Fyodor dreams in sequence of Misha Berezovski, a poplar tree by a church, and his father's return – a dream which also concludes with "a moan and a sob" and (this is new) a paternal embrace. And while in this scene the dream appears as if "from nowhere," it is in fact prepared well in advance, anticipated during the lengthy Grunewald narrative, in the scene with the five nuns and the flower stalk that links up with eerie precision to the day of Konstantin's departure, through the swaying stalk of grass that calls back the earlier scene: "a shoulder continued to stoop and fingers sought a stalk of grass (but the latter, merely swaying, remained to gleam in the sun ... where had this happened before – what had straightened up and started to sway? ...") (G 344, ellipses original). As this scene is developing, we find Fyodor's attention drawn by "an old tree that had seemed to have beckoned to him – 'show you something interesting.' A little song sounded among the trees, and presently there came into view, walking at a brisk pace, five nuns"; admiring the balletic progression of the nuns across the wooded clearing, Fyodor exclaims, "how much skill there was in everything, what an infinity of grace and art, what a director lurked behind the pines." The whole scene encompasses a single sentence of Proustian length, spanning some twenty-seven lines of text in the English translation, and this virtuoso sentence does its best to mimic the flowing artistry of the moment. Once the straightening, swaying grass has done its work, the ladies are dismissed, "and now they all departed through the trees" (G 344). Only the question, "where had this happened before" hints that there is something especially meaningful carried by this image. But once one discovers the early referent, and aligns the poplars, pines, and birches linking the two episodes, hundreds of pages apart, the artistic structure stands out in stark relief. It is this sort of moment Nabokov referred to when he talked about seeing a novel as if it were a painting, moving the eye, instantaneously, between widely separated focal points (LL 3–5). As an afterthought, we should keep in mind, too, that the entire Grunewald episode – about twenty pages – presents itself as Fyodor's mythical return to the primordial forest (glimpsed through scraps and layers of Berlin vulgarity, trash, and trivia). Even the fantasized incarnation of his literary confrere and rival, Koncheyev, he finds sitting "on a bench beneath an oak tree" (G 337), the oak rich in cultural traditions generally, but also, of course, recalling the epigraph's oak, and the one from which an angle-wing butterfly flew to Fyodor's sweaty chest (G 332), as well as *Quercus*, Pushkin's oaks, the Vyra oaklings, and Aikhenvald.[27] The walking stick held by the perceptive watchman by the lightning-split poplar described at Konstantin Kirillovich's last departure is a "dubinka," verbally echoing the dub/oak motif at that crucial moment. One could belabour this point, but it is enough simply to urge the reader's attention upon the entire episode with its many trees accompanying Fyodor in this Orphic journey to the underworld of his artistry, inspiration, and paternal heritage.[28]

Trees, Love, and Knowledge

Following the way Nabokov's works ask that we resist chronology and linearity, this same scene – the nuns, the swaying stalk – offers a useful transition back again to the earlier one, to which it provides a kind of reader's trap door, almost a wormhole (in the anachronistic sense popular in more recent science fiction), or, as Nabokov might prefer, a time machine. As earlier research has shown, the two scenes are linked not just by swaying stalks, but also – and most importantly – by the traces of Fyodor's father in his life: his departure from it in 1916, in chapter 2, and the anticipation of his dream-return, in chapter 5. I want to draw attention here to the way, especially in the earlier scene, the visit to the woods after Konstantin's departure, the ecological setting's emphasis on trees and butterflies leads towards a distinct cognitive proposal:

> The divine meaning of this wood meadow was expressed in its butterflies. Everyone might have found something here. The holidaymaker might have rested on a stump. The artist might have screwed up his eyes. But its truth would have been probed somewhat deeper by knowledge-amplified love: by its "wide-open orbs" – to paraphrase Pushkin. (G 132)[29]

The subsequent paragraph is the fulfilment of this promise, ending with Fyodor's tears by the birch trunk, quoted above. For the moment, we should pause and consider the efficacy of this love for the natural world, which here becomes "knowledge-amplified" (*znaniem umnozhennaia liubov'*).[30] One almost wants to reverse the epithet into "love-amplified knowledge," but that is not what is given, and *love* is the core element of the moment and the act; the *knowledge* (to which we will return with full kit in the next chapter) allows the *love* to reach its most rich and complete engagement with the physically present components of the natural world. The converse may also be true, or implicit in the scene. Fyodor, a *curieux* as he says in "Father's Butterflies,"[31] *loves* this natural world, as does his father, following the tradition of Pushkin. The words pull us back to the early poem proclaiming "I love the beasts, the trees, and God,"[32] and also anticipate the way Nabokov will discuss love in *Speak, Memory.*[33] The description here works to expand the concepts of both love and knowledge.

However, what is most intriguing about the formulation is the way it intertwines knowledge and love into a single relationship to the world. The senior Godunov-Cherdyntsev, who both "names the nameless" (G 119) and exemplifies "something difficult to convey in words, a haze, a mystery, an enigmatic reserve … an aura of something still unknown but which was perhaps the most genuine of all" (G 114–15), whose life epitomizes the human urge to know the world, helps to inaugurate a stage of Nabokov's career that appears especially interested in epistemology: a trail which we will pick up at this same spot in the next chapter.

80 Nabokov's Secret Trees

One final note. We saw that in the scene of Konstantin's final departure, and in that of the dream-reunion, a poplar stands discreetly to the side in each case. There are relatively few poplars in *The Gift*, so we should check on those that exist to see if they continue to bear Godunovian associations. It turns out, indeed, that they do. The first one appears in chapter 1, as Fyodor returns home from the Chernyshesvkis' April First soiree, about to learn that he is locked out of his new building. The scene has been well-examined: it is when he passes "the square where we dined and the tall brick church and the still quite transparent *poplar*, resembling the nervous system of a giant" (G 53, emphasis added).[34] These items are all in the dream as Fyodor makes his way back to this same apartment in chapter 5, where Frau Stoboy presents his returned father to him (G 352–3). Aside from the clear anticipation of the later scene, one struggles at first to find anything specifically related to Konstantin Kirillovich here, near the chapter 1 poplar. However, once Fyodor learns he is stuck outside, he begins pacing, and in the process discovers inspiration for the remainder of a poem he had been attempting to compose that day, whose first line explicitly encodes the idea of "father": "Thank you my land," or, in literal translation from the Russian, "Thank you, fatherland" (G 56; *otchizna*, deriving from the word for father, *otets*). The composition occurs while he is "somnambulistically talking to himself as he paced a nonexistent sidewalk" (G 55); the word "somnambulistically" is added here, and echoed in the poem (only in the English translation), a fact that clearly and deliberately reinforces the link to the narrated night journey that will occur in chapter 5 as Fyodor walks to the dream-reunion. Thus, his father's presence – not necessarily a factual, spectral presence, but at a minimum an inspiring presence for the "demency" of the composing poet – is multiply confirmed in this early scene.

There is yet another, utterly hidden and abstract poplar, in the first butterfly described in chapter 2: "huge ..., flat in flight, bluish-black with a white band" (G 78); this unnamed butterfly, Dieter Zimmer demonstrates, is the poplar admiral (*Limenitis populi*), described exactly the same way in *Speak, Memory* (SM 133).[35] As the first butterfly in a chapter mostly devoted to the life of the father-lepidopterist (and with the father close-by in the text, as well), the link seems firm; it is amplified by a complex image-cluster that combines the arc of a rainbow, the cupola-like arc (*kupolka*) of a cuckoo's song (*kukushka* in Russian – note the multiple *K*s here, phonetically and graphically suggesting Konstantin Kirillovich), and a "supernaturally smooth arc" traced by the butterfly itself (G 77–8). In case we were not paying attention, Konstantin himself emphasizes the point a page later by shooting the letter K into a board with seven shots from a Browning (G 79) – though, as noted above, this board is near a lyre-trunked birch, not a poplar.[36]

There is something enticing about that "transparent poplar, resembling the nervous system of a giant," especially once we associate the tree with the senior

Godunov-Cherdyntsev. Although a tree-as-nervous system is a rough analogy and does not specifically reference the brain, it does hint at the fact that it is through stimuli received by our branching nerves that we know the world: the tree is the conduit through which we perceive the world. By analogy, trees themselves play a special role in the relationship of the human mind to the world and knowledge of it.

Inasmuch as Konstantin Godunov-Cherdyntsev, an explorer and naturalist, embodies the human mind's urge to know its surroundings, it is unsurprising that his character helps launch considerations of epistemology. In the next chapter, we will stay with *The Gift* briefly as we explore how Nabokov uses trees as artistic tools to think about human knowledge.

Chapter Four

"Knowledge-Amplified Love": Trees and Epistemology in Nabokov's Worlds

Before fully shifting into a discussion of Fyodor's (and Nabokov's) approach to epistemology by way of trees in *The Gift*, it's worth stepping back again to consider how Nabokov used trees in some of his broader, even originary, discussions of trees as focal points of and models for knowledge of the world. I am particularly interested in Professor Jack of the Arnold Arboretum, quiet hero of *Speak, Memory*'s chapter 15, and I want to return to him for a moment. We know from various stories (discussed in the introduction) that Nabokov was surprised and disheartened by most people's obliviousness to and disinterest in specific trees around them, matching their failure to notice butterflies. Contrariwise, he sets (attentive and caring, even loving) knowledge of the "given world" and "Visible Nature" as the *sine qua non* of artistic creation. But Professor Jack's knowledge – this was of a special kind, a step beyond the ordinary, beyond, even, the scientific specialist: to know, blindfolded, species based on the sound made by a tree's swished branchlets (SM 304). This must be among the most *useless* types of knowledge imaginable, and yet, simultaneously, one that most powerfully demonstrates the idea of a loving relationship between conscious subject and natural object. There is no goal, no purpose to the knowledge, except to perceive, to affirm, to bask in the existence of this other complex thing. A non-utilitarian, profound depth of concern for the full reality of any object: this seems to be Nabokov's ideal. Again and again he brings it to us through the image of trees.[1] "Knowledge-amplified love" is the mental state Fyodor brings to his natural surroundings, in the moments immediately following his father's departure on his ill-fated last exploration. As we saw in the previous chapter, Fyodor's instantaneous grasp of a large number of ecological details leads him to lean on a birch trunk and "burst into tears" (G 133). He sees the world; he knows the world; he loves the world; and all of this combines into an overflow of emotion whose outlet is tears. Konstantin Kirillovich lives to discover (and name) unknown butterflies and moths; his restlessness at home and the vastness of his physical wanderings make for a taut parable of the relationship

"Knowledge-Amplified Love"   83

between mind and world. In one tradition, at least, knowledge began with the Garden of Eden's Tree of Knowledge,[2] and if a tree's bare branches resemble "the nervous system of a giant," it is but a short step to think of various other ways that trees represent or hint at epistemological reflections. In this chapter, we will see how this interest in human knowledge radiates outward from *The Gift* into the second half of Nabokov's career.

The Trees of Chernyshevski

Nabokov's attention to epistemology achieved particular focus with his work on *The Gift*, and within that project, it may have been sparked by his study of Nikolay Chernyshevski. (It would be interesting to know when Nabokov first drew attention to others' ignorance of tree species, a personal quirk that became increasingly common in his American years – but was already present in *The Real Life of Sebastian Knight*, written in Paris in 1938.) The novel's presentation of epistemology explores a convergence of love (by some definition) with empirical knowledge. Although the specific theme of empirical knowledge is centred on Konstantin Kirillovich and his scientific study of lepidoptera, the abundance of trees in the work reminds us that this, too, is a rich field for a naturalist's exploration. Our nervous system has a branching, inverted tree-like structure; structures of knowledge, as well, take on the same familiar form – as in taxonomic and genealogical trees, or other hierarchical representations of knowledge and information. Empirical knowledge, by definition, relates to the material world, and the philosophical arguments between materialists and idealists are among the well-known motivating forces behind *The Gift*'s complex forms. Sergei Davydov called the novel an "aesthetic exorcism of Chernyshevski," and the "radical" critic in this phrase stands in for all of social-ist materialism.[3] There is not a great deal of attention paid to trees in Fyodor's book "The Life of Chernyshevski," but what attention there is stands out in stark relief, relating specifically to the question of knowing the world – and the epistemological foundations of such questions. To Fyodor as well, it turns out, trees are definitive of the relationship between the mental and non-mental sides of physical reality.

Fyodor's first approach to the materialists' conception of "world" comes with at least a hint of irony regarding his own mastery – not just of the empirical world, but even of the world of words he is crafting. After relating that "the landscape hymned by Gogol passed unnoticed before the eyes of the eighteen-year-old Nikolay Gavrilovich," a strange shift in voice occurs, a kind of frame-breaking variation on Romantic irony: "Here the author remarked that in some of the lines he had already composed there continued without his knowledge a fermentation, a growth, a swelling of the pea ..." (G 214). Ostensibly an admission of the fallibility even of the attentive mind towards things

84 Nabokov's Secret Trees

it cares most about, these words prepare the way for discussion of a more extreme kind of alienation from the world of things: Chernyshevski travels with his mother from Saratov to St. Petersburg, and he "reclines beside her reading a book – and a hole in the road loses its meaning of hole, becoming merely a typographical unevenness, a jump in the line – and now again the words pass evenly by, the trees pass by and their shadow passes over the pages" (G 216). Language and life strain to escape the writer's control, while Chernyshevski, as portrayed, is oblivious to the material world outside the books he reads. The allusion to Plato's cave hardly needs mention here, but it is worth noting that much like the "unevenness" caused by a hole, the trees' shadows are imagined to be not perceived as such, but rather only as temporary occultations of the page or changes in lighting. The trees are "there," they are "real," but they are completely unknown to Chernyshevski, unnoticed even, except for their effects that hamper the reading process – and, thus, mark an important contrast to the first scene of *The Gift*, with its many and varied tree shadows.[4] Fyodor's narrator speaks of Chernyshevski's "belief in knowledge," his honesty ("the man was as straight and as firm as the trunk of an oak, 'the most honest of the honest' (his wife's expression)" – for all of which "he was returned a negative hundredfold" (G 217). This narrator may wish to cast doubt on "knowledge" as a perfectible possibility (as Nabokov later famously would in his interviews, e.g., SO 11),[5] and that "trunk of an oak" as a symbol of straightforwardness might raise eyebrows – but the image is deceptive, for that straightness gives way to all the usual chaotic branchings, and thus it is another trick played by the narrator on Chernyshevski, or on materialistically inclined readers.

When it comes time to define Chernyshevski's epistemological relationship with his world, Fyodor finds that for the materialist thinkers, trees were in fact a central explanatory aid, as well. However, the nature of their analogy (yet another strange revision of Plato's cave) inspires not confidence, but rather mockery:

> "We see a tree; another man looks at the same object. We see by the reflection in his eyes that his image of the tree looks exactly the same as our tree. Thus we all see objects as they really exist." All this wild rubbish has its own private hilarious twist: the "materialists'" constant appeal to trees is especially amusing because they are all so badly acquainted with nature, particularly with trees. (G 243)

Later in his book, Fyodor accentuates this point by noting that Chernyshevski "would forget his cigarette case under a larch, which he was some time in learning to distinguish from a pine" (G 289). Although most readers of *The Gift* will not have noticed just how well acquainted Fyodor is with trees, they will be aware of his "knowledge-amplified love" of nature, and are likely to remember at least some of the emotional evocations of lindens, poplars, birches, pines, and firs – not to mention their shadows – in the other four chapters. A strong contrast presents itself. Fyodor's "Chernyshevski" also includes extensive treatment of the latter's conception of *love*, and although it is beyond the scope of the present work to explore the matter, it would be worthwhile to make an extended juxta-position of the clear delineation of knowledge and love within Chernyshevski's described world, as against their constant intertwining in Fyodor's own.

Of course, one of Fyodor's goals is to suggest that art is, in fact, a more "hon-est" approach to "knowledge," despite its imprecision (or maybe even because of it), since "art," "knowledge," and "love" may turn out to be continuous and non-delineable in Fyodor's conception (and even Nabokov's). It is suddenly not so surprising that trees appear also within the "Life"'s critique of the materialist treatment of art:

> A couple of columns, a couple of trees – not quite cypresses and not quite poplars – some kind of urn that holds little attraction for Nikolay Gavrilovich – and the supporter of pure art is sure to applaud. Contemptible fellow! Idle fellow! And indeed, rather than all this trash, how could one not prefer an honest description of contemporary manners, civic indignation, heart-to-heart jingles? (G 223)

Trees, their artistic representations, and their shadows have no importance to Fyodor's Chernyshevski, no strong presence within his mental landscape or consciousness. But as phenomena, they are significant in Fyodor's "Life" of the radical. We find them in the guise of trees unseen outside Chernyshevski's car-riage; as shadows, unnoticed as such on the pages of books; as reflections on the surface of the human eye, as if this reflection demonstrates the concrete reality of mental life; as ambiguous locations to misplace needed items; their vague, indefinite image in art seen as frivolous, idle decoration, a distraction from contemporary social concerns. Meanwhile, in Fyodor's own life, trees (and their shadows and other light effects) are constantly noticed, identified, valued, loved, and transformed into engaged individual responsiveness, which, here and for him, means art. Can art and knowledge really be identified in this way? This is a question that Nabokov will be exploring throughout his career. A hint at the answer may be found in the inverted sonnet Fyodor uses to clasp his "Chernyshevski": in the poem's closing lines before the narrative's start, a personified Truth holds something in her hands, but shields it from our view with her own shoulder (G 212).

A much simpler – highly simplified – version of truth appears in the full nov-el's epigraph, with its series of basic equational statements, beginning with "An oak is a tree." These elementary identifications represent the first stage of hu-man epistemological activity – naming, creating useful empirical or taxonomic categories for phenomena. The final example, "Death is inevitable," is not truly parallel with the first five, and this incongruity surely amused Nabokov when he found it, whether or not he intended to imply here an indirect refutation of

86   Nabokov's Secret Trees

its meaning. It also creates a moment of doubt about the supposedly obvious certainty of the preceding examples (the penultimate, especially, which was no longer true, strictly speaking, at the time of *The Gift*'s writing: "Russia is our fatherland," inasmuch as the Russia named in the sentence no longer existed). Thus, in a strange way, the grammatical demonstration presents a muted introduction to the novel's epistemological meanderings, along with a subtle nod to the problems attendant upon the human quest for knowledge (some things change; some are unknowable).

We should not neglect *Invitation*'s *Quercus* in this connection. It is valuable both because of its emergence from the same creative broth as *The Gift*, and for its participation in the oak theme itself. Cincinnatus's world, after all, is a kind of epistemological dystopia: every person must be "transparent" and fully comprehensible to the penetrating rays of others, "understood ... at the first word" (the law Cincinnatus by his nature violates): "*That which does not have a name does not exist*. Unfortunately everything had a name" (emphasis in original, IB 26). The very next line is a graffito on the cell wall: "Nameless existence, intangible substance," seemingly in mockery of the words just before it, and perhaps of Cincinnatus as well. *Quercus*, too, offers a particular (certainly, limited) approach to knowing the world, and this approach constitutes its entire conceit: that a stationary oak tree (remember Chernyshevski's "firm, straight trunk"), used as a focal point to examine six hundred years passing in one limited space, provides a lens through which to create a useful imaginary knowledge-picture. And while there is no need to deny that such a detailed history could indeed be interesting and valuable, its self-limitation simultaneously, and perhaps inadvertently, exposes the narrowness and paucity of knowledge delivered. (Notice, too, how the *Quercus* episode offers symmetry with *The Gift*'s epigraph: the oak is indeed a tree, and Cincinnatus's one enduring impression from the huge novel is that the author's *death is inevitable*.)[6]

Krug's Oak: Epistemological Modelling in *Bend Sinister*

Judging from his art, beginning around the time of *The Gift*'s creative inception, in 1932–3, Nabokov became increasingly interested in epistemological questions.[7] Within this area of curiosity, we can subdivide into *questions of knowing the world*, which likely came fully to his attention as he read the materialist critics and philosophers while preparing to write the Chernyshevski chapter, and *questions of knowing other human beings*, hinted at in *Invitation* and *The Gift*, and then foregrounded in *The Real Life of Sebastian Knight* (as well as the important 1937 "Pushkin" speech). While *The Gift* appears to set up a multi-part contrast between scientific and artistic approaches to knowledge of the world, with an emphasis on the latter, *Invitation* and *Bend Sinister* approach the same problem with more attention to the materialists' epistemological presumptions.

"Knowledge-Amplified Love"   87

The Chernyshevskian theme in *Invitation to a Beheading* has been explored by several critics.[8] *Bend Sinister* follows this same line with greater subtlety, but it provides clear hints to its engagement with that cultural tradition. Not only does Padukgrad's Ekwilist regime enforce a brand of radical egalitarianism explicitly proscribing non-average behaviours, thoughts, or achievements, but it voices a direct expression of Chernyshevski's philosophy: in a speech the regime prepares for Adam Krug to make in exchange for his freedom, we find a paraphrase of the materialist's definition of reality by means of trees: "Whatever I have thought and written in the past, one thing is clear to me now: no matter to whom they belong, two pairs of eyes looking at a boot see the same boot since it is identically reflected in both" (BS 150). Chernyshevski's tree is now a boot, but the larger scene in which this passage is set inflicts even greater ridicule upon his thought.[9] The scene is one of several reminders that the novel sets materialist and idealist interpretations of the world against one another. Although we can recall that Nabokov later claimed to consider himself a monist, and all available context suggests this to imply an idealist monism, that does not preclude some playful reflections upon Platonic dualism as well, and we find the most significant dualist/idealist allegory in the chapter 7 discussion of Ember's translation of *Hamlet* and its attendant hypothetical oak tree, "individual T."[10]

The digressive chapter on *Hamlet* sticks out in the flow of *Bend Sinister*'s plot. Both of Nabokov's dystopian novels, it turns out, feature an inset oak embedded as a complex figure for art, boundary-crossing, and knowledge. *Bend Sinister* is the third major novel to include a prominent oak (recognizing that the epigraph's oak in *The Gift* is prominent only in its placement); it is the fourth (completed) novel in a row to include an imaginary, hypothetical, or simply non-existent oak.[11] These oaks function as a sign of word/referent slippage and remind us of the troubled relationship between putatively denotative language and the knowledge it claims to proffer.

I want to pause for a moment to consider the context of the oak tree analogy in *Bend Sinister*. This is one of the most-discussed parts of the novel, owing to its metafictional qualities, the way it embeds references to another artwork which itself encodes artistic embedding and self-referentiality[12] – that is, *Hamlet*'s Hamlet's "The Mouse Trap," staged for his mother and King Claudius. (The fact that Hamlet's play is interrupted by Claudius's angry departure, similarly to Ember's relating of his new translation and its interruption by his sudden arrest, extends the relationship between the two works.) This seventh chapter is the centre of the novel, spanning its midpoint, almost always a fertile and charged location in Nabokov's works. The chapter is variously about artistic representation, translation, and thus, inevitably, epistemology. Through the two scholars' conversation, we learn of recent critics' *interpretations* of the play, in harmony with the victorious Ekwilist regime's ideology; several pre-existing *translations* of the play, which foreground the knot of problems surrounding

88 Nabokov's Secret Trees

philosophy of translation itself, an area Nabokov was already becoming more and more involved in (and had been engaged in since earliest adulthood);[13] Ember's new translation of the play, which takes into account some unknown degree of engagement with the above-mentioned philosophical challenges; and Krug's reaction to that translation, in an abbreviated and philosophical form: not a phrase-by-phrase or word-by-word reaction, but a reaction to the whole and its general success, considered with the help of an analogy – the oak, and a metaphorical translation of the oak and its shadow. At the heart of the matter resides the question: can a translation grant any access to any knowledge of what the original artwork offers in its essence?[14]

Needless to say, the epistemological becomes ontological here. Once we begin talking about trees and their shadows, a quick digression into the world of Nabokov's scientific work of the same era beckons. In the 1945 "Notes on Neotropical Plebejinae," his important paper revising the taxonomy of a large and confusing group of South American butterflies, Nabokov had mapped a group of related species within a subfamily of butterflies, and suggested that today, though geographically dispersed, they can be organized according to the apparent archaic or novel qualities of their sexual organs. Nabokov thus concluded that the species with more archaic-style structural features – which to him seems to have meant simpler and more symmetrical – are "older," and those with novel or derived organ structures or forms (more asymmetrical, more complex) are "newer." The practice of looking at evolutionary lineages produces an evolutionary or "phylogenetic tree," like a genealogy or family tree for evolution; this is, of course, a metaphor- and analogy-based nomenclature, and one need not think about real trees while contemplating such things. But Nabokov did think about them. Aware that modern, concurrently existing species cannot really form an "evolutionary tree," even if their structures seem chronologically marked, he cautions: "This scheme of course is not a phylogenetic tree but merely its shadow on a plane surface, since a sequence in time is not really deducible from a synchronous series."[15] The dead metaphor "ascends from the grave, squaring its shoulders" ("The Circle," CS 375).

Not long after writing about the "shadow" of a phylogenetic tree "on a plane surface," Nabokov launched into the use of a related, but even more elaborate, metaphor relating other things in the world to trees and their shadows.[16] Drawing such a link between the scientific passage and a literary one, and one not even about taxonomy, might seem like a stretch, but the simple fact is that Nabokov *was* thinking a great deal about phylogenetic trees in those years, and it is not hard to imagine that his playful, shadow-casting taxonomic tree had a direct role in stimulating *Bend Sinister*'s image of a tree's shadow, and its careful reproduction, somehow representing the idea of a literary work in one language and its translation in another. Especially noteworthy is the fact that Krug's analogy, like Nabokov's scientific one, involves not just a tree as metaphor, but a tree that exists as a tree and a non-tree, that is, on two conceptual planes simultaneously.[17] Here is Krug's description of how Ember's translation seems to work:

> This process entailed a prodigious amount of labour, for the necessity of which no real reason could be given. It was as if someone, having seen a certain oak tree (further called Individual T) growing in a certain land and casting its own unique shadow on the green and brown ground, had proceeded to erect in his garden a prodigiously intricate piece of machinery which in itself was as unlike that or any other tree as the translator's inspiration and language were unlike those of the original author, but which, by means of ingenious combinations of parts, light effects, breeze-engendering engines, would, when completed, cast a shadow exactly similar to that of Individual T – the same outline, changing in the same manner, with the same double and single spots of suns rippling in the same position, at the same hour of the day. (BS 119–20)

Thus, in *Bend Sinister*, we have another tree (imagined by an imaginary character in response to an imaginary translation of a real play), a copy of a tree, and two shadows – one from each tree (real and mechanical). It is not surprising that Nabokov had Krug choose a tree as his metaphor for the artwork, in light of the ways we have seen Nabokov connect trees with artistic inspiration and creation going back to his earliest days as a writer. This choice also makes a subtle argument for the artwork as an organic product of nature, rather than as an artefact – a version that accords with Kant's definition of artistic genius. The idea Krug is contemplating results in a triple-layered metaphor: the artwork is like a tree; the artwork's effect is like a shadow (tacitly admitting that knowledge of things, even artworks, is mediated by the sensory and psychological reality of the audience). The artwork could be copied with as much precision as possible, but to do so neglects necessary attention to its *shadow*, or effect, its impression on the person consciously engaging it. Thus, more important than the exact details of the original must be (Krug perhaps surmises, or imagines Ember deciding) the shadow it casts – hence, the project works backward from the most perfect shadow to create whatever artificial mechanism will cast that shadow. It may be that Nabokov saw his *Onegin* translation-plus-commentary as somehow similar to this monstrous "tree," and hoped that, through force of its extreme artifice, it could cast a shadow much like Pushkin's own Russian work.

In his highly valuable annotations to the Shakespearean allusions in this chapter, Robert Bowie presents some of the key epistemological problems posed by Krug's idea:

> ... for the rest of this paragraph Nabokov ponders the possibilities and impossibilities of literary translation. The translation motif ... is used to question the possibilities of art itself. The question is: to what extent can art, "by means of ingenious

90   Nabokov's Secret Trees

combinations of parts, light effects, breeze-engendering engines ... cast a shadow exactly similar to" the shadow cast by the "real" transcendental world that is out there somewhere beyond the boundaries of mundane life? Or is art simply a poor translation of "reality" just as the workaday world is a poor translation of the masterpiece that is the real world? Is art (including the art of this book) simply "an exaggerated and spiritualized replica of Paduk's writing machine"?[18]

Bowie's interpretation strikes me as too insistently dualistic in its leanings, though the considerations he raises are certainly also part of the broader context, and deserve attention. The model – that is, Krug's model – here is once again Platonic, with its shadows and hidden, inaccessible forms (or Forms) of reality. What Bowie glosses over, to my mind, is the fact that we know for certain that the world beyond our senses, beyond the phenomenal – the "thing-in-itself" world – is a place we can barely even conjecture about, and, following Kant, we cannot make any scientific statements about it. Even physicists of those days in the 1920s and 1930s wrote about such epistemological puzzles (see Eddington, especially, and his discussion of *Hamlet*, in this exact regard);[19] serious thinkers, and serious scientists, generally accepted that knowledge about the "real" is a project of approximation.[20] The exceptions were the materialists – primarily, the socialists, as represented by Nikolay Chernyshevski and others in *The Gift*, with their certainty that objects reflected on the surface of the eye are perfectly and unvaryingly represented within every human mind – and they are revisited, as noted above, in the line about boots in the official speech intended for Krug.

It seems to me that Krug's question quoted by Bowie – is Ember's translation "an exaggerated and spiritualized replica of Paduk's writing machine"? – has a different emphasis, one that relates directly to Chernyshevski's eyeball-reflected trees. If Ember's translation really aspires to create a perfect copy of the original's shadow, and if I am right to read that shadow as the work's reception by a reader or viewer, the implication seems unambiguous: that this *shadow* is the same for all recipients of the artwork. Inadvertently, this proposition makes the same mistake as the one made by Chernyshevski: he had proposed that the tree's reflection – seen by one bystander – on the surfaces of the eyes of two individuals looks the same, and therefore, the two individuals see exactly the same tree exactly the same way. Krug's understanding of Ember's version, in parallel, suggests that the "shadow-translation," presumably the mental experience of the work of art, is similarly identical in the mind's eye of all viewers (or readers) of the translated work. The implied question, behind Krug's, is, Can a translation, no matter how elaborate, create exactly the same impression upon a reader of language B as the original made on a reader of language A – let alone all readers of B and A? (Nabokov's friend Yuli Aikhenvald argued that even *within* language A, the uniqueness of each reader's impression is paramount.)[21]

"Knowledge-Amplified Love"   91

If it could, this feat might seem miraculous, but it also implies a uniformity – a sameness – of each consciousness confronting the artwork.

This was the very claim that Fyodor in his biography sought to refute, and, it seems, Nabokov with him.[22] It is for this reason, I argue, that Krug can't shake the nagging doubt that for all its ingenuity, Ember's translation is "an exaggerated and spiritualized replica of Paduk's writing machine," the Padograph. At its heart, the translation somehow falls into the trap of believing in unitary and universalized perception; it attempts to limit the reader's freedom and creative artistic engagement with the artwork itself, whatever its language and state. (This reading resists the widespread interpretation of Nabokov as a "tyrannical" author who sought to control his readers and their responses.) To reiterate: in the logic of Krug's reflections here, the original artwork, *Hamlet*, is *equivalent* to a tree, and we can attach to that comparison all the value that has accrued to trees in Nabokov's previous work. The artwork so identified is something complex, indefinite, beautiful, beloved, temporally deep, and – subjectively and partially – known. The more a translation attempts to control its own shadow (its reception, or secondary impression), the more it resembles the Padograph and its perfect imitation of individuals' handwriting, reducing selves to a trivial and fully replicable sliver of their complete identity and essence.

Twigs, Selves, Infinity

In Fyodor's Chernyshevski work, trees' reflections and their shadows feature significantly in the argument against materialists' logic, and by implication also against their philosophical position. So it is, too, in *Bend Sinister*. The novel's first brief paragraph leads us carefully and abstractly into a series of tree images, showing first their parts and sheddings, and eventually the trees themselves. We enter the novel through a reflection of a tree – a compression that offers a striking implicit rebuttal to the eye-reflected trees in Chernyshevski's theory:

> An oblong puddle inset in the coarse asphalt; like a fancy footprint filled to the brim with quicksilver; like a spatulate hole through which you can see the nether sky. Surrounded, I note, by a diffuse tentacled black dampness where some dull dun dead leaves have stuck. Drowned, I should say, before the puddle had shrunk to its present size. (BS 1)

It lies in shadow but contains a sample of the brightness beyond, where there are trees and two houses. This scene is exceedingly hard to visualize at first, despite its detailed specificity. A footstep-shaped puddle; a reflected sky, house, and trees; surrounded by tentacles and leaves.[23] What are the tentacles? Most likely, they are cracks in the asphalt, but they could be shadows of twigs (there is still sunshine for the moment), and they certainly prefigure the twigs that will

92   Nabokov's Secret Trees

be mentioned soon after. The description of the puddle, its contents, surroundings, and reflecting surface continues for several paragraphs. In the fifth, we learn that the nearby trees are poplars (which the narrator, who may be Krug at this point, qualifies with "I imagine"). We read their detailed description standing near the puddle, and then we are shown their reflections:

> ... bright richly furrowed bark and an intricate sweep of numberless burnished bare twigs, old gold – because getting more of the falsely mellow sun in the higher air. Their immobility is in contrast with the spasmodic ruffling of the inset reflection – for the visible emotion of a tree is the mass of its leaves, and there remain hardly more than thirty-seven or so here and there on one side of the tree. They just flicker a little, of a neutral tint, but burnished by the sun to the same ikontinct as the intricate trillions of twigs. (BS 2)

There are several striking elements in this loaded passage. As the contrast between "immobility" and "spasmodic ruffling of the reflection" passes by, one is unsure whether the perceiving eye, too, is now looking at the tree in its reflected form, rather than at the physical tree. That "spasmodic ruffling" of the reflected image gives way to the "visible emotion of a tree," but we learn that this tree's "visible emotion" is diminished, almost absent, since only thirty-seven (strange number: the age of Pushkin at his death?) leaves remain. They flicker, "burnished ... by the same ikontinct." Attention here to the tree's *emotion* is unexpected and noteworthy; we learn, in the next paragraph, that the speaking voice is experiencing the shock of loss: his wife *will die*, presumably any minute. The emotion contained by the speaker is suppressed; this moment of looking at trees brings to mind the history of "pathetic fallacy" scenes in literature, but somehow still makes us believe in the "visible emotion of a tree," forcing us to think of trees not directly in terms of human metaphors (such as "the fierce branches raged in the wind"), but clinically, as though these emotions are not human projections but really belong to the tree; as though they are simple objects of observation.[24] As the chapter continues, we read of the trees' "alembic ascending shadow bands," and after the sun sets, what is probably the "dead black" reflections of their limbs in the puddle, which has faded to a "dull liquid white"; as the daylight grades into dusk, an image reappears: "the trillions of twigs are becoming extremely distinct." Again, we are not quite sure whether these are direct twigs or reflected ones, but either way, "the glass of the puddle is now bright mauve."

By this point in the chapter's "action" (the sun setting, the light reflecting and fading, the observer taking in these changes), in this semifinal paragraph, the speaker (Krug, presumably) must be describing the trees' appearance against the sky, without the puddle's help – but it is still a little bit uncertain, as presumably the "bright mauve glass" could include within it the reflected "extremely distinct" twigs against the sky. The ambiguity is barely noticeable, but it may be important, as it creates an indistinct liminality to the trees' status.[25] Indisputably important, however, is the phrase "trillions of twigs," repeated three times during these few pages. The word "trillions" catches; in fact, considered carefully, it must absolutely *not* be true that even the largest tree (or even the two largest trees side by side) possesses "trillions" of twigs. That number, as a mathematical figure, must be at least eight orders of magnitude larger than the actual number of twigs, which would be at most in the low tens of thousands, in a single tree. The triple repetition speaks for itself, and of course we can accept that the word "trillions" means simply "uncountably many," or the colloquial notion of "infinite" – an honest hyperbole.[26] Curiously, the word "trillions" does not appear much in this book – or in any of Nabokov's novels, for that matter. (John Shade uses it once in his long poem: "And there's the wall of sound: the nightly wall / Raised by a trillion crickets in the fall" (PF 37); Van Veen uses it once, mentioning a distance of "trillions of light years.")[27] *Bend Sinister* marks the first appearance of this word in Nabokov's English lexicon; the word occurs five times in the novel – three in the first chapter already noted, and twice in chapter 16, as Krug reflects on his love for David:

> Ah what agony, thought Krug the thinker, to love so madly a little creature, formed in some mysterious fashion (even more mysterious to us than it had been to the very first thinkers in their pale olive groves) by the fusion of two mysteries, or rather two sets of a trillion of mysteries each; formed by a fusion which is, at the same time a matter of choice and a matter of chance and a matter of pure enchantment; thus formed and then permitted to accumulate trillions of its own mysteries; the whole suffused with consciousness, which is the only real thing in the world and the greatest mystery of all. (BS 188)

The narrator has the confusing habit of delivering Krug's verbalized thoughts without quotation marks; it seems that all, or nearly all, of chapter 1 constitutes such an inner monologue (even though the thoughts are linguistically, stylistically similar to the voice of the narrator throughout the novel). "Trillions" is almost certainly Krug's word, and in this later passage we find him applying it to his theory of self, personality, love, and consciousness – "the only real thing in the world," an explicitly idealist position. But his application of the word "trillions" both to trees' twigs and to the mysteries within persons unites these two phenomena; the trees, described with such detail and anguish during and perhaps after Olga's last moments, offer him something mysterious during the wrenching experience of loss; their "trillions" of twigs express or show solidarity with the trillions of mysteries being taken away through the death of the loved one. This link appears in part to be spiritual, but it is epistemological,

94 Nabokov's Secret Trees

too, in that the innumerable twigs and the innumerable mysteries of a human being represent the *beyond* to which human knowledge cannot go in rational, logical form – but love (or perhaps, recalling from *The Gift*, "knowledge-amplified love"), as expressed and explored by Nabokov, does breach that limit in some intangible way.[28] The repetition of the word "trillions" by Krug, as he processes the most intense feelings his life has offered, demonstrates that he, too, considers trees as more than just emblematic of such depths. It is striking that he (apparently) imagines the "first thinkers" among "olive groves," as if trees themselves are the precondition for philosophical thought.

As I have claimed, the mid-1930s launched a period – a lengthy one, it seems – during which Nabokov and his art devoted significant attention to problems of various kinds of knowledge. We don't see the same epistemological focus in *Mary*, *The Defense*, or even *Glory* – there, the emphases fall more on such matters as memory, creativity, and individual consciousness in a broader, existential sense. But in the post-Chernyshevski works (as I'll call them for convenience), including *Invitation to a Beheading*, knowledge becomes central in various ways: knowledge of the world ("everything, unfortunately, had a name" [IB 26]), and knowledge of human beings as complex and elusive walled-off bundles of consciousness, creativity, experience, and memory. We see this tendency with particular vividness in *The Gift* and the 1937 Pushkin speech; in *The Real Life of Sebastian Knight*'s quest to find the "quiddity" of another (though, here, only obliquely accompanied by trees, as with the twigs in the corner of Sebastian's portrait [RLSK 119]); in *Bend Sinister*'s more abstract but unmissable explorations of epistemology and ontology (which develop upon themes abandoned in the incomplete novel "Solus Rex," especially its "Ultima Thule" chapter – which is explicitly devoted to the question of *ultimate knowledge*, the greatest epistemological riddle of all). These matters do not fade completely in most of the works (*Lolita, Pnin, Pale Fire, Ada*) from the peak of Nabokov's English-writing career. *Pale Fire* represents a first new step *away* from epistemology – which is not to say that it is completely absent, but it is perceptibly outside that novel's main concerns. In *Lolita*, however, epistemology is still front and centre, especially as it relates to the knowledge of other human beings close to us, and this story of knowledge finds part of its telling in the novel's many trees.

Epistemology and Trees in *Lolita*

Humbert's narrative includes a Nabokovian average representation of trees – about twenty species, across around eighty-seven individual references (compare *The Gift*, of similar length, with its thirty or so species and about one hundred fifty individual references). Some of the trees are bystanders, while others play a more active role – active, at least, in their identifiable connection

"Knowledge-Amplified Love"   95

to the novel's themes. The chief epistemological concern in *Lolita* doubtless relates to Humbert Humbert's knowledge of Dolores Haze – or, more pertinently, his lack of such knowledge: as he himself recognizes quite late, "I simply did not know a thing about my darling's mind" (L 284). One of the more famous scenes where Humbert's knowledge of the physical world itself is called into question occurs when he mentions "hundreds of gray hummingbirds in the dusk, probing the throats of dim flowers" (L 155) – referring, of course, to hummingbird hawkmoths ("Sphyngids," as Nabokov often calls them). But this mistake is not the only example of his gappy knowledge of or attention to the natural world (which, in Nabokov's art, typically implicates the empirical domain generally). This example comes from the haphazard chronological list of attractions and motels visited during the first year-long criss-crossings of the (then) forty-eight United States (L 155–9). Humbert's attention during this journey is entirely on his captive "Lolita," occasionally on her peers at motel pools, "whatever other nymphets parsimonious chance collected around her for my delectation and judgment" (L 161).

A paragraph before the hummingbirds, Humbert produces a subtler example of his world-blindness. In the introduction, we saw how he hinted at his indifference to trees by declaring that he was "no Kilmerite" (L 155). This item is the fourth in the list of places visited, and the second instance (after "Magnolia Gardens") among twenty-one actual trees mentioned during the first journey, plus five references to literary ("enormous, Chateaubriandesque trees"), imaginary ("innumerable lovers ... in so many beech forests"), or painted ones ("retouched palms"). One might think that Humbert's dendrological performance indicates that he knows trees and nature well, but then one might have thought the same of his hummingbirds. The "Poplar Cove, N.C." example turns out to be cryptically emblematic, in a multi-layered and especially striking way: here we have both a literary allusion to trees (Joyce Kilmer's "Trees"), and a geographical location identified with a type of tree (and Humbert has already mentioned poplars at least eight times previously). The boulder and plaque add specificity – they exist in "real life," too, as do references to this location in the guidebooks Nabokov used to help him construct Humbert's tour, and which Humbert used while writing his "confession." To Humbert, literary man, perhaps the monument to a poet is especially significant (even though he is "no Kilmerite"), but the real point here is what he is missing: the plaque is located in this spot because the forest itself is extraordinary, with some of the largest trees in the eastern United States, and the largest angiosperms (flowering plants) in North America. The trees at what is now (and was then) the Joyce Kilmer Memorial Forest, which included Big Poplar Cove, were "one of the finest stands of its type in America" by 1939, the year of one travel guide's publication.[29] Two items of note: first, Humbert says not a word about the trees themselves; and, second, the poplars for which the location is named – tulip tree or tulip poplar – are not true poplars at all, but in fact belong to the magnolia family (not closely related to poplars).[30] Whether or not other poplars mentioned by Humbert are accurately identified elsewhere in the novel, his failure to engage the reality of the magnificent trees around him here, at one of the most striking forest stands in the United States, produces yet another significant silence. Later in the same paragraph we are reminded he can't see the trees: "A forest in Arkansas and, on her brown shoulder, a raised purple-pink swelling (the work of some gnat) which I eased of its beautiful transparent poison between my long thumbnails and then sucked till I was gorged on her spicy blood" (L 156). Ozark National Forest, or Ouachita perhaps? We can't be sure. The phenomenal world and its trees and their "trillions of twigs" are blocked out by Humbert's blinding passion. Juxtaposed with Nabokov's fantasy of the same era – knowing a tree blind, from the swish of its twigs – Humbert's sensitivity to trees appears, temporarily at the very least, to be essentially non-existent.

Humbert's somewhat extensive and varied invocation of trees creates a kind of dissonance, or the possibility of one. He is behind Fyodor in *The Gift*, but produces more types than the *Bend Sinister* narrator, or V. in *The Real Life of Sebastian Knight* – the two immediate predecessors. If he can rattle off twenty-tree names – more than most of his readers, according to Nabokov's view of things – surely he must be an observant and competent naturalist?[31] However, phrases like "Chateaubriandesque trees" and "though no Kilmerite" remind us of the essentially, and perhaps exclusively, literary quality of Humbert's knowledge of trees. (Two more of his tree species are mentioned only within literary titles: "Love under the Lindens" and "Cherry Orchard" (L 229), further reducing the number of species he allegedly identifies around him). The Kilmer poem "Trees" and Humbert's apparent rejection of it are also telling: while the poet famously proclaimed, "I think that I shall never see / A poem as lovely as a tree," he ends the work with a note of self-deprecation: "Poems are made by fools like me / But only God can make a tree." Humbert's self-exclusion from the Kilmerite camp suggests, obliquely, not so much that he does not value the poet as an artist (which may also be true), but rather that he disagrees specifically about the relative value of poems and trees.

Humbert says late in his "confession" that he has "camouflaged everything, my love" (L 267), apparently meaning mostly personal and place names, so as not to bring unwanted attention to "real" (in his world) people and towns. Thus, "Ramsdale" and "Lawn St." should be his inventions, but what about the poplars that stand by the Haze house at number 342? Poplars take on a thematic role in the novel, but we cannot tell whether Humbert correctly identifies these trees.[32] The options for poplar in "New England," all named elsewhere by Nabokov, are Lombardy poplar and black poplar (ornamental exotics), eastern cottonwood (not common in the northeastern United States, except in major river valleys; it appears in *Pnin* in a painting at the Sheppards', as will be discussed in chapter 5), and possibly, again, the non-poplar "tulip"(-tree) poplar. Aspens are in the poplar genus, but Humbert (like Nabokov) names them separately. "Lombardy poplar" appears in *Pnin*, *Ada*, and *Speak, Memory*, and the Russian "*topol'*" most commonly refers to European black poplar (*Populus nigra*), of which the Lombardy poplar is a varietal. In fact, among the native poplars of the eastern United States, the quaking aspen, bigtooth aspen, and the tulip "poplar" are the most common around "Ramsdale"; but of course Lawn St. is a suburban place, and exotic landscaping is more than likely. Nevertheless, our awareness that Nabokov knew several poplars, and Humbert either knows only one (which may not be a poplar) or conflates them all serves as a reminder that the natural world is not as well-described as it seems. We will return briefly to the "poplar theme" in *Lolita* in the next chapter.

The Flight of the Unknown: Chestnuts in *Lolita*

In general, we often have little reason to doubt Humbert's identification of trees; when he recalls orange trees, and a mimosa grove from the first interrupted love scene by the Hotel Mirana, this memory seems plausible but of course it, too, might be stylized. "Poplar Cove" is a real place – so it seems he has not renamed it, curiously; however, it is not a town, but rather a named feature of the forest. Chestnut trees, on the other hand, present a problem. They vie with poplars for the novel's lead in frequency: each is named thirteen times (including hotel names, place names, and colour names), a strange coincidence. "The Enchanted Hunters" hotel, which *should* be a name changed by Humbert, includes an anagram of Chestnut. And "Chestnut Court," which should also be his coinage, sits in Kasbeam – also a changed name, we must presume, itself a somewhat oblique and underscoring mutation of the chestnut's genus, *Castanea*, or its German translation, *Kastanie* (etymologically close, Russian is *kashtan*), plus "-beam" as in the tree species "hornbeam" (e.g., *Carpinus caroliniana*, the American hornbeam). All well and good. Of the Chestnut Court location, Humbert relates, "Our cabin stood on the timbered crest of a hill, and from our window you could see the road winding down, and then running as straight as a hair parting between two rows of chestnut trees, towards the pretty town, which looked singularly distinct and toylike in the pure morning distance" (L 212). The problem: chestnut trees were essentially wiped out across North America beginning in 1904, when an invasive fungus from Asia arrived at a park in the Bronx; the resulting decimation of the chestnut trees was essentially complete, and widely discussed, by the mid-1930s, with the exception of a very few isolated, generally secret or at the time unknown, stands.[33] It is impossible, or nearly so, that Humbert saw any chestnut trees in the United States. Chestnuts were important to Nabokov throughout his adult life, appearing in

Chestnut leaves, flower, fruit (g. *Castanea*). Credit: *The North American sylva, or A description of the forest trees of the United States, Canada and Nova Scotia ... to which is added a description of the most useful of the European forest trees ... Tr. from the French of F. Andrew Michaux*, acquired from https://commons.wikimedia.org/wiki/File:NAS-104_Castanea_dentata.png.

Horse chestnut leaves, flowers, fruit (g. *Aesculus*). Credit: Prof. Dr. Otto Wilhelm Thomé Flora von Deutschland, Österreich und der Schweiz 1885, Gera, Germany, via https://commons.wikimedia.org/wiki/File:Illustration_Aesculus_hippocastanum0.jpg.

his early poems, in his letters to Véra and in his first poem after spending time with her, in the memoir (from personal experience at Cambridge, amplified by covert reference to Tennyson, as Olga Voronina has recently discovered), as well as in novels and stories ("The Return of Chorb," *The Gift*, and others).[34]

There are a few ways to resolve this contradiction, but the most efficient starts with the town's name: since Humbert is committed to changing this name like all others, we might presume that like "not Coalmont," it too has been mutated from a related word, or is a word derived from the local environment. Humbert, indifferent as he is to nature's nuances, cares not what trees adorn the road, and – ignorant that chestnuts no longer exist in the United States – places

"Knowledge-Amplified Love"   99

them here; if the town was something like "Oakwood" or "Poplar Grove" or "Pinedale," and the streets lined with matching trees, his choice here would mimic the world he saw before him. Alternatively, the town had an unrelated name but many trees that Humbert somehow mistook for chestnuts.[35] However, the main point may be that, as at Poplar Cove, North Carolina, Humbert does not really see or care what the trees are.

Thus, one way or the other, Humbert has chosen a practically non-existent tree as the emblem for the Kasbeam misadventure, and he probably does so out of ignorance (an ignorance that reverberates with his inattentiveness towards his barber's story of loss, and of course towards Dolly herself). Since chestnuts appear several times in the novel besides the Kasbeam episode (and suspiciously match poplars one-for-one), we should examine them all for clues. They represent a strange anomaly in Humbert's vision; he does not know them, but he sees them almost everywhere.[36]

The word "chestnut," with varying associations, occurs at crucial inflection points within the narrative. It first appears at the moment Humbert steps out onto the "piazza" and lays eyes on unsuspecting Dolly, who immediately becomes a reincarnation of Annabel: "It was the same child – the same frail, honey-hued shoulders, the same silky supple bare back, the same chestnut head of hair" (L 39). The word is just a colour here (although, notably, it is not used in the scenes describing Annabel herself); it will go through subtle transformations/reincarnations as the story progresses. It is also worth noting that in Humbert's decades living in Europe, he could indeed have seen real chestnut trees in his environment – in fact, there is every reason to suppose that he did, although we do not know a great deal about the natural surroundings of his various locales, except for the few scenes with Annabel he gives us.

The narrative rushes past the entire initial period of Humbert's acquaintance with Dolly and Charlotte, through his marriage to the latter and their visit to Hourglass Lake, where after a swim Mr. and Mrs. Humbert are surprised by Jean Farlow, who emerges from the trees nearby:

> She always felt a traitor to Cavall and Melampus for leaving them roped on such gorgeous days. She sat down on the white sand between Charlotte and me. She wore shorts. Her long brown legs were about as attractive to me as those of a chestnut mare. She showed her gums when she smiled.
>
> "I almost put both of you into my lake," she said. "I even noticed something you overlooked. You [addressing Humbert] had your wrist watch on in, yes, sir, you had."
>
> "Waterproof," said Charlotte softly, making a fish mouth. (L 88–9)

This otherwise unassuming scene stands out not just for the strange (and strangely mythological) names of the dogs, but also because it is the moment

100 Nabokov's Secret Trees

right after Humbert's near-attempted murder of Charlotte, and its would-have-been witnessing by Jean, hidden in the trees.[37] Charlotte's response to Jean's comment about the watch, "Waterproof," is echoed in Humbert's memory hundreds of pages later, in Coalmont, when Dolly reveals to him Quilty's identity (which is nearly pre-revealed in the scene above, stifled by John Farlow's interruption). The later scene is one of the "secret points" that Nabokov mentions in his "On a Book Entitled Lolita," a fact that darkens the shading on this minor instance of "chestnut," which here again is just a colour – again, hair, but this time on a horse. The two scenes are further united by Humbert's abortive intent to murder – he arrives in Coalmont planning to kill Dolly's husband, whom he assumes to be the person she absconded with in Elphinstone.

Stepping back to the original timeline, things become more substantial – but still ethereal – as Humbert and his "stepdaughter" approach the Enchanted Hunters hotel. After some difficulties and confusion finding the place, they finally – almost magically – emerge into the light:

> The Park was as black as the sins it concealed – but soon after falling under the smooth spell of a nicely graded curve, the travelers became aware of a diamond glow through the mist, then a gleam of lakewater appeared – and there it was, marvelously and inexorably, under spectral trees, at the top of a graveled drive – the pale palace of The Enchanted Hunters ... Under the arclights enlarged replicas of chestnut leaves plunged and played on white pillars. I unlocked the trunk compartment. (L 117)

Notice: we *almost* have actual chestnut leaves here, implying real chestnut trees as well.[38] However, we don't *really* have them (even if they could have been chestnut, which, again, they cannot); rather, we have their "enlarged replicas" – that is, their shadows, enlarged by the distance and positioning of the arclights: once more, a Platonic tease.[39] By the time the reader – who most likely does not remember that chestnut trees have perished throughout North America – encounters these shadows, they draw little attention; a slight backwards glance, however, makes them still more interesting to the *re*-reader. Trees are mentioned twice during the final approach to the hotel, and the last instance, the very sentence that delivers the travellers to the hotel, also describes what presumably casts shadows on the pillars: "spectral trees." (Shortly beforehand, the trees in the park around the hotel – unnamed species – were "dripping.")[40] The word "spectral" is used exactly twice in the novel, once here and once at the time of Humbert's return to the hotel in part 2, chapter 26 (referring, it seems, to his own shoulder in the newspaper photograph of Dr. Braddock [L 262]). Although Humbert may be, almost certainly is, referring exclusively to the eerie, nighttime ghostly quality of the trees in the strange hotel lighting, his word choice is oddly appropriate for a species decimated by blight. (As he and Dolly leave Briceland the next day, he feels "as if I were sitting with the small ghost of somebody I had just killed.")[41]

The rest of their journey around the United States, recircling twice, over the course of that first year of Dolly's captivity passes without any sightings, or at least namings, of chestnuts or their colour, and so does the entire school year at Beardsley – right up to the day Dolly (with Quilty's secret help) decides to persuade Humbert to head off on another cross-country tour. After their great loud battle, which ends when Miss East calls to protest and Dolly runs out the door and pedals away on her bicycle, Humbert follows on foot to eventually find her on the phone in a booth at the drugstore: "A tepid rain started to drum on the chestnut leaves. At the next corner, pressing Lolita against an iron railing, a blurred youth held and kissed – no, not her, mistake. My talons still tingling, I flew on" (L 206). Here he refers to the chestnut leaves themselves as physical things for the first time (whatever the species might really be). The previous – shadow, spectral – reference to the chestnuts marked the beginning of Humbert's entrapment of Dolores; this latest one, physical, marks the beginning of her thralldom's end.[42] The peak of the liberation process will be in Kasbeam, and the final moments – at Elphinstone.

During the Kasbeam episode, the word "chestnut" appears six times: once to refer to the "two rows" of the trees leading from the lodgings to town, and five instances describing the collection of cabins, with the appended nouns "court," "crest," and "castle." As already noted, the town name "Kasbeam" is a furtive echo of the chestnut theme, and it appears three times in this vicinity, all in the paragraph describing the much-dicussed visit to the barber.[43] Thus six of the novel's thirteen "chestnuts" appear within just five pages, part 2 chapters 16 (4), 17 (1), and 18 (1), with three "Kasbeams" accompanying like harmonic reverberations (or increasing the total to nine). With such dense repetition, we must wonder – what is the novel trying to tell us?[44] The insistent reiteration of the word here serves, at the very least, to draw attention to it and suggest its role in some pattern (Eric Naiman has suggested that its anagram may be part of a bawdy language motif, for example).[45] Since my present concern is epistemology, I want to emphasize that the drubbing repetition stands the strongest chance in the novel's flow of reminding at least an American reader that the trees being named here cannot exist in this place in this way. From one point of view, this tells us either that Humbert does not know what he is looking at (if he has renamed the place based on the trees he thinks he sees), or that he does not know that chestnuts had been wiped out (if the toponym was related to another tree, and he chose a tree name that was familiar to him). Either way, this is a scene that, in more dramatic fashion than the "hummingbirds" of the first journey, demonstrates Humbert's failure of knowledge, and his use of words that do not describe the reality that he alleges to be describing – do not even describe a *possible* reality, in this case.

This failure aligns, as already noted, with his obliviousness during his time at the "Kasbeam barber's," so named in "On a Book entitled *Lolita*" (L 316). The

102 Nabokov's Secret Trees

scene marks Humbert's ignorance in another, more significant (to him) way. As if evolving from the chestnut trees mentioned earlier – invisible except for their leaves in the rain as Dolly plotted her escape – these trees, now fully formed and visible, show the next key stage in the process of her "liberation": her first clandestine private meeting with Quilty during the trip west, most likely involving sex of some sort.[46] Dolly's distance from Humbert reaches a new peak in this scene, as does her safety from his knowledge: earlier, he "simply did not know a thing" about his "darling's mind"; now, she "dreamily brimmed with a diabolical glow that had no relation to me whatever" (L 214), and he "knows" her mind less than ever. Or, to put it a little differently, he now, suddenly and with even greater clarity, knows that there is something very important that he does not know. He rapes her passive body in his attempt to learn this thing, but, he finds, "the scent I traveled upon was so slight as to be practically undistinguishable from a madman's fancy" (L 214). (Later, in Elphinstone, her pillow will carry the scent of "chestnuts and roses," on which more in a moment.) It may be argued that this scene is the pivotal one, in which Humbert transforms from a man who thinks he knows things – lives under the delusion that he knows at least many important things that give him control over his world, and over Dolly – into a man who suddenly recognizes the illusory quality of his knowledge. The false, drubbing presence of chestnut trees reinforces this shift. Much of the novel's remaining nineteen chapters will be devoted to Humbert's quest to discover the elusive secret behind "my Lolita." The secret, of course, turns out to be a parody of himself, embodied by Quilty.

The Kasbeam episode fades away by means of the rather amusing sentence that opens chapter 18, with one final drumbeat on the keyword: "The reader must now forget Chestnuts and Colts, and accompany us further west" (L 216). That combination of trees and guns also fits a pattern – the Chestnut Court episode includes the introduction of Harold Haze's gun with its recent history, reminders of John Farlow (who showed Humbert how to use the gun [L 79]) and Hourglass Lake, and its trees (pines, not chestnuts) through which Jean, with her "chestnut mare" legs (L 89), nearly witnessed a murder and heard the word "waterproof" – a word later echoed in Humbert's mind years later, "Colt" in pocket, in Coalmont, a day after he receives John Farlow's and Dolly's letters. But the sentence opening chapter 18 is, itself, gratuitous, purely rhetorical, an apostrophic, indirect address to the reader highlighting, one might suppose, the two key features of the preceding episode. It serves no other purpose but clumsy (and clichéd) transition, and to emphasize the chestnuts and the gun. The command to "forget" about these things is ironic, though perhaps effective, and we do not see either item again for about twenty-five pages.

There are, of course, many pivots and inflection points in the novel, but we and Humbert see his separation from Dolly, her installation at the Elphinstone hospital, to be one of the most crucial of such moments, her illness creating the spark for Humbert's fever, and her own clandestine escape. Having delivered

"Knowledge-Amplified Love"   103

ailing Dolores to the hospital, and having waited some hours to sober up enough to drive, Humbert heads back to the motor court ("Silver Spur"):

> I found the highway at last, and then the motel, where millions of so-called "millers," a kind of insect, were swarming around the neon contours of "No Vacancy"; and, when, at 3 a.m., after one of those untimely hot showers which like some mordant only help to fix a man's despair and weariness, I lay on her bed that smelled of chestnuts and roses, and peppermint, and the very delicate, very special French perfume I latterly allowed her to use, I found myself unable to assimilate the simple fact that for the first time in two years I was separated from my Lolita. (L 241)

Various structural echoes grab one's attention here: another hotel with bright lights (now neon, rather than arclights), the "millions of millers" recalling the "hundreds of powdered bugs" at the Enchanted Hunters accompanying Humbert's first eerie dialogue with Quilty. And he lies on her bed, bringing back to us (if not to him) the day she left for Camp Q, when he first burrows in her unwashed clothing in the closet, and then gets into her bed. But the strangest part: how can Dolly's bed in Silver Spur Court smell of chestnuts? Is it because her hair is "chestnut," like Annabel's, and takes him back to a European childhood where things might in fact occasionally have smelled like chestnuts? (The other scents he detects are all completely ordinary, even if that of "roses" retains somewhat mysterious origins and fits rather too neatly with the novel's expansive "rose" pattern, including the "experts in roses" from the Enchanted Hunters [L 122]). Here, once again, the "chestnut" is completely removed from any physical object; the smell itself must be an illusion or trick of mind or memory, unless, somehow, the sick Dolly really *does* smell like chestnuts – not something we have been told before, nor would we expect it. However, her absence from his side does bear a functional similarity to the absence of actual chestnut trees from the landscape (that both were removed by disease could be a deliberate echo, too).[47] The fact that we have here a scent – even if an imagined or illusory one – preserves a partial concreteness to the *idea* of the chestnut, but attenuated now in comparison with the alleged presence of the named trees back in Kasbeam and Chestnut Court, and the dripping leaves in Beardsley. However, it is striking that Humbert's hotel adventures with Dolly begin with the "spectral" and dripping chestnuts at Enchanted Hunters, and end with the "scent" of chestnuts at Elphinstone.

The final step attenuates the word yet again, as it clasps the beginning and end of Humbert's "cryptogrammic paper chase" (L 250). At its start, we read the following: "I have a memo here: between July 5 and November 18, when I returned to Beardsley for a few days, I registered, if not actually stayed, at 342 hotels, motels and tourist homes. This figure includes a few registrations between Chestnut and Beardsley, one of which yielded a shadow of the fiend ('N. Petit, Larousse, Ill.')" (L 248). There follows the long list of motel guest register riddles, puns, and

104 Nabokov's Secret Trees

literary references, a series that concludes with the line: "But the most penetrating bodkin was the anagramtailed entry in the register of Chestnut Lodge 'Ted Hunter, Cane, NH'" (*sic*; L 251). As a formal matter, Humbert has opened and closed his list with "Chestnut." The opening "Chestnut" appears to conflate the name of the lodge with the name of the town (Kasbeam), hinting at their etymological connection. (See Dieter Zimmer's "Lolita, USA, Trip 2," which makes note of at least the equation, if not the etymology.)[48] That first use, naming the town or motor court rather than their trees, produces one layer of abstraction; the final mention, now of the "Lodge" with its full title, redirects us from referential language into anagrams, and takes us right back to the Enchanted Hunters, where the first "spectral" chestnuts with their enlarged shadows had appeared in the novel. If this is one of those moments where, by mentioning both Shakespeare (via the bodkin) and anagrams (directly in the word "anagramtailed"[49] and the easily solved "Ted Hunter, Cane, NH) Nabokov is encouraging his reader to find still more anagrams and related puzzles (just as "bodkin" will become "Kinbote" in *Pale Fire*), we might notice that the actual hotel name "Enchanted Hunters" does enclose within it an anagram of "chestnut."[50] We are now at the level of completely abstracted language play, with all referentiality removed from the scene. Humbert moves from Chestnut to Chestnut (at least in his text), hoping to find clues to the abductor's identity, and finally knowledge, but finds only playful words "signifying nothing" – to quote a different Shakespeare play that makes some appearances elsewhere in the novel.[51] "Oh my Lolita," he laments elsewhere, "I have only words to play with" (L 32).

No more chestnuts (noun or adjective) appear by name in the rest of the novel, but there is one final muted echo when, though with Rita and having "given up all hope of tracing [Dolly's] kidnaper and her" (L 261), Humbert had "a curious urge to relive" his stay at the Enchanted Hunters; the attempt fails, and he tries at least to catch some trace of the earlier visit in the library's collection of newspapers, which had printed photographs of the florists' and theologians' conventions at the hotel in August 1947 (by now, it is 1952). When he emerges from the library, Rita is upset by the thought that Humbert would soon leave her, as others have left her, and amid consolations he strings together some "fugitive rhymes" to amuse her:

The place was called *Enchanted Hunters*. Query:
What Indian dyes, Diana, did thy dell
endorse to make of Picture Lake a very
blood bath of trees before the blue hotel? (L 263)

Those trees should be the same ones that Humbert had earlier called chestnuts, indirectly through their leaves' shadows. Here too, we "see" only a nightmarish reflection in "Picture Lake," not the leaves or trees themselves. If anything, the trees have become even more indistinct, now transformed into a vague image enclosed within "fugitive rhymes"; as Humbert does not visit the hotel itself, unable to bear facing the actual site, the poem reflects only memory, not something Humbert had lately seen. Why does he not name the chestnuts, and why do chestnuts not appear at all in the last sections of the novel? (Similarly, only the elms of Ramsdale are described on that last visit; the poplars of 342 Lawn St., so frequently evoked in the first months described in the novel, are invisible when he returns to the house before heading to Parkington and Pavor Manor to kill Quilty.)

Why, we should ask, does this "chestnut theme" rise to its Kasbeam climax and then fade away completely, reduced to a "bloodbath reflection," present at the final visit to the Enchanted Hunters? This question is not easy to answer; future researchers may discover more on this matter than I have. However, the beginning of an economical answer is available: the chestnut tree is largely associated with Quilty and his elusive, unknowable presence behind much of the text. Once he becomes an explicit actor on the novel's stage (if not its director), when Dolly names him in Coalmont, Humbert "knows" his "other" or his "brother" (as he also calls him) as more than a shadowy force and source of angst and doubt. Knowing Quilty also stands for Humbert's own self-knowledge, something foregrounded both by the "double"-like qualities of their relationship, and by many features of the Pavor Manor scene that bring the characters even closer together (not just their blood-and-sweat tumble, but also the décor: a davenport here, a purple silk robe or polar bear rug there, etc.). Knowing Quilty, Humbert also comes to know himself, it seems, and killing his double is also a figure for suicide – linked to the tragic genre, and provoked by the horror of the acts only belatedly understood. The tree disappears as figure and intermediary, as the subject/object struggle becomes literalized in the character of the brother/other/doppelgänger. The chestnuts stand in for Humbert's blindness, in other words; when his eyes are opened, the chestnuts fade away.

I have been arguing in this section that *Lolita* is a novel largely driven by epistemological concerns; such matters are frequently related to love in Nabokov's implied worldview, as we saw in *The Gift*.[52] And in large part it is Humbert's failure in non-erotic human love that prevents him from truly seeing and knowing – both his prisoner Dolly Haze, and his natural surroundings. As has been discussed by many, Humbert "sees" (thus, knows) mainly the bars of his own cage – that is, his passion, his sexual obsession.[53] Just as Nabokov's 1937 Pushkin lecture lays out the significance of love-filled vision in any attempt to represent Pushkin, Russia's most beloved poet, his novel shows how Humbert's inability to love *humanely* prevents him from knowing Dolly as a person, and from honouring her complete personhood adequately within his "confession," although by his story's end he may be approaching such a love and its partial fulfilment in his prose. Perhaps the process of writing has helped him along.

The Elusive Man: *Pnin's* Mystery Trees

I'm going to return in a moment to treating trees and epistemology in greater detail, in *Pale Fire* and (to a lesser extent) *Ada, or Ardor*, but first I want to address a brief flickering of this topic in *Pnin*, which I (for the most part) do not read as a novel largely concerned with epistemology, but rather, as one mostly engaged with ethics – especially the ethics of stories we tell about other people. Knowledge (i.e., epistemology) is tucked away in there too, though, because in some respects to call a narrative "*Pnin*" is to claim to offer knowledge about that person, even if – for us readers of the novel – it's a "suspended disbelief" kind of knowledge. And so, while I read *Pnin* to be primarily about human relationships, and art, and – especially – the ethical efficacy of *love* (and not its epistemological efficacy, such as we explored in *The Gift*), there is one tree-related episode in *Pnin* that speaks directly to both knowledge and the ethics of narration. (I will treat the novel at greater length with an eye on its trees' relationship to art in the next chapter.) This tree is the one growing next to the house Timofey almost buys, the rented one on Todd Rd., which appears in chapter 6.

Pnin contains thirty-four species of named trees and shrubs.[54] For such a small book, it is a large number – probably the most densely wooded work of all, though *Glory* comes close. The tree I want to examine appears in the middle of chapter 6, section 4. The narrator relates that "a tall deciduous tree, which Pnin, a birch-lime-willow-aspen-poplar-oak man, was unable to identify, cast its large, heart-shaped, rust-colored leaves and Indian-summer shadows upon the wooden steps of the open porch" (Pn 145).[55] When I first wrote about this tree in an earlier article, I felt uncertainty about what species it might be, and over the years I have seen a few (unsuccessful, to my mind) efforts to identify it definitively.[56] But before diving into that question, we should examine carefully the rhetorical situation here, as well as the epistemological one. The narrator suggests with his six-tree list that Pnin can identify very few trees, though surely he can identify a few more types than this – certainly fir and pine, probably maple as well – so V.V. is being ungenerous here, one of his "nasty" moments.[57] Because the narrator names thirty-four species of tree before the novel ends, the reader is encouraged to believe that he, unlike Pnin, can identify this tree. On the other hand, if he has (or will have) identified thirty-four species, such a large number, why not identify this one too, if he knows it? Leaving it a blank seems gratuitous, deliberately mysterious, or just plain suspicious.

This moment radiates uncertainty, and amplifies a feeling of ignorance on the part of the reader. Of course, we can try to figure it out: I previously proposed either mulberry (probably red) or basswood (American linden, *Tilia americana*), and I offered some justifications for each of those. Basswood, as a variety of linden or "lime" (see the hyphenated list of Pnin's tree-knowledge, above) must after all be excluded; *T. americana* is similar enough to the lindens

Pnin *would* know (*T. cordata* or *T. europaea* or *T. grandifolia*) that he would surely have thought it to be one of the same trees. Gennady Barabtarlo has also suggested the mulberry genus.[58] Another possibility is the catalpa (there are two varieties, southern and northern; northern would be the main possibility in Waindellville's locale, which appears to be upstate New York). But the catalpa's leaves, like those of all the other tall trees with heart-shaped leaves, turn yellow in autumn. Some rusting is possible (I saw it in autumn of 2019 at the Brooklyn Botanic Garden), but it is not typical, and probably never enough to call the tree's leaves "rust-colored" as a general statement; the yellow still dominates. Paulownia has been mooted in private correspondence, but its leaves fall dead, fully wilted, and nearly black – certainly never rust-coloured and heart-shaped.[59] By now, after years of reflection and study, the two most enticing possibilities are 1) this is a fantastical tree, invented by the Implied Author (over V.V.'s head), *a tree the narrator, like Pnin, does not know*; or 2), it is some variant or freak version of a catalpa (mentioned in chapter 5) or, perhaps, red mulberry – *which is never mentioned* by the narrator in the novel, so it is possible that he does not know it (such ignorance is highly unlikely in the case of mulberry, however).[60]

The point, once again, is that we are faced with a part of nature, and the possibility of knowing, in a taxonomic or strong empirical sense, what that natural thing is. Pnin, apparently, does not. We, the reader, *can* not, because we have only its description. The narrator, for all we know, *may* not. Why set this situation up this way, and why draw so much attention to it?

In fact, the narrator, being a bit of a show-off, would almost certainly identify the tree if he could. For some reason, Nabokov has placed his "serial self" in an awkward spot, where he cannot name a tree and conceals the gap by drawing attention to Pnin's alleged limits as a naturalist. In this novel about love, and about relationships with others, and about the ethics of narration, one likely reason stands out: just as the narrator does not "know" this tree, so he also does not fully know Pnin. This tree, like the trees in *Bend Sinister* with their trillions of twigs, aligning as they do with the trillions of mysteries making up human individuality, stands for all those things in Pnin that must remain mysterious, out of reach, beyond the narrator's penetrating eye. In the novel's next and final chapter, that trait, Pnin's elusiveness and resistance to total narration, will become the dominant theme.

Following *Lolita*, *Pnin* represents a new approach to capturing – literally and "literally" – a person in a web of narrative. This problem, as such, has concerned Nabokov significantly at least since the time when he was writing *The Gift* and its Chernyshevski chapter, which Fyodor juxtaposes with *biographies romancées* (fictionalized biographies). This same concern dominates the 1937 essay "Pushkin, or the Real and the Plausible,"[61] and achieves its first complete realization in *The Real Life of Sebastian Knight*, which places the epistemological challenge

108   Nabokov's Secret Trees

right at the head of its title. *Lolita*, in turn, demonstrates the conflict between passion and knowledge, how passion obstructs or distorts love, thus preventing knowledge and rendering impossible anything like "knowledge-amplified love" (G 132). Though nominally "about" "Lolita," Humbert's narrative reveals mostly his failure to know her (that is, Dolly) beyond the level of his own sensual stimulation. In *Pnin*, also named after a central character and object of the narrator's fascination, that same problem continues to linger, but Nabokov's artistic treatment of it here is becoming more abstract and more generalized. Just as Zina warned Fyodor in *The Gift* against "mass executions of friends and good acquaintances" (G 364), the Implied Author of *Pnin* (our imagined "Nabokov" persona, not the narrator) appears to be exploring the ethical consequences of, as well as the ego-driven motives behind, the description of another human being (even a fictional one). The fictitious V.V. presents his "*Pnin*" as a study, a portrait: he wishes to examine his subject, to describe him, to "spread and pin" him, perhaps. To do this as well as possible (drawing on Fyodor, and also on Bakhtin), he must *love* this other.[62] But even so, following Adam Krug's logic (and also, again, Bakhtin's), he cannot completely know and represent this other's true essence. Does V.V. love Pnin? Maybe; I might even say – probably, despite the "nastiness" that Nabokov himself drew attention to in his comments on the novel (SL 150). But to imagine Pnin as a complete human being is to imagine him free and full of mysteries, off the page; hence the unnamed tree, and Pnin's escape – from Waindellville, V.V., and the metaphorical "axe" – at the novel's end. This sense of mystery, even miracle, is deepened by a tree in the novel's final scene, as Jonathan Rowan has stunningly demonstrated: here Nabokov (or V.V.: it is unclear whose mischief this is meant to be) uses a Lombardy poplar to trigger the eventual discovery that the sun has *risen in the west* on the novel's last day.[63] This amusing detail, combined with the final words describing Pnin's escape – "where there was simply no saying what miracle might happen," their echo of "Mira" in "miracle" – propels Pnin and the reader out of the narrative and out of ordinary reality, into a world of beauty and possibility.

Trees and the Hide-and-Seek of Knowledge in *Pale Fire*

That central concern with the power of narrative to contain and communicate some "truth" about "life" continues in *Pale Fire*, but it takes on a radically new shape, with major complications and embellishments. The novel steps back from the key question of *portraying a person*, and foregrounds instead the matter of how stories represent other stories: how Shade's poem represents (and fails to represent) Kinbote's "Zembla" tale, related to him orally (at least in theory), and how Kinbote's commentary represents Shade's poem and his creative work on it, in the context of Kinbote's alleged efforts to influence that work. The novel's (surely planned) dissolution into a "who invented whom" interpretive

"Knowledge-Amplified Love" 109

vortex is a further step in the epistemological problem of knowing other human beings and knowing texts. Who, after all, is Shade, who is Kinbote, and who, most mysteriously, is Vseslav Botkin?[64] The idea of a known objective world, an empirical field for epistemological grounding, recedes deliberately in this work. Trees remain, however, and move more significantly into the foreground, even while diversifying out into multiple tiers of signification. Some of them do help structure *Pale Fire*'s artistic treatment of epistemological problems. (The ultimate problem, of "who-whom," is probably not one of them.)

There are several prominent trees in *Pale Fire* (the shagbark, the trees in Shakespeare Avenue, the yew and the ginkgo), but I want to focus in this brief section on some deliberately obscured ones, and return to the others in the next chapter, in other connections. Two of the key ways that Nabokov engages epistemology in his works, I argue, are 1) to highlight misidentification (such as Humbert's mistake about the hawkmoths, or the chestnuts; the apparent mislabelling of Sebastian Knight's street; Chernyshevski's inability to name trees) and 2) to highlight complete failures to see things, either because they are concealed (insects with object-resemblance camouflage, find-what-the-sailor-has-hidden drawings and situations, to take two common examples), or because of a defective approach to seeing. Such shortcomings relate, again, to Chernyshevski's failure to see trees while travelling – he sees only their unidentified shadows – or to Humbert's failure to see the huge tulip trees by the Joyce Kilmer memorial or, most significantly, Dolly's human autonomy. The earliest pages of *Pale Fire* pursue both of these strategies.

The last (signature) line of Kinbote's "Foreword" and the first line of John Shade's poem "Pale Fire" each hide a secret tree, and the two trees are the same. Kinbote signs his foreword "*October 19, 1959, Cedarn, Utana*" (italics in original, PF 29).[65] The fictitious toponym "Cedarn" is probably doing a few things simultaneously, but one of them is certainly to hide the tree name "cedar" in plain sight. As Nabokovian puzzles go, this one is so easy as to look, well, not even very puzzling – so much so that it is easy to dismiss. The poem's immediate take on this tree is a bit more subtle: "I was the shadow of the waxwing slain / by the false azure in the window pain," the poem's narrator declares, pausing at a semicolon at this point and then rolling on. The hidden cedar, of course, comes from the bird's full name, "cedar waxwing," which is scrupulously avoided here and elsewhere in the novel. The missing word, however, escapes Kinbote's attention (or so it seems), and leads to a fascinating trail of not-quite-complete information. When we reach the end of this trail, we will learn that these lines are variously involved in the epistemological "mistaken identity" motif, in addition to the more obvious "hidden pictures" game being played here.

Taken together, the two lines offer a subtle combination whereby the mutated word in Kinbote's signature ("Cedarn") offers a thinly veiled, yet also strangely well-hidden, hint to notice the missing word in the poem's first line. In a way, the

110   Nabokov's Secret Trees

missing word, too, is obvious: many people, and all people who care about birds in North America, know the cedar waxwing.[66] Our attention subconsciously drawn to the cedar, the poem moves on, and returns to the waxwing in lines 131 and 181, and according to Kinbote also in its (invisible) last or missing – 1,000th – line. Along the way, it passes by some cedars late in Canto Two – and we will return to these; they are not accompanied by any birds, and they will not be particularly noticed by the first-time, fifth-time, or hundredth-time reader, if that reader is not as interested in trees as Nabokov clearly was.

Kinbote's reaction to the first line's bird is intriguing:

> We can visualize John Shade in his early boyhood, a physically unattractive but otherwise beautifully developed lad, experiencing his first eschatological shock, as with incredulous fingers he picks up from the turf that compact ovoid body and gazes at the wax-red streaks ornamenting those gray-brown wings and at the graceful tail feathers tipped with yellow as bright as fresh paint. When in the last year of Shade's life I had the fortune of being his neighbor in the idyllic hills of New Wye (see Foreword), I often saw those particular birds most convivially feeding on the chalk-blue berries of junipers growing at the corner of his house. (See also lines 181–2.) (PF 73)

As it turns out, Kinbote does not name this bird as a "cedar waxwing," or give its scientific name – a fact we will be reminded of later in the text (especially in the index, but elsewhere too). He gives a beautiful description of its appearance, and assures us that it is based on his eye-witness account, that empirical solid ground: he has seen it! Indeed, that he often saw them feeding on juniper berries at Shade's house produces an important contrast to the bird's name – apparently unknown to him.[67] He mentions lines 181–2, where Shade says early in Canto Two, "Today I'm sixty-one. Waxwings / Are berry-pecking. A cicada sings" (39), closing the circle, as it were, between Shade's experience and Kinbote's. Are we meant to be curious about the fact that Kinbote's birds are eating berries from junipers, not from cedars? I think we are. I want to preface the coming exploration by remembering that in nature, a tree is never just a tree; it is the centre (maybe, or just a part) of a whole complex ecosystem; host, food source, symbiont, and rarely – a parasite. Nabokov's trees are the same – both in their relationships to other organisms in the described world, and as artistic units within a complex text and its extended aesthetic ecosystem. When we read about trees in Nabokov, we can't neglect either side of the question – that is, we must at least test to see what is going on at both the biological-ecological level, and eventually on the aesthetic-ecological one. The two spheres may meet in philosophy – metaphysics/ontology or epistemology, depending on the situation. For now, let's move into Shade and Kinbote's exploration of the ecological action surrounding the cedar waxwing.

"Knowledge-Amplified Love" 111

Bird, tree, berry. This is the combination we are given implicitly in the poem, lines 1 and 181, and explicitly in Kinbote's commentary. He sees junipers in those trees (he mentions them again, p. 290, commentary to lines 993–5, along with "laurel shrubs," just before Shade's death). At this point, we should return to the poem's one reference to cedars: "And suddenly a festive blaze was flung / Across five cedar trunks, snowpatches showed, / And a patrol car on our bumpy road / Came to a crunching stop. Retake, retake!" (lines 484–7, PF 50).[68] We are assuming Shade's poem to be literally autobiographical, and accurate as far as that goes in his world (aside from name changes to "protect the innocent"); that decision is somewhat arbitrary, and even conditional, but we should follow this choice to its logical conclusion and see what it gets us. This image in the poem describes the scene – introduced almost cruelly with the words "festive blaze" – just moments before the Shades will learn of their daughter's death. It is heavily freighted, and part of that freight is cedar trees, at the Shade driveway. Could these in fact be the very trees, called "junipers" twice, that Kinbote saw waxwings dining upon throughout his stay in New Wye? I believe that they are, and as such they provide a curious play on the "mistaken identity" motif – one, in fact, that includes an extra acrobatic twist.[69]

The first thing to mark is that Kinbote does not comment on the cedar trees named by Shade in his note to this part of the poem, creating an inverted lapsus: here, we have the "cedars," but lack the birds and the berries. It is midnight in late winter, after all, and birds would be out of place in the scene. However, the very next sentence – three lines of the poem – includes reference to "Exe," which Kinbote chooses to annotate thus: "Exe obviously stands for Exton, a factory town on the south shore of Omega Lake. It has a rather famous natural history museum with many showcases containing birds collected and mounted by Samuel Shade" (PF 218–19). This detail is intriguing, as the factory and the museum have no obvious relevance to the poem or the novel.[70] The pointed reminder of Shade's father and his scientific work on birds, in such close proximity to the unremarked cedars and their absent waxwings, begs for attention. Luckily, Kinbote's edition of Shade's poem has an index, and it will help us.

We have been delaying our visit to the index entry for "waxwings" until we had the right equipment, which now is in place (there is no entry, strangely enough, for "Shade, Samuel"). Kinbote offers: "*Waxwings, birds of the genus Bombycilla, 14, 131, 1000; Bombycilla shadei, 71;* interesting association belatedly realized" (PF 315). This little entry is just bursting with juniper-fruit flavour. First of all, once again, "waxwings" are here lacking any reference to their "Cedar" common name or that species' binomial, which, given the scientific pretentions of the note, presents a problem.

One wonders, too, why in his careful listing of text locations here, Kinbote leaves out line 181, the one that specifically refers to berry-pecking and, just afterwards, a cicada. The proudly and pedantically offered "*Bombycilla shadei*"

112   Nabokov's Secret Trees

only compounds the situation: if we go to line 71, we will not find this bird, though we learn there (next line, really) that Shade's parents were ornithologists, and that they died when he was an infant (PF 35). The commentary to this line helps, informing us that the poet's father was honoured or commemorated by another scientist who named this bird *for* him (we do not know anything about the bird itself, except that it is a fictitious species of waxwing, sibling of the cedar and Bohemian in the same genus).[71] The absence of *B. shadei* from these lines in "Pale Fire" is matched by the absence of any such bird from nature itself – at least, from nature in the world *outside* the novel, which makes it interesting that, let us say, Nabokov has taken the trouble to invent this bird for this role in his novel.[72] So what is going on here?

The "interesting association belatedly realized," of course, is that the waxwings (in the *Pale Fire* world) include a species newly discovered during or after the life of, and named for, Samuel Shade, the poet's father. The realization is "belated," because had Kinbote known and spoken about this as he wrote the commentary to lines 1, 131, 181, and 1,000, we would have been thinking about the connection, in the poet's mind, between waxwings and Shade's dead father, and between waxwings and scientific discovery (epistemology); and at line 181, we would also be thinking of waxwings (and departed scientists) along with cicadas (and departed Aunt Maud). This last step is something which, to his credit, Kinbote does encourage us to do in his note to lines 181–2, which he heads "waxwings ... cicadas" (PF 163, ellipsis in original), with comments pointing forward to more cicadas at lines 236–44, and the alleged present-absent waxwing at 1,000.[73] That is a lot of toggling between presence and absence, which seems a dominant feature of this "cedar waxwing" theme throughout the work. And even after this scientific *précis*, and the Museum of Natural History, we are still missing the common and scientific names for the cedar waxwing (*Bombycilla cedrorum*), the bird that fed regularly at the junipers-not-cedars of the Shade property.[74] Another clue appears in the way Kinbote discusses the taxonomic name, which "Professor Hurley" had mentioned in a "retrospective article" as "*Bombycilla Shadei*," to which Kinbote retorts, not yet knowing that this is a waxwing, "(this should be *shadei*, of course)," highlighting his greater awareness of taxonomic convention, but also extending the theme of "mistaken identity," if here only by means of a slight typographical change.[75] In a novel featuring "word golf," such changes cannot be ignored.[76]

There is, most likely, a special kind of coding taking place in relation to when, and how, scientific nomenclature is used in *Pale Fire*. At the very least, the invisible pressure here to fill in the gap with "*B. cedrorum*" and "cedar" seems overwhelming. Since that "cedar" takes us from birds back to trees, we are left, again, considering the place of this tree in the novel. Aside from the five fleeting and "festive" trees in the poem, the word "cedar" appears once more – in the all-important "Shakespeare Avenue," as described in the note to line 998, "*Some neighbor's gardener*" (PF 290–1). That entry includes a partial listing of the trees in the avenue (although Kinbote has earlier told us that he has with him, in his notebook/pocketbook, a transcript of all the inscriptions from that alley of trees (PF 154). Thirteen trees(!!) are listed, their Shakespearian homes tagged obliquely, among them exactly two with the genus named: "... a phoenix (now datepalm), a pine and a cedar (*Cedrus*), all insular; a Venetian sycamore tree (*Acer*)" (PF 291). Why are these two, and no others, listed with their genus? The reason, it turns out, is that these are two types of trees whose common names and their scientific names have a tendency to diverge. Thus the Venetian sycamore is an *Acer*, that is, a species of maple, and the cedar (from *The Tempest*) is, well, a cedar.[77] What this little scientific digression draws glancing attention to is the fact that the tree in North America known as eastern red cedar, one of the common food plants of cedar waxwings (and the plant for which they are presumably named), is not from the genus *Cedrus*. In fact, there are no native plants of that genus indigenous to North America: no true cedars at all. And so, it turns out, contrary to John Shade's knowledge of his own yard and common American nomenclature, the trees along his drive are not *Cedrus* anything, but rather a form of juniper, the eastern red cedar, *Juniperus virginiana*, a.k.a. pencil cedar (one of the species once commonly used to make pencils).[78]

We have here a tangle of scientific names, common names, and the real natural entities they denote. There also some instances of mistaken identity, if not outright disguise or imposture (remember that the waxwing genus sports a mask): the "cedar waxwing" is named for a cedar which is not a cedar, but in the poem, its name is hidden. Kinbote is correct: he sees the birds eating blue juniper berries (which, in turn, are actually not berries, but cones), and when he calls the trees junipers, scientifically speaking, he is not wrong, though in the local parlance he *is* wrong. In important ways, we can see how these problems of naming and identity relate to the most controversial and challenging theme in the novel, that of the inner creator's or creators' identity (or their layering), but by framing the matter through this scientific, naturalistic lens, one juxtaposes the difficulty of establishing precisely *what the narrative structure of the novel is* with the larger difficulty that *our epistemological life and task set for us at every phase of existence*. All this, from a darn cedar!

The multiple layers and systems of meaning in Nabokov's works always interweave in complex and various ways. The cedars/junipers, as we have seen (and as amply discussed by Boyd), blend into the metaphysical theme through the death of Shade's father, Shade's musings on death, and his daughter's death, news of which is brought to him by "festive lights on the cedars" (and these are also linked with the cicada case on the pine, adjacent to the report of Aunt Maud's death).[79] The junipers (cedars) reappear, along with laurels, moments before his own death.[80] Of course, what happens after death is one of those things we absolutely cannot know, and as such it is outside the scope of epistemology.

114   Nabokov's Secret Trees

Nevertheless, Shade's yearning to know about such things is *related* to our desire and effort to know more worldly, empirical things, and so it is no surprise that cedars, waxwings, berries, and junipers all fly together in a "false azure" that really is a mirrory glass wall, separating us in life from that unknown *potustoronnost'* (otherworld – or, extremely literally, "on-the-other-sideness").

A Tree Not Like the Others

Many other trees in *Pale Fire* are more blatantly metaphysical in their implications – the shagbark tree (hickory), the churchyard yew evoked by I.P.H. and "*L'if*, lifeless tree" (PF 52), the pine holding the empty cicada casing the day of Aunt Maud's death (PF 40–1), the "elf-haunted alderwood" (PF 239). For the moment, however, I want to draw attention to the epistemological overtones of one more of the most mysterious yet somehow unobtrusive trees in the novel: *Ginkgo biloba*, the ginkgo tree. This tree appears nowhere in the main poem, but Kinbote launches into a teasing discussion of ginkgos after Shade's use of the word "shagbark" at line 49: "A Hickory. Our poet shared with the English masters the noble knack of transplanting trees into verse with their sap and shade" (PF 93). By means of free association he then produces, from a letter sent to him by Queen Disa, John Shade's poem "The Sacred Tree," which turns out to be about the ginkgo:

> The ginkgo leaf, in golden hue, when shed,
> A muscat grape,
> Is an old-fashioned butterfly, ill-spread,
> In shape.[81]

Kinbote shifts abruptly from the short poem to a puzzling and mysterious series of statements: "When the new Episcopal church in New Wye (see note to line 549) was built, the bulldozers spared an arc of those sacred trees [ginkgos] planted by a landscaper of genius (Repburg) at the end of the so-called Shakespeare Avenue, on the campus" (PF 93). The free association that produces the poem, in the commentary, also exists inside the poem, and continues after it in the discussion. Thus we learn that a) Shade wrote a poem about ginkgos; b) there is an arc of ginkgos at the end of Shakespeare Avenue; 3) by the arc of ginkgos there is a church, whose construction "spared" the arc: the string of elements, from Shakespeare to bulldozers, is another palpable manfestation of one of Nabokov's favourite Gogolian quirks.[82] These statements are successively less pertinent to the poem "Pale Fire" (which is never a limiting consideration for Kinbote, but we may as well note it, as the step-by-step distancing is in fascinating evidence here). Kinbote then returns to the short lyric, offering interpretive tidbits: "I do not know if it is relevant or not but there is a cat-and-mouse game in the second line, and 'tree' in Zemblan is *grados*" (PF 93). "Cat-and-mouse game" refers to "muscat"; "grados" may foreshadow "Gradus" and death; but both comments seem quite distant from Shade's poem, though nominally (verbally, onomastically) rooted in it.[83] The ginkgo and this poem are revisited on page 257, in King Charles's letter to Disa, which he annotates awkwardly ("see, I mean the reader should see again") by sending the reader back to the original note and poem on page 93. The fascinating connections of this poem to Goethe's poem "Ginkgo biloba," discussed especially well by Gerard de Vries,[84] play vividly (once again) into the inner-author-identity question. But the fact that Goethe, another artist-scientist (perhaps the artist-scientist par excellence), had written a poem about the ginkgo immediately returns us to the sphere of the epistemological. In fact, the scene as described creates an economical conjunction of the major significances underlying the many trees in Nabokov's career: the metaphysical ("sacred tree," next to a church), the artistic (abutting Shakespeare Avenue, so placed by a "landscaper of genius"; the subject of poetry); and the scientific-epistemological, mainly brought forward by the riddle-like quality of Shade's poem, and the strangeness of the trees' placement at the end of Shakespeare Avenue. There is something to be enquired about, and learned: What are these trees doing here? How do they fit in with Shakespeare's trees?

The answer to this question turns out to relate to both knowledge (knowledge of the past, and knowledge of past knowledge) and art. The placement of an "arc" of ginkgos, and assigning this act to "a landscaper of genius," seems provocatively emphatic. A little bit of armchair research (equally easy for *Pale Fire*'s first readers with a home encyclopaedia) reveals that the ginkgo was not known in the West, or by Westerners generally, in Shakespeare's time. A ginkgo was first seen by someone from Europe around 1690–2, when Engelbert Kaempfer worked in Nagasaki, Japan, for the Dutch East India Company, visiting temples and travelling twice to Edo. By 1730, the tree was brought to Belgium and was soon found to be easy to reproduce and grow.[85] I suspect that the placement of these trees at the end of Shakespeare Avenue by Repburg (an allusion to English landscaper Humphrey Repton, 1752–1818)[86] represents *genius* precisely in the juxtaposition of all(?) the trees Shakespeare mentioned in his works with an arc of trees whose existence he could not have even imagined.[87] The fact that the ginkgo, though new to Western science in the late seventeenth century, is in fact a "living fossil" and of a much more archaic biology than all other modern deciduous trees, makes the juxtaposition all the more extraordinary.[88] Ginkgos represented both the future *and* the past at the same time, but not the present, from the standpoint of a time-traveller resting in Shakespeare's England.[89] Whether or not Kinbote thought this way about the ginkgos in New Wye, it seems likely that Nabokov did (seeing into the deep temporality of things was central to his scientific work as well as his experience of the world). Coming as

116 Nabokov's Secret Trees

they do at the end of Shakespeare Avenue, the trees relate to the artistic theme in yet another way – but I will leave that curious discovery for further discussion in the next chapter.

Shakespeare Avenue, capped by the arc of ginkgos, ties together themes of art, science, and epistemology more generally. As a catalogue of trees, the avenue serves as an embodiment (in the most literal sense) of knowledge about Shakespeare's trees. The trees' tags, with Latin binomials and poetic locations, deepen that commitment to study, knowledge, and systematization. And the ginkos fanning out at the alley's end display a more recent fruit of scientific exploration and the advance of knowledge, now in an anachronistic tree whose artistic life expands into works of Goethe, Shade, and Nabokov.

The ginkgo is one of several exotic tree and shrub species named as present in New Wye, and it is one of the favourite trees of Queen Disa (her other favourite is an austral exotic, the jacaranda). The tree has fascinated Westerners since they learned of its existence, and especially since its status as a "living fossil" was established.[90] It fits within *Pale Fire* along several thematic threads: its "exotic" (exilic, alien) status aligns with King Charles Xavier the Beloved's exiled state – and as a living fossil it is also an exile in time; its "bi-lobed" leaves, sung by Goethe, reflect the novel's play with multiple identity (seen also in the "mistaken identity" theme, above).[91] That Goethe connection, along with the John Shade poem "The Sacred Tree," places it in a tradition of literarily celebrated (and described) trees, to be treated more fully in the next chapter. Its strange biology taps into the epistemological concerns of any scientific endeavour and its inclusion in a landscaping project by "Repburg" carries it into yet another realm of artistic expression. Notably, this is the first work in which Nabokov mentions the ginkgo (it soon features again significantly in *Ada*, his next novel).

In *Pale Fire*, trees straddle the boundary between epistemology and metaphysics, something also embodied in Shakespeare Avenue's progression towards the "sacred trees" and the new Episcopal Church, and similarly in John Shade's jokes about "*L'if*, lifeless tree," the yew, as part of his quest for knowledge about the "hereafter" and his daughter's fate.[92] In *Ada*, the connection between trees and knowledge takes a different route, through the idea of *forbidden knowledge* and radiating from the arboreal heart of the Garden of Eden. We turn now to a discussion of how the trees in *Ada* develop and amplify this theme, intertwining with the novel's weightiest elements.

Ada, or the Arbor of Terra-ble Knowledge

Ada, or Ardor: A Family Chronicle is the fifth and final of Nabokov's novels to place a character's name at the heart of the title (although his unfinished novel "The Original of Laura" would have returned to this practice abstractly, if it kept the title when published). The multiple title raises the question: is this novel meant to be a portrait of an individual, a portrait of an *ardor*, a family chronicle, or all three? And since "ardor" refers essentially to "heat" and hence passion, we can wonder whether "love" is to be part of the story. Is the novel tempting us with knowledge (of Ada, of the family), with forbidden fruit (of ardour)? How does a novel that contains a "shattal apple" from "Eden National Park," which "really was the tree of knowledge," bring us to the boundary of epistemological concerns? At minimum, the very concept of knowledge itself must be a focus of parodic attention, and possibly even of philosophical reconsideration. And, indeed, the novel appears to toy with the possibilities of knowledge in the most difficult areas: the "texture of time," and the possibility of a remote reality, a world or "Terra" whose epistemological trace reaches the consciousness of only a few denizens of *Ada*'s world. Van is a psychiatrist and a philosopher, and he is a passionate brother (forbidden knowledge in that fact, too). But what if all of that is distraction? What if the novel is really about love and, to revisit Fyodor's terminology in *The Gift*, knowledge-amplified love? (Or, maybe, their exact inversion?)

The novel actually begins with a metaphorical Tree of Knowledge, though it holds spurious as well as forbidden knowledge: the family tree.

A text that (after its title) begins with a diagrammatic family tree (and then its textual reconstruction and elaboration, "leafing out") must have as one of its undercurrents an engagement with modes of epistemology. Of course, a "family tree" is yet another incarnation of "tree," this time completely figurative, like the phylogenetic tree mentioned in Nabokov's scientific papers. The most rudimentary scheme of what a family "is," a family tree lays out certain very simple facts that are completely available to knowledge. The only trouble is that even in such a simple case, the epistemological tree is prone to error, due to the vagaries of human deceit and mendacity. And so it is with the novel's introductory tree: it hides a mistake that is slowly (and rather opaquely) revealed in the course of the novel's early chapters, which produce a verbose and more accurate telling of the actual family relationships and their consequences. From that family tree, we eventually reach ... the shattal apple, the Tree of Knowledge where Van and Ada begin the process of knowing each other in the biblical sense.

The ginkgo leaf introduced on the novel's earliest pages helps situate the epistemological context, which at this late point in Nabokov's career appears to have become essentially playful. The leaf is introduced in Marina's "herbarium" (A 7), but is annotated with the information that it arrived in a copy of "The Truth about Terra" in 1869, the first reference to the two-planet structure of the novel's universe. Above, I argued that the ginkgo abutting Shakespeare Avenue in *Pale Fire* represents the past and the future simultaneously in that context; compare Nabokov's exposition of the Terra-Antiterra relationship: "a more complicated and even more preposterous discrepancy arose in regard to time ... because a gap of up to a hundred years one way or another existed between the two earths; a gap marked by a bizarre confusion of directional signs at the crossroads of passing time with not *all* the no-longers of one world corresponding to the not-yets of the other" (A 18). Although the ginkgo, clearly, is both a tree and a discovery of the past on Antiterra (as on Terra), it nevertheless already contains strong temporal energies, due both to the tree's very ancient genetics and its thematic connection to scenes far in the novel's future (Van's contemplation of suicide at Maidenhair station in 1888, and Lucette's suicide in 1901, her maiden's hair "tentaclinging" as she loses strength and life). That the leaf emerges from a book whose title begins with "The Truth" links it to the fairly hopeless epistemological quest by Antiterrans to know the facts about their sister world – a quest which, in the practice described in the novel, is much more closely related to parapsychology than to empirical science.[93]

As will be discussed at much greater length in chapter 6, entirely about *Ada*, the novel's very first tree, the figurative "family tree" that precedes the text, lays out one strategy for organizing knowledge, while also hinting at the taxonomic facets of knowledge that Ada herself, especially, pursues. The key element of this early device is the paulownia tree (revealed on p. 43); the way that this tree is hidden behind the family tree stands in both as a variant of the "find what the sailor has hidden" motif, and also as a precursor of the "wrong tree" motif, yet another instance, so frequently invoked by Nabokov, of human ignorance and obliviousness towards trees (among other things). Brian Boyd devotes much attention to this theme in his *AdaOnline*; aside from this paulownia and its much later (A 522) confusion with a mulberry, Boyd details the oak-elm confusion rehearsed several times in *Ada* along with its precursors in *The Real Life of Sebastian Knight* and the *Eugene Onegin* commentary.[94]

The playfulness I'm referring to in the novel's approach to epistemology – almost amounting to silliness – moves through the "wrong tree" motif into the iconic image for this theme, the "tree (or apple) of [terrible] knowledge" (A 16, 95). The shattal apple tree (where Van and Ada fall into near-intimacy) is, on the one hand, "really" the Tree of Knowledge, according to Ada, imported from "Eden National Park" in Iraq. However, it is the "wrong tree," too, because it is not an apple at all and, as the memoirists admit in their nineties, there was no National Park in Iraq, nor any apple trees, at that time: it appears that they make up these details in their old age, but immediately revise and retract them. The tree's fruits are "drupes," not apples (see the discussion in chapter 6), although this fact does not mean that the tree cannot be the same type as Adam and Eve's; Genesis does not name the tree's species, and apples are merely a modern convention introduced in pictorial representations during the Renaissance, followed by those of Milton. The scene's focus on the tree and its heritage looks to be a deliberate spoof of the way stories (especially stories about trees) make claims to present anything approaching knowledge. Just as the family tree at the opening presents false information, like the taxonomic trees Nabokov inherited when he started studying Polyommatus butterflies in the 1940s, the biblical Tree of Knowledge, parodied here, becomes entangled in a web of uncertainty, error, and ignorance.

This unknowable tree of knowledge illustrates a functional limit to the epistemological impulse. The explosion of trees in *Ada* expresses the problem from a different angle: with some sixty-four species of trees and shrubs, the novel embodies that same urge Nabokov experienced when he attempted to create guides to all the butterflies of Europe and North America. The ever-increasing tree counts in his works up to 1969 demonstrate how much this one corner of nature's storehouse meant to him, and how persistently he expanded his own knowledge of it.

In *Ada*, Van's last described epistemological adventure – his *The Texture of Time* – is punctuated near its end by a striking image of a Lombardy poplar that seems to become part of a painting. We turn now to a sustained look at the many, many trees in Nabokov's works that appear ekphrastically – framed within embedded artworks and related phenomena.

Chapter Five

Trees in the Frame: Art about Art about Trees

Up to this point, I have been discussing primarily trees that appear within the narratives as part of dominant Nabokovian themes (memory, consciousness, knowledge, love), occasionally also looking at trees that are mentioned through metaphors or analogies (such as hair colours, scents, taxonomy), or are mistakenly identified (and thus absent). Here and there, I have touched on trees that exist on a separate artistic plane *within* the works themselves – that is, as parts of embedded works of art (for example, the novel *Quercus* in *Invitation*), without discussing that status in detail. I want to focus now on trees presented this way as a separate category; they constitute a major element of Nabokov's artistic exploration of trees, and they force us to confront particularly interesting aspects of their signifying potential. Because trees, "in the wild" of the works' surface-level stories, do so much hidden work in weaving patterns that relate to individuality, artistry, and consciousness, trees within any sort of frame become a cryptic *mise en abyme*, a version of what Nabokov called a "picture in a picture: *The Artist's Studio* by Van Bock" (SO 73).

From the earliest days of Nabokov's adulthood, trees figured prominently in the blendings, interpenetrations, and grey zones between "art" and "reality" within his work. We have seen this already in the 1921 poem "The Quill," the wood-sprites themselves becoming agents delivering the fire of creativity to the poet.[1] So it is no surprise that trees figured within art or similar frames begin to take on a subtle and significant place in Nabokov's early novels; this role would only grow over time. We saw in *Speak, Memory* and its precursors that Nabokov, in early childhood, was aware of the trees in a painting over his bed, with a trail running into the portrayed forest, and that this painting tugged at his imagination (on which more in a moment). The first painting in his works that contains trees, as far as I can determine, appears in *Mary*: hanging in the room of Ganin's boarding-house neighbour Klara is a reproduction of Arnold Böcklin's then-famous painting *Isle of the Dead* (c. 1880, it was produced in several versions by him over a period of years), in which cypresses feature prominently on the rocky island that awaits Charon and his passenger, approaching in a small boat. *Despair*'s narrator observed that this painting was "found in every Berlin home."[2] Its trees, never mentioned explicitly, may not have been of specific interest or import to Nabokov – though he does mention "funereal cypresses" more than once in various contexts. *Mary* also includes a photograph of a subject that becomes a leitmotif in Nabokov's works; this photograph, showing "chocolate brown palms against a beige sky," hangs on a cruise company's wall. These framed pictures of palms, set in the context of the drudgery of ordinary life, appear as windows looking onto the cliché of bourgeois vacations.[3] *The Defense* has a similar photograph, and related motifs, and we will return to them below.

Thinking biographically about trees in Nabokov's life, we can remember first of all the avenue of oaklings ("framed" by a landscape artist) and the patterns of shadows they cast, accompanying the awakening of childhood consciousness. A later scene in *Speak, Memory*, as we saw in chapter 1, recounts the bath-and-bedtime routine of a slightly older Nabokov, and it is here, in the "My English Education" portion of his life, that he presents the image that became a key artistic motif in several works at various stages in his career. If it is true (as he describes) that the dream of entering a painting and its forest trail originated in his own bedroom and his bedtime ritual, that fact presents, chronologically, a second formative stage to the role of trees in Nabokov's creative biography. Their first marked presence, in the oak avenue at the awakening of consciousness, was literal, and Nabokov felt himself "plunged abruptly into a radiant and mobile medium that was none other than the pure element of time" (SM 21) – that radiance and mobility sliding metaphorically from the trees themselves into the conscious experience of temporality, in a shift that echoes Nabokov's later-in-life interest in Henri Bergson's concerns about the spatializing of time, and perhaps metamorphosing into *Pale Fire*'s "Shakespeare Avenue."[4] The watercolour above Nabokov's childhood bed, with its central and powerfully inviting forest, represented yet another metamorphosis: in that painting, not only are the trees transformed into an artistic image of trees, that is, *art*, but the painting also becomes a window opening onto a new dimension, a new mode of being, one that is guided by imagination and inspiration, rather than by practicality or utilitarian concerns.

Aquarelle: A Path in the Woods (*Glory* and Other Early Works)

In this way, we can see that there is a tentative, not specifically emphasized, background hum of trees vaguely connected to artistic representations in these earliest works. When we reach *Glory*, the device comes out into the open, and here we see the first demonstrative incarnation of the watercolour, later ascribed to Nabokov's childhood, now transported into the early life of Martin

122   Nabokov's Secret Trees

Edelweiss. The trees in the painting – unspecified types – are not the novel's first; linden shadows appear on the novel's first page, and we saw earlier that the village of Martin's mother, Olkhovo, derives from Russian for "alder," suggesting already an arboreal origin of a different sort.[5] The painting itself is immediately echoed by a secondary reflection of the exact same scene, but now mediated through language:

> On the bright wall above the narrow crib ... hung a watercolor depicting a dense forest with a winding path disappearing into its depths. Now in one of the English books that his mother used to read to him (how slowly and mysteriously she would pronounce the words and how wide she would open her eyes when she reached the end of a page, covering it with her small, lightly freckled hand as she asked, "And what do you think happened next?") there was a story about just such a picture with a path in the woods, right above the bed of a little boy, who, one fine night, just as he was, nightshirt and all, went from his bed into the picture, onto the path that disappeared into the woods. (Gl 5)

The multiple layering and inter-reflection of representation here is striking, and it may be the first instance of such an elaborate structural metaphor (certainly the first based on trees) in Nabokov's works. To schematize, we have a painted representation of trees and path, and a boy (Martin) who imagines climbing into the picture's world;[6] this scene is duplicated within the book read by Martin's mother, with a description (now framed within a book) of a similar painting of trees, which is magically entered by a boy in the story.[7] A story about imagination and art bumps up against a child's own imaginary experience with an "actual" artwork. Martin's anxiety over his mother's possible discovery of the coincidence demonstrates his vague awareness that an important boundary is at hand, even if it is not quite the one he thinks it to be.[8] We know that somehow, *this* forest path in *this* artistic incarnation, above his bed, is beckoning to Martin, and finds a particular resonance in his spirit. The careful expression of that resonance becomes the unfolding of the novel.

All at once *Glory* gives us both painted trees and verbally described trees (trees as part of a written story, though even within that inner text they are also framed – in a painting – and then they are imaginary, or simply magical, as the boy in the story crosses into the painting). The notion of imagination-tugging distances, scenery, and especially paths in the woods remains central to *Glory*; it brings Martin to his final journey and the novel to its close, even though by that point in the work we are no longer reading about *represented* trees and trails (we, too, have entered the painting).[9] Such deliberate, and deliberately layered, enframing of trees creates also a layered simulacrum of some of the experiences that Nabokov is probing in his art more generally, and which he seems to associate especially with his personal connection to trees. Regarded this way, it becomes apparent that it is the early, painted forest trail that leads Martin out of his world – that tugs him off the well-worn path of utility and onto another path with a mysterious, never-to-be-known destination. This mysteriousness is something that trees (as metaphorical images) provide better than almost anything, and is also something that sits right at the core of Nabokov's artistic (even philosophical) outlook. Maybe it is the primordial mystery beyond the deepest layers of mind (as later echoed in the analogy between a tree's branches and a "giant's nervous system" in *The Gift*, or descried in Nabokov's infant son's iris, "which seemed still to retain the shadows it had absorbed of ancient, fabulous forests" [SM 297]) – or maybe something else, but whatever it is, we can be confident that the novel does not exclusively, unequivocally imply that Martin perishes at the hands of Bolsheviks when he enters the woods. Too many of Nabokov's other works share the same structure, with the same part-ominous, part-mysteriously-liberating implications. As often as not, these structures are developed from a dominant tree motif – with *Invitation* and "The Ballad of Longwood Glen" offering archetypal examples. Martin's name, which includes "art" – mARTin – in this very Anglocentric novel appears deliberate, and anticipates the thematically related character from "Longwood Glen," Art Longwood. For now, staying within the rubric of artistically represented or enframed trees, *Glory* marks the beginning of a more deliberately structured design in which the inner, creatively portrayed trees serve as special markers of life's depths and secretly permeable boundaries.

The Bedroom Painting in Some "Real" (Fictional) Lives

I want to digress for a moment to show how this painted path in the forest hovers in the background of nearly all similar paths in Nabokov's works. As it turns out, this painting's first embodiment in Nabokov's works is not as a painting at all, but rather as a real forest with a path. That initial instance occurs in *King, Queen, Knave*, a path through a beechwood that Dreyer traverses as Franz and Marthe row to meet him with the intent of drowning him on the return trip home (recall that Nabokov's *Speak, Memory* version of his forest-trail painting renders it a beechwood).[10] As Dreyer proceeds through the wood, he appears to be affected by something magical in the space, and he even dreams about it (and the dream itself might be considered an unusual sort of frame, too):

> When he went to bed that night he could not go to sleep – an unusual occurrence ... Wooing sleep, he lay with closed eyes and saw the circular moat they had been digging to make their beach booth stand more cozily; ... If instead of following the concave brink of the bay one takes a concentric path slightly inland as I am doing now, Rockpoint is reachable, I think, in twenty minutes or less ... I traverse a hamlet and continue through a beech grove for a couple of kilometers. How quiet, how

124   Nabokov's Secret Trees

> soft ... He stopped to rest on a bed in the grove but then gave a start and again saw
> the vertical line of burning pain. (KQK 235–6, second ellipsis in original)

This semi-dream, as he tries to sleep through the pain of his severely sunburned back, represents his mental practice run through the beech grove as part of a planned race against the others in their rowboat. Finally, the real event takes place, and "Quickening his step almost to a trot, he entered the beechwood" (KQK 241). Once they are in the boat together for the return journey, during which Marthe and Franz plan to toss him out (he can't swim), he waxes poetic about his walk: "Ah, children, it was glorious in the woods ... The beeches, the gloom, the bindweed. Keep in rhythm!" (KQK 245). However, he initially resisted the boat journey homeward: "Oh, I'll return the same way. It's wonderful in the woods. I made friends with a squirrel" (KQK 244). But Marthe convinces him that the boat ride home was part of the bet; during the trip, just before he would have been ejected, Dreyer by chance announces the huge business deal he will close the next day in Berlin, and this story saves his life. It seems, somehow, that his magical trip through the wood has armed him with this phrase that saves him from death: "Tomorrow, I'm making a hundred thousand at one stroke" (KQK 247).

The fact that it is a beechwood, and that Nabokov at various times associated such beechwoods with magic and with the mysteries of art, connotes that the grove Dreyer passes through either confers or simply emblematizes some special quality that enables him,[11] as if by accident, to escape the murderous plot.[12] The special energy surrounding this scene is heightened by changes Nabokov made in the translation, as well. Before the beginning of the race, Nabokov has inserted his own anagram: Dreyer is reading through the hotel's guest list, and Marthe, eager for the kill, says, "Let's go." Dreyer keeps reading the list: "'Blavdak Vinomori,' read Dreyer triumphantly" (KQK 239). The name remains a running joke for the next page ("Franz ... with sunglasses over his usual spectacles and his bright red robe ... looked like Blavdak Vinomori should look. 'Don't get drowned, Blavdak,' said Dreyer and began his second roll" (KQK 240). Another authorial cameo is added when Dreyer tries to beg off the boat trip back to the hotel. He suggests that he will walk back through the trees, adding, "We'll meet at the Siren Café" (KQK 244). "Siren" (not in the original Russian) is a near mythological match for the Russian "sirin" (some consider the two words to be equivalent) – Nabokov's pen name in 1928, of course.[13] Nabokov's anagram cameos (like Vivian Darkbloom in *Lolita*) are renowned and invite various interpretations. In this case, the dual authorial signatures bookending the walk through the beechwood ("book" derives from the proto-Indo-European word for beech tree, which is "buk" in Russian) are usefully viewed as underscoring a kind of vague metaphysical instability that, as if through the magic of the trees, winds up protecting Dreyer from murder.

Now, because the forest path in *King, Queen, Knave* is not associated with childhood, it feels very distant from the early "forest path" theme in Nabokov's life, although its magical element (along with the beech trees) makes the connection inevitable. A new incarnation of the "forest trail" theme occurs already in the very next novel, *The Defense*, although here as well the painting itself is not specifically present. Still, "forest paths" become a key motif in Luzhin's life, forming the foundation of his return to the manor house in the novel's first chapter, which sets up his later, breakdown-impelled quest for the "wood," "trail," and "home" after the interrupted match with Turati in Berlin – right after the novel's midpoint, thus echoing the placement of the first half's forest path. Luzhin's relationship to paintings is curious, notable from the game he plays upon entering the manor's drawing room (through the window): he sees his grandfather's portrait, and shifts to an oblique viewing angle so that reflecting light causes the painted image to disappear, "a melancholy amusement he never omitted" (Def 23) upon entering that room (and the painting contains a wooden object – the violin). The primary trees mentioned at the resort where Luzhin meets his future wife are beeches, reminding us of the somewhat magical trees in *King, Queen, Knave*, and anticipating the later, autobiographical memory of beeches and their trail from *Speak, Memory*'s chapter 4.

In any event, there *is* something strange and almost magical about both of Luzhin's journeys on the forest paths: the first takes him past the wood mill, and ends (when he is finally discovered in the house) with his extraction by a bearded peasant reminiscent of Tolstoyan figures. The second pathway itself is doubled, existing in part as a real path in a Berlin parkland, and in part as Luzhin's childhood world more or less psychotically projected onto the scene around him, and leading to his full loss of consciousness lasting, it seems, for days. The idea of a quasi-magical transformation by means of this journey is deepened (and simultaneously undermined) during his awakening at the sanatorium. His "magical" journey through the trees appears to have brought him to a happier, safer place, but this appearance is deceptive and false, as we and Luzhin eventually learn. Luzhin's life is certainly a story of an existence torn between two planes of being: in his case, these are the plane of mundane reality and the plane of "chess forces," instead of the plane of art or pure imagination. Despite this knight's-move deployment, as it were, we can see how Nabokov continues to develop this forest path image: the artistic, painted path quietly and consistently hovers behind Luzhin's "real" world, a latent expression of the challenges surrounding consciousness in life and its many manifestations.

The sanatorium marks a change: all the trees presented from the hospitalization forward are somehow or other artificially, though not artistically, framed: there is the palm in the newlyweds' apartment, and palm trees in travel brochure photographs they peruse; there is a Christmas tree. None of the natural or even park-nurtured trees from the novel's earlier scenes reappear after

126   Nabokov's Secret Trees

Luzhin's release and "rescue" from his "chess ideas." Curiously, even the chess pieces he encounters cease to be made of wood: unlike the carved set from his father's study during the musician's phone call, the set he discovers accidentally in his jacket lining has celluloid pieces, anticipating and reverberating with the material of cinematic production to which Luzhin will be led next when Valentinov tracks him down.[14] Those photographed and potted palms appear to represent a degree of distancing, almost unreality, as if those trees are not, themselves, trees at all, but rather some kind of ossification into a cultural stereotype, or, worse, a cliché of an utterly emptied culture. Taken together, these images combine to form a sense in which Luzhin yearns for the world of the comforting forest trail and its trees, but somehow his life or the people in it keep drawing him away from that kinder, more magical world into which he, like Martin, tried to escape.

Quercus: Framing the Oak

Following a period of relative muting after *Glory*, the painted, drawn, or bound-and-printed subcategory of Nabokov's artistic fascination with trees reaches its next crescendo in *Invitation to a Beheading*, in the already familiar inner novel *Quercus* and its protagonist, a six-hundred-year-old oak tree.[15] Like those forming Martin's forest path over his bed, this tree exists only inside an artwork, not physically in the protagonist's own world. Like Martin's painted path, this tree clearly beckons outside the bounds of fiction that supposedly circumscribe it, creating a different set of metaphors, but with significant overlap between the two works as well. First of all, the oak of *Quercus* is not just the "hero" of its story, but is also its key structural device: the life of the tree becomes the life of the book (rather as the imaginary path in the woods "becomes" the real pathways that Martin and Darwin encounter at *Glory*'s end). In what could be seen as a time-bending allusion to Dziga Vertov's "Kino-eye" form (*Invitation*'s narrator imagines a photographer in the tree), the tree itself is the principle behind and the excuse for – and even the subjective source of – the narrative it also names. (Instead of a "Man with a Movie Camera," we have a "Tree with a Photographer.")[16] It is both matter and material, form and content, on metaphorical as well as literal levels (consider the material source of books' pages, also called "leaves" in Russian). This tree also breaks its frame, and Cincinnatus hears its leaves rustling overhead within his cell, and a large – albeit dummy – acorn falls from out of nowhere onto his bed. To the extent that Cincinnatus's execution is part performance, part burlesque reality, both the axe handle and the execution block (the latter explicitly made of oak) represent offshoots of the *Quercus* oak; when the whole world's stage set collapses at the last moment, other trees – the poplars we have seen earlier in the novel – are shown to be themselves artificial, part of a mock-up world, and they tumble with the rest of the scenery. The oakwood execution block, both a synecdoche of *Quercus* and an artefact in its own right, is itself Cincinnatus's portal – apparently not to death, but to "beings akin to him."

This *Quercus* text looks to be the first time that Nabokov has moved a tree into such a dominant position within any of his novels (although several early poems and his first story, "The Wood-Sprite," provide early models).[17] We should pay special attention to the fact that the oak is not just in a book, but in a library, and arrives together with other books; most readers seem to agree that the librarian is one of the characters in *Invitation* who appear to share some of Cincinnatus's "illicit" traits, if managing to hide them more effectively. The novelized tree may be understood as a smuggled-in token of nature, and art, and hence a sign of some kind of higher freedom, things that the fortress otherwise seeks to suppress or obliterate. Curiously, the inset novel's genre – a kind of documentary fiction popular among Soviet writers of the 1920s and 1930s – appears to encourage a negative interpretation of its role (frequently seen in the scholarship, in fact), but it may be that Nabokov wishes to set something primordial or mythical about the oak into tension with recent cultural appropriations of it.[18] It is as if, notwithstanding its presence within a flawed artwork in an even more deeply flawed political regime, somehow the tree ennobles the work and enables, or at least gestures towards, an escape from those flaws.

This is a particularly apt moment to jump ahead to the 1957 poem, "The Ballad of Longwood Glen," which Nabokov in fact composed and revised over a period of several years and considered his best English-language poem.[19] Although the poem's tree is not initially contained within an inner artwork or narrative, its function and plot significance overlaps in striking ways with what we find in both *Glory* and *Invitation*, and it requires some attention here. The poem has the feeling of a text-within-a-text, something that may be fostered by its metrical qualities as well as the distanced and satirical tone with which the lyric voice treats the material; the tree's more-than-natural qualities – it had been "passing by," and it "turned and stopped" – also add to this otherness. It is also true that by the poem's end, the oak has reached the status of artefact, if not art: "They varnished the stump, put up railings and signs. / Restrooms nestled in roses and vines." And, of course, the glen is renamed for the man who climbed a tree and disappeared into the ether. But what is most intriguing is the repetition of theme between these three works (and also, to an extent, *The Defense*): an impractical, dreamy protagonist follows a path with woody associations (literal or figurative) that leads him out of worldly existence.[20] The "Ballad" is possibly the last variation of this theme in Nabokov's work, and it is the most explicit: Art ("art") climbs a tree and magically shifts into a transcendent realm, where "delirious celestial crowds / Greeted the hero from earth in the snow of the clouds" (SP 151–2). This oak, unusual in many ways, serves as a direct and unambiguous link between "earth" and some superior world, with

128   Nabokov's Secret Trees

"art" as the connecting impulse. The felled tree, as varnished stump, is reduced to barely a trace of its former grandeur; the tendency of the world to reject and expel things that don't conform – "Art" – creates a pessimistic impression. What is left behind for the final lines is a space of artifice without art. Perhaps this was Nabokov's fear for the world in his darker moments; we can only guess. The poem may represent a deconstruction and final distillation of a concept that had driven the three earlier works.[21]

The Gift's Quiet Frames

In *Glory* and *Invitation to a Beheading*, the enframed trees play major and definite roles in the works' plots and structure. By contrast, *The Gift* has just one distinctive tree contained within an artwork, and its role seems minor, even fleeting. It also has several vague, non-specific, or doubly illusory artistically framed trees, if we take into account all references to trees in Fyodor's book "The Life of Chernyshevski," and consider it as an artwork rather than as a biography (as far as I know, the question of its aesthetic status in the novel's world has never been discussed – except as an "aesthetic exercise" or "exorcism"). Finally, as we shall see, it also includes a fascinating tree-related photograph near the novel's end.

Reflecting upon the one very clear and specific enframed tree in *The Gift*, we find something quite intriguing. This tree appears in a painting by Fyodor's fellow émigré, the artist Romanov, whom Fyodor dislikes, but who shares key traits with both Fyodor and Nabokov. This painting is "his best work to date" and "had already been extensively reproduced," with the title "Four Citizens Catching a Canary": "All four were in black, broad-shouldered, top-hatted (although for some reason one of them was barefoot), and placed in odd, exultant, and at the same time wary poses beneath the strikingly sunny foliage of a squarely trimmed linden tree in which hid the bird, perhaps the one that had escaped from my shoemaker's cage" (G 58–9). The tree in this painting offers several intriguing elements: it echoes the linden from *The Gift's* first pages; it is intentionally shaped into a topiary (thus, aesthetic) form – we might consider it a work of arboreal cubism; it is hiding something which the men are seeking. The painting containing the tree tempts the reader with still more teasing questions: Why is one "citizen" barefoot? What should we make of Fyodor's joke that perhaps the hiding canary is the same one that escaped from a previously mentioned empty cage at his shoemaker's shop (whose owner is named Kanarienvogel, or "Canary-bird")? Romanov probably frequented the same shoemaker, and produced this curious artwork from his impression in that shop; the shoeless man, perhaps, was in the middle of having his new shoes fitted when they all ran out to catch the bird. More important, though, is the way the painting continues the theme of creating a bridge between reality and artwork, as well as between narrative and painting: here, the bird that has gone missing from the store appears to have entered the painting (and its tree). This is a recapitulation, in the opposite direction, of the opening scene's shadowed linden branches on the moving van, which strove to break out into three dimensions, but failed at the last instant as the clouds again covered the sun; it also reprises, comically, Martin's fantasy of entering the forest in the painting over his bed, in *Glory*.[22]

The branch shadows on the van do not quite count as a framed or artistically transformed tree, though they seem as though they *ought* to be considered "framed trees." These shadows are immediately reframed into a mirror, where their possible artistic status comes into play, explicitly:

> As he crossed toward the pharmacy at the corner he involuntarily turned his head because of a burst of light that had ricocheted from his temple, and saw, with that quick smile with which we greet a rainbow or a rose, a blindingly white parallelogram of sky being unloaded from the van – a dresser with mirror across which, as across a cinema screen, passed a flawlessly clear reflection of boughs sliding and swaying not arboreally, but with a human vacillation, produced by the nature of those who were carrying this sky, these boughs, this gliding facade. (G 6)

They also offer a preview of a similar scene in *Pnin*, as we shall see below, and some important intermediate developments. But these shadowed and reflected branches are, in their swaying, pulsing illumination and tentative framing, tightly connected to the novel's early thematic exploration of artistic inspiration and creative seeing. We can think of those early, not-quite-stabilized or captured branches as an embryonic, inchoate stage of artistic consciousness and production.

Strikingly, and symmetrically, the final "framed tree" in the novel is also not quite a tree (it's just a shadow), and it is also connected to a linden: it occurs in the first of three photographs of Zina, which she pulls from her bag and shows to Fyodor:

> He took them from her cold fingers. Zina standing in the street before her office, with legs placed tightly together and the shadow of a lime trunk crossing the sidewalk, like a boom lowered in front of her; Zina sitting sideways on a windowsill with a crown of sunshine around her head; Zina at work, badly taken, dark-faced – but to compensate this, her regal typewriter enthroned in the foreground, with a gleam on its carriage lever. (G 361–2)

The allegorical nature of this triptych, once one looks for it, is both heavy-handed and a bit puzzling. As we learn about her in chapter 3, Zina emerges "out of the shadows," and so here too, in this case from behind the "boom" (or *shlag-baum*) of a linden trunk's shadow in the first photograph, her pressed-together

130   Nabokov's Secret Trees

legs almost comically chaste; the halo-like crown of sunshine around her head in the second; and her disappearance back into the darkness in the third, as the typewriter takes the leading (even tyrannical, "regal") role. Is the shadow darkening her in the final photo deliberately related to the linden's shadow in the first, and the ones on the van's side in chapter 1? Most likely it is: her role in the novel as a whole is shadowy, hard to discern (deliberately so), but hard to unsee once seen, too. Since the shadows of trees are among the places where Nabokov frequently encodes potent artistic fermentation, it makes perfect sense that the series of photos should hint at this connection.[23] Of course Zina, like Véra, is her future husband's typist (in addition to being his muse and animating force: the crown of sunlight itself connects her with the chief source of shadows).[24]

I want to touch again briefly on "Life of Chernyshevski," whose trees – strictly speaking, "framed" within this inner text – serve consistently to underscore the inner book's contention that the materialists were out of touch with "matter." As discussed in chapter 4, when trees' shadows appear in Fyodor's book, they merely glide across written (theoretical, presumably Marxist) text held in Chernyshevski's hands; when their reflections appear, it is part of a proof that "we see objects as they really exist" (G 243). Fyodor's book presents scarcely any actual, named trees – they amount to a birch, a rowan, and a larch, and these hundred pages constitute one of the most barren patches of Nabokov's writing. The few trees in the "Life" appear to be designed to emphasize their dominant absence from Chernyshevski's consciousness, and the absence of nature itself from the worldview represented by him and his followers.

A final, minor note on inset trees in *The Gift* returns us to the epigraph. The oak leading the epigraph, and thus the entire novel, marks a strange and special case. Although the epigraph is itself something of a framed, embedded work, this particular text – Smirnovski's *Grammar* – is not at all a work of art, and the "oak" it names is purely abstract, demonstrating and standing not so much for a tree as for the platonic idea of a tree. However, its place at the head of the six-equation syllogism demonstrating Russian-language "to be" elisions gives it an almost mysterious, elusive weightiness. There is nothing one can do with it, yet it cannot be ignored. The "green oak" in the first line of "Ruslan and Lyudmila" is a plausible and almost comical intertext; the possibility of a reference to Iulii Aikhenvald, also, cannot be excluded.[25]

The shadows of branches on the moving van reappear in various ways in many works; they transform also into reflections in this novel and elsewhere, and, as we have seen, they smuggle their way into enframed artworks as well. Late in *The Gift*, trees receive an inverted reflection in the Grunewald lake as Fyodor tilts his head back; in *The Real Life of Sebastian Knight*, the one portrait presented of Sebastian, painted by Roy Carswell, includes a "delicate trellis of twigs" in its corner – a minor, easily overlooked detail, but all the more important for that, within Nabokov's artistic practice. This is the portrait which, in its broader form, shows Sebastian's face reflected, "Narcissus-like," on a pond's surface, an apt image for the author of *The Doubtful Asphodel*: asphodels are sometimes confused with narcissi, even by Shakespeare.[26] The "delicate trellis of twigs" is in one corner – we do not know which; a "withered leaf has settled on the reflected brow," and aside from this, the portrait's background has a "mysterious blueness" (RLSK 119). The water spider, the leaf, and the twigs (clearly, twigs at the ends of a tree's branches, possibly reflected) create a natural setting for the writer's face. Taken in the context of other twigs in Nabokov's works, these appear to form a signature of the portrait's painter, and also a sign of Sebastian's own artistic gifts; the presence of the twigs reinforces the identity of each of them in the broader Nabokovian arboreal picture. As a refraction of Nabokov's own evolving self-conceptualization as an artist, the image is not surprising: just as Fyodor enmeshed the artistic beginnings of his story in *The Gift* with the workings of branches and twigs, their shadows and reflections, Nabokov made them crucial in the remembered birth of his consciousness and the onset of his poetic activity, just a decade or so later, in the related chapters of his memoir.

Framed Trees in *Pnin* and "The Vane Sisters"

Reflected and painted trees, as hinted already, receive another intriguing permutation in a key episode of *Pnin*, at the moment where Victor, the novel's young artist, is developing his skills with the help of "Lake," the art teacher at St. Bart's school. Lake, it appears, has convinced Victor that if Degas could immortalize a calèche, why could not Victor Wind do the same to a motor car?

> One way to do it might be by making the scenery penetrate the automobile. A polished black sedan was a good subject, especially if parked at the intersection of a tree-bordered street and one of those heavyish spring skies whose bloated grey clouds and amoeba-shaped blotches of blue seem more physical than the reticent elms and evasive pavement. Now break the body of the car into separate curves and panels; then put it together in terms of reflections. These will be different for each part: the top will display inverted trees with blurred branches growing like roots into a washily photographed sky, with a whalelike building swimming by – an architectural afterthought; one side of the hood will be coated with a band of rich celestial cobalt; a most delicate pattern of black twigs will be mirrored in the outside surface of the rear window; and a remarkable desert view, a distended horizon, with a remote house here and a lone tree there, will stretch along the bumper. (Pn 97)

Apparently this description presents a painting, or an idea of a painting (we can't tell whether it was in fact realized by Victor, and it doesn't really matter).

132 Nabokov's Secret Trees

As in the portrait of Sebastian, here we have a mix of tree and water motifs, the "mysterious blueness" now developed further into "rich celestial cobalt," and the "delicate trellis of twigs" in Sebastian's portrait corner, now a "delicate pattern of black twigs ... on the outside surface of the rear window." This fourth chapter of *Pnin* is devoted to showing the reader Victor's qualities, demonstrating both his intellectual-artistic gifts as well as his personal affinity for Pnin himself, to whom he has no blood relationship. The details of the painting concept cement Victor's place in the genealogy of serious, Nabokovesque artists, despite his youth (he is fourteen when we meet him).[27] Strange as it might seem, Victor is listening to a story about another painting, portraying another tree – this is now a triple framing – at the moment Pnin falls down the last few stairs of the Sheppard home where he lodges, interrupting the presentation. The crucial part of the scene begins with Bill Sheppard speaking:

> "Now that picture there," deaf Mr. Sheppard was saying, pointing with a didactic finger at a large muddy water colour on the wall, "represents the farm where my brother and I used to spend summers fifty years ago. It was painted by my mother's schoolmate, Grace Wells ... Well, that tree there, behind that barn – you can just make it out –"
>
> A terrible clatter and crash came from the stairs: Pnin, on his way down, had lost his footing.
>
> "In the spring of 1905," sad Mr. Sheppard, wagging his index at the picture, "under that cottonwood tree –"
>
> He noticed that his brother and Victor had hurried out of the room to the foot of the stairs. Poor Pnin had come down the last steps on his back.
>
> ...
>
> Pnin smiled and said: "It is like the splendid story of Tolstoy – you must read one day, Victor – about Ivan Ilyich Golovin who fell and got in consequence kidney of the cancer."
>
> ...
>
> The Sheppard brothers were both awake in their adjacent beds, on their Beautyrest mattresses; ... the elder lay thinking of silence, of a green damp churchyard, of an old farm, of a poplar that years ago lightning had struck, killing John Head, a dim, distant relation. (Pn 107–8, 110)

The painting shows a cottonwood (surely eastern), a type of poplar; we learn obliquely, a few pages later, that under this tree Bill Sheppard's distant relative John Head was killed, when it was struck by lightning. The moment, the painting, and the tree become all the more eerie and portentous when one realizes that the joke Pnin makes after his fall, about the protagonist of Tolstoy's "The Death of Ivan Ilyich," produces a hidden pun with the interrupted and unfinished story Bill Sheppard had been telling: "Ivan Golovin" translates almost perfectly to

"John Head" in English.[28] The uncanny connection between the painted tree, the deaths of the two John Heads, and Pnin's dangerous fall and hat tip to Tolstoy produces a knot of meaning and coincidence that none of the characters notice, and which, had Pnin in fact died in the novel as Nabokov claimed to intend when he began work on it, would have been a clear instance of foreshadowing, and a strange example of art predicting "life." Instead – in a different kind of foreshadowing – life here escapes from the fateful tentacles of art.[29]

Notice how this one chapter moves from an imaginary, perhaps hypothetical painting with trees to a completed painting of a fateful tree, whose description is truncated and then resumed outside the frame, as a dreamy memory. Both of these two paintings with trees represent boundary or transformative situations, and use trees as key parts of this representation. The painting assigned by Lake brings freshness to the artwork by letting the curves of the automobile generate the "strange-making" by means of their reflections of surrounding nature; this is the "mimetic and integrative process Lake called the necessary 'naturalization' of man-made things" (Pn 97), whereby nature and mechanical artefact are merged in the artistic consciousness and on the canvas. The Sheppard painting's cottonwood, on the other hand, concealing its tale of lightning strike and death, and the Ivan Golovin/John Head pun, represents the boundary of earthly life, and its precariousness.

A similar intonation appears in chapter 5, as Pnin unwillingly reflects on his now-dead former love, Mira Belochkin, as he sits among "The Pines," and remembers her "artistic snapshots," including one of "the shadows of birches on wet-sugar snow" (Pn 133). The fact that two pages later we learn that she died at Buchenwald (beech forest), perhaps (as Pnin or the narrator imagines) "burned alive … on a gasoline-soaked pile of beechwood" (Pn 133), may serve as a deliberate counterpoint to earlier, more positively inflected invocations of pathways through beech groves.[30]

Not too long before inventing Victor Wind, Nabokov had created another artist-character who enjoyed combining trees with automobiles. The narrator of "The Vane Sisters" speaks of Cynthia Vane's "artistic gift," which, he says, sets her apart from all her ancestry; his one example of her work has intriguing similarities to the one painting described in Victor Wind's creative biography in *Pnin*: "my favorite, *Seen Through a Windshield* – a windshield partly covered with rime, with a brilliant trickle (from an imaginary car roof) across its transparent part and, through it all, the sapphire flame of the sky and a green-and-white fir tree" (CS 624). Unlike the later painting (possibly) created by Victor, or the earlier one by Roy Carswell in *The Real Life of Sebastian Knight*, this

134   Nabokov's Secret Trees

painting has nothing to do with reflection. It does, however, combine a transparency, partly obscured by ice, and melting water, allowing a view of azure sky, snow, and fir. The dripping ice melt on the car links directly to the dripping icicles of the story's first paragraphs, later attributed to Cynthia's spectral influence; the fir might be seen to hold reference to immortality or rebirth, through its solstice and Christmas associations. As we saw in the introduction, the fir is also one of the trees named in "An Evening of Russian Poetry" as one of the speaker's favourites from his homeland (SP 136). The painting, described as if by chance, once again includes key elements that carry the weight of the story's various implications, with a tree as focal point. The snow-laden fir tree, seemingly a side note in the painting, also echoes Nabokov's very early sonnet discussed in chapter 1, "The cloudless heights and silence ... (1917), in which the speaker empathizes with a similarly snow-burdened tree. The fact that the artist included a tree, augmented by the narrator's reference to it as part of his favourite painting by Cynthia, connects the two with the world of trees that seems to unite all of Nabokov's sensitive characters.

Lolita: Ominous Trees

Lolita is a work whose ekphrastic trees are mostly enframed within textual works, rather than visual ones; after a brief look at the handful of visually framed trees, we will turn to focus on trees bounded within its embedded texts. Paintings of trees in *Lolita* are few in number, and less pronounced than the ones in *Pnin*, but they perform similar functions. In fact, there is only one complete painting, or perhaps a set of them: the murals at the Enchanted Hunters restaurant, which include "a medley of pallid animals, dryads, and trees" (L 121). When, immediately upon introducing their initial sex act, Humbert's faux "seduction" by Dolly and his debauchery and rape of her, he turns to misdirection, wishing, instead of describing the sex scene, to recreate the moment by means of his own revision of the hotel's mural: "Had I been a painter, had the management of The Enchanted Hunters lost its mind one summer day and commissioned me to redecorate their dining room with murals of my own making, this is what I might have thought up, let me list some fragments" (L 134). The images tend towards the gruesome and hint vividly at the brutality of the scene we are missing, but they also include the primary loss of innocence from the "davenport scene," which is now "poplars, apples, a suburban Sunday." That painting, of course, never came to be, and perhaps similarly unfulfilled was Jean Farlow's painting of Hourglass Lake which she was studying for when, through the trees, she spied Humbert and Charlotte swimming as he imagined drowning his wife. This projected painting, again, would have included trees, and might have shown the lake through the trees (we learn that they are pines at the chapter's beginning [L 82]).[31] In our image of Jean's hypothetical painting, it also includes the secret idea of Humbert drowning Charlotte. Although the painting is unfulfilled in the novel, it anticipates the Sheppard painting, thematically, from *Pnin*: a painting with trees and a secret (nearly) fatal story within. (Sheppard's painting, itself, invisibly concretizes the notion of "picnic, lightning.")

Lolita, taken as a whole, shifts into a mode which places more emphasis on trees contained within literary works. Part 2 opens with a reference to "Chateaubriandesque trees" (L 145), which, according to Alfred Appel, emerge from Humbert's reading of *Atala*.[32] Some of the most striking enframed trees in the novel occur in relation to a poem already discussed above, in another context, which the novel alludes to but does not quote, right near the novel's exact centre. We might say this tree is doubly enframed: it is in the poem "Trees," by Joyce Kilmer, which Humbert and Dolly encounter in "Poplar Cove, N.C.," which in "real" life (then and now) refers to the Joyce Kilmer Wilderness and Forest. Kilmer's poem ("I think that I shall never see / A poem as lovely as a tree") does not name a species of tree (he was born in New Jersey, and his family members insisted that he had no one tree or locale in mind);[33] the preserve in North Carolina, full of enormous tulip poplars (*Liriodendron tulipifera*, a.k.a. tulip trees, or yellow poplar), is named as a simple commemoration of Kilmer, the poet-soldier who died fighting in World War I. Humbert does not recite the poem – he could have counted on almost all Americans knowing most of it, or remembering their school-age experience of it – but, as discussed above (introduction and chapter 4), he does confess that he is "not a Kilmerite" (L 155). The passage is understated and obscure, but one of its key features, as I have argued, is that Humbert has utterly ignored the truly massive tulip trees in the vicinity of the plaque; these are some of the largest and tallest trees in the eastern United States (a fact well noted by the guidebooks of the day which Nabokov was using, even if he himself did not visit the spot).[34] Needless to say, Humbert has other things on his mind during this criss-crossing meander around the country, but the present-and-absent trees are placed here, in this central and double-framed spot, as an authorial reminder of the natural and artistic worlds outside of Humbert's solipsistic mind. We could propose various reasons for why Nabokov does not have Humbert present the poem (he presents other poems, after all). True, he is not a Kilmerite, but it is also likely that Nabokov wanted to hide between the lines such sentiments from the lyric as "Poems are made by fools like me, / but only God can make a tree." Without concerning ourselves with the metaphysical implications of the last line or Nabokov's unknowable thoughts on them, we can see the vast gap implied between the human creation of art and the essence of the natural world. As Nabokov wrote to his mother in 1925, artists are "translators of God's creation, his little plagiarists and imitators."[35] The sentiment is echoed in a minor key when he calls his translation of *Eugene Onegin* "dove droppings on [Pushkin's] monument" (PP 175).[36]

136   Nabokov's Secret Trees

Building on the site of Humbert's "fall" and the elaborate murals, Quilty's play "The Enchanted Hunters" takes place in a woodland setting, with the final kiss to be set at "the farm behind the Perilous Forest" (L 201) – a kiss which, in theory, would prove to the "poet" (the seventh hunter) that the nymph Diana was real, and not the poet's invention. In this theatrical frame, we find sylvan qualities dominating moments where boundaries of art and reality are being teased and probed most insistently. Quilty's play, it seems, makes a subtle argument against solipsism – but also creepily, tragically echoes and inverts the scene that had taken place in room 342. Later in the novel, after Dolly has escaped and Humbert has spent years seeking her and finally giving up, more vague trees occur within his brief poem, which also includes the hotel's name. The verses are created for Rita as they travel away from Briceland in early autumn of 1951 or 1952, where Humbert searched for a "portrait of the artist as a younger brute" in the local newspapers from his visit there with Dolly years before:

> The place was called *Enchanted Hunters*. Query:
> What Indian dyes, Diana, did thy dell
> endorse to make of Picture Lake a very
> blood bath of trees before the blue hotel? (L 263)[37]

This scene and snippet of verse come just two paragraphs before Humbert receives Dolly Schiller's letter from Coalmont, initiating the novel's dramatic final episodes, which include a blood bath for the author of the "Enchanted Hunters" play (about Diana in a dell: note the many coincidences). It is worth observing that here, additionally, the trees are both reflected in a lake and transposed by metaphor into blood, simultaneously compressing images of the past (recall the blood in Humbert's imaginary mural) and creating a hallucinatory glimpse of the imminent future. The subtle connection to Jean Farlow's unpainted lake image – a "picture" of "Hourglass Lake," set amid a pine forest (L 82), with nearly attempted murder – seems deliberate on Nabokov's part. These are all key moments in the novel's unfolding (the play, of course, brings Dolly and Quilty together, and helps her learn the skills she needs to deceive and escape from Humbert), and their close association with trees – even when non-specific ones – fits a pattern in many of Nabokov's works. Trees are the real backdrop, the enduring earthly witnesses to passing events and passing intentions. Taken as a set, these framed trees produce a sequence that conveys a quiet undertone to the violence at the core of the novel. The art of all three – Jean, Quilty, and Humbert – places trees within or just beside the crucial action. They may not do so with special intent, but for Nabokov the trees' presence is clearly essential and meaningful, as a nearly hidden marker and reminder of "something else" that the characters often do not see.

Trees and Meta-Trees: *Pale Fire*

If the few "framed" trees from works of the 1950s – in *Lolita*, *Pnin*, "The Vane Sisters," "The Poplar" – are encapsulated in a relatively clear way, those in *Pale Fire*, with its multiple frames, reframings, and frame-burstings, present a much more challenging situation. One faces, first of all, the question, Should all trees within the poem "Pale Fire" be treated as "enframed," since they are framed by the poem? While this approach seems justified, it may not be the most helpful; "Pale Fire" stands as something of a primary inner text, and although the novel is a "frame novel" in a modified sense, the narrative poem at its heart is – for the purpose of its trees – best viewed as a text existing alongside the commentary, foreword, and index. This approach is supported by the poem's predominantly realist mode. Viewed from this angle, the poem itself does not include any enframed trees, just several actual trees that are significant within the autobiographical story John Shade is crafting.[38] Kinbote's commentary, however, presents us with numerous artworks, real and imagined, that contain or depict trees; beyond that, it includes – nearly concludes in – a work that is made of living trees, and these also open onto yet another level.

The embedded (or reframed) artworks that include significant trees within the commentary are John Shade's short poems "The Sacred Tree" (ginkgo), "The Swing" (shagbark hickory implied), "Mountain View" (pines), and "The Nature of Electricity" ("tree so green").[39] Outside of Shade's works we find several more. By association of strong allusive pressure, Goethe's poem "Ginkgo biloba" is also implicated in "The Sacred Tree."[40] In part this connection is justified owing to the fact that another Goethe poem is openly referenced several times, its content woven into both the poem "Pale Fire" and Kinbote's narrative of King Charles's escape: "Erlkönig," featuring the king of an alderwood and of the elves, who steals the life (or soul) of a boy travelling in the woods with his father. Goethe's poem also mentions "old willows so grey," which the father suggests are the reality behind the terrified boy's image of the Erlking's daughters (willows, too, connect to death elsewhere in the novel, especially in Kinbote's discussion of the Institute of Preparation for the Hereafter, and in Shakespeare Avenue, discussed below).[41] The Shades' vigil for the doomed Hazel (implicitly in the poem, and by name in the commentary) also evokes Robert Frost's poem "Stopping by Woods on a Snowy Evening," which Kinbote calls "one of the greatest short poems in the English language" (PF 203).[42] In fact, nearly everything surrounding Hazel's death is underscored by secondary texts featuring prominent trees: the Shades, even as they wait for her (as described in the poem), watch a cosmetics commercial on television (also a frame), which plays on an image of Belinda sitting in a wood, from Pope's "The Rape of the Lock" (thus, a very diluted moment of framed trees); the scene also includes a concealed double reference to T.S. Eliot, mainly his *Four Quartets*.[43] In a way,

138 Nabokov's Secret Trees

Hazel's very name is a framed tree taken from literary history: "hazel shade" comes straight out of Walter Scott's *Lady of the Lake* – whose title, for at least two reasons, can be applied to Hazel herself.[44] Elsewhere in the novel, there is Aunt Maud's painting "Cypress and Bat."[45] During Kinbote's escape we learn of a painting that implies a tree metonymically: Eystein's painting depicting a halved walnut, concealing a secret compartment with real walnut shell fragments. Most emphatically framed of all are the trees of Shakespeare Avenue, capped with an arc of ginkgo trees by Repburg, a "landscaper of genius." This Shakespeare Avenue represents a special case: these trees are growing in life but are also drawn from works of art – they are like arboreal quotations; even in life, they are arranged in a framed-off fashion, forming the boundaries of the landscaped grassy avenue. The arc of ginkgos (Repburg's touch) adds to that avenue; we will revisit it at the end of this section.[46]

Some of these trees, especially the Shakespeare collection, are doubly – even trebly – framed. More subtly, perhaps, the same could be said of a book about trees that features in the Sherlock Holmes story alluded to by John Shade in the poem: although Kinbote doesn't figure it out, the story intended is "Adventure of the Empty House," in which a disguised Holmes makes a scene by demonstratively dropping several books, and among these the only one named is *The Origin of Tree Worship* – thus, a book about trees within another book, which is alluded to within the poem.[47]

The presence of noteworthy trees in so many embedded texts or hidden references helps to confirm their broad thematic (or perhaps more accurately: systemic) importance in *Pale Fire*; it is also clear enough on the novel's surface, and of course in the poem itself, which almost immediately introduces the shagbark and the "ghost of [Hazel's] swing" beneath it, in the shade of which "white butterflies turn lavender" (PF 34–5).[48] The shagbark leads – by means of quirky, Gogolian logic – to the ginkgo in the commentary, and the ginkgo connects directly to the Shakespearean trees (via another knight's move), because of the ginkgo arc's situation abutting (or crowning) the avenue: since Shakespeare's *Timon of Athens* is the source of the novel's title, this link is surely important. In a similarly braided structure, Pope's "The Rape of the Lock" intertwines with Frost's "Stopping by Woods on a Snowy Evening," with time "forking" and Hazel's Ophelia-like (but flowerless) death emerging in the poetic lines at the end of Canto Two. Perhaps most significantly, the shagbark also leads to Goethe, through the cryptic allusion offered by Shade's otherwise irrelevant poem on the ginkgo (PF 93), and Goethe's "Erlking" becomes an important motif both in Shade's "Pale Fire" in the lines surrounding Hazel's death, and during the king's escape over the Bera Range (PF 138), with another echo the commentary to line 894, a "quirk of alderwood ancestry" (PF 266). There is indeed an "eerie note" (PF 266) that somehow unifies these far-flung elements of the novel, but the spectre suggested by the "ghost of my little daughter's swing" under the shagbark may be only the most obvious and superficial of its overtones. Of all the tree-laden external sources implicated in these scenes, Goethe's seem the most insistent – and this pressure receives reinforcement from the repetitious "g" as the king approaches the mountain pass (with thrice-gnarled *Griff*, and his daughter Garh, named five times).[49] The "g" might also point to Gradus, or death (one step away from "grados," "tree" in Zemblan, as Kinbote has told us in his analysis of the ginkgo poem).[50] Omry Ronen has suggested that Nabokov's interest in a key facet of Goethe's thought increased in the latter part of his career, centred on the poem "Blessed Longing" and the phrase "stirb und werde" (die and become/transform), which includes praise of the yearning for death, embodied in the poem through the image of a moth self-immolating in a flame. If Ronen is right that Goethe came to hold this primary significance for Nabokov, as the singer of "blessed longing" for the afterlife, then his presence here (directly through his tree poems "Ginkgo biloba" and "Erlkönig/Alderking," and indirectly through the unmentioned "Blessed Longing") appears to offer one way to approach or understand Hazel's act after the failed blind date.[51] As noted previously, such an approach places Hazel more clearly among a string of "noble suicides" (Luzhin, *Martin, Krug, Aqua, Lucette, perhaps Kinbote himself, and, ambiguously, Hugh Person; the asterisk represents a case where death was not intended and may not have occurred). It also aligns her, by means of her tree-derived first name, with Art Long*wood* in "The Ballad of Longwood Glen," who ascends to the heavens by climbing an oak, disappearing from the world below.

There is still more to be said about the ginkgo's role in the novel's arboreal patterns. As already noted, we first meet the ginkgo within a frame – Shade's poem – which evokes another frame, Goethe's poem about the same tree. After that first introduction, our attention is drawn to the arc of "those sacred trees" planted and, later, spared by the church-builder's bulldozer at the end of Shakespeare Avenue. As part of a landscape design, the trees here are framed as well, and as a "crown" to the avenue of Shakespeare's trees, they represent a very special part of the landscape artist's creative work. Although these various trees appear in the text as if "by the way," an effort to explore how they fit together into a pattern will reap rewards.

Notice that the pattern is launched by the shagbark in Shade's poem, and this leads to Shade's "Sacred Tree" in the commentary. This, in turn, gestures tacitly to Goethe, openly to Shakespeare's trees (and the avenue collecting them), and also openly to the arc of ginkgos topping the avenue. Shade's ginkgo poem comes up again much later, in Kinbote's letter to Disa in the commentary to line 768 (PF 257), which reminds us that ginkgo is one of Disa's favourite trees – along with the jacaranda – and owing to her role as a spurned woman, which she shares with Hazel, this letter and its concluding reminder about the ginkgo, and its instruction to the reader ("see again – I mean the reader should see again – the note to line 49") draws great attention to this chance tree.[52] The

140 Nabokov's Secret Trees

attention is all the more intriguing, as no actual ginkgo plays a role in any of the strands of real or fantastical action in the novel. The invitation to loop back to line 49's commentary will, if followed, remind readers of the ginkgo arc, and Shade's poem, and Shakespeare – suggesting it is something we should bear in mind and not forget. Another teasing coincidence resides in the fact that Shade's poem on the ginkgo mentions a figurative butterfly ("is an old-fashioned butterfly, ill-spread, in shape"), whereas Goethe's poem "Blessed Striving" references a moth (drawn to the flame: fire).[53] In some elusive way, the ginkgo appears connected with Hazel. I propose that the solution to this riddle lies in a hidden metaphor built into the structure of the work, by Nabokov – not by Kinbote or Botkin. The arc of ginkgos we have been cautiously eyeing represents a puzzling extension of Shakespeare Avenue: not only are they not in Shakespeare's works, but the trees (as was discussed in chapter 4) were unknown to Shakespeare and other Europeans during the Elizabethan era. Since, as we know, Shakespeare represented for Nabokov a pinnacle of human genius, this crowning of all of *his* trees with something utterly beyond his ken, and his world's epistemological horizon, the ginkgos here represent unimagined hopes and possibilities. Just as Nabokov does, the Bard clearly strove to include much of nature in his works; yet discovery and knowledge, as Nabokov repeated on many occasions and in many ways, always have further to stretch. One might say that the ginkgos atop the avenue are one kind of manifest transfiguration of Shade's truism: "Life is a great surprise; I see no reason why death should not be an even greater one" (225).[54] The ginkgo species' historical and epistemological relationship to the avenue of trees embodies a "surprise" that came to Europe after Shakespeare's death. The arc of ginkgos brings about yet another unexpected transformation of the avenue, to which we will return – again! – shortly.

There is a circularity or recursiveness that Kinbote himself seems not to notice as he approaches the fatal, climactic moment in his commentary. Not only does he miss that his (African) gardener "trundling an empty barrow up the lane" in the poem's line 998–9 more than echoes Shade's *memento mori* (the clockwork toy) in the poem's line 143, which had been enthusiastically commented upon by Kinbote because he had seen the object and heard Shade tell its story;[55] he also does not notice that Shade's echo of this scene very late in his poem (drawn from the living gardener) may be deliberate – almost certainly *is* deliberate, as it fits the poem's architectonics so well. And, of course, Kinbote does not see the link between the gardener's role in the murder scene and any of these previous motifs: he is too busy praising the gardener, describing him sensually and biographically, and then, describing the murder scene itself, which he perceives as his own intended assassination.[56] The gardener refers to Gradus using some mysterious word – perhaps "death"; whatever the word, Kinbote calls it "strange" and "dark," and he superstitiously refrains from uttering or writing the word himself (or the gardener's name; contrast this to Griff and Garh, named three and five times respectively). Since in Kinbote's view the gardener has saved *his* life, it makes at least some sense that he is distracted, while describing the scene, from these key connections. He, instead, makes another connection, wanting badly to round out the poem's would-be final couplet and proper 1,000-line symmetry, by positing a missing repetition of line 1, which of course returns us to the cedar waxwing's shadow and death, offering a different layer of logic. In the midst of all this heightening action, as the suspense builds, Kinbote digresses to "enumerate ... a few kinds of those trees" in Shakespeare Avenue (PF 291).[57] These are the very trees that are tended by his barrow-trundling gardener, the living embodiment of Shade's memento mori.

"Shakespeare Alley," also "the most famous avenue in New Wye," in fact offers us a new cascade of tree framings, reframings, and frame bursts. Like Goethe's "Ginkgo biloba" and Shade's own "The Sacred Tree," or perhaps even more like his "The Swing" and "The Nature of Electricity," and, likewise, Frost's "Stopping by Woods on a Snowy Evening" and (in *Lolita*) Joyce Kilmer's "Trees," all of which are not cited in full, the Shakespeare plays referenced in the commentary to line 998 include various trees, but the works themselves, like the latter three poems, are barely excerpted. In a sense, the structure of representation is now reversed, because the trees have been, as it were, transplanted from the plays onto the avenue, and through the trees (and their accompanying plaques, one presumes) we learn which play, and which scene, is the source for each one in the avenue. Life (living trees), here, points to art (Shakespeare), but of course it is the art which inspired this particular planting of "life" at this location in New Wye, and the directionality of the art-life-art reference becomes deliberately confusing.

The centrifugal and centripetal forces both at play here can be seen in two further nuances of the situation: centrifugally, "Shakespeare Avenue" is itself a work of landscaping, design, perhaps art; centripetally, we see that among the thirteen examples mentioned, four are themselves already *framed trees* (or tree products) within Shakespeare's plays. The sycamore and one willow come from Desdemona's song in *Othello*;[58] the "mulberry, inviting to tarry,"[59] is from the embedded staging of the play "Pyramus and Thisbe" within *A Midsummer Night's Dream*; and the concluding cypress comes from a song sung by the Clown (Feste), on request, in *Twelfth Night*.[60] Most of the remaining nine are uttered rhetorically, not denotatively, in the plays (exceptions are the willow in *Hamlet* near which Ophelia drowns, and the enchanted linden trees that guard Prospero's prisoners in *The Tempest*).[61] But it also seems likely, and terribly like Nabokov, that this assemblage of Shakespearean tree allusions is trying to tell its own new story as well.

Shakespeare's works refer to fifty-nine kinds of tree all told, not counting uncertain diverse species of oak (genus *Quercus*) and the like. So New Wye's alley should have at least that number; more, if there were an (unlikely) attempt to identify precise species. However, Kinbote's "few examples" suggests that

142 Nabokov's Secret Trees

the avenue may contain one tree for every tree-naming line in Shakespeare's plays, since there are three non-specified oaks, and two willows, in his short list (making his list give in total only ten types of tree, out of the total). If that were the case, there would be a number much larger than sixty (pomegranate trees receive three mentions, plum trees seven in the Bard's plays, for example).[62] It is hard to imagine such an "alley" retaining anything like realistic proportions for an American college campus: even if the number is "only" one hundred eighty, could there really be an alley of ninety pairs double-file? This seems doubtful, but that's not really the point, since Kinbote has carefully chosen (or been prodded by ghosts to choose) his thirteen trees, and these and some of the rest may be part of his phantasms. The key question is: Why these thirteen, with their corresponding snippets of Shakespearean mummery? (In fact, it is eleven discrete passages of text, and ten tree types; "willow" from *Othello* produces the largest number of referents, as the word is repeated by both Desdemona and by Emilia, who reprises the song at the murder scene, before her own death; see note above). Remember, these trees are tended by Kinbote's gardener, living embodiment of the clockwork toy, that "memento mori" seen in Shade's basement – a Black gardener whom Kinbote would like to dress up "according to the old romanticist notion of a Moorish prince, had I been a northern king – or rather had I still been a king (exile becomes a bad habit)" (PF 292). Though Kinbote lists them off as if by chance and in a hurry, the trees seem to have something to say: they ask us to pause.

Let's take note of the precise location of these trees in the Shakespearean texts – locations that are marked clearly enough by Kinbote as far as the source texts are concerned, but might have required a little page flipping in the pre-internet era, or a trip to the library, to discern exactly which lines Kinbote found on the plaques.[63] The series begins with three oaks, and although these appear in seventeen of the plays, only *King Lear* and *The Tempest* are presented by Kinbote. In all three cases, the image is violent: Prospero has "given fire and rifted Jove's stout oak / With his own bolt" in calling up the tempest and other magical events;[64] he threatens Ariel that, "If thou more murmur'st, I will rend an oak / And peg thee in his knotty entrails till / Thou hast howl'd away twelve winters."[65] King Lear, raging against the storm on the heath, cries, "You sulphurous and thought-executing fires, / Vaunt-couriers to oak-cleaving thunderbolts, / Singe my white head!"[66] Here we have two figures – one creating violent weather, the other fighting against it; one an exiled duke and magician who imprisons a king (and threatens to entrap a sprite), the other a king going out of his mind, soon to lose his throne and his life. They encapsulate well the two urges Kinbote is experiencing throughout his time in the novel: on the one hand, to create a magnificent story about his kingdom and exile, but also his apparent madness and self-destructive urges. Immediately after these comes the linden (line/lime), a grove of which imprisons King Alonso and his followers under Prospero's magic.[67] This image is complicated, and multivalent from the point of view of *Pale Fire*, but I propose that the exiled magician, and the captured and bewitched king, offer a parallel for the strange relationship between Shade and his charmed and deranged neighbour-publisher-commentator.

Kinbote's list of trees returns from *Lear* to *The Tempest*, next referencing a moment where the bewitched Alonso, Antonio, and Gonzalo are tricked and teased by Ariel, who conjures magical creatures that deliver food, which disappears as the men approach it, causing them to exclaim that they would believe they are seeing a "phoenix' throne."[68] This "phoenix' throne" is a date palm (*Phoenix dactylifera*) and aside from the distinct motif of death (notably, in fire) and rebirth, the word "throne" describing the imaginary tree may draw Kinbote to it, along with the promise of immortality the bird carries.[69] Still in *The Tempest*, Kinbote's next two trees return to the same speech that produced the first tree he mentioned, Prospero's celebration of his awesome conjuring powers in act 5 scene 1, through which he "by the spurs pluck'd up / the pine and the cedar."[70] This cedar, significantly, is marked by Kinbote (presumably copied from its accompanying plaque) "*Cedrus*," one of only two trees in the list whose genus is given: this one will be the cedar of Lebanon, most likely.[71] The specificity is significant, because it is the moment that gives readers a clue that not all cedars are in the genus *Cedrus*, a matter of confused identity that recurs in many ways throughout *Pale Fire* and is of course central to Kinbote's own life. The very next tree, from the moment in *Othello* where Desdemona introduces her song, is the second one with the genus specified: "sycamore (*Acer*)" – the genus of maple trees. Both of these scholia are intriguing, because there are no non-*Cedrus* cedars, and no non-*Acer* sycamores in Shakespeare; thus Kinbote is apparently flaunting his knowledge of trees, and/or helping his American readers, who will be more familiar with trees of different genera having these names: the "cedars" in New Wye (again: eastern red cedar) are true junipers, *Juniperus virginiana*, and North American sycamores are in the genus *Platanus*, like European plane trees.[72] Kinbote apparently knows this distinction, though it is strange that after such a recent arrival in the United States he would be aware of these nuances – unless through detailed discussions with this gardener.[73] However that may be, Shakespeare's trees here echo Kinbote's struggles with his own identity and amplify that theme which has already been quietly woven into the text from the very beginning.[74] Desdemona's sycamore is the tree under which her mother's maid, Barbary, sang her death chant, about the willow – which Desdemona and *her* maid Emelia each also sing before they die. Kinbote, in his presentation, follows this willow immediately with the one from *Hamlet*, which oversaw Ophelia's drowning, as described by Queen Gertrude (presumed a suicide, but she was also mad at the time, in another parallel with Kinbote). Next, we see "a midsummer elm, its barky fingers enringed with ivy": this refers to the figurative words of the bewitched Titania, as she lies

144   Nabokov's Secret Trees

down and sleeps with Bottom, the two entwined like ivy. In classical mythology, the elm is the tree of dreams, having associations also with death and Hades; the transformed head of Bottom again foregrounds the theme of hidden (or mixed) identities.[75] The relationship between ivy and tree (tree of dreams and of Hades) resonates with the way Kinbote's commentary twines about Shade's poem, in what seems to aim – as he thinks – at a kind of benign parasitism.[76] *A Midsummer Night's Dream*, of course, is a comedy, and thus the shift within Kinbote's tree list to its "midsummer mulberry" is deceptive: the tree appears in the myth-within-a-play-within-a-play of "Pyramus and Thisbe," and is the site of bloody misunderstanding and two suicides, revisiting both the theme of embedded drama (Hazel's *Four Quartets* chat with her parents, her three nights at the barn, her role as "Mother Time"), and that of self-destruction, central to both Hazel's and Kinbote's story arcs – and perhaps a deliberate clue, on Nabokov's part, to Kinbote's final end. And just as *Midsummer* deceives with its comedy veneer, the next and final tree named by Kinbote, a cypress, does the same: *Twelfth Night*'s Clown, Feste, is asked to sing a song, and it becomes a song of death: he sings, "And in sad cypress let me be laid," the cypress here being either the wood of a coffin, or, possibly, a bed of twigs from the tree, which might have decorated a coffin's interior.[77] The word "clown" in Kinbote's reference is some-what diverting to anyone not commanding full memory of Shakespeare's play, but in ending his series of trees with an unambiguous reference to a funereal corpse, he matches the flow of his narrative perfectly, again, possibly foretell-ing Kinbote's end.[78] With the hidden stories behind the trees of the avenue, Nabokov has created a harmonic overtone to his novel's major themes.

As I mentioned above, Shakespeare Avenue is centrifugal in its identity as an artefact or artwork that faces outwards, towards an audience and towards future creative responses. The most important of these elements, within the novel, is the "spared" arc of ginkgos planted at one end of the avenue by the "landscaper of genius," Repburg. These ginkgos appear as a non sequitur or knight's move in the commentary to line 49 (PF 93), and until one is focus-ing on trees, one hardly pauses to wonder why the ginkgo arc is given such attention, and how this might be illustrative of Repburg's "genius" (and if it is not, why mention Repburg at all?). I propose that the trees in this location have a dual significance, separate from the interpretations suggested by Shade's, Frost's, and Goethe's poems. Crucial to note here is that the arc of trees is placed at the end of Shakespeare Avenue, and yet, as we saw, there are (and could be) no ginkgos mentioned in Shakespeare. So the ginkgo, it turns out, has nothing at all to do with Shakespeare, and in a way this is the point: it is a tree he could not have even imagined, something that did not even exist in his world and its plant lore. As I argued in the previous chapter, the ginkgo was, in Shakespeare's lifetime, both a tree of the past (the very deep past), and a tree of the future – something yet unknown, and hence unreal, to European science.

Trees in the Frame 145

Figure 5.1. Conceptualization of Shakespeare Avenue with ginkgo crown, showing the eleven tree types mentioned by Kinbote.

146 Nabokov's Secret Trees

This fascinating, dually anachronistic placement of ginkgos alongside Shakespeare's trees marks one side of the landscape design's genius. The other side is rather more hypothetical: we are told it is an arc of trees; if we imagine that the diameter of this arc is longer than the avenue is wide, we can envision a situation looking something like fig. 5.1, from a bird's-eye view (maybe a waxwing's): in other words, I suspect that Repburg saw the avenue as the trunk of a tree, and decided to craft a crown for that tree using an arc of ginkgos.[79] This is an act of genius (and a centrifugal one), because it continues the artistic flow outwards: Shakespeare's trees inspired the avenue; the avenue inspired Repburg, who expanded the collection with a bidirectional temporal vector, and the creation of a self-referential image (the group of trees constituting, en masse, the image of a tree – a bit like the tale that forms a mouse's tail in *Alice's Adventures in Wonderland* – which, of course, Nabokov had translated).[80] The pronounced (if defocalized) emphasis on the avenue so near the novel's end helps to solidify this connection; we can also see a parallel, even a fruition, here between Shade's poem "Electricity" (connecting explicitly to Shakespeare) and his "Sacred Tree" (connecting to Goethe – although apparently Shade wrote his ginkgo poem earlier than "Electricity": still, he had been hanging around that crowned avenue for decades, and the trees, too, have certainly inspired *him*: more centrifugality). Note also how Repburg's crown builds on the (apparently) pre-existing avenue, both adorning it and making something new, much as Kinbote's commentary does in relation to Shade's "Pale Fire."[81] Notice that the gardener comes, as it were, out of the works of Shakespeare – or out of the trees of Shakespeare, at the very least. Having emerged from Shakespeare Avenue, he merges with the clockwork toy, the memento mori, both in Shade's poem and in his life; meanwhile, he (allegedly) saves Kinbote's life. This return to Shakespeare Avenue in the penultimate note in the commentary is the first time the trees are related to specific texts; the passage brings Shakespeare's words, in the most literal sense, "to life" through his trees; it is the last entry before Shade's death, described in the commentary to "Line 1000," at the hand of Gradus (one word-golf step from *grados*, Zemblan for "tree"). The note is the last one based firmly on Shade's text, since the next line, *"Line 1000,"* does not exist in Shade's manuscript, but only in Kinbote's speculation. Whether that speculation is correct or not, the line he places here, the repetition of line 1 with its "shadow of the waxwing," recalls yet again the "cedar" waxwing, and the invisible, missing, misnamed tree from the poem's beginning. Remember, the cedar (genus *Cedrus*) is named in Shakespeare's work and the tree-alley, but the cedars on Dulwich Road and along the Shade driveway are really junipers (genus *Juniperus*), a.k.a. eastern red cedar.[82] Shakespeare, in any case, does not mention junipers or *Juniperus* species; according to Ellacombe, of cedar-type trees he dealt only in the otherwise famous *Cedrus*.[83] Curiously, Ellacombe reports that the laurel, also present as Shade approaches his death, is another tree name with a dual identity – Shakespeare and classical writers applied it to the bay tree, whereas plants more recently called "laurel" (in Europe, at least) are in a different genus or genera.[84]

At all events, we can see that Shakespeare Avenue in *Pale Fire* produces a condensation, a compressed network of border crossings between the worlds of real trees and represented ones, with these border crossings perhaps standing in for metaphysical transitions from life to death, or from "reality" to art, where "curiousity, tenderness, kindness, ecstasy [are] the norm" [L 315]).[85] The trees, as it were, tell their own story, one that is not less important than the surface-level narrative. In light of this fascinating structural centrality in *Pale Fire*, it is not terribly surprising to see the role of framed trees developed further in *Ada*. It had already played a significant role in *Conclusive Evidence* (1951), and expanded further in the revisions that produced *Speak, Memory* (1966). In *Ada*, we find a novel that begins (and in a way ends) with a figurative transformation of a framed tree – now, a metaphorical "family tree" presenting, and hiding, the key characters and relationships between them.

Ada's Framed Trees: A Brief Overview

The fact that Nabokov uses trees so deliberately yet so differently from work to work attests to their significance as a medium of his art. This is true on the level of embedded, framed trees just as much as on that of "real" ones within the characters' worlds.[86] *Ada*, we could argue, begins with three framed trees: the "family tree" before the title page; the twice-framed ginkgo leaf, moved from Aqua's book *The Truth about Terra* to Marina's herbarium; and the "'*mizernoe* and bizarre'" (inner quote from Aqua; "mizernoe" = miserable, pathetic) Christmas tree, also mentioned in the herbarium: this needleless larch, though only implied obliquely, is, like all Christmas trees, also framed within the setting of seasonal decorations, its base, and its own adornments. The next trees are vague "fruit trees," followed by an obscurely framed tree reference, describing the image on a pen: "it was an unknown product of Parmigianino's tender art. It showed a naked girl with a peach-like apple cupped in her half-raised hand sitting sideways on a convolvulus-garlanded support" (A 12). This peach-like apple in the girl's hand implies the fruit's source (the Tree of Knowledge), and also anticipates the "shattal apple" and the drupe-like reality of Eve's "apple," discussed later by Van and Ada, and even referenced by Demon as the "apple of terrible knowledge" (A 16). The early pages directly mention "the black foliage of a family tree" (A 9), and the Christmas larch will reappear via the index of its own stump just a few pages later (A 25). Even the first elm in the novel is framed within a story: "stop that record, or the guide will go on demonstrating ... a silly pillar commemorating, he said, the 'elmo' that broke into leaf when they carried stone-heavy-dead St. Zeus by it through the gradual, gradual shade" (A 23), making five framed trees before we reach, late in chapter 3, the first unmediated ones, a "piney wood" and

148   Nabokov's Secret Trees

"chaparral" (a scrub-oak desert-edge ecosystem), through which Aqua makes her way to her place of suicide (A 28).[87] Almost unnoticeably, Nabokov has made the first three chapters of his novel unfold like a mini-drama of enframed trees.

But let's take another look at that first, doubly framed one, the ginkgo leaf. We have already seen how important this tree was in *Pale Fire*, also multiply framed, and its status as the first species of tree actually named in *Ada*, moved from the pages of one book to the pages of another, must hold some significance. In the earlier novel, the ginkgo had a role that was primarily artistic – as the subject of a poem, as a hidden link to Goethe, and as a "crown" for Shakespeare Avenue in New Wye. Its placement within the leaves of "The Truth about Terra" brings to mind its Latin name (*biloba*, two-lobed, recalling *Ada*'s two-world structure), and, again, its significance for Goethe in his poem about the unusual shape: "Is it One living being / that divides itself within itself? / Is it two that have chosen each other / So as to be seen as One?"[88] Viewed through Goethe's lens of possible doubling, the leaf offers a potent, even poignant echo of the Terra/Antiterra theme in the novel (itself echoed in Aqua/Marina and of course Van/Ada's twin-like, Narcissus-like passion) – a conclusion encouraged by yet another symmetry, Van's book "Letters from Terra" (L.F.T.).[89] As we will discuss in the next chapter, the ginkgo plays other roles in the novel (specifically around the themes of suicide, perhaps also mental breakdown and despair), but this doubly framed and hidden Goethe allusion may be the closest to the heart of the tree's thematic import. Perhaps relatedly, Ada and Van "die into the book," and in this sense they become "one" with it and become two-in-one as well.

There are two categories of framed trees in *Ada*, and it is worth differentiating them here. The first, like those above, comprises actual framings that present a tree, or a part or product of one, within something like a painting, photograph, poem, or book. The second are a series of subtle allusions, by means of trees in this novel, to trees that appear in other works, though those passages of such works are not quoted or even directly mentioned during their oblique presence in *Ada*. In the first category are trees found in cited artworks within the novel, such as those mentioned above (the pen's painting about "Genesis" book 1, the larch, the elm, the family tree) and those found in quoted or referenced works by Andrew Marvell, Arthur Rimbaud, François-René de Chateaubriand (especially an embedded, fictitious poem, unique to Antiterra it seems), François Coppée, James Joyce, Konstantin Romanov, as well as imaginary works such as the poem by "Robert Brown," memorized by Lucette as the lovers practise their craft and examine albums (including the one with the ginkgo) in the attic (A 145–6, cf. 7–9); or in a vague reference to Chekhov's *Cherry Orchard* (A 115, 245), another work with trees sitting at its symbolic and emotional centre.[90] The second type can also be found in moments like the roundlets-of-light scene, which creates an "infusion de tilleul" (linden flower infusion, or tea) as earth is scooped out during the game, a clear if quiet reference to the linden flower tea in the renowned "madeleine" scene of Proust's novel (A 51); the willows which nearly everywhere evoke Ophelia's death (she is named elsewhere, but not near these willows: e.g., "neurotic willows" [217]); the Pushkin-tinged oak *"Quercus ruslan* Chat." discussed above in the introduction.[91] The "green oak" by the sea, for Pushkin, marks the beginning and source of verbal art, spoken and sung, as well as of magic.[92] The poem's introduction goes on to mention a wood-sprite (*leshii*), a water-sprite (*rusalka*), and asserts that "the wood and dale are filled with visions." Just as the cat on the oak's golden chain was the putative source of Pushkin's tale in "Ruslan," trees, especially openly and tacitly enframed ones, help generate and propel the story of *Ada*.

Notice how many of the key steps in Ada and Van's growing intimacy are accompanied by these framed trees. Their first outing includes the Proustian "infusion de tilleul" (among other trees), and a discussion of an "elmo" in Joyce's *Finnegans Wake*; their first intimate physical contact takes place in the shattal tree which was "really the Tree of Knowledge"; the "night of the burning barn" (their first full intimacy) is introduced by a quick reference to Chekhov's *The Cherry Orchard*; a great many of their summer trysts are overseen by (or, indeed, involve tying Lucette to) a willow, near a river, with its Ophelian implications; even the mulberry soap (discussed in greater depth in the next chapter) takes on this role when one recalls the "midsummer mulberry" from *Pale Fire* and its allusion to the suicides of Pyramus and Thisbe in *Midsummer Night's Dream*'s play-within-a-play. Van gives Lucette the fictitious poem by Robert Brown, including an enframed oak and dead lover, to occupy her during yet another adventure (the attic), which reappears yet again by inference in her last letter, sent shortly before *her* suicide.

Van and Ada have their own poetical oak tree refrain, centred on the Chateaubriand-Baudelaire hybrid piece;[93] they compete in the translation of Coppée's "October Morning" (A 127, 247), with oaks and maples, and use poems by Andrew Marvell ("The Garden," with laurel, oak, palm, lilac, apple)[94] and Arthur Rimbaud ("Mémoire," with willows and poplars) as the basis for their secret communicative code (A 161–2) during their separation between Ardis I (1884) and Ardis II (1888). In addition to that series, Lucette is "tied to the willow" not only literally by Ada, but also figuratively by her "green nightgown ... the nuance of willows" (A 64, etc.), so that the tragic scene in *Hamlet* becomes almost inseparable from her. That same absent yet vaguely Shakespearean mulberry (present and absent, again via "Rue Mûrier") reappears at the scene of Van and Ada's failed reunion in 1905 (A 522), and their successful one seventeen years later, after Andrey Vinelander's death (A 554) – a scene apparently watched over by Lucette from an otherworldly perch, as she worked to ensure that the thing would come off, despite difficulties. (One wonders if the poplar, which also appears with such insistence as the lovers reunite, tentatively at first, is also related to Rimbaud's "Mémoire").[95] Finally, Van buries his unsent letter to Ada (after Lucette's death) in a steel box under a cypress; for its funereal associations alone, this location is appropriate, but similarly it evokes Innokenty Annensky's book of poems, *The Cypress Chest*, referenced in *The Gift* in connection with the suicide of Yasha Chernyshevski, and possibly also in *Pale Fire* in connection with the cicada (it includes a poem called "The Steel Cicada"; the book itself is understood by some as an "apology of suicide" or at least an exploration thereof).[96]

A series of trees may be deliberate references to tree myths from classical antiquity: the oak and linden of Van and Ada's first afternoon, cypresses, and the poplars near the end may all be connected with Greek mythology and its retellings by Ovid and others: such references, if useful, belong decidedly to the second, oblique category.[97] However, while the story of all the framed trees in *Ada* could profitably be inserted here, it's just as well to leave some things to the reader's discovery. *Ada*, in fact, as the ultimate flowering of so many things that Nabokov worked to do with trees, deserves its own special treatment as a culmination of his arboreal art. And so we will return to it in the next chapter in a less narrowly focused, more synthesizing mode.

These acts of placing trees within framed spaces (especially artworks) create a network of secondary references to nature. In contrast to his anagrammatic or otherwise playful self-references in various works, in these ekphrastic moments Nabokov embeds artefacts that connect with the broader world – real, literary, and imaginary – through trees and their stories and shadows. Because it is clear that for Nabokov, trees usually represent, or simply are, the most essential and primordial pathway from the isolated self to the larger "all," their inclusion within framed works or images suggests that each of these insets serves as window, a "loophole for the spirit," offering an intimation of a world beyond the self: that "something else, something else, something else" that we cannot quite see or name, mentioned in Nabokov's poem "How I Love You" (SP 95–6).

Just as much as Nabokov made trees a crucial part of his artworks' "present," he also made trees vital to the works' connection with the literary heritage, the artistic "past," and also to an artistic "parallel universe" of imaginary works. It is striking to see, in these examples, how frequently Nabokov uses trees as the vehicle for connecting a current work with a classic precursor, or to underscore an urgent theme through its tree-chaperoned presence in an earlier masterwork. In this way, Nabokov asserts not only his own deep affinity for trees, but identifies their role as a common inspiration for much of the great art that preceded his. These many framings work to demonstrate how human artistry is built, imagined, and inspired from the glories of the natural world, especially its trees.

Chapter Six

Ada's Exuberant Trees

In this chapter, I will discuss *Ada* as the culmination of Nabokov's lifelong artistic engagement with the creative force he saw, and felt, embodied in trees. We have seen through the examples discussed in several chapters how Nabokov used trees as hidden or explicit analogies for creativity, memory, consciousness, epistemology, and metaphysics. *Ada* incorporates all of these themes in what amounts to an elaborate performance in which trees play a dominant, though characteristically understated, frequently ironized, role.

There are at least sixty-two species of trees in *Ada*, the most in any Nabokov work (it appears there was a deliberate crescendo starting with *Pnin*: see appendices for details). Nabokov was partly focused in this work on his young protagonists' heightened mental abilities, their extraordinary capacity for knowledge and, one might expect, understanding or wisdom, not to mention love. The failure of those qualities to coexist, or to blossom at the necessary time, and the failure of freakish intelligence to produce goodness or "knowledge-amplified love"[1] (and its equal potential to lead instead to narcissism, abuse, and destruction) are the central concerns of this novel. The journey from Adam and Eve's tree of blissful-yet-terrible knowledge to Ophelia's willow of despair, and the funereal cypress, is accelerated by Van's compositional shorthand in those early chapters of part 1.

Nabokov set up this novel with at least three underlying tree-related components standing as metaphorical frames for the narrative and its world. The first, at least in a reader's linear-chronological sense, is the family tree that opens the work, and which introduces the important, tree-like concept of family relationships that shapes so much of *Ada*. The second (again, in the linear text) is the oak, particularly in four of its guises: the "great oak," which

152 Nabokov's Secret Trees

is really an elm (evoking the "epistemology" theme); the oak paired with the linden in acrobatic mimicry; "baldy," the oak that supports Lucette's acrobatic swinging as she peeks at Van and Ada's lovemaking; and the tree identified as "*Quercus ruslan* Chat." (A 398), shown by means of a photograph in Kim Beauharnais's album of blackmail photographs. This late, rather oblique oak has a primary significance, because of its very clear and punning invocation of Pushkin's famous early poem "Ruslan and Lyudmila." The reference is significant not only because of the Pushkin lineage it brings, but also because that final abbreviated "Chat." refers (via a multilingual pun on French *chat,* "cat") to the cat reciting songs and tales while ensconced on an oak's *chain* (note also the "*grand chêne*" echo of "chain," another pun) in "Ruslan and Lyudmila"'s opening lines. These stories are the (imagined) original headwaters of Russian folklore – Pushkin mentions the wood-sprite, Baba Yaga, the rusalka, and Tsar Kaschei – and hence, the native source of all Russian literature. (The oak will be echoed, of course, in the Robert Brown poem memorized by Lucette, and recited shortly before her death, discussed below.) The last of the three central trees to appear is the apple, or "shattal apple," also called the "Tree of Knowledge."[2] This tree plays the key role in initiating Van and Ada's physical relationship, while also tying their story back to the creation myth of the Judaeo-Christian tradition: the *genesis* of knowledge of good and evil, and of stories, and of storytelling (emanating from the Holy Land and cradle of civilization in the Fertile Crescent).

These three trees anchor a sprawling network of trees and shrubs, by far the largest number in any of Nabokov's works, and more than the total number in all of Shakespeare.[3] The most significant of the secondary and tertiary layers of trees are the willow (with Shakespearean associations, as we saw in the previous chapter), the paulownia, and the ginkgo, with pines and cedars close behind. The remaining fifty-odd species play varying roles, some crucially thematic (such as the larch, mulberry, poplar, linden, and elm), some, perhaps, more straightforwardly atmospheric (birches).

The Family Tree

The family tree introduces the text before the embedded (secondary, "fictitious") title page, and soon after, it surreptitiously guides the action on the fourth page of the novel's main text, which presents two unnamed, naked children looking through books in an attic and discovering family-tree secrets in a jumble of romantic history. The purpose of these early pages is to reveal and conceal, simultaneously, the children's sexual relationship and their kinship. Their rummagings in the attic ultimately become explorations in and rewritings of the family tree. The first-time reader, however, is not really "in the know." Though the scene is about a loss of innocence (a coming into knowledge, in this case, knowledge of their true sibling relations), the reader's innocence is quite intact, because the information is presented without revealing the most important components: that the children are lovers, and that the evidence they find proves that they are siblings. The jumble of tangled family-tree twigs makes it impossible for a first-time reader to discern the tree's real branchings, even in close proximity to the schematic family tree before page 1.

But the children in the attic – "in the tree" – know. Like their earlier (in time) and later (in the text) "fall" in the shattal apple, their discovery in the attic takes them across a boundary of knowledge, while the uninitiated reader has no way to know that this boundary is an important one. The digression about the progenitor of their line, Ivan Temnosiniy, compares that ancient and princely lineage to "summer sky through the black foliage of the family tree" (A 9), before trailing off into a sub-digression on Proust, a sub-sub-micro digression on prismatic colours, and falling apart completely in Ada's "late hand" critique of the "awkward" phrase "whose hue."[4] It could be argued that the chapter's development is, itself, organic and tree-like rather than linear and logical; the characters follow the logic of the ramifying twigs, and of their own associations. The commentary branches off as if at random, but certain causal connections remain, such that the narrative obeys a different logic from the one that usually guides a story.

Shattal Apple

If the family tree becomes the tree of knowledge of old family sins (and new siblings), the shattal apple takes on a much blunter role in the ancient tradition of the mythical tree, Tree of Knowledge, and (primarily) tree of carnality. This all-important tree blends notions of knowledge, physical intimacy, and self-pleasuring (a reflection of the siblings' manifest narcissism). Just as they figuratively climb the family tree in the attic, here Van and Ada (Ada leading the way) climb the "apple" ("not a true apple tree"; "it really is the Tree of Knowledge") and achieve a "foretaste of knowledge" (A 94–6, 101); some days later, on the Night of the Burning Barn, they consummate their "love" in the library – also a repository of knowledge – which is described soon after as a storehouse of reproductive instruction manuals and sexual lore, so that "a touch of parody gave its theme the comic relief of life" (A 137).

Mlle Larivière is connected to the shattal apple's first appearance in the text and implicated, more or less directly, in the erotic role it plays in Ada's, and consequently Van's, life: "the omission of panties was ignored by Ida Larivière ... who was not above making secret concessions to the heat of the dog-days herself; but in tender Ada's case the practice had deprecable effects. The child tried to assuage the rash in the soft arch, with all its accompaniment of

154   Nabokov's Secret Trees

sticky, itchy, not altogether unpleasurable sensations, by tightly straddling the cool limb of a shattal apple tree, much to Van's disgust as we shall see more than once" (A 77–8). This narrating voice, of course, belongs to Van, but it is corrected as needed by Ada along the way, so we conclude that she assents to this description (elsewhere, occasionally, she protests). She will interrupt on different, scientific and historical, grounds shortly, when in chapter 15 Van describes the "fall" that placed them "lips to lips," as it were. Some of the key details of the scene include the fact that *drupes* fell from the tree as they shook its limbs (apples are not drupes, so this is the first hint that it is not an apple tree); Ada, then, again "straddle[s] her favorite limb"; Van comments (at some indeterminate future-retrospective point which Van-as-narrator blends into this scene) that he removed a silk larva thread from his lip, and criticized Ada's lack of underclothing; Ada identifies (back in the narrative present?) the "apple tree" as the "Tree of Knowledge," "imported last summer from Eden National Park"; Van notes that apple trees do not grow in Iraq, Ada replying – narrative present – "Right, but that's not a true apple tree," confirming the hint from the drupes, but then adds in the *narrating* or other much-delayed review of this information: "'Right and wrong,' commented Ada, again much later: 'We did discuss the matter ... besides, there was no National Park in Iraq eighty years ago" (settling this discussion, now, as about seventy-nine years post-events, or 1963, when Van is ninety-three and Ada ninety-one); "'True,' said Van, 'And no caterpillars bred on that tree in our orchard'" (A 95). This curious descent into technical discussion appears designed to deflate and distract attention away from the erotic content, but also to engage in playful equivocation about the multiple meanings (and degrees) of "knowledge."[5]

The tree and the story they generate from it is mythical in several ways: in its apple identity; in its Tree of Knowledge association, in its origin in Iraq; in its larval occupants, and even (less obviously) in its age: it is hard to imagine how a tree "imported last year" could now be large enough for two children to climb and allow them to see "through the foliage" the hoop being rolled between Lucette and the governess. The episode, as presented, asks readers to become sensitive to the fact that, while some similar event in the Ardis orchard did take place, exactly which tree it was has been thoroughly mythologized by Van and Ada (and it may well have been a mulberry, though mulberries are not drupes either, but this detail could likewise be misremembered by the pair). Ironically but instructively, the scene anchored by the "Tree of Knowledge" reveals more about what cannot be known, than about what *is* known. One thing seems sure: their innocence is lost, and they know it, because they have both rushed, "soon after the foretaste of knowledge," to describe the episode in compromising terms in their diaries (95–6) – though they do not yet each know that the *other* knows it.

Oaks (and a Linden)

It may be significant that when Van arrives at Ardis for the first time, his acquaintance with Ada is centred around two alleged oaks (and a linden) that feature in their initial stroll. The first "oak" in the novel is not an oak, but the "great oak" (A 50) a.k.a. the "*grand chêne* which is really an elm" (A 53–4), set by Mlle Larivière as a tour attraction on Van's first day at Ardis: the governess is "pathologically unobservant" (A 96), which affects her perception of trees. The slip will be echoed later, and seems to have little significance besides its place in the "wrong tree" sequence; it also extends the mostly hidden "inaccurate family tree" motif. Regardless, on that initial outing at Ardis, we do encounter the novel's first full-sized and named oak, partnering a linden in an acrobatic formation.

These trees begin a series that runs through much of the novel, on two tracks. Let us pause for a moment to review how Nabokov uses oaks, in particular, to create a line through this dimension of his story. Oaks exist both on the novel's reality (diegetic) plane, and in a significant group of artistically figured oaks. There is a small progression of real (physically present) oaks:

- chaparral (scrub oak, unnamed, where Aqua dies) (28)[6]
- the old acrobat-oak catching the linden-lady (51)
- "baldy," with Lucette swinging to peek at the lovers in action (212)
- oak-timbered hill, by the secret island for trysts (215)
- scrub oak (cf. chaparral) where Percy dies/is shot (319)
- *Quercus ruslan* Chat., from Ardis, in photo of 1888, viewed in 1892, in Kim Beauharnais's blackmail album (398); thus, it has dual status ["real" Ardis + "artistic," with a caveat]
- oak avenue, the drive into Villa Venus in England (472)

and a sequence of artistically or rhetorically figured oaks:

- the *grand chêne* from the fictitious poem hybridized from Chateaubriand's "Romance" and Baudelaire's "L'Invitation au Voyage" (repeatedly invoked, 127–428)
- from the Coppée poem ("Matin d'Octobre"): oak has copper leaf, maple has blood (127, 247)
- the "dead" oaks in the Robert Brown poem (fictitious) (146)
- *Q. ruslan* Chat. in photo (398) and in Pushkin (implied)
- scrub oak in Van's allegory about The Past in "The Texture of Time" (544)

With the partial exception of the "old acrobat," all of the physically present oaks have some proximity either to physical passion or to death. Even with the "old acrobat," the idea of death exists, because in Ada's imagination, he is

156   Nabokov's Secret Trees

catching his lover every time, although he *aches* – implying the risk that theoretically, if he did not catch her, she would fall – to her death? to a net? This oak is also spatially associated with Ada's game of "roundlets of live light" (A 51), but by implication those come from between the lady's, that is, the linden's, leaves, as they are scooped to produce an *infusion de tilleul*, or linden-flower tea, such as is found in the early scenes of Proust's masterpiece. More on these shortly.

Among the artistically framed oaks, the theme of memory dominates, though in the Coppée poem "Matin d'Octobre," the copper colour of the falling oak leaves appears as foreshadowing, perhaps creating a direct link between the tree and Lucette through the colour of her hair and her eventual plunge from the deck of the Tobakoff. The fictitious poem "Peter and Margaret" (by "Robert Brown") also emphasizes memory, and it is likewise placed so as to reverberate bidirectionally in time. Note, as well, that the oaks named in this invented poem are presented to the reader via a chronological displacement: rather than reporting simply and directly the text of the poem Lucette was given to memorize, Van mentions that she included it verbatim in her last letter, seventeen years later, and his "fatidic shiver" from that late date is proleptically inserted back into the early page mentioning the poem and the attic. However, very strangely, when (350 pages later) Lucette dies, this last letter is not mentioned at all, even though a whole series of letters sent among Van, Ada, their father, and Cordula de Prey are transcribed in full (including one retrieved, after twenty-seven years, from "a steel box buried under a cypress in the garden of Villa Armina" (A 500). Even a putative suicide note by Lucette, attempted on "the flyleaf of Herb's Journal," is mentioned here, though no words were written, and "she tore her blank life in two and disposed of the pieces in the W.C." (A 492).[7] The full scene of Lucette's last moments, which owes much to the scene of Anna Karenina's final thoughts in Tolstoy's novel, is elaborated (or confabulated) artistically by Van, who goes to some lengths to misdirect, at this point in the narrative, away from Lucette's actually written and final letter, whose quoted poem refers to oaks and a ghost. Chronologically in Van's life, this is the very latest oak (artistic or real) mentioned in the novel (though Van mentions scrub oaks figuratively, within an analogy in his *Texture of Time* [A 544]).[8] The letter's extreme displacement from the time when it actually occurred, completing the fatidic pattern, heightens through ellipsis the stress that thus falls upon it.

The fictitious poem by Robert Brown deserves another moment's attention, representing as it does the last words that Van "hears" from Lucette, in that he receives them after her death, and reports them in retrospection of that post-shock reading long *before* her death, in one of those typically Nabokovian moments of time-layering or time-tangling. The series of oaks in *Ada* intersects strongly with the theme of art, especially poetry, but coming in such a fatal position as well, we can't but associate the oak with Lucette's death. In fact, the deaths of Aqua near the chaparral and Percy near another sort of scrub oak deepen this link. This connection continues an association we have seen already in *Invitation to a Beheading* and "The Ballad of Longwood Glen," where it also intimates an otherworldly continuation – as it does here, by invoking the word "ghost" in the adjacent line. In all three works, the oak pulls together themes of art, death, and transcendence – over time, and over physical limits. The oak's role in Pushkin (both in *Ruslan* and in "The Poet," discussed in the introduction), appears to suggest that for Nabokov, the oak has an important figurative role in artistic inspiration and creation, seen as well in his "pen-holder of young oak."[9]

The Linden's Long (and Dappled) Shadow

Let us return briefly to the linden, the "lady" that accompanies the "old man" oak in imagined acrobatics during Van's first day at Ardis. This linden's leaves create the "roundlets of light" from which Ada invents one of her favourite games:

> The shadows of leaves on the sand were variously interrupted by roundlets of live light. The player chose his roundlet – the best, the brightest he could find – and firmly outlined it with the point of his stick; whereupon the yellow round light would appear to grow convex like the brimming surface of some golden dye. Then the player delicately scooped out the earth with his stick or fingers within the roundlet. The level of that gleaming *infusion de tilleul* would magically sink in its goblet of earth and finally dwindle to one precious drop. That player won who made the most goblets in, say, twenty minutes. (A 51–2)

A few things to observe about these shadows and roundlets: the game and its creativity recall Nabokov's own childhood adventures with "lobed sun flecks" (SM 21) under the avenue of oaklings, emblematic of his awakening self-consciousness as a small child. Here, too, the roundlets have special significance for Ada's mental life. Much later, she notices a parallel between her game (which Van scorns as a fourteen-year-old) and Van's *The Texture of Time* (written forty years later): Ada (in part 5) sees the "sun-and-shade games she used to play as a child in the secluded avenues of Ardis Park" as part of the source of "*Texture*" (A 579), feeling that she is "somehow responsible for the metamorphoses of the lovely larvae that had woven the silk of 'Veen's Time'" (that "responsible" possibly hinting through that silk at the mulberry silkmoth caterpillar, and the tree of suicides from *A Midsummer Night's Dream*) (A 579).[10] That game also had its temporal element, as when sometimes a "gentle breeze suddenly eclipsed her fleck" (A 51), so that the light and the shadows and the leaves and the breeze and the clouds and the stick and the scooping fingers all interacted in the increase and decrease of "points." The "*infusion de tilleul*" forces us to think of

158   Nabokov's Secret Trees

the linden, especially, and of Proust's "lost time"; and while we are thinking of literary genealogy, if a reader knows Nabokov well, one can hardly resist thinking of the lindens, so redolent of creativity in "Recruiting," "The Circle," *Glory, The Gift, Speak, Memory*, and many other works.[11] Curiously, this linden is the only real linden in the whole long novel; a lone, playfully literary one appears hundreds of pages later, in the fictitious "*Love under the Lindens* by one Eelmann" (A 403).[12] The disappearance of true lindens after Ardis the First, and their hidden reappearance as (in Ada's view) the sun fleck casting inspiration of *The Texture of Time* and the final reunion of the lovers, with Lucette's apparent blessing, produces a fascinating diminution of the physical presence, yet perhaps a compensatory expansion of the latent emotive and creative presence, of one of Nabokov's most cherished trees.

The Oak in a Bouquet of Allusive Trees: Lucette's Fate

As Boyd's *AdaOnline* shows, the oak tree is largely associated with the novel's "wrong tree" motif. Ada tells Van that "le grand *chêne*" [oak] is really an elm (53–4), and when Greg Erminin asks "I guess it's your father under that oak, isn't it?" she replies, "No, it's an elm" (92).[13] As Boyd notes in his comments to page 92 (lines 31–3), this oak/elm dichotomy was a favourite of Nabokov's, one he returned to more than once, as we have seen in *Real Life of Sebastian Knight* (37), in class lectures, and in his *Onegin* commentary (EO 3:9). While *The Real Life of Sebastian Knight* may be the earliest *playful* instance of misidentifying a tree as a sign of a fundamental failure to observe and know the world, the first rustlings of the motif occur in the Chernyshevski chapter of *The Gift*, where the materialists' blindness was defined precisely by their inability to name trees correctly. The motif appears earlier still, in Albinus of *Laughter in the Dark*, who, having gone blind, regrets that "if, for instance, he recalled a landscape in which he had once lived, he could not name a single plant except oaks and roses, nor a single bird save sparrows and crows, and even these were more akin to heraldry than to nature" (LD 257). Thus, on the one hand, oaks are in a way the entry point for seeing and knowing nature, in Nabokov's schematic of human consciousness. And yet, on the other, oaks are also deeply implicated in art (the novel's poetic and creative themes, particularly), but in key ways this mistaken *grand chêne*, leading back through the series of poetic texts, reconnects to Lucette's tragic final act. And although Ada and Van know their oaks and their elms and their willows, alders, and tulip trees, there are things that they do not know that will prove to be the most important of all.

In something of a sleight of hand, after Mlle Larivière has sent Ada off with Van, instructing her to take him to "the white lady in your favorite lane, and the mountain, and the great oak," the two of them really do arrive at an oak, but not the "great oak" (elm); as mentioned above, the oak's branches are in

Ada's Exuberant Trees   159

picturesque play with those of a neighbouring linden: "Overhead the arms of a linden stretched toward those of an oak, like a green-spangled beauty flying to meet her strong father hanging by his feet from the trapeze. Even then did we both understand that kind of heavenly stuff, even then" (A 51). This "Even then did we both understand" adds a note of Van's latter-day pride at their youthful sensitivity; both boy and girl intuitively saw the poetic, dramatic, and acrobatic shapes held in frozen pantomime by the trees. (Just a moment later, their sensibilities part, as Van responds coldly to Ada's favourite game, with the "roundlets of light" between the shadows of the trees' leaves.) Ada's vision of the two trees is a complete story: "The teil is the flying Italian lady, and the old oak aches, the old lover aches, but still catches her every time."[14] Three hundred and fifty pages later, Lucette (light) flies, no one catches her, but she leaves behind a poem mentioning dead oaks and a ghost. Van, as narrator, does not seem aware of this connection, as he is of so many others; Ada is in some ways the more perceptive of the two, the more advanced (all along, her artistic nature seems truer than Van's, even if she is no less capable of cruelty than he is).

Four years after the first summer, during Ardis the Second, we find a further iteration of the way the oak creates a key thread linking Van and Ada's narcissism with Lucette's tragic life and death: at one point, Ada and Van copulate in a "forbidden pavilion" beside "Baldy, the partly leafless but still healthy old oak," while Lucette, who at first was "gently" riding a swing hung from its branches, "increased her momentum so cannily" that finally she "swooped up and two green eyes leveled at the astounding tandem" (A 213). This scene eerily echoes the acrobatic image of oak and linden, with Lucette here playing the role of the lady-acrobat, held fast by the old oak. She certainly does not recognize that the tree is the same type as the one in the poem she had memorized. On the early occasion, the poem and its tree had kept her away while Van and Ada romped and explored in the attic; in this scene, "Baldy" is passively complicit, an innocent bystander as Lucette's innocence is further compromised. By tying together the scene of the acrobatic trees where Van and Ada first bond – one kind of "astounding tandem" – with this scene of their selfish carelessness, and weaving a braid together with Lucette's two episodes with the "Peter and Margaret" poem and her leap from the Tobakoff, the novel establishes both a subterranean marker of the lovers' culpability, and also (as Boyd has shown) a vivid indication of Lucette's continuing influence on the characters after her death.[15]

Whereas the shattal tree (with Mlle Larivière's help) throws Van and Ada together, it is the governess's sprained back that initiates a sequence of tree-related scenes auguring Lucette's loss of innocence, and even her death. Part I, chapter 23, describes the lovers' efforts to escape the prying eyes of Lucette, unleashed upon them by the bedridden governess. This series begins and ends with gruesome transformations of the tree motif. In the first, Lucette's doll mimics Ophelia's fate in a brook, causing Van to shed his pants "under a

160   Nabokov's Secret Trees

willow" to retrieve it, whereupon Ada becomes aroused and invents a dragon adventure requiring Lucette to be tied to the willow so that the siblings can escape "for a few precious minutes in the dark grove of conifers" (A 143). A brutal detail is added to the scene by the fact that Ada had "perforate[d] for [Lucette] in the slippery orange-red toy" a "little hole" that produced "a fascinating squirt of water"; the doll reappears in Van's memory (not hers) at the scene of her death (A 494) – almost as if Lucette has been transformed into this doll. On the following day, a tryst in the bathroom is accompanied by "mulberry" soap, which comes to represent Van's penis while also (like the willow) evoking Shakespeare and self-destruction (again, through *Pale Fire*'s "Midsummer Mulberry" and the suicides of Pyramus and Thisbe). Soon after (and just two pages later), we find the culminating scene involving the poem "Peter and Margaret" by the fictitious "Robert Brown," mentioned above. Brown was once seen by Van "up in the air on a cliff under a cypress, looking down on the foaming turquoise surf near Nice, an unforgettable sight for all concerned" (A 145). In her room, Lucette has an hour to memorize the "Peter and Margaret" poem, and during this hour, to recapitulate, we learn, if we piece together the clues, after enough readings, that Van and Ada head to the attic and make the "family tree" discoveries, in between sex acts, closing an anticipatory-retrospective doublet begun in the novel's first pages. But this scene reaches forward, as well, and ominously: it does so through the cypress under which Brown stands, a common marker of death (and under which Van will bury his unsent letter to Ada written after Lucette's suicide), and the "oaks" that "may be dead" in his poem.

The chapter closes with narrator-Van's remorseful, very post factum (when he is in his nineties) anticipatory recollection that seventeen years after the attic adventure, after Lucette's suicide which he does not reveal in this (early) narrative moment, he receives from her the note she composed "just in case" (in case Van did not show up on the Tobakoff, leading to her death), which includes the Robert Brown poem in full, written from memory, ending with the couplet, "Oats and oaks may be dead, / but *she* is by my side" (A 146). The poet's position "up in the air on a cliff under a cypress," "looking down on the foaming turquoise surf" are inverted seventeen years later when Van himself, in the Tobakoff search party, winds up overboard, "bobbing and bawling the drowned girl's name in the black, foam-veined, complicated waters" (A 495). The poem (Nabokov's fictitious creation) suggests a ghostly presence in a reminiscing world, in what turns out to be a microcosm of the novel's larger metaphysical structure.[16] (To repeat the obvious for anyone reading this chapter apart from the remainder of the book, I take these "ghosts" and "metaphysical structures" to be at least as likely metaphorical as indicatively supernatural.) The oak and the linden and the light and the flying lady and the willow and the cypress all wrap themselves around the story of Lucette.[17]

The Family Tree's Shadow and the Secret Paulownia

We can detect a steadily deepening complexity in Nabokov's development of the "tree" theme on all planes of his works' aesthetic being, from the literal (or representational) to the abstractly structural. The most elaborate realization of this tendency comes forth in *Ada,* beginning with the "Family Tree," as we have seen already in a few contexts. This tree resides unassumingly on the first pages of the novel's text – before the "Editor's note"; before a second full-title page(!); before a full page announcing "Part One." This "tree" almost slips past our attention on a first reading – it certainly does so *as a tree* – and it camouflages the existence of a secondary, inner and fictitious, title page. The tree itself is stranger than it looks, even before one begins to suspect its inaccuracies, its hidden and overt incestuous liaisons: titled simply "Family Tree," it is not given a primary family identity, such as the "Veen Family Tree" or the "Zemski Family Tree."[18] In light of the fact that the story's main characters are all Veens, it is surprising, retrospectively, that the tree is not Veen-centred, spreading upward perhaps through the Veen line to a Veen patriarch; instead, the two main branches (which are clandestinely merged in reality, at the third tier) lead back to Prince Vseslav Zemski, who at seventy-one married the "barely pubescent" fifteen-year-old Princess Sofia Temnosiniy. Thus, despite its casual appearance, it is by no means an ordinary family tree.

The hidden reason this tree leads back to Zemski (rather than, say, some patriarchal Veen) as the first progenitor is suggested in chapter 6, where we learn that this Zemski is Ada's "favorite" ancestor: "Of the many ancestors along the wall, she pointed out her favorite, old Prince Vseslav Zemski (1699–1797), friend of Linnaeus and author of *Flora Ladorica*, who was portrayed in rich oil holding his barely pubescent bride and her blond doll in his satin lap" (A 43). Zemski was a naturalist, a "friend" of the creator of modern taxonomic systematics – thus, of taxonomic trees. His daughter's marriage to someone named "Erasmus" brings to mind Erasmus Darwin, an important early thinker on evolution and, of course, grandfather of Charles Darwin. Author of several natural history texts (mostly in poetic form), Erasmus Darwin hinted at a theory of evolution in a commentary to his long poem "The Loves of the Plants," a title whose commonality with "Flora Ladorica" cannot be unseen once seen.[19] That his "Loves" was later re-released as half of *The Botanic Garden* makes it a clear precursor of *Ada*, if only by way of thematic echo.[20] Returning to Prince Zemski, presumably he is Ada's favourite ancestor because he, like her, was a naturalist. Through a tangle of obfuscatory language, we learn that he was obliquely connected to the scientific naming of the paulownia tree:

> On the first floor, a yellow drawing room hung with damask and furnished in what the French once called the Empire style opened into the garden and now, in the late afternoon, was invaded across the threshold by the large leaf shadows of a

162   Nabokov's Secret Trees

paulownia tree (named, by an indifferent linguist, explained Ada, after the patronymic, mistaken for a second name or surname of a harmless lady, Anna Pavlovna
Romanov, daughter of Pavel, nicknamed Paul-minus-Peter, why she did not know,
a cousin of the non-linguist's master, the botanical Zemski, I'm going to scream,
thought Van). (A 43)[21]

No wonder Van is going to scream, though our reasons may be different than
his: he is exasperated by the stream of trivial (to him) details; we readers, on the
other hand, are confused to stupefaction by blindingly opaque syntax, digressions, and connections. If we untangle the knot, we find a paragraph ostensibly
describing a room, but as often happens in Nabokov, the "by the way" paren-
thesis may hold crucial, or *the* crucial, information. In this case, the shadows
of the paulownia leaves take us on a tour through etymological error to Anna
Pavlovna Romanov (hence, most readers will immediately see, a member – on
"Terra," at least – of the Russian imperial Romanov family, and in fact Catherine the Great's granddaughter, sister of the czars Alexander I and Nicholas I),
who, in turn, is "cousin" of the "master" of the "non-linguist" who named the
tree (the paulownia). The "master" is the "botanical Zemski," that is, Prince
Vseslav from atop the family tree who, we now know, was the cousin of the
(Terran) Emperor's family. If the family tree had extended just one tier higher,
it would likely have shown this connection explicitly.[22] The imperial family tree
was especially messy and ambiguous at exactly this point in its "growth," during
Catherine's period of ambiguous extra- and post-marital romantic associations.
The probable implication is that Zemski is a cousin through the spouse of Peter
III or that of Paul I.[23]

And so, the paulownia tree (whose connection to "Peterless" Paul is likely
meant to signal extramarital conception) leads us back to the family tree,
which has become much more interesting if we have been paying attention.
Worth noting, too, is the fact that the leaves' shadows draw us (or Ada) into
the digression, and they help us to see a shadow behind the family tree. The
most penetrating and attentive first-time reader, and all returning readers, will
recognize also that the family tree itself is inaccurate, as Van and Ada are full
siblings, while Lucette is their half-sibling; Aqua had no living offspring. These
variations reinforce the notion that, after all, trees are complicated and even
deceptive things; there is no reason their analogues in the world of information
management should be any different.

Larch and Ginkgo: Minor Trees with Deep Roots

The "Family Tree" thus foreshadows, in the very circuitous way outlined above,
one of the "real" trees – the paulownia – around Ardis Manor, and that particular tree (with its characteristic heart-shaped leaves and their shadows)

reappears twice more in the course of the novel. The paulownia in the family tree is a hidden "tree within a tree," and the first two explicitly mentioned trees in the novel are likewise introduced obliquely, contained within, as it were, another work. The very first, in fact, has a history of double-enclosure. To review: in the novel's first chapter, yet-unnamed Van and Ada, "two naked children" (A 6), discover and examine Marina's herbarium album in the attic; the third and fourth entries in that album appear as follows:

> Golden [ginkgo] leaf: fallen out of a book "The Truth about Terra" which Aqua gave me before going back to her Home. 14.XII.69.
> Artificial edelweiss brought by my new nurse with a note from Aqua saying it came from a "*mizernoe* and bizarre" Christmas Tree at the Home. 25.XII.69. (A 7)

The ginkgo leaf is now in an album holding dried plants, but its previous home was another book, "The Truth about Terra." The artificial edelweiss and its Christmas tree appear arbitrary, until one connects them to Ada's revelation two pages later that the tree is a *larch* (a deciduous conifer, hence "bizarre" for a Christmas tree) and learns, two chapters later, that Aqua, six-months pregnant, miscarried after crashing (on skis) over the stump of a removed larch, probably the very same one. These events all feed into the confusion of the "Family Tree," leading as they do to newborn Van's role as a not-so-subtle replacement for the lost stillborn child. That Aqua (in her dreams) marks the stillbirth as an "X" in the bathtub, and the larch is a Christmas (or Xmas) tree, may hint at the illegitimate crossing of the familial lines as Van is passed secretly from Marina to Aqua (whose husbands are also cousins).[24] Meanwhile, we learn much later (as already discussed) that while Van and Ada are in that attic on that particular day, looking at those tree-traces in the herbarium, Lucette is downstairs in her bedroom memorizing the Robert Brown poem, chosen for her by Van, which mentions a wood, and an oak, and ghostly visitations. The poem is in an anthology whose "fly-leaf" drawings by Van echo Marina's herbarium doodles and contents: in both, an ink blot is evolved into a flower, and in Van's book we also find "a delicate leafless tree (as seen from a classroom window)" (A 8, 146). This image parallels both the ginkgo after shedding the found leaf, and the larch, which would have shed its needles by Christmas time. Since Christmas trees are always evergreens, usually fir or spruce, originally a symbol of *re*birth around the time of the winter solstice, the strange if accidental choice of the larch is all too ominous – especially as the stump is implicated in a stillbirth. Larches will witness other tragedies later in the novel.

The ginkgo leaf, too, coming from Aqua's book, is just the beginning of an extended and multi-faceted pattern, linking forward to the "Chinese tree" at Volosyanka/Maidenhair station, from whence Van leaves Ardis after his second summer there upon learning of Ada's infidelities, his head jumbled with

164   Nabokov's Secret Trees

thoughts of duelling, murder, and suicide all at once.[25] Van's echo, in that scene, of Ada's playful mutation of Lear's "never" into "n'est vert" ("is not green"), refers to the ginkgo (a.k.a. "maidenhair") leaf in autumn. The meanings of the ginkgo leaf here bifurcate, appropriately, as Van says "never shall I hear her 'botanical' voice fall at *biloba*" (bilobed; A 300); as "maidenhair," the leaf also reaches forward to Lucette's "tentaclinging" hair as she drowns, technically still a maiden, after leaping from the Tobakoff ocean liner (A 494). The repeated "never"/"n'est vert"/Lear theme also creates an ominous portent of the blinding of Kim Beauharnais, reinforced just a few pages later when Van replaces his walking stick: "the Ardis Hall sliver-knobbed one he had left behind in the Maidenhair station café. This was a rude, stout article with a convenient grip and an alpenstockish point capable of gouging out translucent bulging eyes" (A 305). As Brian Boyd notes, the blinding of Kim and the fatal effects of Van's and Ada's behaviours on Lucette are the cruellest and most tragic consequences of their solipsistic (selfish) approach to the world;[26] Nabokov gathers markers of all these themes together with the ginkgo tree at the Maidenhair station, at the novel's physical midpoint.[27] The ginkgo, therefore, is the novel's first named tree and also emphatically marks its exact midpoint; it occurs again at page 522 during the lovers' failed reunion, and is presumably present (with the paulownia-not-mulberry) but, curiously, not mentioned at the scene of the successful one seventeen years later.[28]

Fateful Trees and Their Present-Absent Reverberations

Sometimes it is helpful to pull together far-flung trees with thematic links, in order to see more clearly how Nabokov weaves them into a pattern. For example, a fairly understated pine-oak-larch-willow complex takes on special meaning once we draw the elements into a single field of view. Aqua's miscarriage is caused by skiing into the stump of a larch; she produces a "surprised little fetus, a fish of rubber" in her bath (A 26). Playing at a brook, Lucette's "fetus-sized rubber doll" escapes into the flowing current; Van sheds his pants "under a willow" to retrieve the doll; Ada is aroused and so ties Lucette to the willow, and lures Van off for hidden sex in a "clump of evergreens" (A 143); Lucette escapes from the willow, and observes the pair in action, watching "through the larches"; she then re-ties herself (loosely) to the willow, where Van and Ada find her when they are done (A 152). The proximity of willow and water clearly evoke Ophelia's death in *Hamlet*, and so becomes part of an ominous motif for Lucette, reinforced by the doll's vivid link to the fetus. Approaching her suicide, Aqua proceeds through a "little pinewood" to "a gulch in the chaparral," a scrub-oak landscape Nabokov most likely knew from Mayne Reid's *The Headless Horseman* and from butterfly hunting in Arizona.[29] It seems worth noting that in *The Texture of Time*, Van describes the "passage of time" as "arollas [a kind of pine] and larches silently tumbling away: the perpetual disaster of receding time" (A 544); this is the final mention of larches in the novel. But notice the proximity of pines and oaks and larches to Aqua's disasters (her miscarriage and her suicide), and their intimate role in Lucette's first acts of successful voyeurism.[30] In Van's treatise, we barely feel the reverberations of these events in their abstract, philosophical echo and his use of the word "disaster."

Several of the novel's key trees recombine in new riddles and puzzles in the scene depicting Van and Ada's brief (failed) reunion in 1905 in Mont Roux, which includes a walkway, reminiscent of *Pale Fire*'s Shakespeare Alley, with seven tree names in one brief stretch spanning just two sentences:

> A boxwood-lined path, presided over by a nostalgic-looking sempervirent sequoia (which American visitors mistook for a "Lebanese cedar" – if they remarked it at all) took them to the absurdly misnamed rue du Mûrier, where a princely paulownia ("mulberry tree!" snorted Ada), standing in state on its incongruous terrace above a public W.C., was shedding generously its heart-shaped dark green leaves, but retained enough foliage to cast arabesques of shadow onto the south side of its trunk. A ginkgo (of a much more luminous greenish gold than its neighbor, a dingily yellowing local birch) marked the corner of a cobbled lane leading down to the quay. (A 522)

This paragraph is distinctive for its concentration of trees, and for how those trees reach out to other parts of the novel.[31] Boxwood appears only in one other place: as Van falls asleep during an earlier reunion with Ada, the one in Manhattan that features the abortive three-way tangle with Lucette, his fading consciousness drifts past or through a dreamed boxwood maze, presumably at Ardis (A 416: this scene features the infamous "album" of erotic photos from Ardis the First, created by Kim Beauharnais and used for blackmail). The "sempervirent sequoia" is unique in the novel, as is the cedar of Lebanon – though that tree is hinted at through the "weeping" or "Sealyham cedar" under which Van sometimes sleeps (A 72), and where the three children, during Ardis the Second, have (at Ada's instigation it seems) a quasi-erotic threesome (A 204–5), which Van and Ada come to regret soon after, because it has only deepened Lucette's erotic fascination with Van (A 211). This significance is marked by "Ada's late note," which laments, "Torture, my poor love! Torture! Yes! But it's all sunk and dead" (A 204). Through that cedar and from its "weeping shadows" Van sees "the Lebanese blue of the sky between the fascicles of the foliage."[32] Of course, this Lebanese cedar does not really exist in the 1905 Mont Roux scene: it is another "wrong tree," conjured by the American tourists, which is surprising since sequoias are indigenous to (western) North America (on Terra, at least), and cedars of Lebanon are, of course, exotic there.[33] Were it not for that Lebanese blue sky, gratuitously inserted into the erotic scene, there would be no clear connection between that tree and this late, Swiss walkway.

166   Nabokov's Secret Trees

Aptly enough, the misidentified sequoia leads them to a street named for another wrong tree: "rue du Mûrier," as Ada notes, indicates a mulberry tree, but what marks the street is "a princely paulownia ... standing in state." This is the second example of paulownia in the novel – the first, discussed previously, is outside the sitting room at Ardis, and links, via the botanist-ancestor Prince Zemski, to the "Family Tree" at the novel's very beginning, with its many hints of criss-crossing very "wrong" or "mistaken" identifications of relationships. The absent mulberry, like the paulownia, has large, usually heart-shaped, leaves.

There are, however, no actual mulberry trees in *Ada*, though the word "mulberry" itself appears on two other occasions.[34] The first is the scene where Van happens past a bathroom where Ada was "washing her face and arms over an old-fashioned basin on a rococo stand ... A fat snake of porcelain curled around the basin, and as both the reptile and he stopped to watch Eve and the soft woggle of her bud-breasts in profile, a big mulberry-colored cake of soap slithered out of her hand" (A 60). This is Van's first encounter with Ada's bare chest; he had glimpsed her nether parts in the previous paragraph, while they climbed to the roof through the attic skylight together. This same "mulberry" soap appears again, as we saw, when the two lovers have installed Lucette in her bath, and are preparing to make love around a corner in the L-shaped room (this L itself feels somehow significant), when she pulls a surprise: "'I'm Van,' said Lucette, standing in the tub with the mulberry soap between her legs and protruding her shiny tummy" (A 144). To recapitulate: we have a street misnamed for a mulberry tree in Mont Roux, calling us back to two earlier mulberry moments (also sans trees) at crucial junctures in Van and Ada's erotic history. Just after Lucette's soap-bar gag and the lovers' quickie (during which, it should also be noted, they have placed her in danger, unsupervised in overly hot water, for fifteen minutes – Marina had ordered ten–twelve minutes maximum),[35] the very next paragraph mentions the "day of the attic," wherein Van gives Lucette the anthology with "Peter and Margaret," with its flash-forward of seventeen years to 1901, as she contemplated suicide should she fail to seduce Van on the Tobakoff – as, of course, she did.[36] The novel takes pains to keep these disparate scenes all linked together through networks of images, with trees prominent among them.

Return of the Paulownia

The real tree in the scene we are exploring, the paulownia, is shedding its leaves, but those that remain aloft are casting "arabesques of shadow," echoing the heart-shaped shadows from that early scene (the drawing room with Ada and Zemski [A 43]). Thus ends sentence number one, with three real and two imaginary trees. Sentence two begins with a real ginkgo of "luminous greenish gold," and concludes with a "dingily yellowing" birch.[37] The ginkgo's first appearance in the novel, as previously noted, is through its leaf, yellow in Marina's album,

Ada's Exuberant Trees 167

and received from Aqua within the book "The Truth about Terra," and thus has associations with "another world." The second instance of ginkgo, as we saw, occurs in part 1, chapter 41, the novel's midpoint, when Van, crushed by Ada's casual infidelity, flees Ardis in a rage, sees the "Chinese tree" at the "Maidenhair" railway station, thinks about its various names and its leaves and colours, about "Anna Karenin'"s nihilistic stream-of-consciousness while riding in a train, and about Ada's translations from *King Lear* (A 299–300).[38] (There is also "Maidenhair Road," in Percy's offer to duel Van, in a letter that Van misunderstands, at the beginning of part 1, chapter 40, physically connecting the "maidenhair/ginkgo" theme with the "peat bog" theme [the road intersects Tourbière Lane; Tourbière and Veen and Torfyanka all mean "peat bog"]).[39] Presumably, the ginkgo in the 1905 Mont Roux scene harks back to Aqua's suffering due to Demon's infidelities, perhaps additionally due to the loss of her pregnancy (in the album, the leaf was dated 12.XII.69, but the date of the gift is unclear: this may be a later date, when the leaf fell out of the book, some unknown time after it was given to Marina); it links to Van's near-suicidal feelings of jealousy and despair in 1888 as he leaves Ardis the Second, and, finally, recalls Lucette as she was drowning, her "maidenhair" tentaclinging, her green eyes, her lemon-yellow blouse (A 492).[40] The neighbouring tree, the birch, it turns out, is particularly associated with Van's arrival at Ardis and the two birthday picnics, one in 1884 en route *to* the picnic (A 78) marking the lovers' first close physical contact (Ada sitting in Van's lap just afterwards); and one in 1888 on the way home *from* the picnic (A 282), which follows Van's fight with Percy and marks the beginning of his and Ada's estrangement. (It is clear that the birches are carefully placed in Nabokov's mind, always appearing when Van is travelling near "Gamlet, a hamlet.") Since these are birthday picnics, 21 July, they also carry one of the dates Nabokov associated with his father (a variant birthday).[41]

Notably, some of these trees have secondary and even tertiary associations. The paulownia, through its apparent misidentification in the street's name ("Mûrier/Mulberry"), falls into the novel's – and Nabokov's personal – "wrong tree" motif; and with its link to the prefatory family tree, and Ada's later explication, it relates in this other way to a motif of *misnamed things* and *mislabelled relationships* (as in the family tree, discussed above). The paulownia also enters into another series stretching back to the very beginnings of Nabokov's life as a writer: heart-shaped leaves. It is intriguing that this exotic tree (from central and western China) is the one casting heart-shaped shadows into the "yellow drawing room" (A 43), rather than the lindens whose cordate leaves populate so many of Nabokov's poems, stories, and novels – and, especially, the "first poem" episode of *Speak, Memory*, which Nabokov revised while working on *Ada* (see chapter 1). Although in the first appearances of these heart-shaped paulownia leaves, any reference to Nabokov's own biography is muted,[42] the tree's "standing in state" next to a public "W.C.," closely associated with Lucette[43]

168 Nabokov's Secret Trees

(and again, seventeen years later), brings to mind the other key element of Nabokov's early creative mythology discussed in chapter 1, beginning with the languorous time young Nabokov spent in the Vyra estate's two "water closets" dreaming up worlds and words.

Tree confusions in this lane continue at a prodigious rate. The "sempervirent sequoia" also enters the "wrong tree" pattern, and the tree it brings forth, cedar of Lebanon, comes with rich folkloric and mythological associations (perhaps most pertinent is the association of Artemis with the cedar – though this was probably meant as the prickly cedar, another juniper: the lore is muddled – along with her connection to the moon and to sudden deaths).[44] The ginkgo is a tree with at least two names in English,[45] one of which quietly foregrounds Lucette's hair; possibly, Nabokov also still thinks here of Goethe's poem and the theme of doubling and, hence, the double world of Terra/Antiterra.[46] The birch alone among these trees lacks any clear associations outside the core narrative, but it is worth remembering that birches were common figures in Nabokov's own early poetry (and in *Mary*), in one case even imagined as a transformed girl: recall how in the early poem "A Birch in the Vorontsov Park," a birch's hanging branches are compared to a maiden combing her hair.[47] If Nabokov had that early poetry and its shopworn trees in mind, perhaps the pallid yellow of these birch leaves represents a mild denigration of his early overuse of this tree – but also its associations with first love and total loss.

Not all trees associated with Van and Ada's love, or their neglectful, damaging treatment of Lucette, are included in this scene: aside from the sequoia and imagined cedar, evergreens generally are missing from the textual vicinity (recall that after being tied to a willow, Lucette escaped to spy "through the larches" to where the other two had retreated into a grove of "evergreens" and "conifers"). There are no willows here either. The "shattal apple" tree that was the scene of Van's first, accidental, physical contact with Ada's crotch, though not a "true apple," is vaguely reflected in these reunion chapters in an apple pastry and what appears to be a poisoning that it causes (in an episode of diarrhoea, A 515–16). At this point in the novel, Lucette has been dead for four years; Ada has been married for twelve, and is just preparing to leave her unloved husband Andrey Vinelander, to return to Van, presumably because their father, Demon, had recently died, ending the ban on their union. This scene's concentrated (if partial) review of so many trees appears to serve as a reminder – or simply a soft echo – of the harm Van and Ada have already done, in some respects a reinforcement of the notion that they do not yet, in 1905, deserve the reward of being together.[48] The novel appears to conspire with that conclusion – as Van puts it, "the friendly Fates took a day off" (A 527), Andrey enters a seventeen-year-long period of languishing and needy illness, and Ada will not abandon him to suffer alone. (Perhaps it is this almost penance-like act that "earns" their final reunion.)

Revisiting Revisited Trees

Let's look through the trees near and on Rue du Mûrier one more time from a slightly different angle, highlighting the multiple ways they refract across several of the novel's temporal and narrative facets; doing so will lead us to one more provocative insight. As was the case with the trees in *Pale Fire*'s Shakespeare Avenue, almost every tree here brings with it something of a surprise.

Each tree, I suggest, includes a certain tension of presence and absence. The boxwoods are present, but elsewhere in the novel they are absent: except oneirically, in Van's dream (of an Ardis maze) just before the traumatic Manhattan threesome, which causes Lucette to leave a note signed, "miserable … pour Elle" (A 421).[49] (At that event, she had been wearing a "willow-green nighty," which Ada removes from her.) Next comes the "sempervirent sequoia," or coast redwood, mistaken by tourists as "Lebanese cedar" (with which it shares little in common, aside from being evergreen). The sequoia is present, its only appearance in the novel, and it is *sempervirent* – always green and flourishing, that is, evergreen. The absent Lebanese cedar, though uniquely named here, recalls the one actual cedar, the weeping cedar where Ada and Van first attempted sexual play with Lucette, hoping to satisfy and put an end to her curiosity. The boxwoods (also an evergreen) lead past the redwood to "Rue de Mûrier," Mulberry Street, whose putative mulberry (absent) is really a paulownia. The paulownia is present, with "heart-shaped, dark green leaves," reminding us of the family's ancestry, and of Van and Ada's first day together. The "mulberry" is absent, but its echo in the name asks us to remember Lucette's soap and two mythical suicides under a mulberry tree. The ginkgo is present, its leaves "luminous greenish-gold," pulling our thoughts towards Aqua's gold ginkgo leaf in Marina's attic-stored herbarium, and indirectly her suicide, as well as Van's thoughts of Anna Karenina and suicide at the Maidenhair station, and, of course, Lucette's hair as she drowns, and her green eyes and green and yellow garments. The ginkgo marks a "cobbled lane leading down to the quay," that is, the water. The "dingily yellowing local birch" is unique both in its exclusive situation within parentheses, and apparently in its "local," native status.

The progression of colours is striking: the boxwood and redwood are evergreen; the paulownia's leaves are "dark green" and shedding; the ginkgo's leaves are "luminous green-gold"; and the birch is "dingily yellowing." The green, especially of the evergreens, recalls Lucette's green eyes (in particular), and the word *sempervirent* appears to hint at something eternal or everlasting. The shift towards gold and yellow may hint at the yellow attire both Aqua and Lucette wore at their suicides. But the adjective "dingily," and the demotion to a parenthetical (where both the gold and the dingy yellow are qualified and sequestered), may suggest that these features are being pushed into the background. Why, by whom, and what should we make of it?

170   Nabokov's Secret Trees

It may also be worth attending to the specific trees that are absent, even if (or especially since) their memory is evoked here: the willow, the mulberry, the cedar, and the larch – the last of which made its appearance right next to the ginkgo in Marina's herbarium, during the initial attic scene.[50] All four of these missing trees are directly associated with harms caused to Lucette; the trees that are present – boxwood, paulownia, coast redwood, and ginkgo – have at most indirect, distanced associations with those harms. Van and Ada pass by these trees after "three or four hours of frenetic love" (A 521), perhaps on each of their ten trysts in Mont Roux during October 1905. Boyd has argued that in general, Lucette's shade appears to be helping to bring the lovers back together.[51] Of course, in this episode, their reunion is foiled, and perhaps we see this in the trees as well, in their "sempervirent" leaves at the start of the path, fading through "luminous greenish gold" to "dingily yellowing": the trees, in a sense, foretell the lovers' fate during this sojourn, while also shimmering lightly with the hurts and harms that still surround their acts and their history.

Curiously, just before the ultimate, successful reunion in July 1922 (when nothing can be yellowing or falling), Van again passes this place, and notes only one tree, calling it by its misnomer, "mulberry": he "saw that the famous 'mûrier,' that spread its great limbs over a humble lavatory on a raised terrace at the top of a cobbled lane, was now in sumptuous purple-blue bloom" (554) – impossible flowers, by the way.[52] Here the tree has flowers that evoke (and for the nonce are named for) the mulberry, whose colour in soap was so pivotal in early quasi-erotic scenes. This one tree, misnamed, stands in as a synecdoche for all the other trees named in 1905, which are not named in 1922, and with all the earlier colour traces here replaced with "purple-blue." The colour (akin to violet) deserves attention, but perhaps the key element to be underscored is the contrast between florescence and senescence. There is, surely, something of Van's artistic touch as memoir-writer here (and perhaps this is why the timing of the flowers is off), but in any case even the trees with negative associations have become optimistic.

The novel's themes and the lovers' strivings culminate in this scene in 1922, at the Trois Cygnes hotel, as Van awaits Ada's arrival for what they hope will be, almost isn't, and then becomes, their ultimate, permanent reunion. Van looks over the lake, the view from his balcony, and the scene takes on a dual state, half "real" and half "painting":

> The wide lovely lake lay in dreamy serenity, fretted with green undulations, ruffed with blue, patched with glades of lucid smoothness between the ackers; and, in the lower right corner of the picture, as if the artist had wished to include a very special example of light, the dazzling wake of the westering sun pulsated through a lakeside lombardy poplar that seemed both liquefied and on fire. (A 555)[53]

Much is concentrated in this scene, but the Lombardy poplar stands out for several reasons. It is the first reference to this specific type of poplar in the novel (and the only physically present poplar in the whole work – though a metaphorical "long row of poplars" from a few pages earlier, elucidating one of Van's temporal concepts, could also have been this type (or not).[54] The tree's presence, blended with the sunlight and the water of the lake, is marked and mysterious: why wait so long to present this type, one of Nabokov's favourites?[55] The energy intensifies even further when a "distant idiot leaning backward on waterskis behind a speed-boat started to rip the canvas; fortunately, he collapsed before doing much harm, and at the same instant the drawing-room telephone rang." That ringing telephone seems innocent and predictable enough – Van is awaiting Ada's call – but if we have attuned ourselves to Nabokov's creative palette, we should notice that this phone call, too, fits into a long-standing pattern: most dramatically, it echoes the moment in *Speak, Memory* when Nabokov and his mother learn (while the reader does not) that his father has been shot at the Kadet Party gathering in Berlin, in March *1922*.[56] On this day in Antiterra's July 1922, Van has strolled past the "mûrier" (paulownia) and "lavatory" (W.C.), and in combination with these it is easy to see how the new scene's *elements* (in both senses of the word: components; earth-fire-air-water) bring Lucette's influence into even starker relief: the sunlight hints at her name, while the lake's water recalls her death. These two features almost literally (if artistically) merge with the tree – "that seemed both liquefied and on fire" – the Lombardy poplar; the scene's combination of elements (the tree being *earth*) brings to mind also the Elements Room at Palazzo Vecchio, in which Lucette had apparently discovered a fresco detail showing the "pear peacock [moth]" (A 400).[57] All time becomes implicated in the scene when Ada finally calls and they speak: "That telephone voice, by resurrecting the past and linking it up with the present, with the darkening slate-blue-mountains beyond the lake, with the spangles of the sun wake dancing through the poplar, formed the centerpiece in his deepest perception of tangible time, the glittering 'now' that was the only reality of Time's texture" (A 556).[58] That small, abbreviated "rip [in] the canvas" by the water skier appears analogous to the near-failure of the meeting over dinner, but just as the "painting" is not fatally spoiled by the skier's wake, so the lovers' reunion survives the momentary discomfiture produced by elapsed time. This reunion is the end of the novel proper – part 5 serves the role of a Tolstoyesque epilogue – and it seems to come with several signs of approbation: from the (implied) author, and from Lucette.

The Lombardy poplar requires still a little more contemplation, in part to demonstrate that it, too, is part of that "authorial approbation." The poplar variety "Lombardy," a cultivar of the European black poplar, makes its first named Nabokovian appearance in *Conclusive Evidence* (1951) – by means of a twig in the hands of Professor Jack at the memoir's end (SM 304). It next appears as the mysterious, mirrory tree in the final scene of *Pnin* (1957), overseeing and perhaps applauding the protagonist's miraculous escape from the narrator.[59] It then finds its way into the expanded (1966) early chapters of *Speak, Memory* – specifically, the description of the window's view from the room at Vyra where Nabokov as a boy did much of his butterfly work. There, what was presented as "three bushy poplars" in *Mary* (in a scene presumably sculpted from these fragments of Nabokov's life) now becomes "five Lombardy poplars" (SM 72); these same poplars may have been the view from the "sumptuous, gloomy" bathroom where Nabokov composed youthful verse (SM 85, cf. *Mary* and *Drugie berega*). Those poplars are by an "old well and rusty pumping wheel" (also repeated in *Mary*), and at least two poplars, though not necessarily the Lombardy variety, are struck by lightning (in *The Gift* and *Pnin* – in the latter it is a cottonwood), adding fire to the immediate cluster of regular associations.[60] In these various elements, we see something like a gathering of Nabokov's treasures, blessing or condoning at last the lifelong union of Van and Ada; it is their union that will eventually spark and enable the creation of the narrative before us (in their world, at least).

One last look at that vivid scene, with strategic emphases, helps clarify Lucette's place both in the moment, and in the novel:

> The wide lovely lake lay in dreamy serenity, fretted with **green undulations**, ruffed with blue, patched with glades of **lucid** smoothness between the ackers; and, in the lower right corner of the picture, as if the artist had wished to include a very special example of **light**, the dazzling wake of the westering **sun** pulsated through a **lakeside** Lombardy poplar that seemed both **liquefied** and on **fire.**

The emphases (one of colour, two of light, three of water, two of sun/fire) bring to mind Lucette's name, her green eyes, her watery end (undulating, lakeside, liquefied – with a hint of an undine), and her red hair (fire, elsewhere called "embers"). Van's transformation of this scene into a canvas, or an explicit imagined work of art (rather than a casually observed landscape), suggests, perhaps, his conscious awareness, in the moment of recollecting and writing, the centrality of Lucette, both in the "memoir's" inspiration and in its larger artistic qualities – hinting at how we might have considered this scene as part of the present study's fifth chapter. The liquefied, fiery poplar blurs the boundaries of the elements;[61] the encompassed landscape blurs the boundaries of art and life; the return of Ada and the current visual saturation of

Lucette blurs boundaries of past and present. (The water skier's canvas ripping terminates simultaneously with the phone call, a coincidence that poignantly suggests an analogy between the skier's "collapse" into the water and Lucette's fatal plunge).[62] The vital necessity, for Van, to evolve Lucette's sad trace into a triumphant tribute of art appears to be born at this moment, echoing the way he had "evolved" an ink blot into a tree in the book of poems he gave her, and as Marina had evolved one into a flower in her herbarium. (That Ada's re-return is inspired at Morges via "a mermaid's message" appears to reinforce this notion, while also supporting a spectral interpretation).[63] In a deliberate ardis of evolution, the main narrative begins with a bare, black-and-white tree (schematic: the family tree) and ends with a multi-dimensional, multi-coloured, multi-elemental tree: a fire-water tree, a tree of art, envisioned as part of an imaginary, mobile painting.[64]

Epilogue: In and Out of the Pines[*]

Why do the trees move? Why do they, for lack of a better word, "ambulate"? I want to return for a moment to consideration of these sauntering, climbing, marching trees.

The first trees to stretch their legs were under duress – leaping into a ravine in "The Fields, the Swamps Float Past" (1917); starting their endless pilgrimage in the poem "Poplars" (1921) and the story "Gods" (1923); beech trunks "leaping by," and other trees "revolving coolly and blandly, displaying the latest fashions" in "Cloud, Castle, Lake" (1937); rowan saplings clambering collaboratively onto a boulder in *The Gift* (1938), scouts and stragglers from the Grunewald late in that novel; the birch that runs up to a window and raises a book in "Fame" (1942); the "grave green pilgrim" in "The Ballad of Longwood Glen" (1952–7); a "panting pine taking a well-earned breather" in *Lolita* (1957, p. 168 – it is fascinating that Nabokov lent this device of perception to Humbert Humbert); and King Charles in *Pale Fire* (1962), during his escape, fights off "an army of conifers" (140). The acrobatic figures early in *Ada* – the old oak catching the flying linden – appear to emerge from this same motif, offering a final new development: more than mere walking, these trees imply *flight*.

In most of these examples, there is a direct implication that the motion-related imagery is somehow *true* in an elusive way. (In the case of *Ada*, as in that early poem, the moments make clear that what we have is a perceptual fancy and an analogy; Humbert, too, knows he is just playing with words.) Obviously, in our lived lives, we never see trees marching around, and perhaps it has never even occurred to us that the trees might be on the move (J.R.R. Tolkien's "ents" notwithstanding). But that tree in "Longwood Glen" is the most intriguing of all, and there is something about the poem itself that demands our attention.

The poem is a quick and pleasant read, and readers who don't know it well might like to run through it before moving on; I won't present the entire text

---

[*] This concluding chapter is dedicated to the memory of John Bartle, thoughts of whom inspired me while writing these pages in June 2022.

176 Nabokov's Secret Trees

here. The poem's "jaunty tone," in Paul Morris's apt description, bounces the reader along,[1] and in a letter presenting the piece to Katharine White, Nabokov observed that the poem may seem "like a weird hybrid between Shagall [*sic*] and Grandma Moses" (SL 209). He further implores her to "stick to it as long as you can bear, and by degrees all kinds of interesting shades and underwater patterns will be revealed to the persevering eye." Marc Chagall, as the name is usually spelled, not greatly admired by Nabokov, produced brightly coloured, vaguely childlike and variously magical, absurdist, folkloristic, and/or surrealistic (subjectively speaking) images. Grandma Moses, of course – who appeared on the cover of *Time* magazine on 23 December 1953 – was famous for her heartwarming, folksy images of scenes of American life featuring rural and small-town landscapes and motifs. (Chagall's work, likewise, frequently shows people outdoors in a rustic village environment, but with a strong hallucinatory twist, in unnatural, overly vibrant colours and sometimes with cubistic elements).[2] Aware of these partial, and deceptive, parallels, Nabokov urged White to look longer and deeper. What did he hope she would see?

Many of those things have been laid out by Boyd and especially by Morris, and I don't want to rehearse all of them here. The poem's wordplay becomes clear as one sits with it (Longwood; DeForest; Art's name, with its implication of "art"; and, of course, the metaphysical shock of Art's arrival among the "celestial crowds," and his revelation, "How accessible ether! How easy flight!"). Like Boyd and Morris, I want to sit for a moment with the crucial couplet, "Silent Art, who could stare at a thing all day, / Watched a bug climb a stalk and fly away" (SP 150). As Morris writes, this moment demonstrates that Art possesses "a heightened, artistic consciousness," the attention to detail, the "all-important 'capacity to wonder at trifles'" that Nabokov values almost above all else.[3] The moment also, in its way, amplifies *this* Art's ability to fuse with an element of the natural world, to stare at it "all day," and thus to achieve a degree of self-transcendence. This habit of his echoes Fyodor's witnessing of a butterfly taking flight from chamomile in *The Gift*, which in turn (as I have suggested) reaches back to the scene of Konstantin Levin, in *Anna Karenina*, watching a bug climb a stalk and fly away, during his own moments of intense metaphysical reflection and epiphany.[4]

"The Ballad"'s metaphysical side, and its cultural critique of philistinism, have been amply discussed by the scholars I've mentioned. One element has not: the tree, an oak – but not just any oak; this one was "passing by," and the ball's appearance among its foliage causes it to "turn and stop." What kind of tree passes by, turns, and stops? No tree of *our* world, within our normal modes of perception at least, does these things. Somehow, this tree follows rules of its own, exists according to another norm.

In that very early story "Gods," the narrator tells his wife, "you," that "All the trees in the world are journeying [*dvizhutsia*] somewhere ... All trees are pilgrims. They have their Messiah, whom they seek. Their Messiah is a

regal Lebanese cedar, or perhaps he is quite small, some totally inconspic-
uous little shrub in the tundra ... Today some lindens are passing through
town. There was an attempt to restrain them. Circular fencing was erected
around their trunks. But they move all the same" (CS 45). This vision, from
1923, is already an echo of the unpublished 1921 poem, "Poplars," discussed
briefly in the introduction. In that poem, we learn, the trees "walk and walk,
never growing closer to their joyous goal." The trees are on the move in some
way we cannot see, but the lyric speaker in "Poplars," like the narrator of
"Longwood Glen," intuits or knows. The early insistence on a unity between
tree and *soul* hints at a metaphysical component to the essence of the trees,
something reinforced by the word "pilgrim" in 1923 and in 1957. The "Gods"
narrator's idea that even though caged, the trees "move [*dvizhutsia*] all the
same," suggests some sort of extra-mundane mode of perception.[5] That context clarifies, very slightly, what this tree in "Longwood Glen" is doing, and
why it is a "grave green pilgrim." Nevertheless, it requires a tremendous leap
of imagination, even a leap into the unimaginable, to contemplate the world
of trees in this way. This is even a greater leap, I think, than the one offered
by Art, who reaches the "snow of the clouds" – an image that is, by contrast,
utterly conventional. Why does Art reach the end of his journey, and the
trees do not?

Maybe this is a deliberate trick of the poem: like Art's family, and all of the
people who look for him and memorialize him by means of the varnished
stump, the reader focuses on Art's destination, and his clear arrival among the
"delirious celestial crowds" (about whom, after all, there is something suspicious). The tree's destruction, its murder, is of course a tragedy, though the humans in the poem don't notice it. But its felling represents more than the loss of
a tree, the death of one item from nature; with the tree ends its mysterious motion, its journeying, and – glancing through various works, but especially *Bend
Sinister* – its "trillions of twigs," aligning with the "trillions of trillions" of mysteries inherent in human lives and in all of life. The tree (and really, any tree)
seems to embody for Nabokov something impenetrable and unknowable in
the world, something we could call "magical" if the word weren't so clearly reducible to particular human concepts. As I mentioned in the introduction, for
Nabokov the "metaphysical" quality of trees relates to all those ways that trees
pull the imagination from the everyday, from the utilitarian, from the orderly,
fixed, and rational. Trees on the move shake us out of our world, or perhaps,
to try another metaphor, they give us a hint of the blinders we are born with.

The most important journeying trees in the history of culture are probably
those enchanted by Orpheus – he who "with songs like these, drew to himself
the trees, the souls of wild beasts, and the stones."[6] This part of Ovid's telling leads directly to Orpheus's death (like Dionysus, torn apart by the Mae-
nads), though there are other places, including Shakespeare's *Henry VIII*, where

Orpheus's musical powers over nature are described. In Nabokov's instances, perhaps inspired by the Orpheus stories, trees are on the move independently of any clear cause (except the implicit teleological cause of a pilgrimage). Regardless of causes or inspirations, this alternative mythological lineage only deepens the strain of supernatural or metaphysical life coursing through trees' tissues.

Throughout this study I have mostly avoided a type-by-type approach, a correspondence between specific trees and fixed meanings or even connotations, although I did get waylaid by oaks for a stretch back in chapter 3. There are several types of trees across Nabokov's career that one might usefully give a comprehensive treatment: lindens, poplars, chestnuts (actually horse chestnuts), and maybe alders look promising. Birches and firs, most likely, are at once too common and too obvious in their associations, though even these are not fixed.

I will not launch into a full-blown examination of trees' thematic trajectories, but I will sketch out a few things and take one deep dive. Birches are common in the early poetry, *Mary*, and *Speak, Memory*, and they appear briefly in most remaining novels (but only eight stories).[7] Poplars, we can tell from chapter 4 of *Speak, Memory*, are connected with Nabokov's earliest memories of his own creativity and, as we see in the early and late poems titled after these trees, they may be the trees he most strongly identified with. There are many puzzling, highly marked poplars throughout the works; perhaps most intriguing of all are the frequently raging poplars outside the Haze home at 342 Lawn Street, in *Lolita*.[8] Lindens, though, compete with poplars in scenes emphasizing the creative consciousness, as well as memory – we see this in "First Poem" (*Speak, Memory*'s chapter 8), in the opening scenes of *The Gift*, in "A Nursery Tale" and "Recruiting"; the linden, though, is also heavily implicated in (authentic) love-related scenes, in *Mary*, in *The Gift*, in *Speak, Memory*, in the story "The Circle." (Horse) chestnuts, too, are often associated with love ("The Return of Chorb," "The Encounter") but they go far beyond that, and the "love" element is more than complicated by the chestnuts' haunting role in *Lolita*.[9] The birch is associated with nostalgia for the homeland and loss in general, especially a lost parent.

These sketches are really just gestures, and there is no reason a reader might not want to follow any one of these paths in greater detail, across the span of Nabokov's creative work, to see what sorts of secondary forms or patterns it reveals. There is no need for any of them to show a strict consistency, but it is likely that the inconsistencies could prove very interesting, as I hope some of this study's chapters have already shown. As promised, though, I do want to make my own effort to take a deeper look into how one rather unassuming tree makes its way across the artistic landscapes of Nabokov's worlds: the humble pine.

Pines, as a distinctive group of trees, appear to have evolved gradually in Nabokov's artistic thought into a particular kind of aesthetic zone, from early origins that were, perhaps, arbitrary and nondescript. Appearing in only eight poems (and only in the early years; none, it seems, after 1924), and sporadically but vaguely in the early stories, pines emerge in clumps in *Mary*, but without a clear pattern. In *Mary*, the "pine coppice" is the boundary land between Ganin's home and Mary's dacha, through which he cycles. This instance seems simple enough, but already Nabokov seems to be trying to work with these pines: notice the wood framing of houses being built on the novel's final pages, which is underscored in a striking way. The structure is a "yellow wooden framework of beams" (M 113), and then soon "the wooden frame shone like gold in the sun" (M 114), and finally, as Ganin finalizes his decision to leave, "the yellow sheen of fresh timber was more alive than the most lifelike dream of the past" (M 114). Nabokov most likely knew that house frames are almost always made of pine, and the repeated highlighting of this glowing frame may well be a deliberate, semi-hidden transformation of the pine wood through which Ganin originally cycled hoping to meet Mary. This instance – call it, perhaps, "pines as a subtext for personal memory and renewal" – does not seem to become a strict template for Nabokov's later works that include pines, but this aspect of their function does reappear later. In *King, Queen, Knave*, pines are rare, but they do surround the hospital where Marthe dies. *Laughter in the Dark* has a few interesting pines, and another pine building. But something really begins to take shape with the writing of *Despair*. In that work, the most fateful location is Ardalion's lakeside plot of land, whose pine-filled environs are mentioned emphatically every time the spot comes into the frame. We first learn that the plot has a "couple of inseparable birches," "several black-alder bushes," and "five pine trees" (Desp 33); later, after they all swim, Hermann and Ardalion sit "in the shade of his best pine tree," where the artist begins working on his portrait of Hermann. The lake's vicinity is primarily a "pine forest" (Desp 36), also a "thick pine wood" (Desp 55), and it is to this spot that Hermann returns: first, to scope and rehearse his murderous plan, and finally to carry it through, during which scene, he intones, "pines, pines, pines" (Desp 162),[10] a rhythm that echoes the "(bump) ... (bump) ... (bump)" during both drives into the forest, and the twice-repeated "ick."[11] This scene, with its pines and its water, begins to coalesce into something of an archetype in Nabokov's

180 Nabokov's Secret Trees

works. In *Despair*, it is the location where Hermann kills Felix (sends him out of this world), but also where he himself undergoes a transformation, nominally "dying" and taking on a new identity, or, in a dark parody of mythological form, dying and coming back to life.[12] I call the scene archetypal, because key clusters of its details reappear in works as diverse as *The Gift*, *Lolita*, and *Pnin*, with refractory elements appearing in *Pale Fire* and *Ada* as well.[13] Although I have not figured out why, precisely, this image cluster (pine grove, water, metaphysical hints and feints) came to have the recurring form it does, it may have something to do with Nabokov's time in Berlin and his frequent summertime visits to the Grunewald and its lake amid a pine forest.[14] The place settled into Nabokov's creative alembic well before the murderous reality of the Nazis was fully expressed, but already some sort of darkness or metaphysical wobbliness was associated with it, even though it was also the environment where Nabokov mentally composed much of his work in the 1920s.[15] Clearly, it was a place of human extremes: flights of creativity, alongside grotesque littering and leering (one scene in *The Gift* animates "the male gaze" most comically: a sunbathing girl lies in the middle of a "magic triangle" of lechers, "and it seemed that these three pairs of eyes striking the same spot would finally, with the help of the sun, burn a hole in the black bathing tights of that poor little German girl, who never raised her ointment-smeared lids" (G 335–6).

Though pines dominate the Grunewald as described by Fyodor, they are interspersed with other types and grades into other tree stands here and there. Fyodor comes to the forest mainly to sunbathe in clearings, to swim and walk and enjoy nature, but he also contemplates death directly: at one place, we learn that "on the right was a ravine overgrown with oakbrush and bramble. And today, just as every time that he came here, Fyodor descended into that hollow which always attracted him, as if he had been somehow guilty of the death of the unknown youth who had shot himself here – precisely here" (G 337). Fyodor's deep sense of connection to, even (especially) responsibility for, Yasha Chernyshevski's death, and his mother's mourning afterwards, reveals to us a new side of his personality. As we saw in chapter 3, there are elements of the Grunewald sojourns that point to Fyodor's own father's demise, and this section of the novel has a distinct Orphic, underworldly quality to it, framed by the pines and the lake. Koncheyev's surprise (and imaginary) appearance under an oak, in black, extends the pattern further,[16] and immediately after the Grunewald episode Fyodor's father makes his appearance in Fyodor's dream, as if returning from the beyond. One of Nabokov's most ecologically rich lyrical passages, Fyodor's experience among the pine barrens distils and focuses many of the novel's most important themes.

We note in passing that V., in *The Real Life of Sebastian Knight*, "stumbles" through a pine wood on his way to the hospital where his brother is dying, or has just died (more the latter than the former, but both versions are relevant) – the only pines in that novel.[17] This combination that I'm calling an "archetype" makes its next real appearance in *Lolita*, at Hourglass Lake. It should be remembered that this lake hovers, mirage-like, over many of the early chapters of the novel. It is repeatedly dangled as a reward to Dolly for good behaviour, revoked for backtalk, or cancelled due to weather. Humbert thinks it is "Our Glass Lake," only later learning its real name; when they finally reach the nearly mythical destination, Dolly has left for camp and Humbert has married Charlotte, to solidify his proximity to his target when she gets home at summer's end. The newlyweds proceed "down a path cut through a pine forest to the lake" (L 82).[18] There, Charlotte tells Humbert that "Lo, I'm afraid, does not enter the picture at all, at all. Little Lo goes straight from camp to a good boarding school" (L 83). To process his shock and grief, Humbert retreats back to the car purportedly for his sunglasses; once there, "For a while, purple-robed, heel-dangling, I sat on the edge of one of the rude tables, under the wooshing pines," and reaches the conclusion that the "natural solution was to destroy Mrs. Humbert. But how?" (L 84). Humbert *thinks* he has the perfect occasion to murder her by drowning, here by the pines, in Hourglass Lake; but, he reports, "what d'ye know, folks – I just could not make myself do it!" (L 87). They do swim, vaguely recalling the bathing of Hermann et al. (*Despair*), and of Fyodor in the Grunewald (*The Gift*).[19]

A few pages after the Hourglass Lake scene, Charlotte of course does perish. Nabokov does not create a direct physical, causal link between this pine-water-death archetype and Charlotte's demise, but the proximity of imagined death and actual death is not accidental, either. The lake scene does present the very first instant of his murderous intent; his hidden thoughts about Dolly, made physical in his diary, become the real trigger.[20] Through this rather elaborate and drawn-out mechanism – something of a Rube Goldberg device as fictional murder-sequences go – Humbert's trip to the lake in the pine forest leads him to the *other side*, to the mad world where he could have everything he ever dreamed of, with his "Lolita." This life takes on its own form of irreality, and it might merit an extended treatment as another sort of parodic Orphic journey. However, this is not the place for that adventure. What unites the three versions of the archetype we've examined so far is the notion of a person in close proximity to an important metaphysical boundary, and this boundary shows up in the fates of characters around the central one (Felix, Charlotte, Yasha all die or have died), as well as in the continuing life of the central person: Hermann, Humbert, and Fyodor all enter into a new state of being after their "visit" (Fyodor, to be explicit, envisions his version of *The Gift* itself during his piney excursions and swims).

Nabokov's next novel, *Pnin*, continues this archetypal engagement and gives it additional twists and nuances. The novel's fifth chapter, famously, is situated entirely in, or around, an estate called "The Pines," belonging to the wife (Susan) of Russian émigré Alexandr Kukolnikov, a.k.a. Al Cook, where many

182 Nabokov's Secret Trees

fellow émigrés were invited to spend some vacation time on alternate summers. Pines are only one of eleven types of trees mentioned in the chapter, but they dominate, albeit in a fairly quiet way. The environment of the entire chapter is somewhat otherworldly: Pnin loses his accent (because he is speaking Russian), and he becomes a master of wit, esoteric knowledge, and sport. The Pines is a sort of antipode to the existence of the misfit Russian in America; everything is tinged with a bit of magic.

But there is also darkness. It begins before Pnin even arrives, with his very approach to the retreat. As he winds his way through the surrounding forest and near Mount Ettridge, Pnin is watched by an imaginary observer from a fire tower on the mountain (or by the ant up there). This tower, however, through a series of associations in close proximity – especially "Ettridge" – subtly evokes a guard tower from a Nazi concentration camp.[21] But this dark hint is not really apparent on a first reading; it takes time with the novel to bring it into focus.

The mood, on the whole, appears festive at first. We have "The Pines," and we have various pines (Pn 111, 117, 121, 122, 127, 131, 133, 136). Most important, as a contintuation of the "archetype," is the "natural swimming pool under the alders and pines," a place where the local stream broadens and deepens owing to the changes in elevation, with rock formations as natural dams (Pn 127). We need to examine this scene at high magnification and with some attention, because many things happen, almost at once. Pnin, ready to swim,

> glowed in the dappled sunlight of the riverside grove with a rich mohagany tint. He removed his cross and his rubbers.
>
> "Look, how pretty," said observant Chateau.
>
> A score of small butterflies, all of one kind, were settled on a damp patch of sand, their wings erect and closed, showing their pale undersides with dark dots and tiny orange-rimmed peacock spots along the hindwing margins; one of Pnin's shed rubbers disturbed some of them and, revealing the celestial hue of their upper surface, they fluttered around like blue snowflakes before settling again.
>
> "Pity Vladimir Vladimirovich is not here," remarked Chateau. "He would have told us all about these enchanting insects."
>
> "I have always had the impression that his entomology was merely a pose."
>
> ...
>
> He noticed he still had his wrist watch – removed it and left it inside one of his rubbers. Slowly swinging his tanned shoulders, Pnin waded forth, the loopy shadows of leaves shivering and slipping down his broad back. (Pn 128–9)[22]

The presence of alders alongside the pines is intriguing; alders have featured, throughout Nabokov's career, at moments associated with poetic creation (in *Speak, Memory*, and prefigured in *Mary* and *Glory*). "Dappled" before he enters the water, and caressed by "loopy shadows of leaves" as he wades, Pnin is fully enmeshed in this world of pine, alder, and water. Humbert had kept his ("waterproof") watch on to swim; Pnin removes his: is it because this world he occupies is timeless? The digression on blue butterflies (the Karner blue, as it must be, a resident of "pine barren" ecosystems and their lupine host plants), with its allusion to the narrator (and to Nabokov), adds a quirkiness to the scene, to which I will return in a moment.[23] For now, notice how much attention is given here to the physical process of Pnin's preparation, his entry into the water, and his motions of swimming: "He swam with a rhythmical splutter – half gurgle, half puff. Rhythmically he opened his legs and widened them out at the knees while flexing and straightening out his arms like a giant frog" (Pn 129). The whole description probably takes almost as long to read as Pnin actually spends in the water (two minutes). The scene gives a rather intense moment of artistic focus. Why?

Next in the action comes the croquet game, in which Pnin has been transformed as if by magic: "From his habitual, slow, ponderous, rather rigid self, he changed into a terrifically mobile, scampering, mute, sly-visaged hunchback" (Pn 130). This moment of comedy, however, leads into the novel's heaviest moments. Immediately after the game, after "Pnin had tolled the stake and all was over ... [he] quietly retired to a bench under the pines. A certain extremely unpleasant and frightening cardiac sensation, which he had experienced several times throughout his adult life, had come upon him again. It was not pain or palpitation, but rather an awful feeling of sinking and melting into one's physical surroundings – sunset, red boles of trees, sand, still air" (Pn 131). This passage introduces one of the most frequently discussed scenes in the novel: Pnin's reaction to Roza Shpolyanski's reminiscences about Mira and her family members, and their fate during the Holocaust. When Madame Shpolyanski walks off, Pnin falls – without narrative markers – into a reverie of his youthful days with the Belochkins, and his own parents. He reimagines the present estate as the one from the past, and envisions Mira coming towards him, and "this feeling coincided somehow with the sense of diffusion and dilation within his chest. Gently he laid his mallet aside and, to dissipate the anguish, started walking away from the house, through the silent pine grove" (Pn 133). There follow two pages of summary of his history with Mira, and then a forceful, moving account of Pnin's psychological negotiations with his painful memories and knowledge of the recent past ("during the last ten years") (Pn 133–4). We learn of his efforts to discover Mira's exact fate, and we are led through his ever-multiplying nightmare visions, where "since the exact form of her death had not been recorded, Mira kept dying a great number of deaths in one's mind" (Pn 135). As the visions and memories fade, tarnished at the end by crass remembered words from Pnin's departmental protector Dr. Hagen, Pnin again "slowly walked under the solemn pines. The sky was dying. He did not believe in an autocratic God. He did believe, dimly, in a democracy of ghosts" (Pn 136).

184 Nabokov's Secret Trees

Let's take a moment to unpack what we have covered here. Under the pines, Pnin undergoes a physical and metaphysical contortion. He comes face to face with ghostly memories, even as he feels himself "melting into his physical surroundings." He sees, or imagines seeing, people long dead. He thinks through his relationship to these people, and the history of his feelings for them. As his reflections close, still – it is repeated – under the pines, we read a definition of his metaphysical beliefs, even if only "dim" ones. Whereas The Pines is itself a kind of special, separate world for exiled Russians, the *chapter* about The Pines is for Pnin a quasi-metaphysical visit to his personal underworld. (The Orphic quality of this particular episode resides in the fact that he dips into memory to revisit his first love, Mira, though, unlike Orpheus, he knows that he can never retrieve her.) The chapter then ends, with a return to the theme of artistic craft, internally and externally: a romantic couple of the offspring's generation is "silhouetted against the ember-red sky," on the "distant crest of the knoll, at the exact spot where Gramineev's easel had stood a few hours before." The narrator speculates which young lovers these might be, noting that perhaps they are, after all, "merely an emblematic couple placed with easy art on the last page of Pnin's fading day" (Pn 136). Here the narrator-as-artist obtrudes, again, just as he had done in the brief vision of the blue butterflies by the swimming hole. That brief "entomology" moment, referencing "Vladimir Vladimirovich" and the butterflies he loved (and properly described and named), creates a ripple in the metaphysical surface of Pnin's world. This pines-and-water moment destabilizes the narrator's identity, destabilizes the whole structure of coherent narrative art. One need not follow this image all the way to assertions that Nabokov also held Pnin's metaphysical views ("There is no reason to speak here of Nabokov's negative or positive views, of which no one knows anything," he wrote in corrections sent to Bobbie Ann Mason for her book).[24] But as a minimalist position, it seems hard to deny that Nabokov enjoyed imagining and depicting human worlds with slippery, wobbly, unstable metaphysical places.[25]

It's worth pausing as well to note that this artist-in-the-scene device, perhaps evocative of Nabokov's beloved Van Eycks, is a feature of all of the "archetypal" pine-water-death complexes presented above. In *Despair* Ardalion, under the "best pine" by the lake, sketches Hermann's portrait; *The Gift*'s Fyodor is an artist himself and imagines a "someone" staging the artistry around him (such as the five balletic nuns); at Hourglass Lake, after Humbert fails to murder Charlotte, Jean Farlow emerges from the trees, where she was painting a study of the landscape; and at The Pines, as noted, the artist Gramineev is in a knoll (presumably pine) painting a barn, tree, and cows as Pnin heads to the swimming hole. Stated more plainly, the pine-water-death complex also always includes art and an artist. At the end of chapter 5 of *Pnin*, the artist's easel practically turns into two young lovers.

The question of why this Grunewald-inspired image retained a fluctuating thematic role for so long in Nabokov's career has no obvious answer. Perhaps the dark forces that Nabokov felt in German culture and then Nazi rule, especially from 1933, led him to associate that woodland – with its human detritus and crass behaviours – with the underside of being, just as it also connected him, at times, to moments of creative clarity, insight, and early love (the side we see through Fyodor's experiences, even while he remains sensitive to the presence of death). Fyodor, while basking, contemplates life's strangeness, its variety, its darkness, its richness. It is not implausible that as a result of spending so much time in that space, as observer of human and natural life, and as imaginative creator of art, Nabokov came to endow his experiences of it with an archetypal mythology all their own. This nexus may be seen as a contact point between worlds: in ancient times, the "upper world" and the "underworld," but for Fyodor and Nabokov, something more like the interface between the world of ordinary being and that of creative imagination. This boundary, and its crossing, are among the more frequent of Nabokov's motifs, never more visible than in his, and in Martin Edelweiss's, childhood dreams of entering a painting of a forest trail.

A final brief note on pines. Nabokov seems to have folded up the pine-water-death-artist archetype after completing *Pnin*. But the cluster's harmonics do reverberate in the following works. In *Pale Fire*, John Shade's Aunt Maud, an artist who painted such works as "Cypress and Bat," spent her last days in Pinedale, where she died. Of her passing, we read, "Espied on a pine's bark, / As we were walking home the day she died, / An empty emerald case, squat and frog-eyed, / Hugging the trunk; and its companion piece, / A gum-logged ant" (PF 41, poem lines 236–40). Shade's imagery is none too subtle here. More scraps of the traditional association might be pieced together during King Charles's flight across the mountains: he passes a reflective pond and has an existential shiver, "*alfear* (uncontrollable fear caused by elves)" (PF 143), and soon after passes the "pine groves of Boscobel" (Boscobel was made famous for the large oak in which the original King Charles II hid, while fleeing revolutionaries in his own time). No artists appear in the vicinity. In *Ada*, too, there are scenes intently centred around pines, and scenes with water; the closest one gets is at the scene of Van's duel with Captain Tapper, where all the pieces fit together in an almost perfunctory manner (also echoing the early stories "The Fight" and "An Affair of Honor," where combat takes place on similar terrain). Here, Van's "foot touched the pine-needle strewn earth of the forest road, a transparent white butterfly floated past, and with utter certainty Van knew that he had only a few minutes to live" (A 310). Live he does, however, and he convalesces in the "Lakeview (Lakeview!) Hospital" (*sic*; A 311), until his release into the care of Cordula de Prey. Nabokov does, indeed, seem to be reworking and deliberately playing with his favoured "archetype," as if mocking and deconstructing his own mannerism. I leave a full exploration of this late interpolation to future investigators; here, I have tried merely to provide evidence that even in *Ada*, he still found the conjunction in some way productive, albeit in self-parodic form.

In this study, I have worked to present the depth of Nabokov's fascination with trees, and his tendency to allow that fascination, that love, to give shape to his art in highly various ways. When I started this project, by chance really, as a riff on the elm Victor Wind thinks about in *Pnin*, reflected upside-down on a car's hood, I had no suspicion at all that trees formed such an immense – that is the right word – part of Nabokov's artistic ferment. What I thought would be a single, rather narrow if fun, conference paper quickly presented the prospect of something much larger: as soon as I scratched the surface of these arboreal patterns, I could clearly see that something major was going on, hidden among the many other rich patterns Nabokov weaves.

Every close reader I have asked, and I myself for twenty years, had not thought about trees as an expansive medium of artistic communication in Nabokov's work.[26] This obscurity, this invisibility is appropriate to the world as we live in it, at least to the extent that people tend not to notice trees too much; it is also appropriate, because Nabokov seems to love nothing more than to create meaningful layers of art that are virtually undetectable to the casual eye. Once we become attuned to the trees' significance, it seems both obvious and essential: how could Nabokov, a naturalist with an intense connection to the environment and a deep knowledge of many butterflies' ecosystems, *not* want trees to play a vital role in his art? Once seen, they can't be unseen.

Because of their beauty, their longevity, their fascinating structure and natural history, their complex ways of being in the world and their environments (including their layered relationships with light and water), trees pull us in, as they seem to have pulled Nabokov in from his earliest youth. But that's not exactly what they do within Nabokov's art, where, after all, they are not really trees, but words naming trees, or sometimes just naming things that are *like* trees. So a question remains to be answered: how does a sensitivity to all this naming of trees, and the mentioning of forests and coppices and groves and woodcraft, change how we experience and understand Nabokov's work?

Like any critical or interpretive device, trees provide us with an angle, a perspective. Without awareness of their importance to Nabokov – without knowing that he once wrote, "My soul is an alley of poplars" – we pass his trees by, like other trees around us. But once we sense their weight and heft, and start to approach the works anew, from the angle of the trees, something shifts; the works change.

As I hope I've shown with some success, the patterns of trees do encode meanings that Nabokov intended us to feel or find; the trees really do conceal secrets. The trees unexpectedly tie together far-flung scenes and even works; once noticed with care, they add emotional depth and substance to many passages one might simply pass through like a beautiful but vague landscape. But to get at these deeper places of feeling and response, of "knowledge-amplified love," one has to look long and hard, and peacefully, at the words on the page and the images behind them. Like Art Longwood, one has to "stare at a thing all day."

The trees in these works offer us a task: Sit. Listen. Stare. Reflect. Or, as Nabokov wrote to Katharine White, "Stick to it as long as you can bear, and by degrees all kinds of interesting shades and underwater patterns will be revealed to the persevering eye" (SL 209).

Appendices

Nabokov's Invented and Real Trees, in Images

Nabokov invented at least nine trees and shrubs; eight are represented here (missing is the "kiroku," which, within the story "Natasha," was never published in his lifetime). Seven artists have generously offered their original conceptions of these trees.

Acreana bush ("Terra Incognita," CS 299)
Beauvais Lyons (from the Hokes Archive)

Porphyroferous and black-leafed limia trees ("Terra Incognita," CS 298)
Randy L. Arnold (Island Home Press)

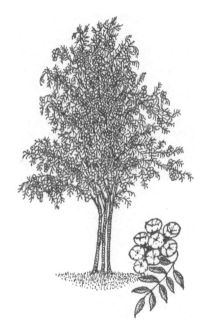

Vallieria mirifica ("Terra Incognita," CS 297)
Susan Elizabeth Sweeney

Nabokov's Invented and Real Trees, in Images 193

Pyrospodia (Foreword to LS)
Valerie Hird

Quercus ruslan Chat. (A 398)
Eric Pervukhin

Shattal apple (A 95–6, etc.)
Tatjana Bergelt

High-mountain willow, semi-extinct (A 55)
Alexandra Kent

Nabokov's Invented and Real Trees, in Images 195

196 Appendices

Bog Bilberry	*Black Birch*	*Paper Birch*
Silver Birch	*Bird Cherry (racemosa)*	*Bladder Senna*
Blueberry	*Boxwood*	*Brazil Nut*
Cactus	*Catalpa*	*Weeping Cedar*

Nabokov's Invented and Real Trees, in Images 197

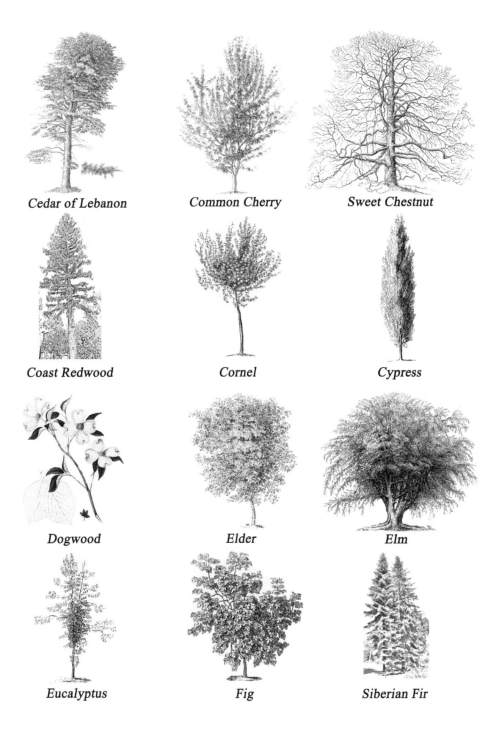

198 Appendices

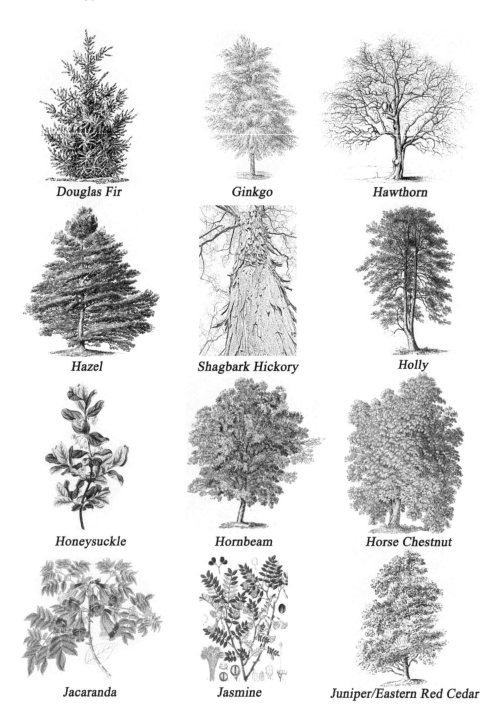

Nabokov's Invented and Real Trees, in Images 199

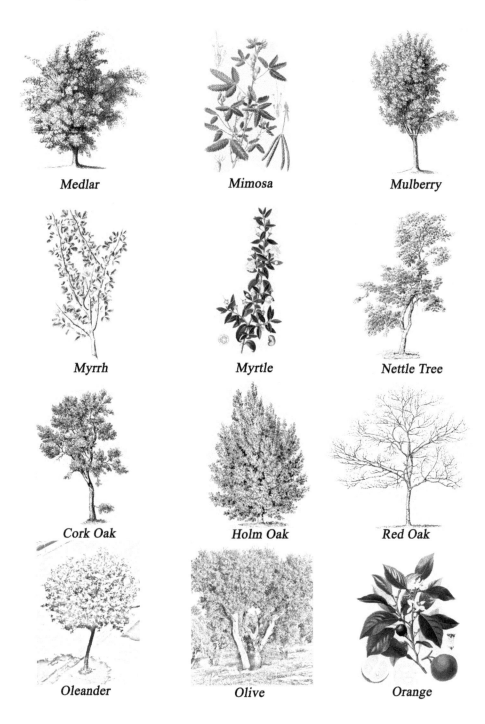

Nabokov's Invented and Real Trees, in Images 201

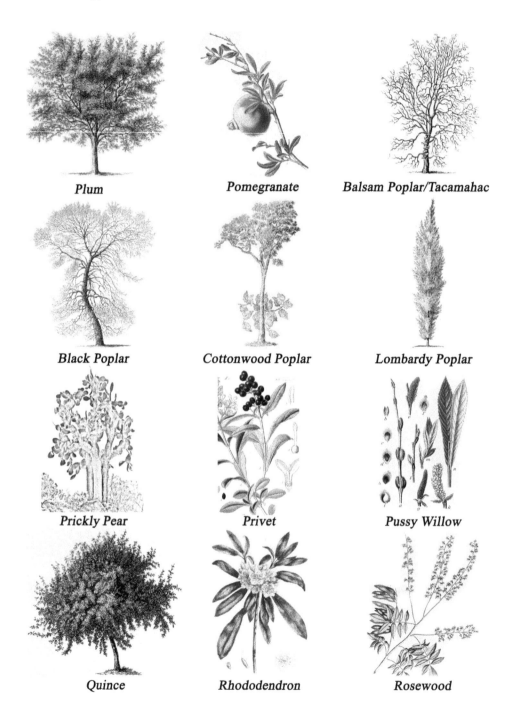

Nabokov's Invented and Real Trees, in Images 203

204   Appendices

Image Credits

Acacia, alder, apple, apricot, arborvitae (thuja), arbutus, pine, ash, aspen, bay (laurel), beech, birch (silver), birch (paper), catalpa, cedar of Lebanon, cherry, chestnut (sweet/American), common quince, cornel, cottonwood, cypress, eastern red cedar, elder, eucalyptus, fig, ginkgo, hackberry (=nettle tree), hawthorn, hazel, holly, hornbeam, horse-chestnut, larch (European and American [=tamarack]), linden, locust, magnolia, medlar, mountain ash, mulberry, oak, oak (cork), oak (holm), pear, plane, plum, poplar (black), poplar (cottonwood), poplar (balsam=tacamahac), poplar (Lombardy), bird-cherry (=racemosa), sycamore (European, g. *Acer*), juniper (=thuja or eastern red cedar), tuliptree (=liriodendron, poplar), walnut, willow (white), willow (weeping), yew: J.C. Loudon, Thordarson Collection, *Arboretum Et Fruticetum Britannicum or: The Trees and Shrubs of Britain Native and Foreign Hardy and Half-Hardy Pictorially and Botanically Delineated and Scientifically and Popularly Described*, 2nd ed. (J.C. Loudon, 1844). Biodiversity Heritage Library. https://doi .org/10.5962/bhl.title.59079

Almond: *Chambers's Encyclopaedia; A Dictionary of Universal Knowledge for the People*, vol. 1 (Philadelphia: J B. Lippincott & Company, 1871; Edinburgh: W. & R. Chambers). https://onlinebooks.library.upenn.edu /webbin/book/lookupid?key=olbp74709

Araucaria: C.A. Johns, *The Forest Trees of Britain*, 2 vols (London, 1847). https://www.biodiversitylibrary.org/item/255342#page/436/mode/1up

Avocado: *Flora Medica Oder Abbildung Der Wichtigsten Officinellen Pflanzen. Mit Berücksichtigung Der Presussischen Und Andrer Neuerer Pharmacopöen Herausgegeben Von David Dietrich. [Heft 1-18]* (1829). https://www .biodiversitylibrary.org/title/6155.

Bilberry: Jan Kops, *Flora Batava,* vol. 14 (Amsterdam, 1872). HathiTrust. https://catalog.hathitrust.org/Record/009707094

Bladder Senna: H.G.A. Engler and K.A.E. Prantl, eds., *Natürliche Pflanzenfamilien*, vol. 3, part 3 (Leipzig: Verlag von Wilhelm Engelman, 1891). https://bibdigital.rjb.csic.es/idurl/1/10935

Blueberry: Amédée Masclef, *Atlas des plantes de France* (1891). https:// commons.wikimedia.org/w/index.php?curid=5767687

Box, myrtle, privet, spiraea: Otto Wilhelm Thomé, *Flora von Deutschland, Österreich und der Schweiz* (Gera, Germany, 1885–). Biodiversity Heritage Library. https://doi.org/10.5962/bhl.title.5360

Brazil-nut tree: Aadapted from Dana B. Merrill. https://commons.wikimedia .org/wiki/File:Vista_Parcial_de_Porto_Velho,_Acervo_do_Museu_Paulista _da_USP.jpg

Cactus: Amante Darmanin from Malta, CC BY 2.0. https://commons
.wikimedia.org/wiki/File:Pachycereus_pringlei_(5782057703).jpg
Cedar, weeping: Ryan Somma, Occoquan, USA, CC BY-SA 2.0. https://
commons.wikimedia.org/wiki/File:Bonzai_Blue_Atlas_Cedar
_%283889954116%29.jpg
Coast redwood: Famartin, CC BY-SA 4.0. https://wellcomecollection.org
/works/kxy3ydks
Date palm: Pearson Scott Foresman. https://commons.wikimedia.org/wiki
/File:Date_palm_2_(PSF).png
Dogwood: Joseph Carson, J.H. Colen, and Robert P. Smith. https://commons
.wikimedia.org/wiki/File:Illustrations_of_medical_botany_(Plate_XLII)
_(7929240990).jpg
Douglas fir: R. Rice et al., *The North American Sylva* (Philadelphia: Rice,
Rutter & Co., 1865), vol. 5, pl. lcxv. https://www.biodiversitylibrary.org
/bibliography/34741
Elm, pine, ponderosa pine: Richard Piper, *Trees of America* (Boston: W. White,
1855–8). https://www.biodiversitylibrary.org/page/37546655
Fir: Crusier, CC BY-SA 3.0. https://commons.wikimedia.org/wiki/File:Abies
_sibirica_HDR.jpg.
Honeysuckle: Curtis plate 1965, via Biodiversity Library, vol. 45, 1818,
Lonicera caerulia. https://www.biodiversitylibrary.org/page/483358
#page/67/mode/1up
Jacaranda: P. Stroobant, *L'Illustration horticole*, vol. 11, t. 391 (1864). https://
commons.wikimedia.org/wiki/File:Jacaranda_puberula.jpg.
Jasmine: Govindoo (art); Robert Wight (text). https://commons.wikimedia
.org/wiki/File:Jasminum_humile_Govindoo.jpg
Lemon: Charles Dessalines d' Orbigny, *Dictionnaire universel d'histoire
naturelle* (Paris, 18479). Biodiversity Heritage Library: https://doi
.org/10.5962/bhl.title.23115
Lilac, palmetto, peach: "Arbres d'ornement," *Larousse du XXème siècle*, 1932.
https://www.flickr.com/photos/149521109@N03/31196536225/, CC0
Lingonberry: Carl Axel Magnus Lindman. https://commons.wikimedia.org
/wiki/File:Vaccinium_vitis-idaea_L.jpg
Mahogany: Mark Catesby, CC BY 4. https://commons.wikimedia.org/wiki
/File:Leaves,_flowers,_fruit_and_seed_pods_of_Mahogany_tree,_1731
_Wellcome_L0035348.jpg
Mangosteen: *Curtis's Botanical Magazine*, v.81=ser.3:v.11 (1855) [no. 4825–90].
Biodiversity Heritage Library. https://www.biodiversitylibrary.org/page
/467747
Maple: British Museum. https://commons.wikimedia.org/wiki/File:Recueil
_d%27%C3%89tudes_d%27Arbres_(BM_1932,1205.12).jpg

206   Appendices

Mimosa: D. Bois et al. *Favourite Flowers of Garden and Greenhouse*, 1896, vol. 1, pl. 70. Biodiversity Heritage Library. https://www.biodiversitylibrary.org/page/36442614

Myrrh, orange, palm, pomegranate, spruce: Gustav Pabst, ed., *Köhler's Medizinal-Pflanzen in naturgetreuen Abbildungen mit kurz erläuterndem Texte* Gera-Untermhaus, Germany, 1887; images from https://commons.wikimedia.org/wiki/Category:K%C3%B6hlers_Medizinal-Pflanzen

Oleander (rose tree): Nicholas Gemini. https://commons.wikimedia.org/wiki/File:Nerium_oleander_in_Catanzaro_19.JPG

Olive: RNBC. CC BY-SA 3.0. https://commons.wikimedia.org/wiki/File:Olea_europaea_subsp_europaeaOliveTree.jpg

Paulownia: Siebold/Zuccarini, *Flora Japonica* (Kurt Stueber, 1870). http://www.biolib.de

Pea-tree: Pierre-Joseph Redouté. https://commons.wikimedia.org/wiki/File:T2_19_Robinia_caragana_par_Pierre-Joseph_Redout%C3%A9.jpeg

Pine, Tauric/Austrian/black: London J. White. *A Description of the Genus Pinus: Illustrated with Figures, Directions Relative to the Cultivation, and Remarks on the Uses of Several Species* (London, 1828–34). Biodiversity Heritage Library. https://doi.org/10.5962/bhl.title.44704

Pisang: François-Pierre Chaumeton et al., 1775–1819. https://commons.wikimedia.org/wiki/File:Banana-Chaumeton,_Fran%C3%A7ois-Pierre.jpg

Prickly pear: Adapted from Joanne Goldby, Birmingham, UK, CC BY-SA 2.0. https://upload.wikimedia.org/wikipedia/commons/7/78/Giant_Prickly_Pear_Cactus_%28Opuntia_echios%29_-_Santa_Fe_Island_-_Gal%C3%A1pagos_Islands_-_Pacific_Ocean_-_14_Sept._2011_-_%281%29.jpg

Pussywillow: Johann Georg Sturm. https://upload.wikimedia.org/wikipedia/commons/c/c0/Salix_purpurea_Sturm25.jpg

Rhododendron: Miller et al., *Figures of the Most Beautiful, Useful and Uncommon Plants Described in "The Gardeners Dictionary"* (London 1760). Bibliothèque nationale de France. https://gallica.bnf.fr/ark:/12148/bpt6k15198147/f215.item#

Rosewood tree (*Dalbergia nigra*): Adapted from Hendrik van Reede tot Drakestein. Wellcome foundation. https://wellcomecollection.org/works/bhb5cy5v

Rowan tree (European): Adapted from Eeno11, CC BY-SA 3.0. https://commons.wikimedia.org/wiki/File:Rowan_tree_20081002b.jpg

Satinwood: Govindoo, in R. H. Beddome, *The Flora Sylvatica for Southern India*, vol. 1, 1873. Biodiversity Heritage Library. https://doi.org/10.5962/bhl.title.57884

Shagbark hickory: Adapted from Plant Image Library, Dcrjsr, CC BY 3.0. https://commons.wikimedia.org/wiki/File:Duke_Forest_shagbark _hickory_trunk.jpg

Sycamore, American (g. *Platanus*): Ernest Haskell, CC0. https://commons .wikimedia.org/wiki/File:Giant_Sycamore_MET_DP846197.jpg

Yucca: Adapted from Bernard Gagnon, CC BY-SA 3.0. https://commons .wikimedia.org/wiki/File:Soaptree_Yucca.jpg

Lists of Trees in Nabokov's Works

Trees, shrubs, and tree-like plants in Nabokov's works

acreana (invented)
alder
almond
apple trees
apple, shattal (not apple, invented)
apricot
araucaria
arborvitae
arbutus
ash
aspen
avocado
bay laurel (*Laurus nobilis*)
beech (American, European)
birch (red-barked, Chinese)
birch, paper
birch, white/silver
black alder
bladder senna
bog bilberry
boxwood
brazil nut

burnberry (invented)
cactus
catalpa
cedar of Lebanon
cedar, weeping (blue Atlas cedar, cultivar)
cherry tree
chestnut, sweet (European) or American
coast redwood (*Sequoia sempervirens*)
cornel
cottonwood poplar
cypress
dogwood
Douglas fir (genus *Pseudotsuga*)
eastern red cedar (=juniper)
elder
elm, American
elm, European (or English)
eucalyptus
fig

fir (unspecified; genus *Abies*)
giant sequoia
ginkgo
hackberry (=nettle tree)
hawthorn
hazel
hickory, shagbark
holly
honeysuckle
honeysuckle, Peruvian
hornbeam (probably American)
horse chestnut
hydrangea shrub
jacaranda
jasmine bush
juniper (general)
kiroku or kiruko (invented)
larch (Eurasian)
larch (tamarack)
laurel (prob. *Kalmia latifolia*)
lemon
lilac (=syringa)

Lists of Trees in Nabokov's Works   209

lilac, Persian
limia, black-leafed
    (invented)
linden
lingonberry (*brusnika*)
locust
magnolia
mahogany
maple (undifferentiated)
medlar
mimosa
mountain ash, American
    (g. *Sorbus*, like rowan)
mulberry
myrrh
myrtle
oak (general)
oak, *Quercus ruslan*
    Chat. (invented)
oak (scrub)
oak, cork
oak, holm
oleander
olive
orange
palm
paulownia
pea-tree
peach

pear
pine (karakul-like)
pine, arolla
pine, general
pine, northern
pine, ponderosa
pine, Tauric (=black,
    Austrian)
pisang
plane tree
plum
pomegranate
poplar (unspecified)
poplar, balsam
    (tacamahac)
poplar, black
poplar, Lombardy
porphyroferous
    (invented)
prickly pear
privet
Pyrospodia (tree or
    genus, invented)
quince
racemosa (old-world
    bird cherry, *Prunus
    padus*)
rhododendron
rose tree

rosewood
rowan (European)
satinwood
spiraea
spruce
sycamore
    (American,
    g. *Platanus*)
sycamore
    (European, *Acer
    pseudoplatanus*;=
    Russian явор
thuja (=arborvitae)
tulip tree
    (=liriodendron)
Vallieria mirifica
    (invented)
walnut
willow, white (=sallow)
willow – high
    mountain
    (invented)
willow, palmoid
willow, pussy-
willow, weeping
    (=Chinese,
    Babylonian)
yew
yucca

All Trees (and Effects) in Nabokov's Poems, by Year

1916	1917	1918	1919	1920	1921	1922
acacia (2)	birch (4)	**almond**	alder (1)	alder (1)	alder (1)	apple (2)
alder (1)	fir (1)	**(1)**	**apple (1)**	birch (4)	birch (6)	birch (2)
aspen (2)	**honeysuckle**	birch (5)	birch (3)	chestnut,	**cedar**	cherry
bird	**(1)**	bird	bird	horse (1)	**Lebanon**	(1)
cherry (1)	linden (2)	cherry	cherry (1)	cypress	**(1)**	cypress
birch (6)	maple (1)	**chestnut**	**cherry (2)**	(1)	**cornel (1)**	(1)
fir (3)	**pine (1)**	**(horse?)**	cypress (1)	**elm (1)**	cypress (1)	fir (2)
lilac (4)	**rowan (1)**	**(1)**	linden (1)	fir (1)	fir (3)	lilac (1)
linden (4)	willow (1)	**cypress**	maple (1)	lilac (1)	lilac (2)	linden (2)
maple (1)	tree, leaves,	**(2)**	**oleander (1)**	linden (1)	linden (1)	maple (1)
oak (1)	etc (6)	**hazel (1)**	olive (1)	oak (2)	lingonberry	oak (1)
poplar (2)		lilac (2)	**palm (1)**	oleander	(1)	olive (1)
willow (1)		linden (3)	**pear (1)**	(1)	maple (3)	pear (1)
shadow,		**mimosa**	**pussywillow**	pine (1)	**medlar (1)**	trees,
dapple		**(1)**	**(1)**	rowan (1)	oak (2)	leaves,
(3)		oak (3)	trees, forest,	willow (1)	palm (1)	etc (5)
tree, foliage,		trees,	etc (4)	trees, etc	pine (2)	shadows
etc: (6)		leaves etc		(6)	poplar (1)	etc (2)
		(5)			willow (2)	
					trees,	
					leaves,	
					etc (10)	
					shadow (1)	

(bold = first instance in the poetry)

All Trees (and Effects) in Nabokov's Poems, by Year 211

1923	1924	1925	1926-30	1931-40	1941 to 1950	1951 on
apple (2)	birch (1)	birch (1)	aspen (1)	birch (2)	fir (2)	fir (2)
birch (1)	beech (1)	chestnut,	Eur. sycamore	linden	birch (2)	oak (2)
bird	lilac (1)	horse (1)	(1)	(3)	poplar (1)	honeysuckle
cherry (1)	oak (2)	fir (3)	alder (2)	light/	linden (1)	(1)
chestnut,	olive (1)	hazel (1)	birch (1)	shadow	willow (1)	lilac (1)
horse (1)	pine (2)	olive (1)	bird cherry (1)	(1)	**chaparral**	maple (1)
fir (4)	poplar (1)	trees etc	chestnut (1)	trees,	**(oak) (1)**	poplar (1)
linden (2)	trees etc	(4)	**Rhododendron**	etc (3)	maple (1)	tree(s) (2)
lingonberry	(6)	shadows	**(1)**		trees etc	woods (2)
(1)	shadows	(2)	evergreen (1)		(1)	branch (1)
oak (1)	(1)	roots (1)	lilac (2)			
olive (1)			pear (1)			
palm (1)			wooden object			
pine (6)			(1)			
plane			trees, leaves,			
tree (1)			etc (2)			
pomegranate						
(1)						
maple (1)						
poplar (1)						
evergreen (1)						
trees,						
leaves, etc						
(18)						

All Trees in Nabokov's Novels and Stories, by Work

Mary	King, Queen, Knave	Defense	Glory		Despair	Invitation to a Beheading
acacia	apple tree	beech	alder	maple	apple tree	apple tree
alder	(in R:	birch	almond tree	medlar	aspen	elderberry
apple tree	patented	conifer	apple tree	mimosa	bay	juniper
birch	tree)	fir	apricot tree	myrtle	beech	laurel
cypress	ash	lilac	birch	nettle tree	birch	lilac
fir	beech	lime	cedar	oak (English)	black-alder	linden
laurel	birch	magnolia	cedar of	oak (scrub)	cactus	locust
lime	fir/	maple	Lebanon	olive	cherry	(akatsiia)
magnolia	Christmas	palm	cherry tree	orange tree	cork oak	oak
mimosa	tree		chestnut	peach tree	cypress	poplar
palm	larch (not in		(horse)	pear tree	linden/lime	rhododendron
pea-tree	Russ.)		conifer	pine	maple	tamarack
pine	linden		cork (oak)	pine,	mimosas	willow
poplar	magnolia		cypress	Karakul-like	oak (implied)	
racemosa	pine		elm	plane tree	pine	
rowan	rose tree		fig	poplar	plane	
	(in R:		fir	rhododendron	rose tree	
	живое		hazel tree	rowan	sallow	
	дерево)		juniper	sallow (ветлы)	(willow)	
	willow		larch	thuja		
			linden			

All Trees in Nabokov's Novels and Stories, by Work   213

The Gift		The Enchanter	RLSK	Bend Sinister	Lolita
acacia	myrtle	chestnut	aspen	alder	almond
alder	oak	apricot	beech	birch	apple tree
aspen	oak, scrub	(preserves)	birch	boxhedge	aspen
birch	oleander		brazil nut	chestnut	beech
cactus	pine		cedar	cottonwood	birch
chestnut (horse)	poplar		chestnut	cypress	catalpa
cypress	rhododendron		elm	fig	chestnut
elder shrub	rose tree		eucalyptus	fir	conifer
elm	rowan		fir	fir, Douglas	elm
fir	sallow (лозняк)		oak	maple	fig
larch	thuja		palm	mountain ash	juniper
laurel	willow		pine	oak	magnolia
lilac			poplar	olive	mahogany
linden			syringa (lilac)	pine	(table)
locust			willow	poplar	mimosa
magnolia			willow, Chinese	rosewood	mulberry
maple			willow, weeping	willow/salix	orange tree
medlar				willow, weeping	palm tree
					pine
					poplar
					tuliptree
					(implied)
					willow
					yucca

214   Appendices

Pnin		Pale Fire		Speak, Memory		Ada
alder	poplar	alder	myrtle	acacia	oak	alder
apple tree	poplar,	araucaria	oak	alder	oleander	apple tree
avocado tree	Lombardy	aspen	oleander	almond	olive	arborvitae
beech	racemosa*	beech	pine	apple tree	orange tree	arbutus
birch	rhododendron	box tree	poplar	arbutus	palm tree	aspen
cactus	rosewood	(boxwood)	rowan	aspen	pea-tree	birch
catalpa	rowan	cedar	sycamore	beech	pine, Crimean	bladder
chestnut	satinwood	(Cedrus)	(Acer)	birch	pine,	senna
cottonwood	scrub oak	cedar	tuliptree	bog bilberry	Ponderosa	boxwood
elm	spruce	(eastern	walnut	cherry tree	poplar,	burnberry
elm	spruce	red,	willow, green	chestnut	Lombardy	bushes
fir	sycamore	Juniperus)	willow,	(horse-)	racemosa*	(invented)
fruit trees	tacamahac	conifers	hoar-leafed	Christmas	sequoia, giant	cacctus
laurel	willow	cypress	willow,	tree	walnut	cedar, of
lilac	mystery tree	date palm	weeping	cypress	willow	Lebanon
linden	(unnamed)	dogwood	yew	elm	willow,	cedar,
locust		elfinwood		fir	Babylonian	sealyham
mahogany		elm		honesuckle	willow,	(=weeping)
maple		fig		hydrangea	palmoid	cherry tree
nettle tree		ginkgo/		larch	yucca	chestnut
oak		maidenhair		laurel		conifer
palm tree		hazel tree		lilac		cornel
pine		hickory,		linden		cypress
		shagbark		maple		ebony
		jacaranda		mimosa		elm
		juniper				fir
		larch				fruit tree
		lilac				ginkgo/
		locust				maidenhair/
		mulberry				Chinese
						tree
						holly

*racemosa=old world bird cherry

		Transparent Things	*Look at the Harlequins!*	Trees in the stories	
honeysuckle	plum	beech	alder	acacia	lemon tree
jacaranda	poplar	alder	araucaria	acreana	lilac
juniper	poplar,	apple tree	arbutus	alder	lilac, Persian
larch	Lombardy	birch	ash	almond	limia
laurel	pseudoacacia	cedar	aspen	apple tree	linden
lilac	(locust,	cherry tree	beech	araucaria	locust
linden	pea-tree)	chestnut	Christmas tree	aspen	maple
liriodendron	*Quercus ruslan*	fir	horse chestnut	balsa	mimosa
(=tuliptree)	Chat.	juniper	kew tree	beech	mulberry
locust	(oak, invented)	larch	(ginkgo)	birch	oak
magnolia	racemosa*	pine	larch	chestnut	oleander
mahogany	coast redwood	rhododendron	lilac	Christmas tree	palm
maple	(*Sequoia*	rowan	linden	cypress	pine
medlar	*sempervirens*)	willow	locust	elm	plane tree
mulberry	scrub oak/		myrtle	eucalyptus	poplar
myrrh	chaparral		oak	fir	porphyroferous
oak	shattal apple		oak, holm	hawthorn	trees
olive	(invented)		palm	hazelnut tree	quince
palm	spiraea		pine	juniper	rhododendron
paulownia	Tree of		plane tree	kiroku	tuliptree
pear	Knowledge		plum, balanic	larch	willow
pine	walnut		poplar	laurel	yule tree
pine, arolla	willow		prickly-pear		
pine, Scots	willow,		willow		
(*Pinus*	babylonian				
silvestris)	willow,				
pisang	high-mountain				
(plantain,	(invented)				
banana)	yew				
	yucca				

*racemosa=old world bird cherry

List of Trees and Shrubs Mentioned in the Works of Shakespeare

almond
apple (also crab, pippin)
apricot
ash
aspen
balsam and balsamum
bay
bilberry
birch
box
cedar
cherry
chestnut
cork
currant
cypress
dogberry
ebony
eglantine
elder

elm
fig
filbert
gooseberry
harlock (burdock)
hawthorn
hazel
hebanon (possibly yew)
hemlock
holly
holy thistle
honeysuckle
laurel
lemon
lime
locust
medlar
mulberry
musk rose
myrtle

nutmeg
oak
olive
orange
osier (willow)
palm tree
peach
pear
pine
plane tree
plum
pomegranate
quince
senna
sycamore
walnut
willow
woodbine (honeysuckle)
wormwood
yew

Notes

Introduction

1 Appel, "Remembering Nabokov," 13.
2 The number can go much higher – up to, say, at least 250 (5,000 years), but not for trees people are in regular contact with.
3 The longest-lived vertebrates may push to 500 years, along with bivalves; some invertebrates can be many thousands of years old through cloning. https://www .livescience.com/longest-living-animals.html; https://en.wikipedia.org/wiki /List_of_longest-living_organisms
4 The passage goes on to specify how these and other varying forms of subjectivity combine to form reality, which can never really be fully objective.
5 Nabokov, in fact, gives "locust," "false acacia," as well as "acacia" in translations of his own works where *akatsiia* appears, suggesting a similar principle at play. A similar kind of specificity can be found in his treatment of evergreens' cones in *Madame Bovary*: Leopold Reigner reports that in Nabokov's copy of the English translation, he complains about pine cones which Flaubert has located beneath fir trees; see his "History, Geography and 'Reality' in Nabokov's Invented Worlds: The Process of Specialization," in *Nabokov Online Journal* 15 (2021): 15.
6 One wonders whether Nabokov might also have had in mind here the Russian poet Nikolai Gumilyov, author of another poem called "Trees" ("Derev'ia"): one of Nabokov's latest lyrics written in Russian begins, "*Kak ia liubil stikhi Gumileva!*" (How I loved the poems of Gumilyov!). As will be addressed in chapter 1 and elsewhere, poplars (but not this kind of poplar) play a special role in Nabokov's creative biography. One possible source for Nabokov's information about Joyce Kilmer's trees is listed in ch. 4, n. 29.
7 See ch. 4, n. 30.
8 Interview with Douglas M. Davis for the *National Observer* in 1964 (TWS 337).
9 This epigram was included in a letter to his wife Véra on 5 July 1926 (LTV 120). The complete excerpt from the letter, with epigram, is as follows: Something like

218   Notes to pages 9–16

an epigram on Aikhenvald: "He judges nothing as if superior, / amateur of words, the word's lover [language's paramour]. / A Pushkin verse sits in his name: / 'The wide-noised oak grove'* ..." / "Что-то вроде эпиграммы на Айхенвальда. / Он свысока не судит ничего, – / любитель слов, любовник слова. / Стих Пушкина есть в имени его: 'Широкошумная дуброва'* ..." (PV 144, cf. LTV 120; my translation differs from Boyd/Tolstoy's in a few key respects).

*adapted from Pushkin, "The Poet," 1827, final line. In Pushkin, these words are plural.

See also ch. 5, n. 25.

10 Original: "У лукоморья дуб зеленый / златая цепь на дубе том / и днем и ночью кот ученый / все ходит по цепи кругом." I have used the archaisms "golde" and "chaine" to approximate the poetic-archaic "zlataia" (cf. modern *zolotaia*," dominant also in Pushkin's time). Pushkin added this "Prologue" to his narrative poem in 1828 (it was composed in 1824), years after the work's first publication.

11 In the appendices, I provide a chart showing the density of trees over time in the poetry.

12 A little-known photograph of this tree, with Nabokov among its branches, was shot by Henry Grossman for *Life* magazine on 5 October 1964. The Berg Collection improperly, but aptly for this study, labelled it in the finding aid as "Photograph of Vladimir Nabokov standing among pine trees." Cf. Nabokov's comment for a 1965 interview, about the Montreux Palace garden and its tree: "I'm especially fond of its weeping cedar, the arboreal counterpart of a very shaggy dog with hair hanging over its eyes" (SO 55).

13 Noted in Boyd, *AdaOnline*, commentary to 211.01. http://www.ada.auckland .ac.nz/

14 Deleuze and Guattari, *Thousand Plateaus*, 5–25. It is also worth considering what neither Deleuze and Guattari nor Nabokov could have known or suspected: that trees are in fact intimately connected with one another through a mycorrhizal network in the soil, sharing food and information. Suzanne Simard began publishing this work with her team in an article in *Nature* in 1997. See Simard et al., "Net Transfer." This work led to the coining of the term "wood wide web."

15 See the full discussion in Deleuze and Guattari, *Thousand Plateaus*, 22.

16 For three examples across time see, e.g., Couturier, *Nabokov ou la tyrannie de l'auteur* (Paris: Seuil, 1993); Voronina, "Nabokov's Shakespeare"; Frye, "Performing Tyranny, Purloining Authority."

17 A few representative works in this vein: Frank, *Nabokov's Theatrical Imagination*; Hamrit, *Authorship in Nabokov's Prefaces*; Blackwell, "Nabokov's 'The Gift,'" and much of Brian Boyd's work (especially *Nabokov's "Pale Fire"*).

18 Deleuze and Guattari address the rhizomatic quality of the brain, and reject the term "dendrites" for the connecting parts of cells: "What are wrongly called

Notes to pages 16–26   219

'dendrites' do not assure the connection of neurons in a continuous fabric" (*Thousand Plateaus*, 15).

19 Nabokov, emphasis added. Boyd and Pyle, "Nearctic Forms of *Lycaeides* Hüb.," 280.

20 Here too we find "porphyroferous" trees (SoVN 297), which may be merely an adjective suggesting that they held fruits the colour of porphyry. The likely inspiration for these two names turned up by chance during final manuscript preparation: see *Notizblatt des Königl*, 307. (*Bauhinia acreana* and *B. porphyrotrica* appear as consecutive "New Species" descriptions on this page.)

21 Nabokov, *Lolita: A Screenplay*, ix. Andrei Babikov drew my attention to this invented tree over a decade ago, for which I am grateful.

22 Letter to Bobbie Ann Rawlings (Mason), 29 January 1973. In Berg Collection as "Corrections to *Nabokov's Garden* by Bobbie Ann Rawlings."

23 See the notes on firs and spruces in chapter 1, nn. 35 & 38.

24 Helfant, *That Savage Gaze*, xvii.

25 Hodge, *Hunting Nature*, 11.

26 Costlow, *Heart-Pine Russia*, 5.

27 See Blackwell, *The Quill*, ch. 4.

1 Nabokov's Origins in the Poetry of Trees

1 Nabokov, "The Madman," *Selected Poetry*, 94.

2 Exceptions to this neglect include Mason, *Nabokov's Garden*; Boyd (various); Blackwell, "Reflections on (and of) Trees"; Hetenyi, "Lolita as Goddess." For a first fairly deep study of the theme, see a very recent master's thesis: Nemzer, "A Birch." I had completed a draft of this study when I read Nemzer's thesis; a few of our findings overlap, but for the most part our approaches differ. There have also been several related discussions on *Nabokv-L* and thenabokovian.org, with specific observations by Jerry Friedman, Jansy Mello, Dieter E. Zimmer, Alexey Sklyarenko; some of these will be acknowledged at appropriate moments in the text.

3 Some of the others are Robert Michael Pyle, Robert Dirig, Victoria N. Alexander, John Kopper, listed in the bibliography. The neglect of "nature" as a focus of research is ending; by the time this book appears, the French Vladimir Nabokov Society will have hosted the conference "Vladimir Nabokov: Writing Nature / Écrire la nature," in Lausanne, Switzerland, in June 2023.

4 Tudge, *Secret Life of Trees*, 13–16.

5 There were several other discarded candidates for the memoir's title; these are presented by Andrei Babikov in "Nakhodchivaia Mnemozina," and in his book *Prochtenie Nabokova*, 581–2.

6 In the *New Yorker* version, he locates the composition of his *first poem* to this room, rather than "youthful verse," but it is already changed by the time *Conclusive Evidence* (version two) was published. The last part of the sentence is new in *Speak,*

220   Notes to pages 26–32

Memory, where it replaces yet another version introduced in *Drugie berega/Other Shores*.

7 "... later I transported the whole edifice into my first tale [*povest'*], as one transports a disassembled castle across the ocean."

8 One should recall here Pekka Tammi's extremely apt and useful formulation of the relationship between biography and art in Nabokov's case: "A motif originating in the author's own life conjoins a network of subtextual, cross-linguistic, and transcultural echoes. It is very much due to such interlocking that the Nabokovian corpus of fictional and autobiographical writings can be said to assume the shape of a synchronic, multidimensional whole." Tammi, "Reading in Three Dimensions," in *Russian Subtexts in Nabokov's Fiction*, 64.

9 Afanasy Fet, who wrote many poems mentioning the trills of nightingales, such as his poem "Whispers, timid breathing" ("Shepot, robkoe dykhanie," 1850), which is misquoted by Nikolay Chernyshevski in *The Gift* (who gives "shelest," "rustle," instead of "whisper"), as an example of a poem frivolously lacking verbs (G 240; cf SSRP 5:418). The English tranlsation abandons the misquotation.

10 It appears that the cognate word *makhagoni* did not exist or was not in general usage at the time Nabokov was writing; it is not to be found in *Dal'*, *Brokgaus-Efron*, or the mid-twentieth-century four-volume Ushakov dictionary (Moscow: Ogiz, 1930–1940).

11 The last phrase was first introduced in *Drugie berega/Other Shores* (SSRP 5:194), and preserved in *Speak, Memory*.

12 This is my translation of the *Drugie berega* text, which, though it came first, is uncharacteristically more expressive than the later version. In *Speak, Memory*, we find: "long, straight strokes of his elegantly held, incredibly sharp pencil caused the lines of the room he created out of nothing (abstract walls, receding ceiling and floor) to come together in one remote hypothetical point with tantalizing and sterile accuracy" (SM 91). Nabokov clearly wanted to create a more precise and detailed picture of what Cummings would teach (here, the "laws of perspective"), but he also appears to have decided in this case to separate the pencil-based lessons from the themes within the watercolours, such as "magical strokes" and "infinite, far-away points." As seen above, he reintroduced those themes in a new section on the painter's watercolours.

13 *Annotated Lolita*, 414.

14 Boyd, *Nabokov: The American Years*, 392.

15 Boyd makes a similar point about this scene: *Nabokov: The American Years*, 158; see also 138.

16 According to Véra Nabokov, it was awaiting one final pruning at the time of Nabokov's death, and she published the list as it was then.

17 See especially Morris, *Nabokov: Poetry and the Lyric Voice*, 96–8 and 396n1; Boyd, *Nabokov: The Russian Years*, 108–9; and Zholkovsky, "Poem, Problem, Prank," 22.

Notes to pages 32–4   221

18 In Nabokov's late novel *Transparent Things*, the narrator(s) can see the temporal depth, or layered past, of physical objects in the present.

19 This sentence offers a crucial example of the theme of "dappling" in connection with consciousness and creativity, with its first instance (in the autobiography) in the initial scene of Nabokov's discovery of time and his self-conscious "I" (SM 21–2); echoes can be found throughout Nabokov's works.

20 See in particular the discussion in Malikova, "Pervoe stikhotvorenie."

21 The question of "sincerity" has, in my view, been neglected among Nabokov scholars. Although Nabokov publicly scorned the lazy use of terms like "simple and sincere," the concept and its place in his works deserves significant attention.

22 Alexander Zholkovsky incorrectly suggests that the chapter's publication in *Partisan Review* was presented as fiction. "Poem, Problem, Prank," 22. Cf. *Partisan Review* 16, no. 9 (XVI; September 1949), table of contents.

23 Nabokov's translation, NSP 69. The original: "Дождь пролетел и сгорел на лету / Иду по румяной дорожке. / Иволги свищут, рябины в цвету, / Белеют на ивах сережки. / Воздух живителен, влажен, душист. / Как жимолость благоухает! / Кончиком вниз наклоняется лист / И с кончика жемчуг роняет" (PP 18).

24 Boyd makes clear that the 1914 poem was not "The Rain Has Flown" (*Nabokov: The Russian Years*, 108), and that the scene in chapter 11 of *Speak, Memory* does not describe that 1917 poem, though it does seem to evoke it. I will argue for a nuanced palimpsest of memories. Morris, *Nabokov: Poetry and the Lyric Voice*, 396n1, points out the important connection between honeysuckle in the poem (*zhimolost'*, given by Nabokov with the obscure term "caprifole") and the same plant's "curiously whimsical" presence in the memoir's index. Relevant to my formulation here, in one of the indexed references to "honeysuckle" (SM 76), Nabokov is describing his five-year-old self reminiscing about the oak alley and the honeysuckles at Vyra, remembered from a year before; as he says, "The recollection of that recollection is sixty years older than the latter, but far less unusual."

25 See Morris's discussion of debates about this notion (previous note). In *Speak, Memory*, Nabokov claims to have made his first butterfly catch from a honeysuckle: a swallowtail that the janitor Ustin bagged with his cap (SM 120).

26 Of his recent credo, Nabokov writes in *Poems and Problems*, "What about faithfully englishing one's own verse, written half a century or a quarter of a century ago? One has to fight a vague embarrassment; one cannot help squirming and wincing; one feels rather like a potentate swearing allegiance to his own self or a conscientious priest blessing his own bathwater." But, he insists, "a horrid sense of falsification makes one scamper back and cling like a baby ape to rugged fidelity. There is only one little compromise I have accepted: whenever possible, I have welcomed rhyme, or its shadow" (PP 14). In the case of "sallow" and "caprifole," Nabokov does not violate literalism, but he certainly is pushing it to its limit in terms of register.

222 Notes to pages 35–6

27 Nabokov often refers to lindens as limes, after the British tradition.

28 Of course, I may be retrospectively projecting this linden into the poem, based solely on the "evidence" of the other passages, which is not really evidence at all, as far as this poem is concerned. However, the undeniable existence of the parallels between the scenes clearly invites such imaginative leaps by a reader thinking about Nabokov's art

29 The Russian title has a different literal translation; it was an archaic term, a collective singular noun meaning roughly "sprites" (cf. Boyd, *Nabokov: The Russian Years*, 180), or "magical creatures," but perhaps with a hint of life's destruction during the revolution, the form also evokes a negation, as in "not to live" (ne-zhit'). The Russian word is also homonymous with the verb "to be tender" (towards a thing or person). See Dal's dictionary (online) under "nezhiloe": "everything [anthropomorphic] that lives not as a human being, lives without a soul and without flesh, but in the form of a human: house-sprite (*domovoi*), field-sprite (*polevoi*), water-demon (*vodianoi*), wood-sprite (*leshii*), water-sprite (*rusalka*), kikimora [a malevolent house spirit]"; http://slovardalja.net/word .php?wordid=19498. Cf. Ushakov's *Tolkovyi slovar' russkogo iazyka* (published 1934–40), https://ushakovdictionary.ru/word.php?wordid=35108. A.N. Afanasiev collected one of the largest compendiums of Russian folk takes, including many that include wood-sprites. See *Narodnye russkie skazki A. N. Afanasieva: v 3 tt.* (Moscow: Literaturnye pamiatniki, 1984–85 [3 vols.]). A source of the "learned cat" appears in Afanasiev no. 286, in vol. 2, 303–6; online at http://feb-web.ru/feb /skazki/default.asp?/feb/skazki/texts/af0/af2/af2r-296.html.

30 "Зелененьким юрким внучатам / наказывал леший в бору: / 'По черным ветвям, по зубчатым, / жар-птица порхнет ввечеру; // поймайте ее, лешенёчки, / и клетку из лунных лучей / возьмите у ключницы-ночки, / да так, чтоб не видел Кащей.'"

31 Cf. "Koshcheev" in the "Gift 2" draft, a surprising distortion of the character name "Koncheyev," the poet admired by the novel's protagonist. "Dar. Chast' II," in Babikov, *Prochtenie Nabokova*, 338–59.

32 The emphasis on the branches or twigs also echoes Nabokov's twig-driven drawing lessons from Dobuzhinsky.

33 "Но утром, как пламя живое, / на пыльном пороге моем / лежало перо огневое / с цветным удлиненным глазком. / Ну что ж, и за этот подарок / спасибо, лесные друзья. / Я беден, и день мой неярок, / и как же обрадован я."

34 Here and elsewhere, I will follow Nabokov's practice in translating "el' " as "fir," although in fact it is "spruce" in modern usage.

35 Nabokov's poem is not at all like Pushkin's (which contains extensive biblical imagery about the prophet's experience); however, in the context of the poem's historical reception, reading "The Quill" this way has some attraction. See ch. 3, n. 29. Vladimir Solovyov began a tradition of interpreting Pushkin's "Prophet" as an allegory of the poet; Khodasevich rejected this view. With other poems like "The

Poet" (1827) and "The Muse" (1821) in mind, the case seems rather ambiguous. See Vladimir Solov'ev, "Znachenie poezii"; Khodasevich, "'Zhrebii Pushkina'"; also Makarova, "Vl. Solov'ev o 'Proroke.'" Nabokov approached the theme from a more seriously metaphysical angle in his 1923 story "The Word."

36 Cf. *Glory*, whose point is the apparent aimlessness and pointlessness of protragonist Martin Edelweiss's life (Gl x). Martin echoes the magical connection from the firebird's quill, by means of his genealogy in Russian magical lore via the indrik-beast; additionally, his mother spent her childhood summers in "Olkhovo," from "ol'kha," alder. Note also that in a passage explored above, discussing his "first poem," Nabokov placed the conclusion of his first poetic effort in a pine grove, linking that reminiscence to the locale of the wood-sprites' efforts to catch the firebird for the poem's lyric hero. Olga Voronina suggests an alternative, also quite helpful, interpretation, linking the quill's appearance with the "vain gift, chance gift" from Pushkin's famous poem, so important in the *The Gift* and its offshoot called in English "Father's Butterflies"; see especially Boyd and Pyle, *Nabokov's Butterflies*, 234. On this reading, "The Quill," like *The Gift*, offers a rebuttal to Pushkin's pessimistic sentiment in this 1828 poem.

37 Along with the poem-triptych "Skazanie" (A Legend), published the same day in *Rul'* (7 January 1921), see SSRP 1:759. In her commentary to this story, Maria Malikova points out that it also echoes Alexander Blok's lyric poem "Bolotnye cherteniatki" (The Swamp Demonlings, 1905), SSRP 1:759, which notably offers a precursor for Nabokov's "woodspritelings" in "The Quill." The triptych includes the poems "And I saw: the vault of heaven darkened" (I videl ia, kak stemneli neba svody), "Crossbearers" (Krestonostsy), and "Peacocks" (Pavliny), later collected in *The Empyrian Path* (*Gornii put'*), SSRP 1:478, 510, 537, 785–6. The story and poem cycle were published as Christmas texts (appearing on the day of Orthodox Christmas, 7 January). The poem "Peacocks" includes dropped feathers (from which Mary weaves a crown for Christ's head). The combination of this first-person story with its magical visitor, the poems, and the new *nom de plume* Sirin with its similarly legendary overtones, appears to mark a deliberate if lightly veiled "coming out" or arrival of Sirin the writer, after a series of other pseudonymous and non-pseudonymous publications. Boyd's discussion points out that this day, and these two works, mark the first appearances of the name "Sirin," and he quotes Nabokov's early English essay "Painted Wood," *Carousel* 2 (1923): 9, as a sign of "his more unexpected link to Russia's bright supernatural fancies" (Boyd, *Nabokov: The Russian Years*, 181). See also TWS, 28–30. Very likely the later "The Quill," with its fiery feather token bestowed by the wood-sprites, evolved as Nabokov continued, in early 1921, to contemplate the imagery he had presented on his first public day as Sirin.

38 "Сонет. Безоблачная высь и тишина … / Голубоватый снег; оцепененье; / Ветвей немых узорное сплетенье — / Моя страна — волшебная страна. / Когда в снегу сияющем она / Стоит как серебристое виденье — / Душа в

таинственное влюблена, / В душе покой и кроткое смиренье. / 'Березка стройная под дымкой снежной, / Ты заколдована, скажи, навек? / Наверно, девушкой была ты нежной ...' / 'Ты, елочка, устала? Давит снег? / Ну погоди, я осторожно сброшу / С ветвей поникших снеговую ношу ...'" The poem has "elochka," diminutive from *el'*, spruce, but Nabokov most often rendered this word as "fir" in his own self-translations (see note 33, above, on firs and spruces). The trees look similar, and while he did add "spruce" to his English fairly late in life, it seems he did not differentiate between them early on. I thus choose his "standard" translation simply to conform to his practices. The earliest appearance of the Russian word for "fir," "pikhta," in any of his works seems to have been in the English-language story "The Forgotten Poet" (1944), which quotes the title character's lines in idiosyncratic transliteration: "sibirskikh pikht oogrewmyi shorokh s podzemnoy snositsa roodoy"; however, the story provides a divergent translation: "the gloomy sough of Siberian larches communicates with the underground ore" (CS, 572). From the choice of "larch" here in 1944, elsewhere usually given its standard Russian "listvennitsa," we can conclude that Nabokov was still feeling his way among the conifers at this time, or, just as plausibly, the translation is deliberately as rough as the transliteration, or else based strictly on sound contours. The Siberian fir, *Abies sibirica*, is indeed not a larch – which are common in Nabokov's works. "Pikhta" appears to be completely absent from Nabokov's own poetry. It appears that the taxonomy organizing firs (g. *Abies* today) and spruces (*Picea*) was not firmly established in Nabokov childhood and early adulthood (the species in these genera are visually similar, and even scientific botanical volumes conflated them in the nineteenth century).

39 We see a similar empathy in "Osen'" ("Autumn," 1923): "Была в тот день светлей и шире даль, / В тот день упал увядший лист кленовый ... / Он первый умер – дымчато-лиловый, / Весь нежная, покорная печаль ... / Он падал медленно; мне было больно. / Он, может быть, не знал, что упадет / И в тихий, слишком тихий день умрет – / Такой красивый и такой безвольный." Compare also "A Birch Tree in Vorontsov Park" (1918).

40 Unpublished until 1923's *Empyrian Path*. "Son na Akropole," SSRP 1:527.

41 "А там вдали, меж полем и деревней, / я вижу лес, – как молодость, веселый, березовый, бледно-зеленый лес, / и просветы тропинок своенравных ... / Как хочется предаться их извивам, / блуждать, мечтать, срывать кору с берез / и обнимать янтарный, влажный ствол – / льнуть, льнуть к нему и грудью и губами / и кровь его медовую впивать!" Olga Voronina points out an important kinship here with the tone in Pushkin's lyric, "Vnov' ia posetil" ("I visited anew," 1835), with the speaker's extended address to a group of pines (personal communication). The poem's third verse paragraph offers an extended meditation on the pine grove and its evolution: "Here, whenever by them / alone I used to pass on horseback in the moonlight, / their friendly summits soughing in the wind / would greet me wistfully. Now I come

riding / again along that road, and there before me / again I see them loom. they have not altered, / they greet me with the same familiar murmer"; the poet's engagement with the trees continues for seventeen more lines, welcoming the new generation, and imagining his progeny's encounters with the saplings' future grandness (thus, the trees are another example of a source of both recollection and prospective recollection in the future, by one's not-yet-born kin). Nabokov translated this poem in the early 1950s for his cousin Nicholas Nabokov's *The Return of Pushkin: Elegy in Three Parts, for High Voice and Orchestra*; see Nabokov, *Verses and Versions*, 200–3 (esp. 201, 203), and 408–9.

42 For example: "mramornye glyby ... pokhozhi na mertvetsov s purpurnymi rtami."

43 "На кладбище – солнце, сирень и березки / и капли дождя на блестящих крестах. / Местами отлипли сквозные полоски / и в трубки свернулись на светлых стволах. // Люблю целовать их янтарные раны, / люблю их стыдливые гладить листки … / То медом повеет с соседней поляны, / то тиной потянет с недальной реки. // Прозрачны и влажны зеленые тени. / Кузнечики тикают – шепчут кусты, – / и бледные крестики тихой сирени / кропят на могилах сырые кресты" (SSRP 1:461).

44 Discussed at some length by Boris Kats, "'Exegi Monumentum' Vladimira Nabokova: K prochteniiu stikhotvoreniia 'Kakoe sdelal ia durnoe delo,'" *Staroe literaturnoe obozrenie* 1 (2001). https://magazines.gorky.media/slo/2001/1 /8220-exegi-monumentum-8221-vladimira-nabokova.html. Kats identifies a telling parallel between the author's pen name and the tree/shrub's name precisely in the shadow of twigs "on the marble of my arm/hand" – a key image in the post-*Lolita* poem "What is the evil deed"(SP 125). Jane Grayson was one of the first to posit the presence of a Sirin reference in *siren*': "The Russian version [of *Despair*] contained a pun upon Nabokov's surname and his pen-name Sirin: 'malinovoi siren'yu v nabokoi vaze," *Nabokov Translated*, 66n2.

45 *Glory*, 1 and 5; it is hard to find good information in English on the indrik-beast. I recommend loading the Russian Wikipedia page, and machine-translating it. The English page gives minimal information. In all versions, including Dal' (*Tolkovyi slovar'*), it is the "father of all beasts"; https://ru.wikipedia.org/wiki/индрик. Thus, it represents not only a source in the folkloric bestiary, but perhaps in the very origins of folklore itself (or at least of its animal kingdom). Surely it is no accident that the name "Indrikov" appears in *Glory*'s very first sentence.

46 Berg Collection, Prose and Poetry Notebook, Album 22, 126–7.

47 "Моя душа—аллея тополей, / высоких, сумрачных, и мягких, неуклонно / идут они, идут, а к радости своей / не приближаются … но если отдаленной / повеет музыкой из сказочной страны, / и ветер сладостный сквозь траурные сны / тех чутких тополей душисто простр[у]ится, / тогда, исполнившись блаженства и едва, / едва затрепетав, их темная листва / внезапно светится, волнисто серебрится."

48 "Liubliu zverei, derev'ia, Boga."

226   Notes to pages 45–50

2 Trees on the Mind: Consciousness and Memory

1   Most days, in other words, not spent in crowded subways or stadiums and the like.
2   See Nabokov's discussion of "reality" and "ghosts" in *Strong Opionions*, p. 11; compare to this also to Tolstoy's diary discussion of one's habitual non-perceptions of surroundings and actions, mentioned in Viktor Shklovsky, "Art, as Device," 162.
3   Boyd, *Nabokov: The American Years*, 161–5.
4   This tree-driven dappling, we see again and again, is nearly always linked to consciousness. Cf. *The Defense* (discussed below), and *Ada* (discussed in chapter 6).
5   Jack did live a few years longer, so it is conceivable that Nabokov might have met him at a social occasion (he lived in Walpole, dying there in 1949 aged about eighty-eight, and later in life his trips to Cambridge were presumably rare). For a history of Jack's time at the Arnold Arboretum, and his biography, see Pearson, "John George Jack," 2–11. See also "Studying Trees at the Arnold Arboretum," and Jack, "John George Jack."
6   Juliar, "Al'manakh: Dva puti," in *Nabokov Bibliography*.
7   Cf. Brian Boyd's full discussion, *Nabokov: The Russian Years*, 108.
8   See, for example, Foster, *Nabokov's Art of Memory*; an anthology has appeared on the topic: Księżopolska and Wiśniewski, *Vladimir Nabokov and the Fictions of Memory*.
9   See Avital Nemzer's useful and expansive discussion of the complexity of pathetic fallacy in Nabokov (particularly with reference to trees), "A Birch …," 16–19.
10   Nabokov's phrasing here invites a useful contrast with Humbert's comment in *Lolita*, composed a few years after the fact, about having "safely solipsized" his victim: in his case, the real girl dissolves into his fantasy, whereas in Nabokov's case he "parted the fabric of fancy" and embraced the physical and human reality of Shulgin.
11   Cf. Boyd: "For Nabokov, the love of parent and child and man and woman are such extraordinary forces they make more urgent than anything else his question: 'what are the limits of my being?'" (*Nabokov: The Russian Years*, 160). See also Barabtarlo, "Nabokov's Trinity."
12   Cf. Boyd, *Nabokov: The Russian Years*, 112–13; John Burt Foster discusses *Mary* in relation to themes of memory in Nietzsche and Baudelaire: *Nabokov's Art of Memory*, 33–41. For Nabokov's statement, see SSRP 5:193, and translation above, ch. 1, n. 7.
13   Ganin's creative relationship to the beloved also echoes Nabokov's: "Now, many years later, he felt that their imaginary meeting and the meeting which took place in reality had blended and merged imperceptibly into one another, since as a living person she was only an uninterrupted continuation of the image which had foreshadowed her" (M 44, SSRP 2:77). Compare this formulation also to the

reminiscing-hallucinatory arrangement of the late poem "The Poplar," discussed below.

14 Curiously, when Ganin says, "Pull yourself together," in response to his fear that he could die before making it to Saturday and Mary's arrival, his chosen verb, in Russian, is "podtianut'sia" –directly (if perfectively) echoing at a key moment the poet's surname, Podtyagin (cf. *podtiagivat'*, to pull up or tighten).

15 Boyd, *Nabokov: The Russian Years*, 249.

16 Maxim D. Shrayer perceptively notes that that much of the flora in the story matches Orpheus's journey to the underworld in Ovid, and – especially intriguing – that leaves in the Russian that had been "pale" (*vialye*), and "faded," (*bleklye*), became "dead" in the English version. *The World of Nabokov's Stories*, 106–7.

17 Boyd, *Nabokov: The Russian Years*, 249–50.

18 Albeit in the heat of his affair with Irina Guadanini (4 April 1937, LTV 349; cf. *Pis'ma k Vere*, 289). "The Encounter" appears in Brian Boyd's translation.

19 See discussion of *Eugene Onegin* 1.L, in EO 2, 189–92; "A Guide to Berlin," in CS, 160.

20 The "gleaming dot" is apparently ("obviously" to Luzhin, but perhaps not so definitively to the reader) coming from the "telephone support"; however, the "shiny object" that the musician plays with is the box of chess pieces, and could also produce this "dot." More important than the fact that telephones often incorporated wood in those days (around 1910) is the fact that the musician's connection to the phone recalls the ringing that Luzhin hears from the attic (with its cracked chessboard) after his first escape, and foreshadows the insistent, repeated phone calls from Valentinov that initiate his tragic finale. This fatidic role for telephones can be found throughout Nabokov's works, in *Speak, Memory*, *The Gift*, *Lolita*, *Pnin*, and several other novels.

21 Original: "derev'ianno-rassypchatyi zvuk" (SSRP 5:330).

22 Nabokov's geography teacher, mentioned in Boyd, *Nabokov: The Russian Years*, who is transformed artistically in "Orache" (CS 325) and *The Gift* (G 135) as Berezovski, was named Berezin (Nikolai Ilyich), from *berëza* (birch). This figure plays a crucial role in each of his appearances. See Boyd, *Nabokov: The Russian Years*, 100–1. Discussed further in chapter 3. The last line of poetry Nabokov wrote before leaving St. Petersburg forever (November 2 o.s., 15 n.s.) 1917, was "'Tell me, birch …' but the birch weeps" (Berg Collection Nabokov Papers, Stikhotvorenie [Album B], p. 24), discussed in Boyd, *Nabokov: The Russian Years*, 134.

23 As suggested in the introduction, the recurring theme of lilacs (g. *Syringa*, and given as "syringa" in *The Real Life of Sebastian Knight*), may in many cases be intended to invoke the mythological origins of pan pipes.

24 Also significant, the geography teacher (whose absence lets Luzhin witness his first true chess match) is named "Valentin Ivanovich," fatidically anticipating Valentinov, who takes over as Luzhin's "chess father." In the course of the novel,

228   Notes to pages 59–67

Luzhin misplaces three canes, a series echoed by Nabokov forty years later in the story of Van, in *Ada*. See further discussion of Luzhin's canes, below.

25 "The life of the artist and the life of a device in the consciousness of an artist – this is Sirin's theme," as Vladislav Khodasevich famously wrote. Khodasevich, "On Sirin."

26 It is useful to keep in mind that here, "talent" retains primarily its Russian overtones (*talant*): Nabokov means, essentially, "creative gift."

27 Martin's anglophile upbringing leads to the suggestion that his name was chosen deliberately because it includes art, mARTin. This supposition finds support in the much later protagonist of "The Ballad of Longwood Glen," Art Longwood, who meets a metaphysically and narratively similar fate.

3 Twigs, Shadows, and the Ramifications of Art

1 See Marina Grishakova, who explores the oak tree theme in Virginia Woolf's *Orlando* and a handful of late-nineteenth-century texts (*The Models of Space, Time and Vision in V. Nabokov's Fiction*, esp. 241–2); Rachel Trousdale and Priscilla Meyer expand the examination of this oak in Woolf, among other Woolf traces in Nabokov, in "Vladimir Nabokov and Virginia Woolf"; Julian Connolly discusses the thematic implications of *Quercus* in *Nabokov's Early Fiction*, 169–1; Olga Skonechnaia's commentary adds another possible referent: Burt, *Memorials of the Oak Tree*: https://thenabokovian.org/annotations/invitation-to-a-beheading-english, commentary to page 122 of *Invitation*. In a very early treatment, explicitly praised by Nabokov himself, Robert Alter wrote that *Quercus* "is Nabokov's reductio ad absurdum of the naturalistic novel and of the principle of exhaustive documentary realism ... Such photographic realism, in other words, is mindless, formless, pointless, infinitely tedious, devoid of humanity. It denies imagination, spontaneity, the shaping power of human consciousness; subverting everything art should be, it produces the perfect novel of a totalitarian world" (*Nabokov and the Real World*, 159–60; the article first appeared in *TriQuarterly* 17 [Winter 1970]).

2 See previous note.

3 Grishakova, *Models*, 241, 242. According to Grishakova, the novel may also "parody ... the immobile outside point of view in narration" (241); "The parodic metaphor of the immobile 'cameraman' in *Quercus* is symptomatic of Nabokov's approach to fiction. Nabokov avoids fixation on the immobile point of view" (242).

4 Nabokov was presented with an irresistible coincidence while the novel was being translated in 1959: finding himself in Oak Creek Canyon, Arizona, that June, he telephoned his son Dmitri, asking him to send him the translation to check "at once," and wrote and signed his foreword listing that locality. See Boyd's discussion of that time, *Nabokov: The American Years*, 382ff.

5 For example, "The normal periods of inaction were filled with scientific descriptions of the oak itself, from the viewpoints of dendrology, ornithology,

coleopterology, mythology – or popular descriptions, with touches of folk humor" (IB 123).

6 Johnson, *Worlds in Regression*, 168–9.

7 Julian Connolly reads the acorn as carrying unequivocally negative connotations (*Nabokov's Early Fiction*, 170). The acorn's descent caries an intriguing echo of a linden fruit that falls at a marked moment in the story "The Circle" (CS 381), composed the same year as *Invitation*. However, this acorn has at least two other interesting echoes in Nabokov's works, in which seeds from trees almost magically descend into stories: in "The Circle," the "winged fruite of a linden" (*letuchii letunok*, CS 381), and in *Speak, Memory*, in the "lantern slides" chapter, "the small helicopter of a revolving samara" (SM 171). And Maxim Shrayer notes that falling chestnuts in the story "Beneficence" are associated, perhaps, with "cosmic syncronization" and "the otherworld" in *The World of Nabokov's Stories*, 302.

8 Much of this imagery, overlapping with some from *The Defense,* appears in the poem "Ul'daborg (perevod s zoorlandskogo)" (1930). For a thorough review of the puppet-booth theme in Russian culture (culminating in Nabokov), see Senderovich and Shvarts, "Kukol'naia teatral'nost' mira."

9 The most similar is probably Fyodor's narrator in his "Life of Chernyshevski" within *The Gift*, also composed that same year. "The Circle," written just before the "Life," also bears traces of the same approach.

10 Avital Nemzer's thesis, "A Birch …," treats liminality in its second chapter, especially pp. 34–42, and, further, in association with trees in classical mythology, 60–7.

11 A detailed discussion of variously framed or ekphrastic trees appears below, in chapter 5.

12 In "Good Readers and Good Writers," he mentions that the writer and the reader are linked forever "if the book last forever" (LL 2); in a letter to Edmund Wilson about his scientific work, he noted that his discoveries would be obsolete in twenty-five years, and that "herein lies the difference between science and art" (Nabokov and Wilson, *Dear Bunny*, 159).

13 Avital Nemzer's chapter 3, "'A Conspiracy of Poplars': Trees and the Otherworld," addresses this topic extensively across many works; its basic premise, quite different from mine, is that the "otherworld" as a metaphysical belief should guide our understanding of Nabokov and his trees. Nemzer, "A Birch …," 57–90.

14 Leving, *Keys*, 339–41, discusses some implications of the "oak" motif in the epigraph, such as "roots" (= father) and "branches" (= family), as well as the echo from *Invitation's Quercus*. He also suggests that the progression of statements in the epigraph amounts to a circle with metaphysical implications.

15 These leaves with their drops reverberate forward and backward in Nabokov's career, recalling "The Rain Has Flown" and anticipating "First Poem" from *Speak, Memory*, dripping trees in *Lolita*, the late poem "Rain," or the very early story "Sounds," where after a rain "a fiery drop fell from a leaf right onto my lips" (CS 16).

230   Notes to pages 73–8

16 See Blackwell, "A Flurry of Words."

17 See Leving, *Keys*, 345. Firs later also form part of Fyodor's memory connecting the Berlin streetscape to his Russian past (G 80).

18 See ch. 1, n. 45.

19 Also discussed in Leving, *Keys*, 329.

20 It is also especially pertinent to the mid-career story "Recruiting" ("Nabor"), written during *The Gift*'s composition.

21 Notice that this same "appearance from the shadows" motif is associated with the emergence of consciousness early and late in *Speak, Memory* (see discussion in chapter 1), recalling Nabokov's own efforts to discover patterns in his personal story, or concealed objects in life, nature, and art ("Find what the sailor has hidden": walking stick insects, special themes like "matches," the "pursuit" motif in *Eugene Onegin*. Also discussed in Blackwell, *Zina's Paradox*, 130–1). Polina Barskova, "Filial Feelings," suggests that Zina's emergence from her kindred element is a direct reference to Ophelia in *Hamlet*; however, their kindred elements are markedly different (for Ophelia – water, for Zina – shadow).

22 "Близ фонаря, с оттенком маскарада, / лист жилками зелеными сквозит"; "Но вот скамья под липой освещенной"; "Под липовым цветением мигает/ фонарь" (SSRP 4:337, 338, 357).

23 See Blackwell, *Zina's Paradox*, chapter 5 ("Art's Romance in *The Gift*"), for a cultural and philosophical exploration of the connections of love and art in this novel. See also Nemzer, "A Birch …," on trees and creativity.

24 This detail is strangely echoed by *Pnin*'s John Head, a groundskeeper killed by lightning under a poplar. See discussion in chapter 5.

25 On this link, see Blackwell, "Three Notes on *The Gift*," esp. 38.

26 See "At a Village Cemetery," SSRP 1:461, and discussion above in chapter 1; this poem was composed in November 1922, just a few months after V.D. Nabokov's murder, and its birches link both to grief and to poetic inspiration (as well as to the lost home's natural environment). As the birch was the last image recorded in Nabokov's final poem written in Petrograd in 1917, and one of the first recorded in exile ("Dream on the Acopolis," Athens, 1919), this tree may be as emblematic of loss itself for Nabokov as it is of his Russian home.

27 There is another curious detail about Aikhenvald: in *The Gift*'s translation, Nabokov spells his name "Eichenwald," as if the man had one time been German (he never was). It is tempting to think that Nabokov wanted the German word for "oak" to be more visible than it would be in a direct transliteration. He also used the "Eiche-" spelling in *Conclusive Evidence* (216), but changed it to Ayhenvald in *Speak, Memory* (287), just four years after *The Gift* came out in English, in conformity with his preferred phonetic rendering of Russian sounds. Like the oak panelling in chapter 4 of the memoir, it provides an example of how Nabokov's decisions about naming trees were carefully considered and changed over time.

28 On the Orpheus theme, see Dolinin, *Kommentarii*, 183), and Senderovich, "Pushkin v 'Dare' Nabokova," esp. 524–7.

Notes to pages 79–80   231

29 As Aleksandr Dolinin points out (*Kommentarii*, 208), this is a reference to Pushkin's "The Prophet," itself a poem with a varied history of interpretation and, clearly, evocations of the biblical prophets, most commonly linked to the book of Isaiah; however, at the Pushkin Centennial Conferece at Stanford, 1999, Vadim Liapunov proposed an important source also in Jeremiah, relating to the introduction of fire into the prophet (Jeremiah 5.14) (personal communication). Why exactly Fyodor chooses *this* Pushkin poem as his referent has not been explored. See discussion in chapter 1, especially note 35, for critical history of articles by Sergei Bulgakov, Vladimir Solovyov, and Vladislav Khodasevich.

30 In the original, the verb is not in the subjunctive, but, rather, indicative past: "Но несколько глубже проникала в ее истину знанием умноженная любовь: отверстые зеницы" (SSRP 4: 315). This love *did* penetrate more deeply, as is demonstrated by the subsequent paragraph.

31 Boyd and Pyle, *Nabokov's Butterflies*, 203.

32 "What is necessary to my heart" (Chto nuzhno serdtsu moemu) (1923, from *The Empyrian Path*, SSRP 1:497).

33 In particular, "into which rushes all I love" (regarding a natural scene with butterflies; SM 139); "Whenever I start thinking of my love for a person, I am forced" (SM 296).

34 See Alexander Dolinin's discussion, in which he explains convincingly that the "we" here cannot refer to a future dining experience with Zina. "*The Gift*," 164.

35 Zimmer: http://www.d-e-zimmer.de/eGuide/Lep2.1-L.htm#Lim.populi.

36 The K repetition (for Konstantin) is built into the earlier scene, too, as is especially visible in the Russian: "kirpichnaia kirka," brick church (SSRP 4 239) – "kirka" being a less common term for church than "tserkov," though denoting a Lutheran church in the Russian usage (thus, appropriate to Berlin). However, "tserkov'" is used at times to refer to this specific building, including in the novel's third paragraph (SSRP 4:192); at the dream-reunion it is again "kirka" (SSRP 4:529), solidifying the link of these *K*s with Konstantin Kirillovich. The novel's final scene, approaching the second apartment (again unwittingly unbreachable, continuing the cluster of echoes), also includes a "kirka" (SSRP 4:541). Perhaps the K in the word "key" and its Russian, "kliuch," deliberately relates to this pattern. "Kliuch" is also "spring" (water source) in Russian, and associated with Pushkin's poem "The Three Springs"; see Johnson, "The Key to Nabokov's *Gift*." Nabokov translated "The Three Springs" into French while writing *The Gift*. The birch-lyre, it should be noted, combines motifs of loss (Russia, father) with Orpheus (especially via the invented butterfly, *orpheus* Godunov with its lyre-like chastity belt, G 112) and his artistic associations. A surprising discussion of this moment appears in Naiman, *Nabokov, Perversely*, 170–1. See also Zimmer, http://www.d-e -zimmer.de/eGuide/Lep2.1-M-O.htm#orpheusGodunov.

232   Notes to pages 82–7

4 "Knowledge-Amplified Love": Trees and Epistemology in Nabokov's Worlds

1 Compare Brian Boyd: "Questions of knowledge are crucial to Nabokov: our knowledge of our world, our knowledge of ourselves and others, our desire to know what lies beyond human knowledge. These questions may seem to matter less in *Lolita* because we are so urgently preoccupied with Humbert's twisted love for Lolita. Yet in Nabokov questions of knowledge are often inextricable from the intensities of love." "*Lolita*," n.p.

2 According to Brian Boyd, Robert Alter's translation of this part of the Bible is best (Genesis 2:17), where we find "the tree of knowledge, good and evil"; Robert Alter, *Genesis: Translation and Commentary* (New York: Norton, 1996). http://www.ada.auckland.ac.nz/ada115ann.htm, note to 94.01.

3 Davydov, "*The Gift*."

4 Also, accompanying the birth of consciousness in *Speak, Memory*, and the story development in "Recruiting."

5 Tolstoy appears to have crafted an important precursor to Nabokov's epistemological parable in the first epilogue to *War and Peace*, concerning the many ways of knowing a bee, moving from the child, to the poet, to the beekeeper, to a botanist, leading finally to the conclusion that "the higher the human intellect rises in the discovery of these purposes, the more obvious it becomes that the ultimate purpose is beyond our comprehension." Tolstoy, *War and Peace*, 1224–5.

6 This fact, in turn, connects with *Invitation*'s epigraph: "Comme un fou se croit Dieu, nous nous croyons mortels." If the grammatical sequence in *The Gift*'s epigraph undermines the final statement through the logical shift, here the belief in mortality is undermined by the parallel with a madman's thought.

7 There are signs of a shift in this direction already in *Laughter in the Dark/Camera Obscura*, whose original title invokes a model of mind, which Koncheyev echoes in *The Gift* when he says, per Fyodor's fantasy, "Thought likes curtains and the camera obscura" (G 338). The main character of *Laughter*, Albinus, expresses concern about his superficial knowledge of the world (discussed below).

8 Alexander Dolinin summarizes several opposing possibilities in his *Istinnaia zhizn' pisatelia Sirina*. In particular, Dolinin rebuts Nora Buks, who finds that Cincinnatus recalls in some ways the critic's physical person, while the state around him embodies the materialist philosophy and epistemology of the 1860s radicals' worldview (Dolinin, *Istinnaia zhizn'*, 214–15); see Buks, *Eshafot v khrustal'nom dvortse*, esp. 123–4; see also Shapiro, *Delicate Markers*, 134. Dolinin asserts that Cincinnatus is better aligned with Pushkin and the poetic tradition than with Chernyshevski, with even his name recalling (etymologically) Pushkin's curly hair.

9 Could there be some clever analogy play taking place here? "Tree" is to "boot" as "Akakii" (acacia) is to Bashmachkin (famously from "bashmak," a low boot or ankle-high shoe).

Notes to pages 87–90   233

10 Nabokov on monism: *Strong Opinions*, 85, 124. See discussion in Blackwell, "Nabokov, Mach, and Monism"; see also the extended treatment by Dana Dragunoiu, in *Vladimir Nabokov and the Poetics of Liberalism*, 200–11.

11 In *The Real Life of Sebastian Knight,* Sebastian lives at 36 Oak Park Gardens, where V. finds "a couple of elms, not oaks, in spite of the street name's promise" (RLSK 37): thus, the street name appears to name the absent, or tell a false story.

12 See, for example, Johnson, *Worlds in Regression*, 187–219. Johnson also notes that one of the early working titles for the novel was "Game to Gunm," a reference to the tenth volume of the *Encyclopedia Britannica* of the day and thus, among other important possibilities, a play on the compilation of human knowledge (203). The same can be said for the chapter's meta-theme, the identity of the "real" Shakespeare, and the elusiveness of certainty regarding such a would-be simple fact for modern researchers (201).

13 See Raguet-Bouvart, "Ember, Translator of *Hamlet*," https://web.archive.org /web/20110610032121/https://www.libraries.psu.edu/nabokov/raguetb1.htm for an extensive theoretical discussion of the translation theme in *Bend Sinister* and especially in this chapter and its *Hamlet* section. Jacqueline Hamrit also explores the implications of this passage for a theory of translation and of a translator's (or other reader's) relations to a text, producing readings that are "similar and different, endlessly performing and regenerating the difference present within language" (Hamrit, *Authorship in Nabokov's Prefaces*, 46–7); see also Shvabrin, *Between Rhyme and Reason*, 174–7.

14 Of course, this question goes to the heart of some of Nabokov's literary concerns. See Shvabrin's discussion of Nabokov's various writings about the theory of translation, *Between Rhyme and Reason*, 169–70, 201–5; for a differentiation of various Nabokov texts called "The Art of Translation," see ibid., 367–8n26.

15 "Nearctic Forms of *Lycaeides* Hüb.," 280.

16 That is, via *Hamlet* and individual T.

17 In the scientific paper, the two planes are the dead metaphor of the phylogenetic tree, and the playfully derived three-dimensional tree that casts shadows. In *Bend Sinister*, they are the real tree and its shadow, and the un-tree-like "machinery" and *its* perfectly tree-like shadow.

18 Bowie, "*Bend Sinister* Annotations," 119.

19 See Eddington, *New Pathways in Science*; see also discussion in Blackwell, *Quill*, 153–4.

20 A point, again, emphasized in Nabokov's famous lines about "reality" and lilies in *Strong Opinions* (11).

21 For just one suggestive example among many: "Separated from the context of subjective impressions, literature, like art in general, does not exist" – an important example of the way that "the freedom of the reader's reception [is] internally connected to the author's identical freedom of creation." Aikhenval'd, "Vstuplenie," 28, 29. These ideas can be traced at least to German Romantic philosophy. The

234   Notes to pages 90–6

essay's translation is forthcoming as "Theoretical Premises," in *In Praise of Idleness: Selected Essays by Yuli Aikhenvald*, trans. Tatyana Gershkovich and Stephen H. Blackwell (Boston: Academic Studies Press, 2024).

22 Raguet-Bouvart critiques Ember's translational philosophy from a different point of view ("Ember, Translator of *Hamlet*"; see above, note 96).

23 This passage calls to mind words Nabokov said at a New England MLA meeting in 1941, in his talk called "The Creative Writer" (later published as "The Art of Literature and Commonsense"), just a few years before he wrote *Bend Sinister*. Describing artistic inspiration, he offered the following example: "A passerby whistles a tune at the exact moment that you notice the reflection of a branch in a puddle, which in its turn, and simultaneously, recalls a combination of damp green leaves and excited birds in some old garden" (LL 377; see also TWS 199, and editor's note on 191). In some respects, that branch-reflection and those leaves became the central image of his next novel's first pages.

24 Nemzer includes a useful overview of Nabokov's relation to the pathetic fallacy, as embodied in trees especially. Nemzer, "A Birch …," 17–20.

25 For an extensive treatment of trees as markers of liminality per se, see Nemzer, "A Birch …," 34–49.

26 The largest tree crowns are estimated to hold in the low hundred thousands of leaves; each twig typically sprouts several leaves; thus the number must be under 100,000 in even the largest tree.

27 In this case, "per second," a deliberate needling of Einstein and the theory of relativity (A 339); Van also mentions a "trillionth of a trillionth part" (A 220). In all these instances, the number is far from denotative – for these characters, the "number" trillions serves a hyperbolic purpose, not a mathematical one. In *Speak, Memory*, Nabokov uses it once in reference to the sensations of a poet (SM 218).

28 I discuss the ethical and narrative implications of love in "Calendar Anomalies, Pushkin, and Aesthetic Love."

29 *American Guide Series: North Carolina*, 459. See Zimmer, "Lolita, U.S.A.," "Trip One"; Zimmer quotes and cites the *AAA Southeastern Tour Book*, 1947, with some evidence that it was a key source for Nabokov; cf. also "old logging road" in *American Guide Series: North Carolina*.

30 Nabokov was aware of the taxonomic distance: this same species (*Liriodendron tulipifera*) is mentioned twice in the story "Lance" (1951) and the word Nabokov chose for its second appearance there ("liriodendron") evoked objections from editor Katharine White, and a detailed, spirited, and successful defence of the choice, presented in full in Boyd, *Nabokov: The American Years*, 209. Olga Voronina plausibly suggests that the reason for the rare tree name (usually, as elsewhere in the same story, "tuliptree") may be its evocation of "lyre," notwithstanding the real etymological source in "lily" (personal communication). Nabokov tells White that his reason related to the assonances formed by the words "driving rain" and the letters "l," "r," and "dr." He also stated that "'Liriodendron' is as important as the whole thing is'" (Boyd, *Nabokov: The American Years*, 209).

Notes to pages 96–100   235

31 *Speak, Memory*, by contrast, whose early composition began immediately before and overlapped with *Lolita's*, has forty named species of trees and shrubs, distributed through about 160 total references.

32 Recall Nabokov's early unpublished poem, "*Topolia*" (Poplars), and its exclamation, "My soul is an alley of poplars." See also Hetenyi, "Lolita as Goddess," for a close examination of the sources of *Lolita's* trees in classical mythology.

33 There is significant literature on the demise of the chestnut, and efforts to save it, beginning before 1920. The following poignant article came out the year Nabokov fully engaged with writing *Lolita*, and given his connections he might have seen it: Ulm, "Remember the Chestnut." C.A. Reed, writing in 1941, reported that "American and European chestnuts have largely been killed by blight." "The Present Status of Chestnut Growing in the United States." Jenefer Coates proposed in a recent conference paper that the chestnuts in *Lolita* are actually part of a complex web of literary allusions to Spanish medieval culture and literature. "Chestnuts and Juicy Tidbits: Kasbeam's Subliminal Signs," at the Hidden Nabokov Conference, 29 June 2023. If this theory bears out, it would present a phenomenon I have not otherwise classified in this work, whereby Nabokov may use trees to signal not only specific writers or myths, but larger complexes of cultural referents.

34 Olga Voronina in her 2020 "Nabokov Readings" presentation demonstrated that Nabokov's own comments about Cambridge's chestnuts are a direct and deliberate echo of earlier reminiscences; these specific trees appear to have been in reality horse chestnuts (*Aesculus hyppocastanum*), not in the true chestnut family. Voronina, "Tainopis' otkrytym tekstom," manuscript provided by author. Discussed in greater detail below. Now published as part of *Tainopis': Nabokov. Arkhiv. Podtekst.*

35 Horse chestnuts and related buckeyes (see below) would also have likely been covered with the candle-like flowers, in pink, white, or red, that Nabokov loved at Cambridge and in Berlin. Cf. *Speak, Memory*, 211; *Ada*, 470; "Return of Chorb" (CS 150). See, e.g., https://www.uky.edu/hort/Ohio-Buckeye. American chestnuts, however, blossomed much later in that part of the country, when they thrived.

36 In the Russian translation, Nabokov preserved all the original instances of "chestnut" as "kashtan" except the "chestnut mare"; I did not discover whether he also added one "kashtan" somewhere to compensate for the lost chestnut. The French translation by Eric Kahane, overseen by Nabokov, produces a mix of the terms *châtaigne* and *marronier*. My informal queries of native French speakers suggests that while *châtaigne* is always applied only to true ("sweet") chestnuts, *marronier* can be applied both to horse chestnuts and to true chestnuts producing large fruits (such as the *marron glacé*). Maurice Couturier's translation opts mainly if not exclusively for *marron*.

37 On the mythological dogs Cavall and Melampus, see Boyd, "*Lolita*: What We Know and What We Don't," final section, "Annotation and Global Interpretation: Cavall and Melampus."

236   Notes to pages 100–4

38 There is another reason to be sceptical of these trees: a few pages later, Humbert will write, as they drive towards Lepingville, of "a lovely, lonely, supercilious grove (oaks, I thought; American trees at that stage were beyond me)" (L 140). Presumably, they were beyond him earlier, too, when he named poplars, elms, pines, and chestnuts.

39 Note also the connection to the abiding theme of leaves' shadows throughout Nabokov's works, as in *The Defense, The Gift*, "A Nursery Tale," "Recruiting," *Speak, Memory, Pnin*, and *Ada*.

40 Dripping leaves, of course, feature in many key scenes, particularly ones related to the birth of art, or of love (or to Nabokov's biography). See discussion of "The Rain Has Flown" in chapter 1; see also Nabokov's letter to Katharine White on dripping tulip trees in "Lance," Nabokov's last short story, cited in note 29 above. Compare, too, the early poem: "Zimniaia noch'" ("Zimneiu lunnoiu noch'iu molchanie ...") (SSRP 2:571), whose trees anticipate the "spectral" ones in this scene: "Lipy, kak prizraki chernye v riad, / Strannye, grustnye, v inee spiat" (Lindens, like black ghosts in a row, / Strange, sad, they sleep in [a coating of] frost).

41 The spectral theme is continued on the surrounding roads as Humbert tries to sleep that first night in the Enchanted Hunters, among unnamed trees that may be the ones Humbert thinks are chestnuts: "And when finally all the waterfalls had stopped, and the enchanted hunters were sound asleep, the avenue under the window of my insomnia, to the west of my wake – a staid, eminently residential, dignified alley of huge trees – degenerated into the despicable haunt of gigantic trucks roaring through the wet and windy night" (L 130).

42 After passing the rain drumming on chestnut leaves during his pursuit of Dolly, Humbert finds her "waiting for me near the ghostly birch tree" (L 207).

43 Most famously, Richard Rorty's "The Barber of Kasbeam: Nabokov on Cruelty," chapter 7 of his *Contingency, Irony, Solidarity*; see also Leona Toker's reply, "Liberal Ironists and the 'Gaudily Painted Savage.'" https://web.archive.org /web/20211023052418/https://www.libraries.psu.edu/nabokov/tokerp1.htm.

44 It is not, in my view, productive or plausible to assume that Nabokov is imagining a world in which American chestnuts still thrive as part of a fictional universe that includes places like "New Wye" and "Waindellville." After all, *Lolita*'s world still includes newspaper references to such real things as the Sally Horner story and the Joyce Kilmer Memorial Forest.

45 See Naiman, "A Filthy Look at Shakespeare's *Lolita*," in his *Nabokov, Perversely*.

46 Although we later hear that Quilty is "practically impotent" (L 298), this is probably a lie, and not relevant to the present claim in any case.

47 Their cabin, Humbert has told us, is made of pine logs, perhaps invoking the pine trees from Hourglass Lake.

48 http://www.d-e-zimmer.de/LolitaUSA/Trip2.htm. Zimmer proposes that Pisky and Kasbeam are "synthetic," not disguised "real" towns, located in the general geographic vicinity of Decatur, Illinois.

49 *Queue* means "tail" in French; at Pavor Manor, Humbert says, "Reveillez-vous, Laqueue, il est temps de mourir!"

50 One wonders why the S has been left out of the "Ted Hunter" anagram; possibly another marker, now by subtraction, of Shakespeare?

51 On this topic, see Alfred Appel's annotations to 157/3, 251/14, 301/3, in *Annotated Lolita.*

52 Recall Brian Boyd's comment, quoted above in note 1, from "*Lolita*: What We Know and What We Don't."

53 One of the earliest discussions of this theme was by Dieter E. Zimmer, in his 1959 review of the novel from *Die Zeit*, "Humbert Humbert: Ape in the Cage." It has been recently translated by Brian Boyd: https://thenabokovian.org/node/51813, accessed 20 February 2022.

54 It is matched by *Pale Fire*, also with thirty-four, topped by *Speak, Memory*, with at least forty, and almost doubled by *Ada*, with around sixty-four. Nabokov clearly worked to increase this number as his career progressed.

55 Cf. Nabokov's comment to Wilson in October, 1944: " the trees are green and rusty brown, stepwise, like gobelins" (Nabokov and Wilson, *Dear Bunny*, 159). In a chance comment in *Speak, Memory*, Nabokov offers a clue to what his notion of "rust-coloured" might be: he uses this epithet to described the Oak Eggar (SM 132). However, judging from available imagery, this moth (*Lasiocampus quercus*, see Zimmer's *Guide*, http://www.d-e-zimmer.de/eGuide/Lep2.1-L.htm#L.quercus, for description but not for image comparisons) ranges from a beige or light-brown to a truly rusty colour. Therefore, it does not help to settle the exact hue of "rust-coloured" in Nabokov's vocabulary.

56 At that time, I leaned towards basswood. See Blackwell, "Reflections," 30–1.

57 In his letter to Katharine White, Nabokov emphasized the narrative's "nastiness" and "'unpleasant' quality" (SL 150).

58 Barabtarlo, *Phantom of Fact*, 229. In a private communication, the author also mentioned discussing paulownia and catalpa with others.

59 In *Ada*, they appear to fall while green, but that is in Antiterran "Mont Roux." See discussion in chapter 6.

60 The mulberry's case is strengthened by the tree's association with silk, and Pnin's strange garb for his party, a "sybaritic smoking jacket of blue silk" (Pn 151); Rita mentions a "mulberry moth" in *Lolita*, demonstrating Nabokov's predictable familiarity with the role of these trees and moths in the production of silk (L 259). But, once again – their leaves are usually yellow in autumn. The fact that mulberry appears in both *Pale Fire* and *Ada* might push one still further in its direction. Redbud is never mentioned by Nabokov in any work or correspondence.

61 As originally translated and published by Dmitri Nabokov; recently republished (with slight modifications) by Brian Boyd as "Pushkin, or the True and the Seemingly True" (TWS 188–232).

238   Notes to pages 108–10

62   On the relation of Nabokov's notion of love within epistemology, in relation to Pushkin and his own life, see Blackwell, "Nabokov's 'The Gift,'" esp. 18–22.

63   Rowan, "True to Life," 79–80. It is also intriguing that in the *New Yorker* version of the fourth chapter, Nabokov included in a list of words that young Victor would have been exposed to the very obscure "cacuminous," which describes trees "having a pointed top" (*Webster's Second International Dictionary*) – something that accurately describes the top of a Lombardy poplar (as well as various firs, spruces, and cypresses). In the final book version, the word is replaced with "converge" (Pn 91; cf. "Victor Meets Pnin," 39). Nabokov made a special defence of "cacuminous" in a letter to William Maxwell, so his eventual decision to change it is surprising. (Letter of 22 July 1955; Berg Collection, *New Yorker* manuscript box, folder 47). I am grateful to Olga Voronina for directing my attention to this passage in the first version and the letter.

64   Botkin's literary heritage is explored in Meyer, *Find*, 115–17, and on *Nabokv-L* by Alexander Dolinin (https://thenabokovian.org/node/20670). Dolinin also points out the possible connection to Innokenty Annensky's early pseudonym, "Nik. T—o" (evoking "nikto," no one, plus a stray "b" that could be a subjunctive particle in Russian; an echo of Odysseus's self-naming to Polyphemus is apparently intended). The "nikto b" anagram first appeared on *Nabokv-L* on 27 January 1999, posted by "Sersak" (https://thenabokovian.org/node/31705); D. Barton Johnson editorialized that the anagram had been noticed before. Jansy Mello presented a useful summary of discussions of the "nikto b." discussion on 3 March 2012 (https://thenabokovian.org/node/9168), including the following quotation from Victor Fet's 2006 *Nabokv-L* contribution: "It probably was Andrew Field who first noticed 'Nikto' in Botkin in his 'VN' (1986, p. 346)." Andrew Field, *Nabokov: His Life in Art*.

65   Some of these details are discussed by Brian Boyd, in "Shade and Shape in *Pale Fire*," 209–10, in connection with his revised interpretation of the novel centred on Hazel Shade's influence on Shade's and Kinbote's texts (and then Shade's, as well, on Kinbote), in Boyd, *Nabokov's "Pale Fire."*

66   The Bohemian waxwing remains mostly to the north of the United States in North America throughout the year, and does not compete for attention there; it never strays as far south as New Wye. See Robert Dirig's scientific analysis of New Wye's probable location, "Drawing with Words," esp. 208–10. On the Bohemian waxwing's seasonal distributions, and differences from the cedar waxwing, the Cornell Lab's ornithology site is helpful: https://www.allaboutbirds.org/guide /Bohemian_Waxwing/maps-range.

67   However, it was known to Nabokov, who wrote in detail about the linguistic relations between cedars and junipers in English and French in his letter to Raymond Girard, 19 October 1963 (Berg Collection). My thanks to Julie Loison-Charles for bringing this letter to my attention.

68 This line echoes the earlier line about a bird's prints in the snow, "retake the falling snow," which leads to Kinbote's reference to the Sherlock Holmes story "The Empty House," which will be discussed in the next chapter.

69 The "wrong species/genus" motif is picked up by Kinbote himself, when he refers to the "Oriole that is not an oriole," the Baltimore oriole of North America, which is of genus *Icterus* and family Icteridae, unlike the European orioles, genus *Oriolus* and family Oriolidae – in other words, not closely related at all (PF 246).

70 There may be some deliberate connection here to glass production at Corning, NY; Tatiana Ponomareva has also discussed relevant materials about a glass factory in pre-revolutionary Russia, in "On One of the Biographical Sources of *Pale Fire*."

71 See D. Barton Johnson (the leading birder among Nabokovians) on why the poem's bird is a cedar, not Bohemian: "A Field Guide to *Pale Fire*: Waxwings and the Red Admiral."

72 See his comment on inventing a tree for *Ada*, vs. inventing quadrapeds, in *Think, Write Speak*, 467. In fact, he invented three trees in *Ada,* as well as the "*Pyrospodia*" he names in the foreword to *Lolita: A Screenplay*, and at least two in "Terra Incognita" – all discussed briefly in the introduction. As mentioned above, the tree at Pnin's house on Todd Rd. may also be a "new species."

73 Brian Boyd, of course, does discover these things, from a different angle of attack and with different purposes; see *Nabokov's "Pale Fire,"* 190–1. In 2015, Alexey Sklyarenko proposed that the poem "Pale Fire" requires a "coda" of a further two lines to complete Shade's logical flow (https://thenabokovian.org/node/1984), including another mention of the (cedar) waxwing.

74 See Boyd for discussion of the cicada, and the garrulous waxwing: *Nabokov's "Pale Fire,"* 190, 191, 278n34; elsewhere Boyd also presents proof that Nabokov was aware of, and felt the importance of, this difference, in Nabokov's letter to Maurice-Edgar Coindreau of 14 January 1964: "Ce qu'on appele cedar en Amerique n'est pas un cedre mais un genevrier (What Americans call cedar is not a cedar but a juniper)," Berg Collection; quoted in *Nabokov's "Pale Fire,"* 278n34. However, one does not need access to the Nabokov archive to reach this conclusion, as I have tried to demonstrate – a fact which moves the reading more firmly into the realm of those that readers without archival access might happen upon. Boyd asserts that the fictitious *B. shadei* is Mexican, a logical but not direct conclusion from the text: *Stalking*, 347 .

75 Boyd discusses this scene as a fine example of Nabokov's "expertise in piecemeal disclosure of information." *Nabokov's "Pale Fire,"* 178

76 Equally relevant is the theme of "doubled italics"; see Ramey, "*Pale Fire*'s Black Crown."

77 The European sycamore (from the *Merchant of Venice*) is *Acer pseudoplatanus*, and is the type species for Linnaeus's maple genus *Acer* (https://en.wikipedia.org /wiki/Acer_pseudoplatanus). American sycamore is *Platanus occidentalis*, related to other plane trees, and a parent species of the hybrid London plane tree.

240   Notes to pages 113–15

78 This tree was used for making pencils until the 1940s; Nabokov knew of this no later than 1970 when he was writing *Transparent Things,* where he calls the eastern red cedar by an idiosyncratic name: "it shot out and spilled a pencil. This he briefly considered before putting it back. It was not a hexagonal beauty of Virginia juniper or African cedar ... but a plain, round, technically faceless old pencil of cheap pine" (TT 6); see also https://en.wikipedia.org/wiki/Juniperus_virginiana). Also worthy of attention, the tree's specific name, *virginiana*: Hazel, whose death is heralded by the lights on the "cedars," *Juniperus virginiana*, dies a virgin. The species is named (in this case, by Carl Linnaeus) for the territory of its discovery, which in turn is named either in reference to Queen Elizabeth's virginity, or the virgin quality of the new territory when it was first explored in 1584; https://en.wikipedia.org/wiki/Virginia.

79 Boyd, *Nabokov's "Pale Fire,"* 178, 191.

80 Notice how the butterfly *playing and sliding* on the laurel leaf echoes the drop on the leaf in "first poem" scene of *Speak, Memory* ("Tip, leaf, dip, relief").

81 This is the poem Nabokov cited in his interview with Robert Hughes, mentioned in the introduction.

82 What he describes in his lecture on Gogol as "this life-generating syntax ... bridg[ing] the logical, or rather biological, hiatus between a dim landscape under a dull sky and a groggy old soldier accosting the reader with a rich hiccup on the festive outskirts of the same sentence" (*Lectures on Russian Literature*, 20).

83 Kinbote seems to be propelled here by the fact that "muscat" is a grape, which is "vinograd" in Russian, leading to his "tree"/"grados" observation: once, Gradus is called "Vinogradus."

84 de Vries, "*Pale Fire* and the Romantic Movement"; DeRewal and Roth, "John Shade's Duplicate Selves."

85 Crane, *Ginkgo*, 199–203, 218.

86 See, e.g., Roth, "The Composition of *Pale Fire*," 31.

87 Stacey Schiff credits Véra with researching the list of Shakespeare's trees and their place in the plays; one finds the trees and plays listed in her handwriting on cards for *Pale Fire* held in the Library of Congress collection of Nabokov papers. Véra, for her part, may have turned to a comprehensive book such as Henry Nicholson Ellacombe's *The Plant-Lore and Garden-Craft of Shakespeare*, which includes detailed discussion of all the flora in Shakespeare's works, where they appear, and whether and where he might (or might not) have seen them in his lifetime.

88 See Crane, *Ginkgo*, 81–8. On ginkgo's "living fossil" status, see Seward, *Links with the Past in the Plant World*. Seward credits Darwin with the phrase "living fossil." The fossil history of prehistoric ginkgos could be found by general readers as early as Scott 's *The Romance of Plant Life* (1907). Cf. also "Leaf Impressions of Ginkgo Are Found in Rocks of Nearly All Ages Back Even to the Upper Palæozoic," in Stopes, *Ancient Plants*. The eleventh edition of *Encyclopedia Britannica* contained similar information. An early scientific review of the paleontology appeared in Lester F. Ward, "The Ginkgo-Tree," *Science* 5, no. 124 (19 June 1885): 495–7.

Notes to pages 115–21   241

89 This diachronic perspective emerges from Nabokov's most important lepidopterological article, his 1945 "Notes on Neotropical Plebejinae (Lycænidæ, Lepidoptera)" (*Psyche* 52, 1–61): 44.

90 This was established at least by the 1880s: see Ward, "The Ginkgo-Tree"; also "The Ginkgo," *Scientific American Supplement*, no. 979 (6 October 1894), 15,642–3. Nabokov's extra efforts to learn the taxonomic history, and Russian name, of this tree can be found on a card in the "Notes on Various Subjects" binder, Berg Collection. The card appears to include dictionary research conducted by Nabokov's sister Elena Sikorski. I am grateful to Andrei Babikov for reminding me of this card's existence.

91 Goethe's poem had been retranslated into English in *The Scientific Monthly* (soon to be absorbed by *Science*), just a few years before Nabokov began writing the novel, in a publication he was likely to have seen. (Robert Bloch, "Ginkgo Biloba," *Scientific Monthly* 74, no. 4 [April 1952]: 230). But he would, in any case, have known the Goethe poem from its inclusion in the collection *West-Eastern Divan* (1819). The full poem is discussed as an example of a "framed tree" reference in chapter 5, below.

92 The same tendency is evident in the widespread mythological hints and themes connecting the novel's characters to various trees. "Yewshade," by blending the homonym of "you" with the poet's name and a metaphor of "ghost," can be seen as accidentally prophetic on Shade's part; there are other ways to read the figure, of course.

93 Elsewhere, I have argued that Nabokov was specifically interested in moving the boundary of scientific research towards such traditionally inhospitable domains. See Blackwell, *Quill*, 178–80.

94 *AdaOnline*, note to Ada 92.31–3.

5 Trees in the Frame: Art about Art about Trees

1 This origin may have some deliberate connection to Pushkin's "Ruslan and Lyudmila," another poem with a tree and wood-sprites, discussed above in the introduction

2 *Despair*, 56. This observation has become a part of the painting entry's introductory paragraph on Wikipedia. https://en.wikipedia.org/wiki/Isle_of_the _Dead_(painting), accessed 15 March 2022. Böcklin (painting unnamed) appears also in *Glory* (Gl 187, cf. also 138).

3 Palms play this role (potted or in represented images) in *Laughter in the Dark*, *Real Life of Sebastian Knight*, *Pnin*, *Lolita*, *Speak, Memory*, several stories, and elsewhere.

4 Anticipating things a bit, the oak tree in *Quercus* is noteworthy precisely for its durability, its extensive presence across a stretch of time. In this scene in *Speak, Memory*, of course, it is not just space that becomes time, but light, shadow, movement, image, and the elusive quality of an entire moment: Nabokov already

242 Notes to pages 121–6

appears to be working quite consciously to avoid Bergsonian limitations, which were to become central to his thinking in the early 1960s as he began work on *Ada* and its "Texture of Time" chapter.

5 Recall that the linden and alder are both present surrounding the crucial "first poem" episode of the memoir. Martin's part-indrik, part-alder heritage suggests that he is a fantastical creature with a blood relationship to trees.

6 "When, as a youth, he recalled the past, he would wonder if one night he had not actually hopped from bed to picture, and if this had not been the beginning of the journey, full of joy and anguish, into which his whole life had turned. He seemed to remember the chilly touch of the ground, the green twilight of the forest, the bends of the trail (which the hump of a great root crossed here and there), the tree trunks flashing by as he ran past them barefoot, and the strange dark air, teeming with fabulous possibilities" (Gl 5).

7 To be even more explicit, for a moment we have the following situation: the reader of *Glory* reads a book about a boy reading (or hearing) a book about a boy viewing, and entering, a painting of a winding path in the woods.

8 I mostly skip over the important thematic concept of "liminality" as it relates to trees; a thorough treatment can be found in Nemzer, "A Birch …," ch. 3.

9 However, Martin has been studying maps and perhaps other sources concerning hidden trails from the Baltic states to Russia, so there is an implicit representational forest-world here, as well.

10 *Speak, Memory*, 86; see discussion in chapter 1.

11 A decade or so later, *The Real Life of Sebastian Knight* would also include a variation on this "magical beechwood" and its path (88–9), where both Sebastian and Claire, on separate occasions, expect to see a "gnome" or a "brownie."

12 More generalized "paths" of the park at the estate described in *Mary* also serve as a crucial background for the "first love" theme, but these contain pines and birches, not beeches, which are not local to the St. Petersburg area: the beeches were exotic even as flora depicted in Nabokov's bedside painting. They were not just painted trees, but trees of another world or another place.

13 "Siren" is also a near-perfect transliteration of the Russian word "lilac," an iconic small tree in Nabokov's creative biography, as we have seen.

14 Cf. "Celluloid," as defined in OED, dating back at least to 1922: "3. In extended use: film; the cinema as a genre," etc.

15 The represented trees theme goes more or less underground for the next two novels, *Laughter in the Dark* and *Despair*, but even in these there are some subtle gestures: Nabokov turns the writer "Segelkranz" into "Baum" (German "tree") in the heavily revised and translated *Laughter in the Dark*. In *Despair*, Ardalion's portrait of Hermann includes "gallow trees," in Russian just "viselitsy"; and in the first chapter, Hermann follows a trail through "stunted beeches" towards his magical discovery of Felix: the scene presents a travesty of the path in Martin's bedroom painting from *Glory*.

Notes to pages 126–30   243

16 "It seemed as though the author were sitting with his camera somewhere among the topmost branches of the Quercus, spying out and catching his prey" (IB 123). Vertov's film was released in 1929. We can tell from the director's letter to the German press that year that it was shown in Germany, thus, surely, Berlin. Vertov, *The Writings of Dziga Vertov*, 101–2.

17 There is also a less detailed, and possibly less consequential, mural/painting of the distant "view," including its trees, within *Invitation*.

18 On early Soviet "documentarism," see Silina, "The Struggle against Naturalism," and Papazian, *Manufacturing Truth*.

19 See letters to Katharine White (SL 201, 208–9).

20 In *The Defense*, the associations are highly figurative, since in effect it is the wooden chess pieces that lead Luzhin out of his world: as we saw in play the wooden chess pieces fall away from the "chess forces" of the game.

21 Hazel Shade in *Pale Fire* may be another, later mutation of the theme, especially in her role as artistic inspiration (per Boyd) after the end of her – apparently – unhappy life. In a further twist, not only is her first name derived from a tree, but her full name can be traced to an artwork, Sir Walter Scott's *The Lady of the Lake* (Boyd, *Nabokov's "Pale Fire*," 152–3). However, she marks (or aligns with) a shift towards *water*-oriented departures (Mira Belochkin and Lucette Veen are two others), which reach out to Ophelia and to Pushkin's "Rusalka" (river-sprite) heritage. Gerard de Vries notes that Hazel's sinking by the "reedy bank" (PF 51, poem lines 499–500) may be another deliberate echo of the myth of Pan and Syrinx, in Ovid, *Metamorphoses*, book I, "reeds" (Greek "syrinx") being the form into which the wood nymph was transformed, later synonymized with lilac bushes, "syringa." Personal communication.

22 Yuri Leving proposes Pavel Tchelitchew as an important figure standing behind Romanov. Tchelitchew produced several relevant paintings, in particular *Autumn Leaves* and *Hide and Seek*. The latter may have "germinated from some studies of an ancient tree in Sussex made as early as 1934, a tree in which the painter saw a likeness to a large, gnarled, open hand, with its fingers about to close into a grasp; its root system looked to him like a foot." See Leving, *Keys,* 197–202, esp. 201. Leving reports that Simon Karlinsky in 1967 was the first to draw attention to a possible link to Tchelitchew, and that Alfred Appel followed up on it in an interview (SO 171).

23 The list of places where shadows play this creation-related role in Nabokov's works is too numerous to give in full. It begins, biographically, with the "oakling avenue" presented in *Speak, Memory*, and representative examples can be found in the poem "At a Village Cemetery," the stories "A Nursery Tale" and "Recruiting," with reverberations in *Ada* and later. The motif plays a personal role in Nabokov's early letters to Véra, particularly in the lovely series about the acacia in their lodgings' courtyard (summer 1926, discussed in the introduction).

244 Notes to pages 130–5

24 The shadow in this photo appears reminiscent of the shadow on Luzhin's forehead in *his* published photograph. There are many places in Nabokov's works *outside* of framed images where shadows emphatically touch and modify humans in various ways.

25 First proposed in Blackwell, *Zina's Paradox*, 29. Nabokov's oak-related pun on Aikhenvald's name, in an epigram included in a letter to Véra (5 July 1926), is presented in the introduction, note 9. The fact that Nabokov's 1926 epigram links Aikhenvald with oaks as well as with Pushkin strengthens the likelihood that *The Gift*'s epigraph, too, gestures towards both of them. Structural overlap between this epigram and Fyodor's hidden poem to Zina provides further support: "What shall I call you? Half-Mnemo*syne*? There's a half-shim*mer* in your surname too" (G 157; Nabokov's italics, though they are absent in the Russian; cf. SSRP 4:337–8).

26 This might be another instance of the motif of misidentification in nature, seen in the elm-oak substitution on Sebastian's street. On Shakespeare conflating daffodils (narcissi) and asphodels, see Ellacombe, *Plant-Lore*, under "asphodel." For more on asphodels, see de Vries, *Silent Love*, 98–9, 167.

27 The puddle reflecting twigs and trees in *Bend Sinister*'s first pages clearly falls into this same family of meaning; while that puddle does produce a sort of frame for the twigs' image, it is not discussed as, or compared to, an artwork in that novel. A similar puddle appears in "The Return of Chorb": "the small twig-reflecting puddle in the middle of the black pavement resembled an insufficiently developed photograph" (CS 150).

28 "Ilyich," his patronymic, correlates to "Elijah"; in Slavic mythology, Elijah was known as "Elijah the Thunderer." See Belova, "Il'ia sv," 2:405–7. Elijah also is associated biblically with Elisha; in his story "The Thunderstorm" ("Groza"), Nabokov appears to combine the two prophets in his charioteering character Elisha (CS 86–9).

29 In chapter 5, at The Pines, the painter Gramineev is working on a strangely similar canvas: "a view of the valley beyond, complete with quaint old barn, gnarled apple tree, and kine" (Pn 127).

30 There may also be an element of tension between Nabokov and Goethe here; the latter shows up in this same scene, and in a tower that mimics a prison-camp guard tower at the opening of chapter 5 (Pn 111–12). The echo between Mount Ettrick in *Pnin* and Grosser Ettersberg, where Buchenwald was situated, has been noted. Ronen, "Nabokov and Goethe"; see also Liapunov, "*Pnin* and Goethe."

31 Pine woods regularly feature as sites of violence or tragedy: Hermann's murder of Felix (*Despair*) is at a lake in a pine wood; the final departure of Fyodor's father is viewed through pine trees. Pines are in close proximity at the time of Aqua's suicide in *Ada*, as well as that of Lucette's first too-early witnessing of sex, among "a dark grove of conifers" (A 143).

32 If Appel is correct, *Atala* makes for a thematically appropriate but very weird intertext for *Lolita*. It is renowned for descriptions of "Edenic" North American

natural settings (penned by a European), and the star-crossed love of two fugitives (*Annotated Lolita*, 385). This is not the place for a full review, but the parallels deserve attention. See https://en.wikipedia.org/wiki/Atala_(novella).

33 https://en.wikipedia.org/wiki/Joyce_Kilmer#"Trees".

34 See ch. 4, n. 29. For more on this scene from another perspective, see the discussion in the previous chapter.

35 The sentence continues: "*We* dress up what he wrote, as a charmed commentator sometimes gives an extra grace to a line of genius"; 13 Oct. 1925, Berg Collection. Translated in Boyd, *Nabokov: The Russian Years*, 245. Throughout most of the 1920s, Nabokov often used traditional, religiously inflected language and imagery; he moved away from them by around 1930. The early poems are rich with these images, which Nabokov later discussed this way: it was "a period (reaching well into the 1920s) of a kind of private curatorship, aimed at preserving nostalgic retrospections and developing Byzantine imagery (this has been mistaken by some readers for an interest in 'religion,' which, beyond literary stylization, never meant anything to me" (PP 13–14).

36 See also Thomas Karshan's commentary (SP 190).

37 Humbert notes that the verse and the quest for a photograph were actually from two separate trips through Briceland, probably one in 1951 and one in 1952, but he does not say which was which, insisting rather that "such suffusions of swimming colors are not to be disdained by the artist in recollection" (L 263).

38 The poem does hint at some framed trees, for example in the "Sherlock Holmes" story it mentions, and prompts Kinbote to find some of them. And the treatment of the Institute of Preparation for the Hereafter, I.P.H., and Shade's pun on *l'if*, the yew, comes extremely close to being a framed moment.

39 PF 93, 94–5, 115, 192.

40 See discussion by de Vries, "*Pale Fire* and the Romantic Movement."

41 Goethe's "Erlking" is quoted openly at lines 662–4, but the resonance between this scene (especially the concern with sounds in the night, lines 653–9) and the death vigil (esp. lines 479–80) make its latent presence in the latter scene compelling as well. In the commentary to line 629, Kinbote retroactively applies these same lines ("Who rides so late in the night and the wind ... It is the father with his child") to the episode of the king's climb across the Bera range (PF 239, cf. 143). Especially noteworthy is the fact that it is at the very moment when the elf-/alderking theme clandestinely appears in the king's narrative that he sees a lake, with striking colours and reflections, during his flight; Boyd has connected this scene with the imagery surrounding Hazel's "flight" home from a failed blind date and her death in the lake (and with the colours of the waxwing, central in Shade's long poem). Connected this way, Nabokov (through Kinbote) creates a curiously desynchronized presentation of the set of allusions. Per Boyd, regarding the place of Hazel's death, "Lochanhead": "*lochan* is Scottish for 'little lake,'" the very thing in which Kinbote sees coloured reflections (*Nabokov's "Pale Fire*," 152).

246 Notes to pages 137–8

42 Nabokov shares Kinbote's view (TWS 337). Other Frost poems, e.g., "The Road Not Taken" and "Birches," likely caught his attention as well.

43 Both *Four Quartets* and *The Wasteland* include many references to trees; the former appears more apt, with its special focus on time (echoed in Hazel's role as Mother Time, and the night watchman's as Father Time, at Lochanhead/Lake Omega). *Four Quartets*, of course, also seems veiled within the "quartet of bores" who would discuss poetry on television, and who mention Shade "one oozy footstep – behind Frost." *Four Quartets* is moreover the source of Hazel's vocabulary questions on "grimpen" and "chthonic," in cross-talk between Hazel, Shade, and Sybil. Lake Omega itself may also invoke time, by means of the watchmaking company (and the "watchman," line 475 and commentary p. 218). At least later in life, however, Nabokov seems to have worn a Rolex. See https://revolutionwatch.com/vladimir-nabokov-rolex-guy.

44 As discovered first by Mary McCarthy (1962) and refined by Boyd, *Nabokov's "Pale Fire,"* 279n9. The *Lady of the Lake*'s plot has some resonance with *Pale Fire*'s: one can point, at least, to the theme of a disguised king, and to a daughter who is "of the lake" and serves a helping role in the plot's development (even if, in *Pale Fire*, this role was thoroughly concealed until Brian Boyd presented it in 1999). On the other hand, Scott's poem has a generally happy ending and a wedding for its eponymous heroine, something not remotely hinted at in *Pale Fire* (unless one takes Hazel's apparently joyous otherworldly existence, per Boyd, as a similarly positive outcome).

45 Cypress is also mentioned in connection with Socrates and Proust (PF 41) and Shakespeare (PF 291).

46 Because some of the trees from the avenue are identified with a specific Shakespearean text, one could bring in those titles as well, but at this stage in the discussion, we can simply consider this "avenue" a Shakespearean tree-text in a collective sense.

47 For more on the significance of this story's possible role in *Pale Fire,* including discussion of a wax bust decoy, see Brian Boyd's 22 December 1997 contribution to *Nabokv-L*, https://thenabokovian.org/index.php/node/32714. The "reversed footprints" theme was discussed previously by Paul R. Jackson, in "*Pale Fire* and Sherlock Holmes." Jackson asserts that this story contains the only reference to reversed footprints in the Sherlock Holmes corpus. See also Polish, "On the Origin of Tree Worship." Two more examples that will not be pursued further in this study: another, probably not exactly framed, tree reference appears when Shade refers obliquely to Robert Browning's *Pippa Passes*, via his neighbour Paul Hentzner's son who, Shade has told Kinbote, once said, "Here Papa pisses," an allusion reinforced by the Shade and Goldsworth houses' situation on Dulwich Road – "a wood near Dulwich" being the site where Browning's idea for the poem came to him, according to his biographer; Dulwich was also the location of the failed blind date that sends Hazel to her death. Finally, Boscobel, site of the "Royal

Summerhouse" (PF 144, 305), refers to the place where Charles II hid in a tree, now the "Royal Oak," to escape pursuit after the civil war in 1651; after hiding in the tree he made his way to France and lived there in exile for nine years. This is a legend or story featuring an oak, but also just "history." Charles II related the story to several people, three of whom wrote it down. https://en.wikipedia.org/wiki /Escape_of_Charles_II.

48 The importance of this specific tree to Nabokov becomes apparent when he rejects the translation "noyer" (walnut) proposed by Maurice Coindreau in his translation of the novel. The problem is that "shagbark," and even "hickory," as tree and indigenous word, do not exist in France, so Coindreau proposed another tree in the same genus. Nabokov was having nothing of it, and his letter and comments offer a lesson in taxonomic botany. Eventually, the translators used "hickory" as a French word, reverting to the genus level from the specific "shagbark" (*Carya ovata*). See letter to Maurice Coindreau, 14 January 1964 (Berg Collection). See aso Coindreau's response to Nabokov's previous letter, 6 January 1964. Excerpted in Boyd, *Nabokov: The American Years*, 479–80, with discussion. Once again, I am grateful to Julie Loison-Charles for bringing these letters to my attention. The tree which was the apparent model for Shade's tree was photographed in 2013 by Robert Dirig (see Blackwell and Johnson, *Fine Lines*, 199). It seems that the leaf colour and the striated bark, as well as the very particular tree Nabokov knew from memory, drove him to ensure its accurate inclusion in the French edition.

49 The world "gnarled" was apparently first used in a literary setting by Shakespeare in *Measure for Measure* (1604/printed 1616), act 2, scene 2 (114), spoken by Isabella, and applied to an oak. Its repetition in the scene with Griff is extremely curious. In *Henry IV, Part 1* (1592/printed 1623), Shakespeare used the word "gnarling" to mean "gnaw."

50 It seems a stretch, but still worthy of note, that in *Invitation* Nabokov aligns the Cyrillic Г (G) with images of death and "gallows trees." Cf. Gerald Emerald, "heraldic" butterfly (геральдический, гербовый – from герб, coat of arms).

51 Ronen, "Nabokov and Goethe." Kinbote also speaks of a longing for death, but in an ambiguous light counterbalanced by his religious convictions.

52 It may be significant, as well, that the poem within Disa's "green album" represents yet another layer of framing: it is now a tree within a poem within an album. Cf. the ginkgo leaf preserved in Marina's herbarium, in *Ada*, which she had received inside the pages of the book "The Truth about Terra," given to her by her twin sister, Aqua.

53 At his comment to line 90, Kinbote brings us back to the shagbark by means of a deleted variant, referring to the Luna moth's "dead and shriveled-up cocoon," further reporting that "the caterpillar of [this moth] feeds on the hickory" (114). Kinbote imagines that Shade replaced these lines because "Luna" clashes with "moon" in the next stanza, but more likely is its implication of failed metamorphosis, which he perhaps intuitively (or with Hazel's help) rejected.

248   Notes to pages 140–2

54   This quip comes from the note to line 549, to which Kinbote also refers the reader in his discussion of the ginkgo arc (c49): "When the new Episcopal church in New Wye (see note to line 549) was built, the bulldozers spared an arc of those sacred trees planted by a landscaper of genius (Repburg) at the end of the so-called Shakespeare Avenue, on the campus" (PF 93). The note to 549 is also urged upon us at c101 (116) and c169 (148), and garners three mentions in the Index. The c169 item is especially noteworthy in that its contents are so spare and unambiguous:
   "*Line 169*: survival after death
               See note to line 549."

55   From the poem: "One day, / When I'd just turned eleven, as I lay / Prone on the floor and watched a clockwork toy – / a tin wheelbarrow pushed by a tin boy – / Bypass chair legs and stray beneath the bed, / There was a sudden sunburst in my head" (PF 38). Kinbote's remark: "The boy was a little Negro of painted tin with a keyhole in his side and no breadth to speak of ... and his wheelbarrow was now all bent and broken. He said, brushing the dust off his sleeves, that he kept it as a kind of *memento mori* – he had had a strange fainting fit one day in his childhood while playing with the toy ... now the clockwork shall work again, for I have the key" (PF 137).

56   Unless, that is, there is a hidden agenda, and his early, mysterious claim, "the clockwork shall work again, for I have the key," hints at some secret machinations.

57   Schuman, "Nabokov and Shakespeare's Trees," identifies the trees' sources.

58   *Othello*, act 4, scene 3 (41): "*Desdemona* (singing) – The poor soul sat sighing by a Sycamore tree. // Sing all a green Willow; / Her hand on her bosom, her head on her knee, / Sing Willow, Willow, Willow. / The fresh streams ran by her, and murmur'd her moans; / Sing Willow, Willow, Willow. / Her salt tears fell from her and soften'd the stones, / Sing Willow, Willow, Willow. / Sing all a green Willow must be my garland."

59   "*Prologue*. Thisbe tarrying in Mulberry shade." *Midsummer Night's Dream*, act 5, scene 1 (149).

60   "*Clown*. In sad Cypress let me be laid." *Twelfth Night*, act 2, scene 4 (51).

61   "*Queen*. There is a Willow grows aslant a brook, / That shows his hoar leaves in the glassy stream. / There on the pendent boughs her coronet weeds / Clambering to hang, an envious sliver broke." *Hamlet*, act 4, scene 7 (167). "*Titania*. The female Ivy so / Enrings the barky fingers of the Elm." *Midsummer Night's Dream*, act 4, scene 1 (48). For some valuable exploration of the Ophelia theme in another Nabokov work, see Rakhimova-Sommers, "Nabokov's Mermaid," in *Nabokov's Women*, 58.

62   There are about twenty-three oak trees evoked in the works, plus an additional five references to acorns.

63   Or, more efficiently, one could simply have used Henry Nicholson Ellacombe's quite thorough *The Plant-Lore and Garden-Craft of Shakespeare*.

Notes to pages 142–4   249

64 "*Prospero.* To the dread rattling thunder / Have I given fire, and rifted Jove's stout oak / With his own bolt." *Tempest*, act 5, scene 1 (44).

65 "*Prospero.* If thou more murmur'st, I will rend an Oak, / And peg thee in his knotty entrails." *Tempest*, act 1, scene 2 (294).

66 *King Lear*, act 3, scene 2 (5).

67 "*Ariel.* All prisoners, sir, / In the Line-grove which weather-fends your cell." *Tempest*, act 5, scene 1 (9).

68 "*Sebastian.* That in Arabia / There is one tree, the Phoenix' throne; one Phoenix / At this hour reigning there." *Tempest*, act 3, scene 3 (22).

69 There was an extensive *Nabokv-L* discussion in 2006, originally started by Jerry Friedman in 2002, about the date palm's inability to survive in the New Wye climate, and various interpretations this fact might produce. Interested readers should conduct a phrase search for "date palm" at https://thenabokovian.org /search/node, using the "advanced search" function and, using the check-boxes below, limiting the search to *Nabokv-L.*

70 "*Prospero.* And by the spurs pluck'd up / The Pine and Cedar." *Tempest*, act 5, scene 1 (47). Jerry Friedman and Jansy Mello discussed the cedar/juniper deliberate confusion on *Nabokv-L* in 2006 (e.g.: https://thenabokovian.org/node/19308).

71 Ellacombe believes that Shakespeare never saw one of these trees, but they were of course trees of great renown throughout much of history (*Plant-Lore*, 52). Cedars (of Lebanon) are mentioned in the Bible, and the *Epic of Gilgamesh*; however, the cedar referred to in classical mythology is thought to be the prickly cedar, another juniper: *Juniperus oxycedrus*. See "Plants of Greek Myth," https://www.theoi.com /Flora1.html.

72 For more on the cedars in *Pale Fire*, see discussion in chapter 4.

73 Cf. also his comment about the "Oriole which is not an oriole" (PF 246).

74 "Sycamore" has a tempting etymology and a tempting history as a tree name: it derives from Greek, *sikon* (fig) + *moron* (mulberry), and the earliest use of this tree name was apparently for a fig tree whose leaves resemble those of the mulberry (the sycamore fig, *Ficus sycamorus*). Thus, in a sense, the name "sycamore" already includes *four* species of tree in its genealogy, with the mulberry present as one of "nature's rhymes," as *The Gift*'s Konstantin Godunov-Cherdyntsev might have put it. That Nabokov was aware of this etymology is suggested by the fact that the next tree but one is the mulberry itself.

75 "Myth 1: Tree of Dreams. The Oneiroi, spirits of dreams, roosted on the branches an elm tree near the entrance of Haides." (Source: Virgil). https://www.theoi .com/Flora1.html. Gerard de Vries suggests that Shakespeare may borrow his image from Ovid, *Metamorphoses*, book 10, the passage about Ardis. Personal communication.

76 In classical mythology, ivy is associated with the protection of Dionysus in infancy.

77 Shakespeare may have adopted his phrase "sad cypress" from Spenser, who used it in *The Faerie Queene* in 1590 (ii.i. sig. N7v: "The great earthes wombe they open to

250 Notes to pages 144–7

the sky, / And with sad Cypresse seemely it embraue." See "cypress, n.1, 1.c.," OED Online (Oxford University Press, March 2022), www.oed.com/view/Entry/46669. There is some disagreement over whether the word "cypress" in *Twelfth Night* refers to the tree or the fabric; Nabokov – or his fictitious avenue designer – clearly thought it was the tree, though his most likely source for his list of trees asserted that it was the fabric. I am grateful to Heather Hirschfeld for providing insight and guidance into this Shakespearean usage.

78 It is especially intriguing that in the example cited from *Othello*, if one includes the references to "willow" in both Desdemona's song and in Emilia's, two extra layers of nesting occur: Desdemona is already *quoting* Barbary's song (which took place under a sycamore), and Emilia, finally, is quoting Desdemona's quoted version. One wonders if Shakespeare scholars have noted this nested framing effect; it seems anticipatory of Lermontov's "triple dream," which Nabokov so loved.

79 Nabokov's interest in the shapes made by groups of trees can be seen in the alley at Vyra that forms a T with the "path of the Sphingids" (SM 26), which Avital Nemzer helpfully associates with the T formed by Todd and Cliff Roads in *Pnin* (Pn 120–1), roads which also have a full complement of variously described and animated trees. See Nemzer, "A Birch …" 47–9. Nemzer's full discussion of the Vyra avenue as a "channel of life in the branching system of his perennial childhood memories" is enlightening.

80 In fact, Nabokov mentions this very scene as one of the "fragmentary little pictures" he managed to recall when revisiting Cambridge after a seventeen-year absence: "Lewis Carroll's Dormouse, unexpectedly starting to tell a tale" (SM 273, unchanged from *Conclusive Evidence*).

81 The parallel between the "crown" of a tree and the "crown" of Kinbote's imagined royalty is also tempting.

82 Apparently, however, the confusion has its sources in ancient nomenclature. See "Cedar, Prickly or Juniper, Prickly," at "Plants of Greek Myth," https://www.theoi .com/Flora1.html.

83 The hickory, too, is not a Shakespearean tree, though it is closely related to both the walnut and, in ancient lore, to the hazel tree – the latter two were both "karya" in ancient Greek, *Carya* being today the genus for hickory, which is in the same family as the walnut's, *Juglans*, but not at all the hazel's *Corylus*, which is in the birch family, Betulaceae, vs. Juglandaceae for both walnut and hickory. (They are all in the order Fagales.)

84 "The Bay tree gives us a curious instance of the capriciousness of English plant names. Though a true Laurel it does not bear the name, which yet is given to two trees, the common (and Portugal) Laurel, and the Laurestinus, neither of which are Laurels – the one being a Cherry or Plum (*Prunus* or *Cerasus*), the other a Guelder Rose (*Viburnum*)." https://www.gutenberg.org/files/28407/28407-h/28407 -h.htm#Bay.

85 Or, to consider another boundary or border the trees might span, as Brian Boyd writes: "Art and science, he always insisted, meet at their highest level, because art

Notes to pages 147–50   251

and nature merge at their deepest. Art and nature certainly fuse throughout the worlds within worlds of *Pale Fire*" (Boyd, *Nabokov's "Pale Fire*," 243).

86 Notably, the first difference Van observes between the Ardis he sees as he approaches it for the first time, and the painting of it he had long seen in his father's dressing room, is between the "amplitude and animation of great trees" in the real present, contrasted with "regular rows of stylized saplings (thrown in by the mind of an architect rather than observed by the eye of a painter)" (A 35).

87 Nabokov seems to have learned of chaparral from Mayne Reid's *The Headless Horseman* (which he read in childhood), judging from his poem "To Prince S. M. Kachurin" (1947): "Isn't it time / to return to the theme of the bowstring, / or to what is enchantingly called 'chaparral' in *The Headless Horseman*" (SP 122).

88 "Ginkgo Biloba" (*sic*: Goethe correctly had "biloba" start with lowercase). In Goethe, *West-Eastern Divan*, 197. In his annotation, Ormsby states that this is the best-known poem in *West-Eastern Divan*.

89 By the novel's last pages, there are hints of "the secret Government-concealed identity of Terra and Antiterra. Demonian reality dwindled to a casual illusion. Actually, we had passed through all that. Our world *was*, in fact, mid-twentieth-century" (A 582).

90 But, cf. earlier boy in a cherry tree (A 35).

91 The "Chat." had a circumflex in the first edition, later removed. See Mason, *Nabokov's Garden*, 177, and discussion thereof in Boyd, *AdaOnline*, notes to *Ada*, 2–7.

92 In *Lectures on Literature*, "Good Readers and Good Writers," Nabokov asserts that the writer should be part storyteller, part teacher, and part enchanter, but "it is the enchanter which predominates and makes him a major writer" (LL 5).

93 According to Brian Boyd this poem "hybridizes François-René de Chateaubriand ... and Charles Baudelaire ... and their most famous poems, Chateaubriand's 'Romance à Hélène' from *Les Aventures du dernier Abencérage* ... and Baudelaire's 'L'Invitation au voyage'" (commentary to 106.11–26). Nabokov, in his *Onegin* commentary, points out that "*René*, a work of genius by the greatest French writer of his time ... was, he says, thought up under the very elm at Harrow, in Middlesex, England, where Byron 's'abandonnait aux caprices de son âge' (*Mémoires d'outre tombe*, ed. Levaillant, pt. I, bk. XII, ch. 4)" (EO 3.98).

94 See especially the first eight lines: "How vainly men themselves amaze / To win the Palm, the Oke, or Bayes; / And their uncessant Labours see / Crown'd from some single Herb or Tree, / Whose short and narrow verged Shade / Does prudently their Toyles upbraid; / While all Flow'rs and all Trees do close / To weave the Garlands of repose." (Available with basic commentary at Wikipedia, https:// en.wikipedia.org/wiki/The_Garden_(poem))

95 On Rimbaud and his poem, see Boyd's *AdaOnline* commentary to Part One, ch. 10, especially beginning at 64.15.

96 The cicada is associated with Aunt Maud's death metonymically through its abandoned case on the pine tree near the place where she died; the cypress was

252   Notes to pages 150–7

in one of her named paintings. The "steel cicada" as death emblem may also find a kind of echo in Shade's "clockwork toy," his metallic *memento mori*. Dolinin discusses the death theme in Annensky's *Cypress Chest*, especially in juxtaposition to life and art celebrated by Khodasevich in his *Heavy Lyre*, in his commentary to *The Gift*, *Kommentarii k romanu Nabokova "Dar,"* 114–17; also available in "'Dar': Dobavleniia k kommentariiam (chast ' vtoraia)," *Nabokov Online Journal* 2 (2008), 2ff, https://www.nabokovonline.com/uploads/2/3/7/7/23779748/v2_13 _dolinin.pdf.

97 The mythical subtext to this scene was first brought forward by Nemzer: see "A Birch …," 28–30.

6 *Ada*'s Exuberant Trees

1 See discussion of this topic in chapters 3 and 4, in relation to Fyodor in *The Gift*.

2 To reiterate – "not a true apple tree" (A 95), both in *Ada* and in "Genesis."

3 Shakespeare, however, reached sixty without any inventions; Nabokov's novel includes only fifty-eight real types (unless one were to include the peach tree, which I did not, alluded to in the novel only via its fruit, and as an abstract comparison through its fruit via buttocks; the fig is also mentioned with similar abstraction). In the lists from both authors, I have included shrubs – woody plants generally. See Ellacombe, *The Plant-Lore*. My compiled list of Shakespeare's trees and shrubs is in the appendices.

4 Boyd (*AdaOnline*) points out that this is a pun on the elitist "Who's who" publications.

5 The larva-web, though denied existence here, may deliberately implicate a mulberry (silk) moth, and produce an extremely subtle hint towards the theme that will entangle Lucette and lead to her death (by means of the "Midsummer Mulberry," discussed in the previous chapter).

6 See note 29, below.

7 Note also the extra parallel with Aqua's leaf in Marina's herbarium.

8 On that occasion, death is not mentioned, but as noted above, scrub oaks situate both Aqua's suicide and Percy's murder.

9 See discussion of the penholder above: introduction (SM, facing 256). Based on the evolution of oaks' appearance in Nabokov's oeuvre, it is tempting to think that even in this broad association with art, memory, transcendence, and death, the tree relates to Aikhenvald in the artist's mind. Aikhenvald's untimely death, caused by a streetcar on his way home from the Nabokovs' flat in 1928, might also figure into the way oaks intertwine with Lucette's sad fate in this novel, and the invented poem bookending, as it were, her story.

10 Nabokov repeats and distorts the recollecting echo in *Look at the Harlequins!*, where Vadim reflects on his own past as reflected in his *Ada*-like novel, *Ardis*, recalling the "avenue of statues and lilacs where Ada and I drew our first circles

on the dappled sand," calling this novel "my most private book, soaked in reality, saturated with sunflecks" (LATH 234). Vadim, of course, worries that his novel, and even his life – these most important scenes from it – "might be an unconscious imitation of another's unearthly art" (ibid.). The recurrence of these words and these motifs (tree-cast dapplings and sunflecks) in Nabokov's mock autobiography reaffirms their vital role wherever they appear in Nabokov's art. The dapple-casting trees in the later work are lilacs, and thus they appear to engage also in that *siren'* (lilac) – Sirin network of playful auto-allusions.

11 Boyd's *AdaOnline* annotations to pages 366 and 367 are especially useful in expanding our sense of the light-and-shadow game's significance. The entanglement of Lucette, too, in themes of light, shadow, and time, appears in the phrase "she inhabited this or that dapple of drifting sunlight, but could not be wholly dismissed with the rest of sun-flecked Ardis" (366–7), with its mix of "dapple," echoing "apple," recent "orchards," "flecks" – which recall the early game's "flecks" and "roundlets" (A 51) and "sunflecks" on Ada's reading (A 279), as well as Nabokov's own "strutting" among sunflecks in *Speak, Memory* (SM 21). See also Rivers and Walker, "Notes to Vivian Darkbloom's Notes to *Ada*," 291.

12 Boyd's annotation to this line (following Darkbloom's gloss) unpacks the tree-filled density of this moment: the referents are Eugene O'Neill's *Desire under the Elms* and Wilhelm Müller's poem "The Linden Tree," presented as a song in Thomas Mann's *The Magic Mountain*.

13 The secondary joke here, invisible to Greg, is that it is not her father, either, though only she knows this fact (via Blanche) at this moment in the text; the "foretaste of knowledge" episode at the shattal apple is less than a page worth of text further along in the novel. It, too, continues the "wrong tree" motif, since it is called an apple, but is not a "true apple tree" (it has drupes [p. 94], similar to peaches, plums, almonds, rather than a seeded fruit like an apple). But Eden's Tree of Knowledge was also not named as an apple tree, and its fruit never called an apple in the Bible. Nabokov may here be drawing on his awareness that the "apple" tradition from the Garden of Eden came late; the book on Shakespeare's flora that Nabokov may have consulted for his *Pale Fire* avenue of trees includes a long discussion of the word "apple" and its surprising history of use referring to other sorts of tree besides the genus *Malus*. See as well Jansy Mello's *Nabokv-L* note on the cat's chain, the *grand chêne*, Chateaubriand, with a side reference to the elm in Chekhov's play *The Seagull*: 29 October 2013, https://thenabokovian.org/node/6094.

14 Nemzer points out the relationship of this scene to Ovid's telling of the myth of Baucis and Philemon, who in old age become a linden and an oak in *Metamorphoses*, book 8 ("A Birch …," 28–30). Nemzer argues that Van and Ada's death "into the book" shows that they "fully merge – like Baucis and Philemon" (30). One might add that dying "into a book" evokes the word's etymology, "buk," beech tree.

15 Boyd, *Nabokov's "Ada,"* 218; also discussed in Mason, *Nabokov's Garden*, 33–4.

254   Notes to pages 160–2

16 In a letter to Bobbie Ann Mason, Nabokov hinted at the special import of this poem, memorized by Lucette: "it is a stylized glimpse of a mysterious person visiting the place, open to tourists, where in legendary times ... a certain Peter T. [Peter Townsend] had his last interview with the Queen's sister. Although he accuses the old guide of being a 'ghost,' it is he, in the reversal of time, who is a ghostly tourist, the ghost of Peter T. himself; ... it should send a tingle down the spine of the reader." Mason, *Nabokov's Garden*, 185 n. 2.

17 In Boyd's efficient summary, Violet Knox (Van's typist) "seems to be – without her or Van's in the least suspecting – Lucette's unconscious letter-carrier (Violet types the book out on the special Atticus paper named after Cicero's *Letters to Atticus*, that also alludes to that first scene of the novel which takes place in the Ardis attic during the time that Lucette learns the poem about a ghost talking to a mortal which she quotes in a letter Van receives from her after her death)" (*Nabokov's "Ada,"* 252).

18 Boyd notes that Nabokov had recently used a similar tree in his translation of the *Lay of Igor's Campaign*. https://www.ada.auckland.ac.nz/ada11ann.htm.

19 Via "l'adore" (love(s) her/him/it).

20 Mason makes a brief introductory study of parallels between *Ada* and E. Darwin's *Botanic Garden* in *Nabokov's Garden*, 170–2, and urges others to follow up on this; apparently, no one yet has done so (although my own look at the text led me to think it not so promising). Erasmus Darwin's text is a poem with an attached and very elaborate commentary by the author (the commentary sections are longer than the sections of poem they explain). Also relevant here is Bosch's "Garden of Earthly Delights," whose connections to *Ada* are widely discussed; see esp. Boyd, *Nabokov's "Ada,"* and *AdaOnline*.

21 Could "Empire style" be intended as a hidden underscoring of the paulownia, elsewhere in the novel called "Imperialis"?

22 However, if Zemski was the cousin of Catherine's granddaughter, that could imply that one of his parents was a sibling to Anna Pavlovna; all of these siblings were of non-Romanov parentage, as Catherine's husband was murdered (with her prior knowledge or tacit participation) and they were raised under different names. Second- and third-cousin relationships are also possible, of course. This interpretation, however, relies somewhat on the Anglo-American tradition of "cousin" meaning "first cousin," with greater distances typically specified as "second-" etc.

23 The cryptic reference to this situation produces several options: they are cousins of *Paul* (meaning perhaps that one of Zemski's parents was a cousin of Catherine II (her mother had several siblings; Peter III apparently had no siblings); or due to the linguistic antecedent, Zemski may be a cousin of Anna Pavlovna, whose mother had eleven siblings (Paul, officially, had none, and his own parentage is allegedly tied to Count Sergei Saltykov, rather than his nominal father Peter III, further muddying that line). Nabokov used an impossibly complex sentence to refer to an impenetrably complex situation in Russia's royal family.

Notes to pages 163–4   255

24 Cf.: "a stillborn infant a half a year old, a surprised, little fetus, a fish of rubber that she had produced in her bath, in a *leiu de naissance* plainly marked X in her dreams, after skiing at full pulver into a larch stump, had somehow been saved and brought to her at the Nusshaus" (A 25). Nemzer discusses Nabokov's dream of the 26–27 December 1964, which features a larch as a Christmas tree, and its realization in *Ada* ("A Birch ...," 67–8). Nabokov's narration of the dream, in *Insomniac Dreams*, 89–90, displays a striking case of trees' place in his conscious and subconscious creativity. In his note, he points out the connection between this dream tree and the yew in *Pale Fire*. For Nemzer and for Barabtarlo, these trees are strongly connected to otherworldly themes ("A Birch ...," 68–9; *Insomniac Dreams*, 89n93). The dream also falls cleanly into Nabokov's extended interest in the "wrong tree" phenomenon.

25 "Volosyanka" derives from Russian *volos* (hair, plural *volosy*). Cf. "-ianka" suffix: https://en.wiktionary.org/wiki/-янка.

26 *Nabokov's "Ada," passim*, esp. 125 and 129.

27 The scene also dresses Ada in the same clothing Aqua had worn for her suicide – yellow slacks and a "black bolero" (A 295, 298, cf. 28). As Boyd notes (*AdaOnline*), Lucette also put on yellow (actually "lemon") and black the night of her suicide (A 492). The ginkgo leaf's green (like Lucette's eyes) changing to yellow (like her and her late aunt's suicidal clothing) appears to be yet another deliberate echo and parallel. Boyd (*Nabokov's "Ada,"* 150) also links the word "maidenhair" with Lucette's maidenhood, and the *souci d'eau* (marsh marigold) theme with the *arbre au quarante écus d'or*, identified as a French name for the tree. However, the true French name lacks the phrase "d'or" (which Nabokov added) and is based simply on the fact that the tree in early years cost forty *écus*, an archaic French coin. These coins existed in gold as well as silver variants. See Crane, *Ginkgo* (220), where one finds the origins of the tree's French name presented in charming detail from a quoted narrative by André Thouin. In brief, the tree's original French acquirer, one M. Petigny, paid 120 francs each, or forty crowns (actually twenty-five guineas, in London), for five small plants grown from seed in 1780. Casual research suggests that the *écus* in wide circulation at that time were silver. The history and value of these coins in that day can be found under the section "French Revolution" of the Wikipedia page: https://en.wikipedia.org/wiki/écu.

28 The fact that the novel's first named tree is a ginkgo, through a leaf taken from (fallen from) "Letters from Terra," may also be a deliberate early trace of Lucette's role in the work (this fallen "maidenhair," given by Aqua to Marina). Such a strategy would echo the encoding of Zina into the first pages of *The Gift* through shadows, poplars, and an angular street. Blackwell, *Zina's Paradox*, 127.

29 Chaparral is a distinct type of shrubby plant ecosystem, characterized by fire-resistant and fire-dependent species. The name comes from Spanish "chaparro," a species of scrub oak (*Q. coccifera*), derived originally from Basque "txapar," "little thicket." https://en.wikipedia.org/wiki/Quercus_coccifera. The Wikipedia

256 Notes to pages 164–7

article on chaparral ecosystems includes a fine bibliography and summary: https://en.wikipedia.org/wiki/Chaparral. Chaparral is also mentioned in the poem "To Prince K.M. Kachurin" (1947), where a source in Mayne Reid's *The Headless Horseman* is revealed (PP 141).

30 The oak supports the swing in the "old baldy" scene, Lucette's second reported eye-witness moment (A 212).

31 In this respect, it reverberates with similarly tree-dense moments in *Pnin*, *Pale Fire*, and *Speak, Memory*.

32 Note also the echo of the weeping willow in this tree; two of the trees that attend Lucette's exposure to sex and erotic play are thus "weeping."

33 Charitably, we can presume that the sequoia here is so young that it is not "giant," though it would not look much like a cedar of Lebanon. Cedars of this type feature in the *Epic of Gilgamesh*, which is noted as the world's oldest surviving piece of literary art. They also feature in the Bible. Cedars featured in Greek myth are actually not cedars (g. *Cedrus*) but junipers, (gg. *Juniperus* and *Thuja*); see discussion of this difference and identification/"wrong tree" problem in *Pale Fire* above, in chapter 4. The "weeping cedar" was one of Nabokov's favourite trees in the Montreux Palace garden, where he often wrote; see *Strong Opinions*, 55.

34 In addition to the *Pale Fire* tree, there is also a "mulberry moth" in *Lolita*, and a metonymic silk (from mulberry-moth silk) dinner jacket in *Pnin*. The mulberry is a particularly Shakespearean tree, as he famously planted one at his home, New Place, which launched a legend and then a small industry in keepsakes when it was cut down in the 1750s (including snuff boxes with the punning inscription, "Memento mori"). See http://theshakespeareblog.com/2014/07/shakespeares-mulberry-and-new-place/.

35 One wonders, does the soap deliberately recall Aqua's miscarriage in the tub?

36 The fictitious ballad itself, as already noted, includes a forest of oaks or ghost-oaks.

37 "Luminous" echoes the "light" component of Lucette's name; "greenish" – her eyes; gold – perhaps the yellow she (like Aqua) wore on the day of her death.

38 Note how Nabokov has created these two separate pathways from the ginkgo to Shakespeare: the maiden's hair "tentaclinging," recalling Ophelia's drowning by (probable) suicide; and the leaves' autumn state, "n'est vert, n'est vert, n'est vert, n'est vert, n'est vert," "not green," from "Never, never, never, never, never," among Lear's last words while dying from grief after Cordelia's murder.

39 See "Motif: peat" at *AdaOnline*.

40 Extensively discussed by Boyd, *Nabokov's "Ada,"* 251–2.

41 "Hamlet/Gamlet" of course points to Shakespeare, and perhaps obliquely to Ophelia's fate. Birches appear only in *Measure for Measure*, act 1, scene 3, as a symbolic threat of corporal punishment. The date Nabokov used for his father's birthday in *Conclusive Evidence* was 21 July.

42 The paulownia's second appearance (under the name "imperialis" – recall, again, the "Empire style" adjoining the first one) evokes, very faintly, "The Rain Has

Flown": " a window flew open all by itself, and a powerful shower started to drum upon the liriodendron and imperialis leaves outside, and the conversation became general and loud. Not long did the rain last – or rather stay: it continued on its presumable way to Raduga or Ladoga or Kaluga or Luga, shedding an uncompleted rainbow over Ardis Hall" (A 68). This rain has clearly flown by (*proletel*, in the Russian); it may not be pure coincidence that just two and three pages later, we find the words "honey" (repeatedly) and "anthemia" (which via *Webster's Second* connects to honeysuckle, and appears directly related to the 1966 foreword to *Speak, Memory* and its mention of the rejected title "The Anthemion"); Boyd concurs, see *AdaOnline*, http://www.ada.auckland.ac.nz/ada112.htm#71.02). As we saw in chapter 1, honeysuckle is a crucial image in "The Rain Has Flown," though in Nabokov's English disguised as "caprifole." The paulownia leaf is heart-shaped, like the leaf in the related "First Poem" episode of *Speak, Memory* (and elsewhere). In these early Ardis scenes, it appears that Nabokov is creating a distorted, distanced (if not estranged) version of his own creative origins.

43 See Grant and Blackwell, "Toilets, Trees, and Inspiration."

44 See also the discussion of cedar in *Pale Fire*, in chapter 4.

45 The novel also refers to it as a "Chinese tree"; another name for it is "Kew tree," which is used in *Transparent Things* (TT 55) and *Look at the Harlequins!* (LATH 75).

46 Van also draws attention to the ginkgo's two Latin binomials, the valid *Ginkgo biloba* and the "sunk" *Salisburia adiantifolia*. See *AdaOnline* at http://www.ada .auckland.ac.nz/ada141.htm#300.06.

47 "Bereza v vorontsovskom parke" (Birch in Vorontsov Park) (SSRP 1:474). See discussion in chapter 1 of use of birches in nostalgic poems about Russia (e.g., "Son na Akropole" [Dream on the Acropolis]).

48 One could wonder, is newly dead Demon in some way influencing the course of Andrey's disease, to keep the two of them apart? Given the novel's suggestion of the deads' ability to play some role in the lives of the quick, we can imagine an argument taking place between Lucette and Demon. The extended episode's emphasis on what looks like protective fate early on, replaced by its exact reversal as Ada must return to nurse Andrei for another seventeen years (though it is first suggested that he is at death's door in the 1905 scene), leaves room for speculation.

49 One wonders if the word "miserable" here is meant as a deliberate echo of the *mizernoe* (Christmas "larch") (A 7), although her meaning here is different from the French and Russian meaning of this word glossed by Nabokov via Vivian Darkbloom ("'miserable' in the sense of 'paltry'").

50 The larch is associated both with Aqua's miscarriage and with Lucette's neglectful exposure to sex from a young age. This scene actually creates a nexus between the mulberry bath scene and the willow, for it is to the larches Lucette steals, spying on the lovers from there when she escapes the willow, causing Van later to exclaim, "that explains the angle of the soap!" (A 152).

258   Notes to pages 170–3

51 Boyd, "Lucette Late in *Ada*," 121, 134.

52 The blooms on this tree may be temporal hallucinations or mnemonic flaws, as paulownias produce flowers in early spring, before they leaf out, and not at all in "July" – even, surely, along Lake Geneva.

53 Note Aqua's "flame-colored nightgown" (A 26). Cf. also *Ada* Annotations 2.5, August 2021, now at *AdaOnline* – especially with reference to the phrase "emblazed trees" at 366.24–5, which Van contemplates through the "northeast casement" of a suite in Kingston; here, too, Lucette "inhabited this or that dapple of drifting sunlight." Lucette is "liquefied" in her death, but "on fire" by means of her hair colour.

54 Aspen, while also genus *Populus* (usually, *P. tremuloides* [N. American] or *P. tremula* [Eurasian]), is always named separately from poplars in Nabokov's works (in Russian, *osina* vs. *topol'*).

55 The Lombardy poplar has key placements in *Pnin* and *Speak, Memory*; non-specific poplars have significant appearances throughout the works, including (as we saw) early and late poems named for them.

56 Cf. also the phone call at the end of "Signs and Symbols," the phone call telling Humbert of Charlotte's death, among other examples.

57 This is *Saturnia pyri*; see Dieter E. Zimmer's very important note (one of his great gems in his monumental work), with his photograph of the fresco in question at http://www.d-e-zimmer.de/eGuide/Lep2.1-Q-S.htm#S.pyri. It will be seen that, in the fresco, the moths are not "in copula" – perhaps a difference between Antiterra and "our world," or one between the worlds of fiction and of fact. According to Zimmer, this same moth appears in *Invitation* and elsewhere. He notes, "Latin *pirum* or *pyrum* is 'pear' and 'apple,'" but one is forced to wonder from the context whether a pun on "pyre" or L. "pyra" is intended in the choice of this exact species by Nabokov in this context. His 1951 letter to Katharine White about "Liriodendron," apparently based on an interlingual phonetic but not etymological pun, lends support to the idea. ("Orpheus's lyre" may be the intended referent in that case.) Boyd describes Nabokov's real-life visit to this room in his annotation to 400.21, currently at https://thenabokovian.org/annotations/ada-2-7.

58 Van's comments about his call with Ada here also seem pertinent to the history of phone calls in Nabokov's works, culminating in this moment.

59 See Jonathan Rowan's discussion of the mirroring quality of this tree and its background: "True to Life," 78–80.

60 The poplar nymph, additionally, was the first butterfly Nabokov found an interesting subspecies of, as a boy in 1908, sending it to the renowned entomologist Nikolai Kuznetsov in hopes that it was a new species entirely (SM 133).

61 Note also that the "elements" here are viewed through the window, just as Lucette had discovered the moth fresco in the window alcove of the Elements Room.

62 There is also something to explore further in the empty face powder container Van finds in the bureau, with a Firebird image on the box; it was the powder Lucette

had preferred, adding to an extended theme of confusion or overlap between Ada and Lucette.

63 However, the fact that they both, or Ada, directly interpret the pun "morzhey" as indicating "a mermaid's message" (A 562) could indicate that much of the Lucette theme in the work is similarly devised by them in the act of artistic creation, as a tribute and commemoration, a transformation of Lucette into art (more than a weak palliative?).

64 Cf., again, the Firebird on the face powder, and note also Nabokov's early poem "The Quill," with its firebird as the source of the writer's art (abetted by the wood-sprite, and all present in Pushkin's "Ruslan" stories told by the cat on the gold chain). See also Brian Boyd's treatment of the "fire" and "ember" themes in his *AdaOnline* notes to page 366.

Epilogue

1 Morris, *Nabokov: Poetry and the Lyric Voice*, 195ff. Morris's discussion, to my knowledge the most in-depth of any scholar's, spans about seven pages and concerns primarily the poem's juxtapositions of rationality and irrationality, this-world and otherworld. Cf. discussion in Boyd, *Nabokov: The American Years*, 303–5. Morris also points us to Fowler, *Reading Nabokov*, 205, as the only significant earlier treatment of the poem, but one which, Morris suggests, is too limited.

2 Brian Boyd suggests another parallel in Norman Rockwell (*Nabokov: The American Years*, 304), and while I can see the temptation for this proposal, I think Nabokov's own formulation is really spot-on and needs no supplement. My main reason for this claim is that, to my eye, Rockwell's paintings – the dozen or two I've just taken time to review and consider – look like stills from a film or from action in "real life"; Grandma Moses, on the other hand, presents pastoral, iconic images that transcend time, or enfold a great swath of it: these are not slices of life. Chagall's images are outside of earthly time altogether.

3 Morris, *Nabokov: Poetry and the Lyric Voice*, 197, citing Nabokov, "The Art of Literature and Commonsense."

4 Blackwell, "Three Notes on *The Gift*."

5 Cf. Vladimir Nabokov, *Polnoe sobranie rasskazov*, 3rd (rev.) ed., edited by Andrei Babikov (St. Petersburg: Azbuka, 2016), 38.

6 Ovid, *Metamorphoses*, book 11.

7 A subject awaiting analysis is why *Look at the Harlequins!* is completely lacking in birches. (They appear about thirteen times in its mirror-text, *Speak, Memory*.)

8 Zsuzsa Hetenyi associates these poplars with the tree's role at the gates of Hades, and the myth of Persephone, which may help explain some appearances – especially in *Lolita* – but far from all (Hetenyi, "Lolita as Goddess," 47).

9 Nabokov's Cambridge-era poem, "Kashtany" (Chestnuts), gives these trees a spiritual aspect: it opens, "Blooming chestnuts, like temples." and ends, "chestnuts,

260   Notes to pages 178–81

delightful temples" (SSRP 1, 532.; ellipsis original). See ch. 4 n. 34, concerning the chestnut blooms' role in earlier writers' responses to Cambridge, discussed by Voronina.

10 It may be significant that Ardalion, in the portrait he is drawing, includes "gallow trees" (Desp 56).

11 The "ick" echoes Felix's "stick" unconsciously; the stick itself is made of linden (Desp 73).

12 In "Nabokov's Wiener-Schnitzel Dreams," I argued that the pine tree is related to myths of Cybele and Agdistis (a god who dies and is reborn). However, I by no means intend to suggest that in general, for Nabokov, pines always point to this specific mythology.

13 The motif is previewed in the story "Perfection," as well, written the same year; there, a tutor (Ivanov) takes his charge to the seaside to swim, through a pine wood that is "dense" (CS 343 and 344); dangers and otherworldly implications abound. The story deserves a full work-up from this point of view.

14 E.g., Boyd, *Nabokov: The Russian Years*, 369, 402, 420. Nabokov visited especially often in the summer of 1926, while Véra was at a sanatorium (see LTV 76, 90, 94, and note on 570). In *Speak, Memory*, he reports that much later, when Dmitri was a toddler, they rarely visited "the popular pine barrens around the lake in Berlin's Grunewald" (SM 303); it had by then, perhaps, become less attractive, or Véra just didn't like it: "You questioned the right of a place to call itself a forest when it was so full of refuse."

15 Boyd, *Nabokov: The Russian Years*, 369, 402, 420.

16 Aleksandr Dolinin notes that the last word in Khodasevich's collection *The Heavy Lyre*, named as one of Yasha's books just after his suicide, is "Orpheus" (Dolinin, *Kommentarii*, 116–17). Nabokov translated Khodasevich's poem, originally called "Ballada," into "Orpheus." See *Verses and Versions*, 344–7. See also discussion in Shvabrin, *Between Rhyme and Reason*, 206. The translation is not literal; as Shvabrin notes, of this poem and "The Monkey," "The calculated liberties they take, however, reveal the presence of a considered agenda" (ibid.). See also Senderovich, "Pushkin v 'Dare' Nabokova," esp. 524–7; Wilson, "Nabokov and Khodasevich," 10.

17 In *Bend Sinister*, pines appear on pages 83, 91, 94, and 95, but without clear thematic unity.

18 This particular episode is actually the last of several "daily" visits they made there in late July.

19 This is the only time we see Humbert swim in *Lolita*: later, when Dolly swims in Champion, Colorado, he "could not swim with [his] heart in that state" (L 236).

20 Curiously, as Charlotte finishes her last letters and takes them to the mailbox, Humbert prepares them each "whiskey and a dram of soda. She had tabooed my pin" (97): "pin" is also French for "pine."

Notes to pages 182–6   261

21 The camp where Mira Belochkin perished was Buchenwald, located on Grosser Ettersberg, near Weimar. See Liapunov, "Pnin and Goethe," as well as Ronen, "Nabokov and Goethe."

22 The passage also describes how Pnin removes his "Greek Catholic" (i.e., Orthodox) cross; Ardalion, in *Despair*, had one as well, which he did not remove to swim.

23 By the time he wrote *Pnin*, a sandy pine barren was already associated with his discovered subspecies (now species), the Karner blue, which he visited annually. Boyd, *Nabokov: The American Years*, 168, 296.

24 Berg Collection, "Corrections to *Nabokov's Garden* by Bobbie Ann Rawlings," p. 5. The well-known book was published under the name Bobbie Ann Mason. I am grateful to the latter for bringing the notes to my attention and sending me a copy.

25 Vladimir Alexandrov's *Nabokov's Otherworld* influentially advocates for a biographical interpretation of various metaphysical figures throughout Nabokov's works; Paul D. Morris (on the poems) and Maxim D. Shrayer (on the stories) offer a similar approach. Brian Boyd's readings, such as in *Nabokov's "Pale Fire,"* present a related but less categorical approach to the problem. For a forceful argument against using Nabokov's art to speculate about his personal beliefs, see Muravnik, "Nabokov's Philosophy of Art," and its excerpted introduction, "Nabokov's Philosophy of Art."

26 Avital Nemzer is an important exception, but I started asking this question, and publishing about it, years before she began her thesis.

Works Cited and Consulted

Works by Nabokov (with Abbreviations)

A — *Ada or Ardor: A Family Chronicle*. 1969. New York: Vintage, 1990.

– — *The Annotated Lolita*, ed. Alfred Appel, Jr. Rev. ed. New York: Vintage, 1991.

– — "The Art of Translation." Letter to the editor. *New Republic* 105, no. 12 (1941): 375. Also in *Think, Write, Speak*, 184.

BS — *Bend Sinister*. New York: Vintage, 1990.

CS — *Collected Stories*. London: Penguin, 1997.

CE — *Conclusive Evidence*. New York: Harper, 1951.

Df — *The Defense*. Trans. Michael Scammell with Vladimir Nabokov. New York: Vintage, 1990.

Desp — *Despair*. Trans. Vladimir Nabokov. 1966. New York: Vintage, 1989.

DB — *Drugie berega/Other Shores*. SSRP 5, 140-335. [Russian revision of *CE*].

EO — *Eugene Onegin*. By Alexander Pushkin. Trans. with commentary by Vladimir Nabokov. Rev. ed. Princeton, NJ: Princeton University Press, 1975. 4 vols.

– — "First Poem." Partisan Review 16, no. 9 (September 1949): 8885–93.

G — *The Gift*. Trans. Michael Scammell with Vladimir Nabokov. 1963. New York: Vintage, 1991.

Gl — *Glory*. Trans. Dmitri Nabokov with Vladimir Nabokov. [*Podvig* 1932]. 1971. New York: Vintage, 1991.

– — *Insomniac Dreams*. Ed. Gennady Barabtarlo. Princeton: Princeton University Press, 2018.

IB — *Invitation to a Beheading*. Trans. Dmitri Nabokov with Vladimir Nabokov. New York: Vintage, 1989.

KQK — *King, Queen, Knave*. Trans. Dmitri Nabokov and Vladimir Nabokov. New York: Vintage, 1989.

LD — *Laughter in the Dark*. New York: Vintage, 1989.

LL — *Lectures on Literature*. Ed. Fredson Bowers. New York: Harcourt Brace Jovanovich and Bruccoli Clark, 1980.

264 Works Cited and Consulted

–   *Lectures on Russian Literature.* Ed. Fredson Bowers. New York: 1981.
LTV   *Letters to Véra.* Ed. and trans. Olga Voronina and Brian Boyd. New York: Alfred A. Knopf, 2014.
L   *Lolita.* New York: Vintage, 1989.
–   *Lolita: A Screenplay.* New York: Vintage, 1997.
LATH   *Look at the Harlequins!* New York: Vintage, 1990.
M   *Mary.* Trans. Michael Glenny with Vladimir Nabokov. New York: Vintage, 1989.
–   "Nearctic Forms of *Lycaeides* Hüb. (Lycaenidae, Lepidoptera)." In *Nabokov's Butterflies*, ed. Boyd and Pyle, 278–88; also in *Psyche* 50 (September–December 1943): 87–99.
–   "Notes on Neotropical Plebejinae (Lycaenidae, Lepidoptera)." *Psyche* 52.1–2 (March–June 1945): 1–61.
–   *Dear Bunny, Dear Volodya: The Nabokov-Wilson Letters 1940–1971.* With Edmund Wilson. Rev. and expanded ed. Ed. Simon Karlinsky. University of California Press, 2001.
PF   *Pale Fire.* New York: Vintage, 1989.
–   *Pis'ma k Vere.* Moscow: KoLibri, 2017.
Pn   *Pnin.* 1957. New York: Vintage, 1989.
PP   *Poems and Problems.* New York: McGraw-Hill, 1970.
RLSK   *The Real Life of Sebastian Knight.* New York: New Directions, 1959.
SP   *Selected Poems.* Ed. Thomas Karshan. New York: Knopf, 2012.
SSRP   *Sobranie sochinenii russkogo perioda v piati tomakh.* 5 vols. St. Petersburg: Symposium, 1999.
SM   *Speak, Memory: An Autobiography Revisited.* New York: Vintage, 1989.
SO   *Strong Opinions.* New York: Vintage, 1990.
TWS   *Think, Write, Speak: Uncollected Essays, Reviews, Interviews, and Letters to the Editor.* Ed. Brian Boyd and Anastasia Tolstoy. New York: Knopf; London: Penguin, 2019.
TT   *Transparent Things.* New York: Vintage International, 1989.
–   *Verses and Versions.* Ed. Brian Boyd and Stanislav Shvabrin. Orlando: Harcourt, 2008.
–   "Victor Meets Pnin." *The New Yorker*, 15 October 1955, 38–45.
SL   *Vladimir Nabokov: Selected Letters, 1940–1977.* Ed. Dmitri Nabokov and Matthew J. Bruccoli. San Diego: Harcourt Brace Jovanovich, 1989.

Archival Material (Berg Collection) (including unpublished poems about trees not discussed in this book)

"And when the tawny woods are full." n.d. [1950s].
"Corrections to *Nabokov's Garden* by Bobbie Ann Rawlings." 1973.
"Pel noch'iu rebenok v lesu." (15 August 1920) [Album 20, v. 2] (p. 395).
"Topolia." Cambridge, 12 November 1921. [Prose and poetry notebook, Album 22] (pp. 126–7).

"Tsarskoe selo." 1917. [Stikhi Album A].

"Veterok." 30 November 1922. [Stikhi Album 7] (p. 64).

"Vot kiparis bezzvuchnyi na lugu" (12 August 1921; [Prose and poetry notebook, Album 22] (p. 58).

"Zvezda nad listvoiu." 9 January 1923 [Stikhi Album 7] (p. 75).

"Allei lipovoi cherneet ulublen'e." 1917 [*sic*] [Album A] (p. 10).

"Nad parkom dozhd' bormochet odnozvuchno." (2 November 1917) [Album B (StikhotvArenie)] (p. 24).

Secondary Sources

AAA Southeastern Tour Book. Automobile Association of America, 1947.

Aikhenval'd, Iulii. "Vstuplenie." In *Siluety russkikh pisatelei*. Moscow: Respublika, 1994.

Alexander, Victoria N. "Hopeful Monsters: Literary Teleology and Emergence." *Emergence: Complexity & Organization* 7 (2005): 95–104.

– "Nabokov, Teleology, and Insect Mimicry." *Nabokov Studies* 7 (2003): 177–214.

Alter, Robert. *Nabokov and the Real World.* Princeton: Princeton University Press, 2021.

American Guide Series: North Carolina. Federal Writers' Project, WPA. Chapel Hill: University of North Carolina Press, 1939.

Appel, Alfred Jr., ed. Notes to *The Annotated Lolita*, by Vladimir Nabokov, 319–457. Rev. ed. New York: Vintage, 1991

– "Remembering Nabokov." In *Vladimir Nabokov: A Tribute*, ed. Peter Quennell, 11–33. New York: William Morrow, 1980.

Babikov, Andrei. "Nakhodchivaia Mnemozina: Arkhivnye materialy k memuaram Nabokova." *Literaturnyi fakt* 2 (2017): 8–52.

– *Prochtenie Nabokova.* Saint Petersburg: Ivan Limbakh, 2019.

Barabtarlo, Gennady. "Nabokov's Trinity: On the Movement of Nabokov's Themes." In *Nabokov and His Fiction: New Perspectives*, ed. Julia W. Connolly, 109–38. Cambridge: Cambridge University Press, 1999.

– *Phantom of Fact: A Guide to Nabokov's Pnin.* Ann Arbor: Ardis, 1989.

Barskova, Polina. "Filial Feelings and Paternal Patterns. Transformations of *Hamlet* in *The Gift*." *Nabokov Studies* 9 (2005): 191–208.

Belova, O.V. "Il'ia sv." In *Slavianskie drevnosti: Etnolingvisticheskii slovar' v 5 t.*, ed. N.I. Tolstoy. Moscow: Institut slavianovedeniia RAN, 1999.

Blackwell, Stephen H. "Calendar Anomalies, Pushkin, and Aesthetic Love in Nabokov." *Slavonic and East European Review* (London) 96, no. 2 (July 2018): 401–31.

– "A Flurry of Words about One Small Dot in *The Gift*." *The Nabokovian* 78 (Fall 2019). https://thenabokovian.org/nabokovian-new-notes/78-2019fa.

– "Nabokov, Mach, and Monism." In *Nabokov at the Crossroads,* vol. 1, ed. Jane Grayson, Arnold McMillin, and Priscilla Meyer, 121–31. Houndmills Basingstoke: Palgrave, 2002.

– "Nabokov's 'The Gift,' Dostoevskii, and the Tradition of Narratorial Ambiguity." *Slavic Review* 76, no. 1 (Spring 2017): 1–22.

266   Works Cited and Consulted

- "Nabokov's Wiener-Schnitzel Dreams: Anti-Freudian Poetics in *Despair*." *Nabokov Studies* 7 (2002/3): 129–50.
- *The Quill and the Scalpel*. Columbus: Ohio State University Press, 2009.
- "Reflections on (and of) Trees in Nabokov." In *Nabokov Upside Down*, ed. Brian Boyd and Marijeta Bozovic, 21–36. Evanston: Northwestern University Press, 2017.
- "Three Notes on *The Gift*: An Intertext, a Revision, and a Puzzle Solved," *The Nabokovian* 40 (Spring 1998): 36–9.
- *Zina's Paradox: The Figured Reader in Nabokov's "Gift"* New York: Peter Lang, 2000.
Blackwell, Stephen H., and Kurt Johnson. *Fine Lines: Vladimir Nabokov's Scientific Art*. New Haven: Yale University Press, 2016.
Bouchet, Marie. "Crossbreeding Word and Image: Nabokov's Subversive Use of Ekphrasis." *MoveableType* 2, "The Mind's Eye" (2006). https://discovery.ucl.ac.uk/id/eprint/1572290/1/Marie%20Bouchet.pdf.
Bowie, Robert. "*Bend Sinister* Annotations: Chapter Seven and Shakespeare," *The Nabokovian* 32 (Spring 1994): 28–53.
Boyd, Brian. *AdaOnline*. http://www.ada.auckland.ac.nz/.
- "*Lolita*: What We Know and What We Don't." *Cycnos* 24, no. 1 (2008). http://revel.unice.fr/cycnos/pdf.php?id=1079&revue=cycnos.
- "Lucette Late in *Ada*," *Nabokov Studies* 17 (2022): 121–35.
- *Nabokov's "Ada": The Place of Consciousness*. Rochester, MN: CyberEditions: 2003.
- *Nabokov's "Pale Fire": The Magic of Artistic Discovery*. Princeton: Princeton University Press, 1999.
- "PF narrator? BOYD." *Nabokv-L*, 22 December 1997. https://thenabokovian.org/index.php/node/32714.
- "Shade and Shape in *Pale Fire*." *Nabokov Studies* 4 (1997): 173–224.
- *Stalking Nabokov*. New York: Columbia University Press, 2011.
- *Vladimir Nabokov: The American Years*. Princeton: Princeton University Press, 1990.
- *Vladimir Nabokov: The Russian Years*. Princeton: Princeton University Press, 1991.
Boyd, Brian, and Robert Michael Pyle, eds. *Nabokov's Butterflies*. Boston: Beacon, 2000.
Buks, Nora. *Eshafot v khrustal'nom dvortse*. Moscow: Novoe Literaturnoe Obozrenie, 1998.
Burlaka, D.K., et al. *V.V. Nabokov – pro et contra: Lichnost' i tvorchestvo Vladimira Nabokova v otsenke russkikh i zarubezhnykh myslitelei i issledovatelei: Antologiia*. Saint Petersburg: Izd-vo Russkogo Khristianskogo Gumanitarnogo Un-ta, 1997.
Burt, Isabella. *Memorials of the Oak Tree, with Notices of the Classical and Historical Associations Connected with It*. London, 1860.
Connolly, Julian. *Nabokov's Early Fiction: Patterns of Self and Other*. Cambridge, UK: Cambridge University Press, 1992.
Costlow, Jane. *Heart-Pine Russia: Walking and Writing the Nineteenth-Century Forest*. Ithaca, NY: Cornell University Press, 2013.
Crane, Peter. *Ginkgo*. New Haven: Yale University Press, 2013.

Works Cited and Consulted   267

Dal', Vladimir I. *Tolkovyi slovar' zhivogo velikorusskogo iazyka: V chetyrekh tomakh.*
Moscow: Progress, 1994.

Davydov, Sergei. "*The Gift*: Nabokov's Aesthetic Exorcism of Chernyshevski."
Canadian-American Slavic Studies 19, no. 3 (1985): 357–74.

de Vries, Gerard. "*Pale Fire* and the Romantic Movement." ZEMBLA (online).
https://web.archive.org/web/20110610044328/https://libraries.psu.edu/nabokov
/devriespf.htm.

– "Zimmer on Shakespeare Alley and NYHT Interview." *Nabokv-L*, 15
November 2006. https://thenabokovian.org/sites/default/files/2018-01
/NABOKV-L-0014057___body.html.

Deleuze, Gilles, and Félix Guattari. *A Thousand Plateaus: Capitalism and
Schizophrenia*. Trans. Brian Massumi. Minneapolis: University of Minnesota Press,
1987.

DeRewal, Tiffany, and Matthew Roth. "John Shade's Duplicate Selves: An Alternative
Shadean Theory of *Pale Fire*." *Nabokov Online Journal* 3 (2009). http://www
.nabokovonline.com/uploads/2/3/7/7/23779748/v3_06_roth.pdf.

Dirig, Robert. "Drawing with Words: The Toothwort White and Related Natural
History Motifs in *Pale Fire*." In Blackwell and Johnson, *Fine Lines*, 201–15.

Dolinin, Aleksandr [Alexander]. "Botkin." *Nabokov-L*, 14 October 2006. https://
thenabokovian.org/node/20670).

– "'Dar': Dobavleniia k kommentariiam." *Nabokov Online Journal* 1 (2007). https://
www.nabokovonline.com/uploads/2/3/7/7/23779748/v1_dolinin_dobavki_1.pdf.

– "'Dar': Dobavleniia k kommentariiam (chast' vtoraia)." *Nabokov Online Journal* 2
(2008). https://www.nabokovonline.com/uploads/2/3/7/7/23779748/v2_13_dolinin.
pdf.

– "*The Gift*." In *The Garland Companion to Vladimir Nabokov*, ed. Vladimir E.
Alexandrov, 135–65. New York: Garland Publishing, 1995.

– *Istinnaia zhizn' pisatelia Sirina*. Saint Petersburg: Akademicheskii proekt, 2004

– *Kommentarii k romanu Vladimira Nabokova "Dar."* Moscow: Novoe izdatel'stvo,
2019.

Dragunoiu, Dana. *Vladimir Nabokov and the Poetics of Liberalism*. Evanston:
Northwestern University Press, 2011.

Dviniatin, F. "Piat' peizazhei s nabokovskoi siren'iu." http://nabokov-lit.ru/nabokov
/kritika/dvinyatin-pyat-pejzazhej.htm.

Eddington, Arthur. *New Pathways in Science*. New York: Macmillan, 1935.

Ellacombe, Henry Nicholson. *The Plant-Lore and Garden-Craft of Shakespeare*.
London: W. Satchell, 1884. https://www.gutenberg.org/files/28407/28407-h/28407
-h.htm.

"Escape of Charles II." https://en.wikipedia.org/wiki/Escape_of_Charles_II.

Field, Andrew. *VN: The Life and Art of Vladimir Nabokov*. New York: Crown, 1986.

Foster, John Burt. *Nabokov's Art of Memory and European Modernism*. Princeton:
Princeton University Press, 1993.

268   Works Cited and Consulted

Frank, Siggy. *Nabokov's Theatrical Imagination*. Cambridge, UK: Cambridge University Press, 2012.

Frye, Mitch. "Performing Tyranny, Purloining Authority: Nabokov's Dictators" *Nabokov Online Journal* 7 (2013). http://www.nabokovonline.com/uploads /2/3/7/7/23779748/2._mitch_frye_final.pdf.

Goethe, Johann Wolfgang von. *West-Eastern Divan*. Trans. and annotated by Eric Ormsby. London: Gingko, 2019.

– "Ginkgo Biloba." Trans. Robert Bloch. *Scientific Monthly* 74, no. 4 (April 1952): 230.

Grant, Paul, and Stephen H. Blackwell. "Toilets, Trees, and Inspiration in *Ada*." *The Nabokovian* 86 (Spring 2024). https://thenabokovian.org/nabokovian-new -notes/86-2024sp.

Graves, Arthur H. "The Present Status of the Chestnut in North America." *Northern Nut Growers: Report of the Proceedings of the Annual Meeting* 20 (1929): 48–63.

Grayson, Jane. *Nabokov Translated: A Comparison of Nabokov's Russian and English Prose*. Oxford: Oxford University Press, 1977.

Grishakova, Marina. *The Models of Space, Time and Vision in V. Nabokov's Fiction*. Tartu: University of Tartu Press, 2006.

Hamrit, Jacqueline. *Authorship in Nabokov's Prefaces*. Cambridge, UK: Cambridge Scholars Publishing, 2014.

Helfant, Ian. *That Savage Gaze: Wolves in the Nineteenth Century Imagination*. Boston: Academic Studies Press, 2018.

Hetenyi, Zsuzsa. "Lolita as Goddess between Life and Death: From Persephone to the Poplars." *Intertexts* 12, nos. 1–2 (Spring 2008): 41–54.

Hodge, Thomas. *Hunting Nature: Ivan Turgenev and the Organic World*, Ithaca: Cornell University Press, 2020.

Jack, Kenneth. "John George Jack (1861–1949)." *Electric Scotland* (website). https:// electricscotland.com/history/world/jack_john.htm.

Jackson, Paul R. "*Pale Fire* and Sherlock Holmes." *Studies in American Fiction* 10, no. 1 (Spring 1982): 101–5.

Johnson, D. Barton. "A Field Guide to *Pale Fire*: Waxwings and the Red Admiral." In *The Real Life of Pierre Delalande: Studies in Russian and Comparative Literature to Honor Alexander Dolinin,* ed. David M. Bethea et al., part 2, 652–73. Stanford Slavic Studies 34. Stanford: Stanford University Press, 2007.

– "The Key to Nabokov's *Gift*." *Canadian-American Slavic Studies* 16, no. 2 (1982): 190–206.

– *Worlds in Regression: Some Novels of Vladimir Nabokov*. Ann Arbor: Ardis, 1985.

Juliar, Michael. *Nabokov Bibliography: All about Vladimir Nabokov in Print*. http:// vnbiblio.com/; http://www.vnbiblio.com/wp-content/uploads/2013/05/Dva -puti.pdf.

Kats, Boris. "'Exegi Monumentum' Vladimira Nabokova: K prochteniiu stikhotvoreniia 'Kakoe sdelal ia durnoe delo.'" *Staroe literaturnoe obozrenie* 1 (2001). https:// magazines.gorky.media/slo/2001/1/8220-exegi-monumentum-8221-vladimira -nabokova.html.

Khodasevich, Vladislav. "On Sirin." In *Nabokov: Criticism, Reminiscences, Translations and Tributes*, ed. Alfred Appel, Jr. and Charles Newman, 96–101. Evanston: Northwestern University Press, 1970.

– "'Zhrebii Pushkina', stat'ia o. S.N. Bulgakova." Vozrozhdenie, no. 4094 (3 September 1937): 9.

Kopper, John. "The Evolution of Nabokov's Evolution." In *Nabokov at Cornell*, ed. Gavriel Shapiro, 219–30. Ithaca: Cornell University Press, 2003.

Księżopolska, Irena, and Mikołaj Wiśniewski, eds. *Vladimir Nabokov and the Fictions of Memory*. Warsaw: Fundacja Augusta Hrabiego Cieszkowskiego, 2019.

Leving, Yuri. *Keys to "The Gift": A Guide to Nabokov's Novel*. Boston: Academic Studies Press, 2011.

Liapunov, Vadim. "*Pnin* and Goethe." Trans. Stephen Blackwell. *The Nabokovian* 81 (2021). https://thenabokovian.org/node/52943.

Loison-Charles, Julie. *Vladimir Nabokov as an Author-Translator: Writing and Translating between Russian, English and French*. New York: Bloomsbury, 2022.

Malikova, Maria E. "'Pervoe stikhotvorenie' V. Nabokova: Perevod i kommentarii." In *V.V. Nabokov – pro et contra*, comp. B. Averin et al., v. 1, 741–71. St. Petersburg: Izd-vo Russkogo Khristianskogo Gumanitarnogo Un-ta 1997.

Makarova, N.G. "Vl. Solov'ev o 'Proroke' A.S. Pushkina." *Inzhenernye tekhnologii i sistemy* 1–2 (2000): 65–8. https://cyberleninka.ru/article/n/vl-soloviev-o-proroke-a-s-pushkina-1/viewer.

Mason, Bobbie Ann. *Nabokov's Garden*. Ann Arbor: Ardis, 1974.

Mello, Jansy. "Lolita's Reversions and Anamorphosis." *Nabokv-L*, 3 March 2012. https://thenabokovian.org/node/9168.

Meyer, Priscilla. *Find What the Sailor Has Hidden*. Middletown, CT: Wesleyan University Press, 1988.

Morlan, Anna. "Frost and Shade, and Questions of Design." *The Nabokovian* 56 (Spring 2006): 19–27.

Morris, Paul D. *Vladimir Nabokov: Poetry and the Lyric Voice*. Toronto: University of Toronto Press, 2010.

Morris, Robert T. "Chestnut Notes." *American Nut Nournal* 32, no. 3 (1930): 41–4.

Muravnik, Constantine F. "Nabokov's Philosophy of Art." PhD diss., Yale University, 2010.

– "Nabokov's Philosophy of Art." *Nabokov Studies* 15 (2017). https://doi.org/10.1353/nab.2017.0002.

Naiman, Eric. *Nabokov, Perversely*. Ithaca: Cornell University Press, 2011.

Nemzer, Avital. "'A Birch-Lime-Willow-Aspen-Poplar-Oak Man': Images of Trees, Temporospatial Liminality, and the Metaphysical in the Works of Vladimir Nabokov." MA thesis, Hebrew University of Jerusalem, 2021.

Notizblatt des Königl. Botanischen Gartens und Museums zu Berlin, bd. 6 (1913–17).

Ovid. *The Metamorphoses of Ovid*. Trans. Henry T. Riley. London: George Bell and Sons, 1893.

Papazian, Elizabeth Astrid. *Manufacturing Truth: The Documentary Moment in Early Soviet Culture*. DeKalb: Northern Illinois University Press, 2009.

270 Works Cited and Consulted

Pearson, Lisa. "John George Jack: Dendrologist, Educator, Plant Explorer." *Arnoldia* 71, no. 4 (2014): 2–11.

"Plants of Greek Myth." https://www.theoi.com/Flora1.html.

Polish, Daniel F. "On The Origin of Tree Worship." *Baker Street Journal* 67, no. 3 (Autumn 2017): 29–32.

Ponomareva, Tatiana. "On One of the Biographical Sources of Pale Fire." *Nabokov Studies* 16 (2019). https://doi.org/10.1353/nab.2019.0002.

Pushkin, Alexander. *Eugene Onegin*. Trans. with commentary by Vladimir Nabokov. 4 vols. 1964. Rev. ed. Princeton: Princeton University Press, 1975.

Pyle, Robert Michael. "Between Climb and Cloud: Nabokov among the Lepidopterists." In *Nabokov's Butterflies*, ed. Brian Boyd and Robert Michael Pyle, 32–76. Boston: Beacon, 2000.

Raguet-Bouvart, Christine. "Ember, Translator of *Hamlet*." ZEMBLA (online). https://www.libraries.psu.edu/nabokov/raguetb1.htm.

Rakhimova-Sommers, Elena, ed. *Nabokov's Women: The Silent Sisterhood of Textual Nomads*. Lanham, MD: Rowman & Littlefield, 2017.

Ramey, James. "*Pale Fire*'s Black Crown." *Nabokov Online Journal* 6 (2012). https://www.nabokovonline.com/uploads/2/3/7/7/23779748/22_ramey_pdff.pdf.

Reed, Clarence A. "Chinese Chestnut in Eastern States." *American Nurseryman* 85, no. 6 (1947): 7–8.

– "The Present Status of Chestnut Growing in the United States." *Proceedings of the American Society of Horticultural Science* 39 (1941): 147–52.

Rivers, J.E., and William Walker. "Notes to Vivian Darkbloom's Notes to *Ada*." In *Nabokov's Fifth Arc: Nabokov and Others on His Life's Work*, ed. J.E. Rivers and Charles Nicol, 260–95. Austin: University of Texas Press, 1982.

Ronen, Omry. "Nabokov and Goethe." In *Cold Fusion: Aspects of the German Cultural Presence in Russia*, ed. Gennady Barabtarlo, 241–51. New York: Berghahn Books, 2000.

Rorty, Richard. "The Barber of Kasbeam: Nabokov on Cruelty." In *Contingency, Irony, Solidarity*, 141–68. Cambridge: Cambridge University Press, 1989.

Roth, Matthew. "The Composition of *Pale Fire*." *Nabokov Online Journal* 9 (2015). http://www.nabokovonline.com/uploads/2/3/7/7/23779748/2_noj_9_2015_roth_composition_of_pale_fire.pdf.

Rowan, Jonathan Bricke. "True to Life: A Study of Lifelikeness in Fiction through Proust, Austen, Nabokov, and Joyce." PhD diss., University of California Berkeley, 2014.

Schiff, Stacey. *Véra (Mrs. Vladimir Nabokov)*. New York: Random House, 1999.

Schuman, Samuel. "Nabokov and Shakespeare's Trees." *Notes on Contemporary Literature* 18, no. 3 (1988): 8–10.

– *Nabokov's Shakespeare*. New York: Bloomsbury, 2014.

Scott, G.F. Elliot. *The Romance of Plant Life: Interesting Descriptions of the Strange and Curious in the Plant World*. Philadelphia: J.B. Lippencott Co., 1907.

Senderovich, Savelii Ia. "Pushkin v 'Dare' Nabokova." In *Figura sokrytiia*, 2:4 93–532. Moscow: Iazyki slavianskikh kul'tur, 2021.

Senderovich, Savelii Ia., and Elena M. Shvarts. "Kukol'naia teatral'nost' mira: K kharakteristike serebrennogo veka: Opyt fenomenologii odnoi kul'turnoi epokhi." In *Figura sokrytiia: Izbrannye raboty*, 1:541–96. Moscow: Iazyki slavianskikh kul'tur, 2012.

"Sersak" (pseudonym). "Query: KINBOT-NIKTO B." *Nabokv-L*, 27 January 1999. https://thenabokovian.org/node/31705.

Seward, A.C. *Links with the Past in the Plant World*. Cambridge: Cambridge University Press, 1911. https://www.gutenberg.org/files/62521/62521-h/62521-h.htm.

Shapiro, Gavriel. *Delicate Markers: Subtexts in Vladimir Nabokov's "Invitation to a Beheading."* New York: Peter Lang, 1998.

Shklovsky, Viktor. "Art, as Device." Trans. and intro. by Alexandra Berlina. *Poetics Today* 36, no. 3 (September 2015): 151–74.

Shrayer, Maxim D. *The World of Nabokov's Stories*, Austin: University of Texas Press, 1999.

Shvabrin, Stanislav. *Between Rhyme and Reason: Vladimir Nabokov, Translation, and Dialogue*. Toronto: University of Toronto Press, 2019.

Silina, Maria. "The Struggle against Naturalism: Soviet Art from the 1920s to the 1950s." *RACAR: Revue d'art canadienne/Canadian Art Review* 41, no. 2 (2016): 91–104.

Simard, Suzanne W., et al. "Net Transfer of Carbon between Ectomycorrhizal Tree Species in the Field." *Nature* 388 (August 1997): 579–82.

Sklyarenko, Alexey. "Coda and Oda in *Pale Fire*." *Nabokv-L*, 11 November 2015. https://thenabokovian.org/node/1984.

Solov'ev, Vladimir. "Znachenie poezii v stikhotvoreniiakh Pushkina." *Vestnik Evropy* 12 (1899).

Stopes, Marie C. *Ancient Plants*. Glasgow: Blackie and Son, 1910. https://www.gutenberg.org/files/43976/43976-h/43976-h.htm.

"Studying Trees at the Arnold Arboretum." *Boston Daily Globe*, 28 June 1903, 49.

Tammi, Pekka. *Russian Subtexts in Nabokov's Fiction. Four Essays*. Tampere: Tampere University Press, 1999.

Toker, Leona. "Liberal Ironists and the 'Gaudily Painted Savage': On Richard Rorty's Reading of Vladimir Nabokov." *Nabokov Studies* 1 (1994): 195–206. https://web.archive.org/web/20110609072203/https://www.libraries.psu.edu/nabokov/tokerp1.htm.

Tolstoy, Leo. *War and Peace*. Trans. Louise and Aylmer Maude, revised by Amy Mandelker. Oxford: Oxford University Press, 2010.

Trousdale, Rachel, and Priscilla Meyer. "Vladimir Nabokov and Virginia Woolf." *Comparative Literature Studies* 50, no. 3 (2013): 490–522.

Tudge, Colin. *The Secret Life of Trees*. London: Allen Lane 2005.

Ulm, Amanda Ann. "Remember the Chestnut." *Smithsonian Institution*, no. 3971 (1949): 377–82.

272   Works Cited and Consulted

Vertov, Dziga. *The Writings of Dziga Vertov.* Trans. Kevin O'Brien, ed. Annette Michelson. Berkeley: University of California Press, 1984.

Voronina, Olga. "Nabokov's Shakespeare: Allusion and Authorial Control." *Literatur in Wissenschaft und Unterricht* 35 (2002): 219–34.

– *Tainopis': Nabokov. Arkhiv. Podtekst.* St. Petersburg: Ivan Limbakh, 2023.

– "Tainopis' otkrytym tekstom. Kommentarii k materialam iz arkhivov V.V. Nabokova v N'iu-Iorkskoi Publichnoi biblioteke i iz Biblioteki Kongressa SShA." Paper presented at Nabokov Readings, Institute of Russian Literature (St. Petersburg), July 2020.

Webster's New International Dictionary of the English Language: Second Edition. Springfield, MA: G. & C. Merriam, 1937.

Wilson, Sarah. "Nabokov and Khodasevich: The Lyre Tightens." *Nabokov Online Journal* 7 (2013): 10. https://www.nabokovonline.com/uploads/2/3/7/7/23779748/4 ._wilson.pdf.

Zholkovsky, Alexander. "Poem, Problem, Prank." *The Nabokovian* 47 (Fall 2001): 19–29.

Zimmer, Dieter E. *A Guide to Nabokov's Butterflies and Moths.* Revised [final] edition 2012. http://www.d-e-zimmer.de/eGuide/PageOne.htm.

– "Humbert Humbert: Ape in the Cage. The Novel of the Nymphet Lolita and Her Cruel, Suffering Seducer." Trans. Brian Boyd. *The Nabokovian*, 6 July 2020. http://thenabokovian.org/node/51812.

– "Lolita, U.S.A." http://www.d-e-zimmer.de/LolitaUSA/LoUSpre.htm.

– "Zimmer on Shakespeare Alley and NYHT Interview." *Nabokv-L*, 15 November 2006. https://thenabokovian.org/sites/default/files/2018-01/NABOKV-L-0014057___body .html.

Index

absence, 13–14, 58, 232 n. 9, 243 n. 23

acacia, 6, 13–14, 51

acreana, 17

Ada, 8, 18, 23, 93, 97, 116–19, 147, 149, 150, 175, 185, 151–73, 228 n. 24, 234 n. 27, 244 n. 31, 247 n. 52, 251 n. 86, 253 n. 11; *Ada-Gift* similarity, 255 n. 28; implied author, 171; main trees in, 152; narrators, 154; pine-water-metaphysics complex, 186; two-world structure 117–18, 148, 167–8, 251 n. 89

Adam and Eve, 151

"The Adventure of the Empty House" (Conan-Doyle), 138, 239 n. 68, 245 n. 38, 246 n. 47

aesthetic ecology, 21

Afanasyev, Alexander, 222 n. 29

"An Affair of Honor" (Nabokov), 185

afterlife, 113–14, 139

Aikhenvald, Iulii (Yuli), 9, 72, 78, 90, 130, 230 n. 27, 244 n. 25, 252 n. 9; reader theory of, 16; *Silhouettes of Russian Writers*, 233 n. 21; VN epigram on, 217 n. 9

alder, 19, 32, 42, 51, 114, 122, 137, 138, 179, 182, 183, 223 n. 36, 242 n. 5

Alexandrov, Vladimir, 261 n. 25

Alice's Adventures in Wonderland (Carroll), 146

Alter, Robert, 228 n. 1, 232 n. 2

anagrams, 124

"And I saw: the vault of heaven darkened" (Nabokov), 223 n. 37

Anna Karenina (Tolstoy), 66, 156, 167, 169, 176

Anna Pavlovna (Romanov), 162, 254 nn. 22–3

Annensky, Innokenty, 238 n. 64

anthemion, 23–4, 31, 257 n. 42

anthropomorphism, 39, 168

Appel, Alfred, 3, 5, 30, 135, 243 n. 22

apple tree, 147, 149

arborescent model, 15; vs nomadic model, 15

arbutus, 46

Arnold Arboretum, 226 n. 5

"The Art of Literature and Commonsense" (Nabokov), 234 n. 23

"The Art of Translation" (Nabokov), 233 n. 14

art-knowledge-love unity, 85

art-nature relationship, 251 n. 85

art-science relationship, 250 n. 85

art, 69, 70, 71, 82, 85, 87, 115, 116, 123, 128, 136, 141, 147, 156, 158, 176, 184, 228 n. 27, 236 n. 40; as portal, 64, 121; creation and, 89; death and, 157;

274 Index

art (*cont.*)
representation of, 108; vs. science, 229 n. 12
art/reality boundary, 72
artist, concept of, 71; cameo of, 124, 184; figure of, 184; as translator, 135
artistry, 76
aspen, 97, 106
"At a Village Cemetery" (Nabokov), 41, 77, 230 n. 26, 243 n. 23
Atala (Chateaubriand), 135, 244 n. 32
Athens, 40, 50
attention, 187
author: in *Ada,* 171; death of, 66; implied, implied in *Pnin,* 107, 108
authorial self-reference, 253 n. 10
autobiography, 111
"Autumn Leaves" (Nabokov), 76
"Autumn" (Nabokov), 224 n. 39
awareness (of nature), 44

Babikov, Andrei, 219 n. 21, 241 n. 90
Bakhtin, Mikhail, 108
Balashov, Sergey, 31
"The Ballad of Longwood Glen" (Nabokov), 10, 12, 18, 39, 42, 64, 69, 70–1, 123, 127–8, 139, 157, 175–7, 187, 228 n. 27, 259 n. 1
Barabtarlo, 107, 255 n. 24
bark, 40
Barskova, Polina, 230 n. 21
basswood (linden), 106
bathroom, 25–8, 160, 166, 172. *See also* W.C.
Batiushkov, Konstantin, 6
Baucis and Philemon, myth of, 253 n. 14
Baudelaire, Charles, 149, 251 n. 93
bawdy language, 101
bay laurel (and -tree), 147, 250 n. 84
beech, 46, 60, 95, 123, 124, 133, 242 n. 12, 242 n. 15, 253 n. 14
beechwood, 29–31, 123–4, 133, 242 n. 11

Bend Sinister (Nabokov), 17, 70, 86, 87, 88, 89, 90, 91, 92, 93, 94, 96, 107, 177, 232 n. 9, 233 n. 12, 233 n. 13, 233 n. 17, 244 n. 27
Berezin, Nikolai Ilyich (geography teacher), 227 n. 22
Bergson, Henri, 121, 242 n. 4
Berlin, 37, 78, 230 n. 17
Bible, 249 n. 70
birch, 12, 19, 20, 32, 37–8, 40–1, 48–54, 60, 77–8, 80, 82, 84, 106, 133, 165–6, 168–9, 178–9, 227 n. 22, 230 n. 26, 250 n. 83, 257 n. 47; absence of, 259 n. 7; and first love, 168, poetry and, 52
"A Birch in Vorontsov Park" (Nabokov), 168, 224 n. 39, 257 n. 47
"Blessed Longing" (Goethe), 139–40
Blok, Alexander, 223 n. 37
Böcklin, Arnold, "Isle of the Dead," 120, 241 n. 2
Bolshevik revolution, 38–9
Bolsheviks, 49
Boscobel, 246 n. 47
Botanic Garden (Erasmus Darwin), 161
"Botkin" (in *Pale Fire*), theories regarding, 238 n. 64
boundaries, 63, 70, 87, 123, 179–81, 185, 260 n. 13
Bowie, Robert, 89–90
boxwood, 46, 165, 169
Boyd, Brian, 22–3, 34, 46, 54, 118, 158, 164, 176, 223 n. 37, 232 n. 1, 238 n. 65, 239 n. 73, 239 n. 74, 243 n. 21, 245 n. 41, 246 n. 44, 255 n. 27, 259 n. 2
Brown, Robert (character in *Ada*), 148, 155
Buchenwald, 133, 244 n. 30, 261 n. 21
buckeye, 235 n. 35
Buks, Nora, 232 n. 8
butterflies, 21, 28, 31, 82, 88, 182, 221 n. 25
butterfly-writing, 21
Byron, Lord, 251 n. 93

Index 275

camouflage, 109, 112

cane/walking stick, 59, 164, 228 n. 24

caprifole. *See* honeysuckle

Carroll, Lewis, 250 n. 80

Catherine II (the Great), 162, 254 nn. 22–3

Cavall and Melampus (myth), 235 n. 37

cedar (*Cedrus*/of Lebanon), 113, 143, 146, 165, 169–70, 176, 240 n. 78, 256 n. 33

cedar (*Juniperus*/eastern red), 113, 143, 146, 240 n. 78

cedar, 109–11, 114, 141

cedar waxwing, 109–10, 112–14

cedar-juniper relationship, 238 n. 67, 239 n. 74, 249 n. 70, 250 n. 82, 256 n. 33

cedar: mythological, 168; prickly, 249 n. 70; sealyham, 165; weeping, 165, 169, 218 n. 12

celluloid, 242 n. 14

centrifugal/centripetal tendencies, 144

Chagall, Marc, 176, 259 n. 2

chaparral, 148, 155, 164, 251 n. 87, 255 n. 29

Charles II (England), 185, 247 n. 47

Chateaubriand, François Renée de, 148–9, 155, 251 n. 93

Chernyshevski, Nikolay, 83, 85, 87, 90, 91, 109, 232 n. 8

The Cherry Orchard (Chekhov), 96, 148–9

cherry tree, 96

chess, 16, 18, 55, 56, 57, 58, 59, 60, 61, 63, 125, 126, 227 n. 20, 227 n. 24, 243 n. 20

chestnut, 97–102, 105, 229 n. 7, 236 n. 38, 236 nn. 41–2; absence of, 101–3; blight, 97, 100, 235 n. 33; chestnut in *Lolita*, translations of, 235 n. 36; Quilty and, 102, 105; scent of, 103. *See also* horse chestnut

chestnut (American), 235 n. 33; flowering of, 235 n. 35

Chestnut (name), 103–4

"Chestnuts" (Nabokov), 259 n. 9

childhood, 46–7

"Chinese tree" (ginkgo), 163

Christmas tree, 163, 255 n. 24

"church," translations into Russian, 231 n. 36

cinema, 242 n. 14

"The Circle" (Nabokov), 72, 88, 158, 229 n. 7; narrator in, 229 n. 8

clairvoyance, 136

classical mythology, 150, 229 n. 9, 235 n. 32

clockwork toy, 146, 248 n. 56, 252 n. 96

"Cloud, Castle, Lake" (Nabokov), 175

coast redwood (*Sequoia sempervirens*) 165, 169–70, 256 n. 33

Coates, Jenefer, 235 n. 33

Coindreau, Edgar, 239 n. 74, 246 n. 47, 247 n. 48

Conan-Doyle, Arthur, 138, 245 n. 38

Conclusive Evidence (Nabokov). See *Speak, Memory* under "versions"

conifers, 160

Connolly, Julian, 228 n. 1, 229 n. 7

consciousness, 4, 24–5, 32–3, 43, 55, 57–8, 60–5, 93–4, 121, 125, 157, 178, 221 n. 19, 228 n. 25, 230 n. 21; art and, 44; artistic, 129, 176; birth of, 23, 45–7; trees and, 44

Coppée, François,148

Corning Glass Works, 239 n. 70

Costantini, Costanzo, 8

Costlow, Jane, 20

cottonwood (poplar), 96, 132–3, 172

Couturier, Maurice, 235 n. 36

craft, artistic/poetic, 75

creation, 243 n. 23

creative mythology, 32

"The Creative Writer" (Nabokov), 234 n. 23

creativity, 37, 41, 43, 57, 64, 65, 82, 89, 94, 120, 129, 130, 158, 178, 221 n. 19, 228 n. 26; and trees, 75

Crimea, 40, 49, 51

"The Crossbearers" (Nabokov), 223 n. 37

276 Index

Cummings, Mr. (drawing master), 30, 220 n. 12

Cybele and Agdistis (myth), 260 n. 12

cypress, 120, 121, 141, 144, 149, 150, 151, 156, 246 n. 45, 249–50 n. 77, 251 n. 96; Lucette and, 160

The Cypress Chest (Annensky), 150, 252 n. 96

D'Annunzio, Gabriele, 8

dapple, 45, 47, 57, 58, 60, 70, 73, 74, 156, 157, 159, 166, 182, 221 n. 19, 253 nn. 10–11, 258 n. 53; consciousness and, 226, n. 4

Darwin, Charles, 161, 240 n. 88

Darwin, Erasmus, 161

date palm, 113, 143

Davydov, Sergei, 83

de Vries, Gerard, 115, 243 n. 21, 249 n. 75

Dead Souls (Gogol), 71

"The Death of Ivan Ilyich" (Tolstoy), 132–3

death-longing, 139, 247 n. 51

death, 77, 113, 133, 139, 141, 143, 146, 155, 156, 173, 177, 180, 183, 185, 185, 245 n. 41, 247 n. 50, 248 n. 55; as surprise, 140

Decatur, Illinois, 236 n. 48

The Defense, (Nabokov), 18, 49, 55–63, 94, 121, 125–7, 227 n. 20, 227 n. 24, 243 n. 20, 244 n. 24

Deleuze, Gilles, and Félix Guattari, on the brain, 218 n. 18

Desire under the Elms (O'Neill), 253 n. 12

Despair, 179, 184, 242 n. 15, 244 n. 31

digressions, 67, 228 n. 5

Dirig, Robert, 238 n. 66, 247 n. 48

Dobuzhinsky, Mstislav, 30–1, 222 n. 32

Doctor Zhivago (Pasternak), 8

documentarism, 127, 228 n. 1, 243 n. 18

Dolinin, Alexander, 231 n. 29, 231 n. 34, 232 n. 8, 252 n. 96, 260 n. 16, 238 n. 64

double (theme), 105, 148

double-framing, 122, 135, 138, 141, 147, 163, 247 n. 52, 250 n. 78

Dragunoiu, Dana, 233 n. 10

drawing lessons, 31

"Dream on the Acropolis" (Nabokov), 40–1, 49, 50, 225 n. 42, 230 n. 26, 257 n. 47

Drugie berega (Nabokov). See under *Speak, Memory*: "versions"

drupe (fruit type), 118, 154, 156, 253 n. 13; vs. apples, 154

dualism, 87, 90

duality, 70

Dulwich (*Pale Fire*), 246 n. 47

early poetry (Nabokov), 31, 48

ecocriticism, 20–1

ecology, 79; aesthetic, 110

ecosystem, 77, 110, 186

écu, old French monetary unit, 255 n. 27

Eddington, Arthur, 90

Eden, Garden of, 83, 116–17, 147, 152, 154, 244 n. 32, 253 n. 13

"Eelmann" (in *Ada*), 158

Einstein, Albert, 234 n. 27

ekphrasis, 67–8, 70, 86, 119, 122, 144, 150

"Elements Room" (Palazzo Vecchio), 171, 258 n. 57

Elijah (prophet), 244 n. 28

Elizabeth I (of England), 240 n. 78

Ellacombe, Henry Nicholson, 146, 240 n. 87

elm, 105, 131, 143, 144, 147, 148, 152, 186, 236 n. 38, 251 n. 93; mistaken identity, 155. *See also* oak-elm motif

embedded drama, 144

empathy, 38, 224 n. 39
The Empyrian Path (Nabokov), 43
"The Enchanted Hunters" (play in *Lolita*),136
"The Encounter" (Nabokov), 54, 98
The Encyclopedia Britannica, 233 n. 12
The Epic of Gilgamesh, 249 n. 70, 256 n. 33
epigraphs, 72, 85–6, 130
epistemology, 79, 81, 152, 232 n. 5, 232 n. 7, 82–119 *passim*; and play, 117
"The Erlking" (Goethe), 138–9, 245 n. 41
error, 117, 119
essence, 70
ethics, of narration, 106
etymology, 162, 253 n. 14
Eugene Onegin (Pushkin), 55, 89, 230 n. 21; Nabokov's commentary, 6, 10, 158
"An Evening of Russian Poetry" (Nabokov), 12, 134
evergreens, 46, 169
evolution, 88
exile, 116
The Eye, (Nabokov), 61–2

The Faerie Queene, (Spenser), 249 n. 77
"Fame" (Nabokov), 175
family tree, 117–18, 147, 151–3, 155, 160–3, 166, 173, 254 n. 18; errors, in 161, 167; secrets in, 254 n. 23
fantastic tree, 107
fate, 76
"Father's Butterflies" (Nabokov), 79, 223 n. 36
Fet, Afanasy, 26, 220 n. 9
Fet, Victor, 238 n. 64
fictitious nature, 112
Field, Andrew, 238 n. 64
"The fields, swamps drift past" (Nabokov), 39, 249 n. 74, 252 n. 3
"The Fight" (Nabokov), 185
Finnegans Wake (Joyce), 149

fir, 12, 19, 32, 36, 38, 56, 57, 59, 60, 64, 74, 77, 84, 134, 163, 230 n. 17
fir-spruce: conflation, 224 n. 38; translation, 222 n. 34
firebird, 10, 17, 35–6, 233 n. 36, 258 n. 62, 259 n. 64
"first love"/"Tamara" (Nabokov), 50
"First Poem" episode (*Speak, Memory*), 9, 32–5, 37, 48–9, 51, 167, 219 n. 6, 221 n. 22, 221 n. 24, 223 n. 36, 240 n. 80, 242 n. 5
folk genres, 36
folklore, 23, 42
folkloric creatures, 35–6, 74
forbidden knowledge, 117
forest, 38, 56, 58, 60, 179
forest path, 29, 31, 40, 56, 60, 62–4, 70, 74, 120–6, 185, 242 n. 6, 242 n. 9, 242 n. 12
"A Forgotten Poet" (Nabokov), 224 n. 38
Foster, John Burt, 226 n. 12
Four Quartets (Eliot), 137, 246 n.43
frame, 62
frame novel, 66, 69, 70–1, 148
frame-breaking, 133
framed artwork/ekphrasis, 87
framed trees, 29, 48–9, 58, 61, 64, 67–71, 74, 95, 119, 120–50, 155, 163, 167, 169–73, 184, 255 n. 28
framing: double (*see* double-framing); implicit, 148; non-artistic, 125; visible, 148
French Vladimir Nabokov Society, 219 n. 3
Freudian reading, 29
Friedman, Jerry, 249 nn. 69–70
Frost, Robert, 144

"The Garden" (Marvell), 251 n. 94
"The Garden of Earthly Delights" (Bosch), 254 n. 20
gardener, 140–2, 146
genealogical tree, 83

278   Index

genealogy, 117, 162, 254 n. 23
Genesis, Book of, 118, 148, 152, 232 n. 2
genius, 115, 140
ghosts, 101, 103, 156, 157, 159, 236 nn.
   40–2, 241 n. 92; narrative influence of,
   255 n. 28; trees as, 100
The Gift (Nabokov), 21, 39, 42, 64–5,
   71–86, 90–1, 94, 96, 98, 106–9, 123,
   128, 129, 131, 150, 158, 172, 175–6,
   180–1, 185, 223 n. 36, 229 n. 14, 230
   n. 37, 232 nn. 6–7, 244 n. 24, 244 n.
   31; narrator of, 229 n. 8
ginkgo, 13, 114, 116, 117, 118, 137, 138,
   139, 140, 144, 146, 147, 148, 162, 163,
   164, 165, 166, 167, 168, 169, 252 n.
   7, 256 n. 38, 257 nn. 45–6; and Hazel
   Shade, 140; history of, 115, 240 n. 88,
   241 n. 90, 255 n. 27; as living fossil,
   240 n. 88; VN research on, 241 n. 90
"Ginkgo biloba" (Goethe poem),
   115, 137, 139, 141, 148, 251 n. 88;
   translations of, 241 n. 91, 255 nn.
   25–7
Girard, Raymond, 238 n. 67
Glory, 21, 41, 42, 56, 62–3, 70, 74, 94,
   106, 121–3, 126–7, 129, 158, 182, 185,
   223 n. 36, 225 n. 45, 228 n. 27, 242
   nn. 6–7, 15; ambiguous ending, 123;
   foreword, 62–4
Glotfelty, Cheryll, 20
"gnarled," word history, 247 n. 49
"Gods" (Nabokov), 12, 39, 175–7
Goethe, Johann Wolfgang von, 21,
   115–16, 144, 146, 244 n. 30, 245 n. 41
Gogol, Nikolai, 83, 114, 240 n. 82
Gogolian digression, 26, 47
"Good Readers and Good Writers"
   (Nabokov), 71, 229 n. 12, 251 n. 92
Grandma Moses, 176, 259 n. 2
Grayson, Jane, 225 n. 44
Grishakova, Marina, 66–8, 228 n. 1, 228
   n. 3

Grosser Ettersberg, 244 n. 30
Grossman, Henry, VN portrait by, 218
   n. 12
Grunewald, 76, 77, 78, 180, 184, 185,
   260 n. 14
Guadanini, Irina, 227 n. 18
"A Guide to Berlin" (Nabokov), 55
Gumilyov, Nikolai, "Trees," 217 n. 6

Hamrit, Jacqueline, 233 n. 13
hawkmoth, 95
hazel tree, 138, 243 n. 21, 250 n. 83
"The Headless Horseman" (Mayne
   Reid), 164, 251 n. 87, 256 n. 29
Heavy Lyre (Khodasevich), 252 n. 96,
   260 n. 16
Helfant, Ian, 20
Hetenyi, Zsuzsa, 23, 235 n. 32, 259 n. 8
hickory, 114, 137–8, 247 n. 53, 250 n. 83;
   French translation, 247 n. 48
hidden picture theme, 46, 47, 186, 109,
   112, 118, 230 n. 21
Hodge, Thomas, 20
Holocaust, 133, 183, 244 n. 30
honeysuckle, 23, 24, 34, 34, 46, 221 nn.
   24–5, 257 n. 42
hornbeam, 46, 97
Horner, Sally, 236 n. 44
horse chestnut, 53–5, 98, 235 nn. 34–5
house-frame, 179
"How I Love You" (Nabokov), 150
"How I loved the poems of Gumilyov!"
   (Nabokov), 217 n. 6
Huckleberry Finn (Mark Twain), 19
Hughes, Robert, 8
Humbert Humbert (*Lolita*), poem by,
   136, 245 n. 37

idealism (philosophical), 44, 83, 87, 93
identity, 70, 113, 116, 148
imaginary trees, 70
implied author: in *Ada* 171; in *Pnin*, 107–8

In Search of Lost Time (Proust), 67, 148
incognito, 112
individuality, 65, 107
indrik-beast, 42, 225 n. 45
innocence, loss of, 159
inspiration, 129, 234 n. 23
interconnectivity, 14
invented flora and fauna, 239 n. 72
Invitation to a Beheading (Nabokov),
    10, 13, 18, 64–70, 72, 74, 86–7, 123,
    127, 157, 228 n. 3, 229 n. 7, 229 n. 14,
    232 n. 6, 232 n. 8, 241 n. 4, 247 n. 50;
    foreword, 228 n. 4; translation of, 228
    n. 4
irony, 67
irrationality, 177, 259 n. 1
ivy, 144, 249 n. 76

jacaranda, 116, 139
Jack, John George (Professor Jack, *Speak
    Memory*), 46–7, 82, 172, 226 n. 5
Jackson, Paul R., 246 n. 47
Johnson, D. Barton, 68, 233 n. 12, 238 n.
    64, 239 n. 71
Johnson, Kurt, 22
Joyce, James, 148
juniper, 110–14, 240 n. 78
Juniperus virginiana, 113. *See also* cedar
juvenilia, Nabokov's, 31

Kadet party, 41, 53
Kaempfer, Engelbert, 115
Kafka lecture (Nabokov), 5
Kahane, Eric, 235 n. 36
Kant, Immanuel, 89–90
Karlinsky, Simon, 243 n. 22
Karner blue (butterfly), 183, 261 n. 23
Kasbeam (synonym for Chestnut, town
    in *Lolita*), 103
Kats, Boris, 225 n. 44
Khodasevich, Vladislav, 71, 222 n. 35,
    228 n. 25

Kilmer, Joyce, 43, 95, 217 n. 6; "Trees"
    (poem), 7, 96, 135, 141
Kilmer Memorial, 95, 109, 135, 236 n. 44
King, Queen, Knave (Nabokov), 55,
    123–5, 179
knowingness, 67
knowledge, 45, 47, 231 n. 29, 232 n.
    1, 233 n. 12; abstract, 96; false, 109,
    119; forbidden, 116, 153; hidden,
    108; literary, 96; love and, 79; non-
    utilitarian, 82; of other, 95; scientific,
    86; terrible, 147; ultimate, 94
Kuznetsov, Nikolai, 258 n. 60

Lady of the Lake (Scott), 138, 243 n. 21,
    246 n. 44
lake, 245 n. 41
landscape, as frame, 121
larch, 84, 147, 148, 162, 163, 165, 168,
    170, 255 n. 24, 257 nn. 49–50
Laughter in the Dark (Nabokov), 158,
    179, 232 n. 7, 242 n. 15
laurel, 20, 51, 111, 113, 146, 149;
    European, 147; types of, 250 n. 84. *See
    also* bay laurel tree
Lay of Igor's Campaign, 254 n. 18
leaves, 37, 51, 71, 91–2, 126, 131, 162;
    analogy with pages, 75; dripping,
    229 n. 15, 236 n. 40, 240 n. 80; heart-
    shaped, 33, 76, 106, 162, 165, 166,
    167, 169; number per tree, 234 n.
    226
Lectures on Russian Literature
    (Nabokov), 240 n. 82
"A Legend" (3 poems) (Nabokov), 223
    n. 37
lepidopterology, 22, 31, 182, 184, 247
    n. 53
Lermontov, Mikhail, "The Triple
    Dream," 250 n. 78
Letters to Atticus (Cicero), 254 n. 17
Leving, Yuri, 229 n. 14, 243 n. 22

280 Index

"The Life of Chernyshevski" (*Gift*), 83–5,
  128, 130
life's strangeness, 185
light and shadow, 253 n. 11
lights, far-off (among hills/trees), 62
lilac, 41, 56–7, 149, 227 n. 23, 252 n. 10
lime, 106. *See also* linden
limia, black-leafed, 17
liminality, 229 n. 9, 242 n. 8
linden (European), 20, 33, 35, 51, 73–4,
  76, 84, 96, 106–7, 122, 128–30, 142,
  150, 152, 155–9, 167, 175, 177–8, 229
  n. 7, 260 n. 11; absence of, 158; and
  Lucette (*Ada*), 160
"The Linden Tree" (Wilhelm Müller),
  253 n. 12
linden-oak story in Ovid, 253 n. 14
lineage, 254 n. 23
lingonberry, 36
Linnaeus, Carolus, 161, 239 n. 77
Liriodendron tulipifera (tulip tree), 135.
  See also tulip tree
liriodendron, 234 n. 30; importance of
  word to VN, 258 n. 57
logic, 153
Loison-Charles, Julie, 238 n. 67, 247 n. 48
Lolita (Nabokov), 23, 39, 43, 94–7, 99,
  100–5, 108–9, 134–6, 181, 183–4, 226
  n. 10, 232 n. 1, 235 n. 31, 235 n. 33,
  236 n. 38, 236 nn. 41–2, 245 n. 37, 256
  n. 34, 259 n. 8
Lombardy poplar, 12, 46, 96–7, 108, 119,
  170–2, 258 n. 55, 258 n. 59
longevity, trees vs. animals, 217 n. 3
Look at the Harlequins! (Nabokov),
  252–3 n. 10, 259 n. 7
loss, 47, 168, 178, 230 n. 26
"Love under the Lindens" (*Ada*,
  fictitious), 158
love, 65, 68, 75, 76, 77, 85, 93, 94, 105,
  108, 117, 186, 226 n. 11, 231 n. 30,
  231 n. 33, 236 n. 40; art and, 230

n. 223; ethical and metaphysical,
  50; knowledge and, 79; knowledge-
  amplified, 82, 187
"Loves of the Plants" (Erasmus Darwin),
  161
Lucette, and trees, 170; in *Ada*, 256 n. 30;
  and cypress, 160; and mulberry, 160;
  and oak, 158–69; and Ophelia, 159;
  and willow, 160
Luna moth, 247 n. 53

Madame Bovary (Flaubert), 217 n. 5
"The Madman" (Nabokov), 22
magic, 74, 122–5, 127, 177, 182–3, 242
  n. 11
magical creatures, 74, 222 n. 29
The Magic Mountain (Mann), 253 n. 12
magnolia, 95–6
mahogany, 28; Russian translation, 220
  n. 10
maidenhair. *See* ginkgo
Maidenhair Road, 167
Maidenhair Station 163, 169
Malikova, Maria, 223 n. 37
The Man with a Movie Camera (Vertov),
  126, 243 n. 16
maple, 59, 113, 143, 149
maps, 242 n. 9
Marvell, Andrew, 148
Mary (Nabokov), 18, 19, 26–7, 49, 50–3,
  75, 94, 120–1, 168, 179, 182, 226 n. 13,
  242 n. 12; tree-key of, 20
Mason, Bobbie Ann, 18, 23, 184, 261 n.
  24; VN corrections to, 18, 254 n. 16
material world, 84
materialism, philosophical, 83, 87
materialists, 84–6, 90–1, 158
"Matin d'Octobre" (Coppée), 155–6
Maxwell, William, 238 n. 63
Mello, Jansy, 238 n. 64, 249 n. 70, 253 n. 13
memento mori, 140–2, 146, 248 n. 55,
  252 n. 96, 256 n. 34

memory, 47–55, 60, 76, 94, 105, 156, 178, 183–4, 221 n. 24, 230 n. 17, 245 n. 37

Metamorphoses, (Ovid), 9, 38, 150, 177, 249 n. 75, 253 n. 14

metaphor, 14, 241 n. 89

metaphysics, 75, 110, 113–16, 127–8, 133–4, 139, 147, 150, 160, 176–7, 180, 181–5, 247 n. 53

Meyer, Priscilla, 66, 228 n. 1, 238 n. 64

mirror as frame, 129

mise en abyme, 122

misidentification, 155, 236 n. 38

mistaken identity, 98–9, 109–13, 116, 118, 143, 149, 152–4, 158, 165–8, 233 n. 11, 239 n. 69, 244 n. 26, 249 n. 73, 253 n. 13, 255 n. 24, 256 n. 33

mobile trees, 39, 176

Moby-Dick (Melville), 19, 67

monism, 87, 233 n. 10

Montreux Palace Hotel garden, 218 n. 12

Morris, Paul, 176, 259 n. 1

mulberry, 106–7, 141, 144, 149, 154, 157, 165–7, 170, 249 n. 74, 252 n. 5, 256 n. 34, 257 n. 50; absent, 169; Lucette and, 160; silk and, 157

Muravnik, Constantine, 261 n.25

music, 55–7

"My English Education" (Nabokov), 25, 28–30

mycorrhizome, 16, 218 n 12

mystery, 107, 123, 177, 185

mystery trees, 106

myth, 23

myth-making, 154

mythology, 23, 50, 144, 241 n. 92, 249 nn. 75–6, 259 n. 8, 260 n. 12; classical, 150, 229 n. 9, 235 n. 32

Nabokov, Dmitri (VN's son), 46–7, 228 n. 4, 260 n. 14

Nabokov, Elena Ivanovna (VN's mother), letters to, 135, 245 n. 35

Nabokov, Nicholas, 225 n. 41

Nabokov, Véra (VN's wife), 13–14, 35, 46, 54–5, 98, 240 n. 87, 260 n. 14; letters to, 217 n. 9, 243 n. 23, 244 n. 25

Nabokov, Vladimir (VN): corrections to Mason, 184; early poems 8, 11, 33, 42, 70, 74, 168; favourite tree, 256 n. 33; last poem in St. Petersburg, 227 n. 22; lepidoptery papers, 117; lepidoptery work, 119, 241 n. 89; organic vs. coherent career, 44; personal creative mythology, 5; tree-poems, 67; tyrannical author, seen as, 16, 91

Nabokov, Vladimir Dmitrievich (VN's father), 41, 53, 77, 167, 230 n. 26; birthday, 256 n. 41

Naiman, Eric, 101, 231 n. 36

naming, 85–7, 113, 140, 143, 168, 230 n. 27

narration, ethics of, 106–7; instability of, 184

narrative, as painting, 4; as representation, 108

narrator: in *Ada*, 154; in "The Circle," 229 n. 8; in *Gift*, 229 n. 8; ignorance of, 107; in *Invitation*, 69; in *Pnin*, 106, 182, 184

"The Nature of Electricity" (*Pale Fire*), 141, 146

nature, 3, 61, 63–4, 67, 79, 176, 186; alienation and, 62; awareness of, 158; invisibility of, 4; knowledge of, 158

nature writing, 20–1

"Nearctic Forms of *Lycaeides* Hübner" (Nabokov), 17, 88, 233 n. 17

Nemzer, Avital, 226 n. 9, 229 n. 9, 229 n. 13, 234 n. 24–5, 250 n. 79, 253 n. 14, 261 n. 26

nervous system, 16

nested frames, 242 n. 7

282   Index

New Place (Shakespeare's home), 256 n. 34
The New Yorker, 24–6, 28, 30, 219 n. 6, 238 n. 63
non-chronology, 79
non-linearity, 79
non-utility, 37
"Notes on Neotropical Plebejinae" (Nabokov), 88
Notizblatt des Königl. Botanischen Gartens und Museums zu Berlin, 219 n. 20
noumenal world, 90
"A Nursery Tale," 74, 243 n. 23

oak, 10–11, 17, 27, 35, 39, 46, 50, 54, 65–72, 78, 84, 86, 88, 106, 126–7, 130, 139, 142, 148, 149–52, 155–6, 158–9, 175, 177, 180, 230 n. 27, 244 n. 25, 247 n. 49; literary history of, 228 n. 1; Lucette and, 158–60; Pushkin and, 8–9; royal, 185, 246–7 n. 47; scrub, 155, 157, 252 n. 8, 255 n. 29; in Shakespeare, 248 n. 62
Oak Creek Canyon, Arizona, 228 n. 4
oak execution block, 127
oak-elm motif, 6, 158, 233 n. 11, 253 n. 13
oakling avenue (*Speak, Memory*), 24–5, 27, 45, 121, 157, 243 n. 23, 252 n. 10
obliviousness, 44, 82, 95, 101–2, 119, 236 n. 38
The Odyssey, (Homer), 238 n. 64
oleander, 46, 59
olive, 46, 94
Omega watch company, 246 n. 43
"On a Book Entitled *Lolita*" (Nabokov), 100–1
"On Translating Eugene Onegin" (Nabokov), 135
One Thousand Plateaus (Deleuze and Guattari), 14–16

openness, aesthetic, 16
Ophelia (*Hamlet*), 141, 149, 151, 164, 256 n. 38, 256 n. 41; Lucette and, 159
orange tree, 46, 59
The Origin of Tree Worship, 138
The Original of Laura (Nabokov), 116
oriole, 249 n. 73
Orlando (Woolf), 19, 66–7
Orpheus, 78, 177, 180, 184, 230 n. 28, 231 n. 36, 260 n. 16; trees and, 178
other: knowledge of, 102; representation of, 108
otherworld, 69–71, 75, 114, 117, 157, 173, 182, 229 n. 13, 229 n. 7, 255 n. 24, 257 n. 48, 259 n. 1; alternative interpretations of, 259 n. 63; and VN biography, 261 n. 25
"The Overcoat" (Gogol), 232 n. 9

painted trees, 29, 30, 49, 121–2, 128–34, 184, 242 n. 12, 244 n. 29, 251 n. 86
"Painted Wood" (Nabokov), 223 n. 37
painting, 148; as portal, 128–9, 185
Pale Fire (Nabokov), 7, 8, 13, 42, 93–4, 104, 108–16, 121, 137, 139, 140–50, 165, 169, 175, 185, 238 n. 65, 239 n. 68, 240 n. 80, 243 n. 21, 246 nn. 43–4, 246–7 n. 47, 255 n. 24; "Commentary," 111; "Foreword," 109; "Index," 111–12; "Poem," 109, 111–12, 114; translation of, 247 n. 48
palm tree, 61, 95, 121, 125–6, 149, 241 n. 3
panelling, wood, 27
parenthood, 46
Pasternak, Boris, 8
pathetic fallacy, 66, 92, 226 n. 9
patterns, in life and art, 230 n. 21
Paul I (Russia), 254 n. 23
paulownia, 107, 162, 165–7, 169–71, 254 n. 21, 256 n. 42, 257 n. 42; and family tree, 161–3; flowers of, 258 n. 52

pavilion at Vyra park, 32, 48–9, 51
pea tree, Siberian, 6
peach tree, 252 n. 3
"Peacocks" (Nabokov), 223 n. 37
pear peacock moth, 171, 258 n. 57
pear tree, 171
pen-holder, oak, 11, 157
perception, 62, 65, 81, 91, 109, 129;
    material/practical/utilitarian, 62
"Perfection" (Nabokov), 260 n. 13
Persephone, 259 n. 8
perspective, in drawing, 30, 220 n. 12
"Peter and Margaret" (*Ada*), 156, 159–
    60, 163, 166, 252 n. 9, 254 n. 16
Peter III (Russia), 254 n. 23
Petigny, M., 255 n. 27
philistinism, 176
Phoenix dactilifera (date palm), 143
photography, 58, 121, 129, 133, 148
phylogenetic tree, 88
physics, in 1930s, 90
pine, 19, 20, 33, 36, 39, 46, 50–2, 78, 84,
    113–14, 134, 136–7, 143, 147, 175,
    179–86, 236 n. 38, 236 n. 47, 240 n.
    78, 244 n. 31; arolla, 164
pine barren, 261 n. 23
pine-cicada-death relationship, 251 n. 96
pine-water-metaphysics complex, 180,
    184, 260 n. 13
"Pinedale" (*Ada*), 185
"The Pines" (*Pnin*), 181, 183
Pippa Passes (Browning), 246 n. 47
Pivot, Bernard, 17
plane, London, 239 n. 77
plane tree (*Platanus*), 46, 143
Platonism, 84, 87, 90, 100
play, 118
Pnin (Nabokov), 17, 42, 54, 97, 106–7,
    108, 131–5, 151, 172, 181–4, 186, 230
    n. 24, 250 n. 79, 256 n. 34, 258 n. 59;
    implied author of, 107–8; narrator of,
    106–7, 182, 184; versions of, 238 n. 63

Poems (1959, Nabokov), 52
Poems and Problems (Nabokov), 32, 34,
    221 n. 26
poet, sources of, 36
poetic creation, 182
poetry, definition, 32; in *The Gift,* 76
poetry writing (verse-making), 26, 32,
    75
point of view, 228 n. 3
Ponomareva, Tatiana, 239 n. 70
poplar, 7, 19, 26–7, 31, 39, 42, 50, 52–3,
    77–8, 84–5, 92, 96–9, 105–6, 126,
    132, 134, 149–50, 171, 178, 230 n.
    21, 236 n. 38, 258 n. 55, 259 n. 8;
    black, 96; and Konstantin Godunov-
    Cherdyntsev (in *The Gift*), 80
"The Poplar" (Nabokov), 13, 39, 40,
    52–3, 227 n. 13
poplar admiral (butterfly), 80. *See also*
    Lombardy poplar
Poplar Cove, North Carolina, 7
poplar nymph (butterfly), 258 n. 60
"The Poplars" (Nabokov), 12, 39, 42–3,
    175, 177, 187, 235 n. 32
porphyroferous trees, 219 n. 20
presence and absence, 112
privet, 46
Proust, Marcel, 39, 67, 148–9, 153, 156,
    158, 246 n. 45
puppet-booth motif, 69, 229 n. 8
Pushkin, Alexander, 6, 8–9, 17, 35–6, 55,
    66, 72, 78, 92, 135, 149, 231 n. 36, 232
    n. 8, 244 n. 25; works: "I visited anew
    …" 224 n. 41; "The Muse," 8–9, 36, 66,
    223 n. 35; "The Poet," 9, 157, 218 n. 9,
    223 n. 35; "The Prophet," 36, 79, 231
    n. 29; "The Prophet" interpretation
    history, 223 n. 35; "Rusalka," 243 n.
    21; "Ruslan and Lyudmila," 9, 10, 35,
    66, 130, 152, 222 n. 29, 241 n. 1; "The
    Three Springs" and VN translation of
    into French, 231 n. 36

284   Index

"Pushkin, or the Real and the Plausible" (Nabokov), 86, 94, 105, 107
"Pyramus and Thisbe" (play in *Midsummer Night's Dream*), 141, 144, 149
Pyrospodia tree, 17

Quercus (fictitious novel in *Invitation*), 13, 65, 67–72, 74, 86, 126–7, 141, 228 n. 1, 228 n. 3, 228 n. 5, 229 n. 14, 241 n. 4, 243 n. 16; *Quercus* oak, spatial extension of, 68
Quercus ruslan Chat., 17, 149, 155
quill pen, 36
"The Quill" (Nabokov), 9, 10, 35–7, 120, 222 n. 31, 222 n. 35, 223 nn. 36–7, 259 n. 64

racemosa/bird-cherry, 40, 51
Raguet-Bouvart, Christine, 233 n. 13
"Rain" (Nabokov), 229 n. 15
"The Rain Has Flown" (Nabokov), 32, 34–5, 37, 48–9, 51, 221 n. 24, 222 n. 28, 256–7 n. 42; critical confusion about, 34
Rakhimova-Sommers, Elena, 248 n. 61
ramification, 21
"The Rape of the Lock" (Pope), 137
reader, 68, 84, 110; creativity of, 91; freedom of, 91; reception by, 90; role of, 16, 90, 222 n. 28
reading, 84
The Real Life of Sebastian Knight (Nabokov), 13, 83, 86, 94, 96, 107, 109, 130–3, 158, 180, 227 n. 23, 233 n. 11, 242 n. 11, 244 n. 26
reality, 70, 83, 136, 141, 147, 233 n. 20; fancy and, 226 n. 10; staged and superior, 68–9
rebirth, 180
reception of art, 90
"Recruiting" (Nabokov), 9, 73–4, 158, 230 n. 20, 243 n. 23

reflection, 73, 76, 85, 91–2, 104, 114, 129–31, 136, 244 n. 27, 245 n. 41
Reid, Mayne, *The Headless Horseman*, 164, 251 n. 87, 256 n. 29
Reigner, Leopold, 217 n. 5
religion, 245 n. 35
René (Baudelaire), 251 n. 93
representation, 87
Repton, Henry, 115
re-reader, 110
"Resound, my faithful verse" (Nabokov), 10
"The Return of Chorb" (Nabokov), 53, 54, 98, 235 n. 35, 244 n. 27
rhizome (vs. tree) analogy, 14, 16
Rimbaud, Arthur, 148, 251 n. 95
Rockwell, Norman, 259 n. 2
Roman antiquity, 66
Romanov, Konstantin, 148
Ronen, Omry, 139
Rorty, Richard, 236 n. 43
Rowan, Jonathan, 108, 258 n. 59
rowan, 34

"The Sacred Tree" (*Pale Fire*), 114–16, 137, 247 n. 52
sallow, 34. *See also* willow
Saltykov, Sergei, 254 n. 23
sap, 40
Schiff, Stacy, 240 n. 87
science, 115–18; boundary of, 118, 241 n. 93; Elizabethan, 144
Science (journal), 241 n. 91
The Seagull (Chekhov), 253 n. 13
"secret points" ("On a Book Entitled *Lolita*"), 100
self, 91; mystery of, 93
self-knowledge, 105
self-referentiality, 87
self-translation, 221 n. 26
Senderovich, Savely, 229 n. 8
Sequoia National Forest, 32

shadows, 16, 17, 24, 32–3, 42, 45, 58, 70–1, 73, 74, 75, 76, 84, 85, 88, 90–1, 100, 106, 129, 130, 141, 141, 146, 157, 161–2, 165, 166, 182, 230 n. 21, 236 n. 39, 243 n. 23, 244 n. 24

shagbark: in Ithaca, 247 n. 48. *See also* hickory

Shakespeare Avenue (in *Pale Fire*), 112–14, 116, 117, 121, 137–42, 144, 146–8, 152, 165, 169, 246 n. 46; visualization of, 145–6

Shakespeare, William, 8, 89, 104, 115, 131, 140, 167, 244 n. 26, 256 n. 38; authorship theories, 233 n. 12; flora, 240 n. 87; number of trees in, 19, 141, 143, 252 n. 3, 256 n. 41, and settings, 144; works: *Hamlet*, 17, 87–8, 90–1, 141, 143, 149, 164, 167, 233 n. 13, 243 n. 21, 248 n. 61, 256 n. 41; *Henry IV, Part 1*, 247 n. 49; *King Lear*, 104, 142–3, 164, 249 n. 66, 256 n. 38; *Henry VIII*, 177; *Measure for Measure*, 247 n. 49, 256 n. 41; *A Midsummer Night's Dream*, 141, 143–4, 149, 157, 160, 248 n. 59; *Othello*, 141–3, 248 n. 58, 250 n. 78; *The Tempest*, 141–3, 249 nn. 64–5, 67, 68, 70; *Timon of Athens*, 138; *Twelfth Night*, 141, 144, 248 n. 60, 249–50 n. 77

shattal apple, 17, 117–18, 149, 152–4, 168, 253 n. 13

Sherlock Holmes. *See* "Adventure of the Empty House"

Shrayer, Maxim, 227 n. 16, 229 n. 7, 261 n. 25

Shulgin, Valentina, 10, 33, 49

Shvabrin, Stanislav, 233 n. 14, 260 n. 16

Shvarts, Elena, 229 n. 8

Sikorski, Elena (sister of VN), 241 n. 90

silk, 105, 154, 237 n. 60, 252 n. 5, 256 n. 34; mulberry and, 157

silk (mulberry) moth, 252 n. 5

Simhard, Suzanne, 218 n. 12

simile, mock-Homeric, 240 n. 82

sincerity, 33, 221 n. 21

Siren (mythical creature), 124

siren-*siren'*-lilac pun, 124, 242 n. 13

Sirin (VN pen name), 37, 41, 223 n. 37; associations, 225 n. 44; first use of, 35; puns on, 124

Sklyarenko, Aleksey, 239 n. 73

Skonechnaia, Olga, 228 n. 1

Smirnovski's *Grammar*, 72

Socrates, 246 n. 45

solipsism, 226 n. 10

Solovyov, Vladimir, 36, 222 n. 35

"Solus rex" (Nabokov), 94

"Sonnet" ("A spring wood shimmers before me … wait") (Nabokov), 38

"Sonnet" ("The cloudless vault and silence …") (Nabokov), 12, 37–8, 134, 223 n. 38

"Sounds" (Nabokov), 229 n. 15

Speak, Memory (Nabokov), 8, 11, 18, 20–1, 29, 32–3, 35, 41, 45–8, 50, 65, 75–6, 79, 80, 82, 97–8, 123, 157–8, 172, 182, 221 n. 25, 230 n. 21, 234 n. 27, 235 n. 31, 240 n. 80, 250 nn. 79–80, 253 n. 11, 257 n. 42, 260 n. 14; alternative titles, 219 n. 5; index, 221 n. 24; versions, 23, 24–7, 28–31, 147, 171, 219 n. 6, 220 nn. 11–12, 230 n. 27

sprites, magical creatures, 74

spruce, 163. *See also* fir; fir-spruce

spying, 159

St. Petersburg, 40

"Steel Cicada" (Annensky), 150

Stikhi (*Poems*, 1916) (Nabokov), 10, 33–5

Stikhi (*Poems*, 1979) (Nabokov), 32, 35, 220 n. 16

"Stopping by Woods on a Snowy Evening" (Frost), 7, 137, 144, 246 n. 42

stories, trees and, 119

strange-making, 133

stream of consciousness, 167

streets with tree names, 74

Strong Opinions (Nabokov), 84, 233 n. 20

suicide, 139, 144, 148, 150, 156–7, 160, 164, 166, 255 n. 27

sunflecks, 45, 57. *See also* dapple

swimming, 181–2

"The Swing" (*Pale Fire*), 141

sycamore, 141; American, 143; etymology, 249 n. 74, European (*Acer*), 113, 143; European vs. American, 239 n. 77

syringa, 227 n. 23. *See also* lilac

Syrinx, in Ovid, *Metamorphoses*, 243 n. 21

talent, 62–3, 65, 228 n. 26

Tamara Gardens (in *Invitation*), 68

tamarack, 68

Tammi, Pekka, 220 n. 8

tangled syntax, 162

taxonomic tree, 83, 119

taxonomy, 85, 112, 239 n. 69, 250 n. 83

Tchelitchew, Paul, 243 n. 22

teachers, art, 30

telephone, 171, 173; fatidic, 227 n. 20, 258 n. 56, 258 n. 58

temporal depth, 221 n. 18

"The Texture of Time" (*Ada*), 157, 164–5, 242 n. 4; sunflecks and, 158

Thouin, André, 255 n. 27

thuja, 256 n. 33

"The Thunderstorm" (Nabokov), 244 n. 28

time, 5, 66–8, 115, 116–18, 121, 136, 144, 156–7, 165, 171, 241 n. 4, 246 n. 43, 253 n. 11; geological, 67; lifespan, 67

Time Magazine, 176

time travel, 79, 115, 241 n. 89

"To Prince S. M. Kachurin" (Nabokov), 251 n. 87, 256 n. 29

Tolkien, J.R.R., 175

Tolstoy, Leo, 125, 171; diary of, 226 n. 2; epistemological parable, 232 n. 5

transcendence, 157, 176

transitions, 179

translation, 34, 87–91, 233 nn. 13–14; changes in VN's works, 68, 80, 124, 231 n. 36, 242 n. 15; literalism in, 34, 221 n. 26

Transparent Things (Nabokov), 18, 32, 221 n. 18

travel guides, 135, 234 n. 29

trees(s), absent, 61–2, 130, 170, 178; ambulating, 39; analogies of, 83, 88, 89, 233 n. 17; of art, 173; birth of art and, 52; colour of, 169; concentration of, 166, 168, 170, 256 n. 31; and creativity 31, 33; definition, 22–3; in dreams, 123–4; in ecosystem, 110; fire-water, 173; harm and, 170; in history of art, 150; and imagination, 31; increasing number, 151; ink-drawn, 173; invented, 17; invisibility of, 3, 19, 96; key of, 18–19; knowledge and, 5; knowledge of, 151; lepidopterology and, 3; in life, 45; light and, 14; lightning-struck, 77, 132, 172; literary, 116; Lucette and, 170; metaphors, 64, 70; mobile, 175; as mystery, 123; mythical, 4; names of, 45; narrated (story), 122; as nervous system, 81; network of, long-distance, 166; non-humanness of, 71; ossified and stereotyped, 126, 176; painted, imaginary, 131; as pilgrims, 39, 42; platonic, 130; as portal, 127, 150; potentials of, 16; presence-absence, 169; reader awareness of, 186; real vs. framed, 155; shadows and, 14; time and, 4; variations of, 178; VN's early overuse of, 168; writing and, 3

tree complex, pine-oak-larch-willow, 164
Tree of Knowledge, 4, 23, 83, 117–19,
    147, 152–4, 253 n. 13
tree stump, 42, 79, 147, 177
tree-art-contraband, 127
tree-author-identity, 115
tree-book analogy, 75
tree-hierarchy, 83
tree-logic, 153
tree-messiah, 176–7
tree-related product (soap), 166, 170,
    256 n. 35
tree-surnames, 42
tree-theme, deepening of, 161
tree-themes, most common, 178
tree-water-fire combination, 258 n. 53
tree-writing, 21
"Trees" (Gumilyov), 217 n. 6
"Trees" (Kilmer), 7, 96, 135, 141
trillion (rare word), 92–4, 177, 234 n. 27
"The Triple Dream" (Lermontov), 250
    n. 78
Trousdale, Rachel, 66, 228 n. 1
truth, 85
Tsïganskie romansï, 33
Tudge, Colin, 22
tulip tree (tulip poplar), 95–7, 234 n. 30,
    257 n. 42. See also *Liriodendron*
Turgenev, Ivan, 20
twig(s), 31, 41, 46–7, 51, 55, 56, 58, 73,
    91–4, 130–2, 153, 171, 177, 222 n. 32,
    244 n. 27
Two Paths (Nabokov), 31–2, 39, 48
two-names theme, 112
two-world structure, dualism, 185, 253
    n. 10. See also under *Ada*
two-worlds theme, 117
typography, 112; italics and, 239 n. 76
tyrannical authorship models, 15

"Ul′daborg" (translation from
    Zoorlandian) (Nabokov), 229 n. 8

"Ultima Thule" (Nabokov), 94
underworld, 184
uniformity, 91
utilitarian thinking, 177

Van Eyck, Jan (paintings), 184
"The Vane sisters" (Nabokov), 131, 133–4
versions of VN publications, 26, 28–31,
    172. See also under *Pnin* and *Speak,
    Memory*
virginity, 240 n. 78
Volosyanka/Maidenhair Station, 163
Voronina, Olga, 98, 224 n. 41, 234 n. 30,
    235 n. 34, 238 n. 63
Vyra, 24, 25, 32, 35, 45, 49, 78, 168, 172,
    221 n. 24

W.C. (=water closet), 25–9, 31, 50, 156,
    167–71
walnut, 138, 250 n. 83
War and Peace (Tolstoy), 66, 232 n. 5
The Wasteland (Eliot), 246 n. 43
water, 180, 182, 184
water-sprite, 149
waxwing: Bohemian, 112, 238 n. 66;
    waxwing, cedar, 146, 239 n. 74; cedar
    vs. Bohemian, 239 n. 71; fictitious,
    112; genus, 112
*Webster's Second International
    Dictionary*, 23–4, 42, 68
weeping cedar, 13, 165, 169, 218 n. 12
"What is the evil deed" (Nabokov), 225
    n. 44
"What my heart requires" (Nabokov),
    43, 79
"Whispers, timid breathing" (Fet), 220
    n. 9
White, Katharine, 176, 187, 234 n. 30,
    258 n. 57
willow, 34, 106, 137, 141, 142, 143,
    149, 151, 169, 170, 257 n. 50; high-
    mountain, 17; Lucette and, 160

288   Index

Wilson, Edmund, 229 n. 12
"Winter Night" (Nabokov), 236 n. 40
wood object, 18, 28, 32, 48, 50–2, 55–9, 63, 78, 147, 157, 164, 166, 179, 182, 228 n. 24, 227 n. 20, 256 n. 34
"The Wood Sprite" (Nabokov), 9, 12, 35, 37, 40, 67, 74, 223 n. 37
wood-sprite motif, 36, 42, 120, 127, 149
"wood-sprite" (title-word) translation, 222 n. 29
wood-wide web, 218 n. 12
Woolf, Virginia, 66, 228 n. 1
"The Word" (Nabokov), 223 n. 35

word-golf, 112, 146
workaday life/*byt*, 71

Yaremich, S.P., 30–1
yew, 46, 114, 116, 241 n. 92, 245 n. 38, 255 n. 24
Yggdrasil, 4

Zemski, Prince (*Ada*), 161–2, 166, 254 n. 22
Zholkovsky, Alexander, 221 n. 22
Zimmer, Dieter E., 22, 104, 22, 236 n. 48, 258 n. 57

www.ingramcontent.com/pod-product-compliance
Ingram Content Group UK Ltd.
Pitfield, Milton Keynes, MK11 3LW, UK
UKHW042052240225
455503UK00002B/29/J